DEcolonial Heritage

Waxmann Verlag GmbH
Steinfurter Straße 555, 48159 Münster
info@waxmann.com

Cultural Encounters and the Discourses of Scholarship

Edited by
Gesa Mackenthun

Volume 10

This series seeks to stimulate fresh and critical perspectives on the interpretation of phenomena of cultural contact in both transhistorical and transdisciplinary ways. It brings together the research results of the graduate school "Cultural Encounters and the Discourses of Scholarship," located at Rostock University and sponsored by the German Research Foundation (DFG). One of the concerns of the volumes published in this series is to test and explore contemporary theoretical concepts and analytical tools used for the study of intercultural relations, from antiquity to the present. Aware of significant recent changes in the ways in which other cultures are represented, and "culture" as such is defined and described, the series seeks to promote a dialogical over a monological theoretical paradigm and advocates approaches to the study of cultural alterity that are conscious of the representational character of our knowledge about other cultures. It wants to strengthen a recognition of the interdependencies between the production of knowledge about unfamiliar peoples and societies in various scholarly disciplines and ideologies of nationality, empire, and globalization. In critically investigating the analytical potential of postcolonial key terms such as "hybridity," "contact zone," and "transculturation," the series contributes to international scholarly debates in various fields oriented at finding more balanced and reciprocal ways of studying and writing about intercultural relations both past and present.

Aníbal Arregui
Gesa Mackenthun
Stephanie Wodianka (eds.)

With the editorial assistance of Lisann Wassermann

DEcolonial Heritage

Natures, Cultures, and the Asymmetries of Memory

Waxmann 2018
Münster · New York

Bibliographic information published by the Deutsche Nationalbibliothek
The Deutsche Nationalbibliothek lists this publication in
the Deutsche Nationalbibliografie; detailed bibliographic data
are available in the Internet at http://dnb.d-nb.de

**Cultural Encounters and the
Discourses of Scholarship, volume 10**

ISSN 1868-1395
Print-ISBN   978-3-8309-3790-6
E-Book-ISBN   978-3-8309-8790-1

© Waxmann Verlag GmbH, 2018

www.waxmann.com
info@waxmann.com

Copy-editing: Sarah Thomas
Cover design: Plessmann Design, Ascheberg
Cover image: 'La Muneca', Yasuní National Park, Ecuador. Photo: Jürgen Vogt.
Typesetting: Satzzentrale GbR, Marburg

Printed on age-resistant paper,
acid-free as per ISO 9706

All rights reserved.

No part of this publication may be reproduced, stored in a retrieval
system or transmitted in any form or by any means, electronic,
electrostatic, magnetic tape, mechanical, photocopying, recording
or otherwise without permission in writing from the copyright holder.

Contents

Introduction
Aníbal Arregui, Gesa Mackenthun, Stephanie Wodianka 7

Soundings:
Three Approaches to the Heritage-Ecology-Coloniality Problematic

Chapter One
Stewarding Disputed Heritage:
Private Property, Tribal Legacy, National Patrimony, Global Commons
David Lowenthal 31

Chapter Two
How Did Climate Change Cause the Collapse of Civilizations in the Historical Past?
Ronnie Ellenblum 55

Chapter Three
Bad Heritage:
The American Viking Fantasy, from the Nineteenth Century to Now
Karl Steel 75

From Individual to Collective Heritage

Chapter Four
Du "Patrimoine national" au "Patrimoine interculturel":
Concepts et formes d'institutionnalisation, depuis la Révolution Française jusqu'au Musée National d'Histoire de l'Immigration
Hans-Jürgen Lüsebrink 97

Chapter Five
Le patrimoine en question(s): Le moment des années 1830 au prisme des "Voyages en France" de Stendhal
Laure Lévêque 115

Chapter Six
From Town to Cultural Site: The Heritagization Paths for Casablanca
Romeo Carabelli 135

Colonial and Decolonial Ecological Epistemologies

Chapter Seven
The Gift of Heritage: Making "Eco" Economical in Nigeria
Peter Probst 151

Chapter Eight
Indigenous Knowledges, Ecology, and Living Heritage in North America
Kerstin Knopf 175

Chapter Nine
Ecological Conservation vs. Big Oil: The Case of Yasuní in Ecuador
Jürgen Vogt 203

Toward an Eco-Cultural Decolonization of Heritage

Chapter Ten
Naturalizing Culture in the Pyrenees: Heritage Processes and the Eternalization of Rural Societies
Camila del Mármol and Ferran Estrada 219

Chapter Eleven
Panarchy and the Cross-Cultural Dynamics of Place in Nineteenth-Century America
John J. Kucich 237

Chapter Twelve
Cultivating the Sky
Aníbal Arregui 257

Contributors 275

INTRODUCTION

DEcolonial Heritage.
Natures, Cultures, and the
Asymmetries of Memory

ANÍBAL ARREGUI, GESA MACKENTHUN,
STEPHANIE WODIANKA

The idea for this volume, and the conference on which it is based, was triggered by an event that is a perfect illustration of the triangulation of decolonial politics, environmental protection, and ongoing discussions about World Heritage. In 2007 the state of Ecuador decided to resist the extraction of oil from underneath an UNESCO biosphere reservoir, the Yasuní National Park, and made an unconventional offer to appease the ecological concerns this project raised all around the world: President Correa promised to retain the national park, including its fauna, flora and human cultures, in its current state provided the world community would recompense this 'service' to World Heritage by transferring to Ecuador the sum of 3.6 billion US Dollars. In 2013, President Correa alleged to have to give up on this unprecedented plan to save the Yasuní Park because only few nations had contributed to the fund (Vogt, "Grünes Licht"; Acosta, "Erdöl oder Leben").[1]

The photo on the cover of this volume (see Fig. 3 on p. 214), shot by our contributor Jürgen Vogt, shows an ancient plug or stopper on top of an oil drill left over from previous, smaller scale extractions in the Yasuní Park, which Texaco and other multinational companies had been undertaking since the 1960s. The "pupa" (puppet), as the local population sometimes calls it, stands in the rainforest like one of those ancient pagan stone monuments that fill the pages of colonial travelogues (Fig. 1), or like a Pacific Coast totem pole confronting European visitors with unfamiliar mythologies and heritages (Fig. 2). The pupa reminds us of the ongoing history of resource exploitation that has characterized the relations between the so-called First and Third World. Yet the recent conflict about leaving the oil in the ground and thus salvaging the area for the sake of global natural heritage indicates a change in these relations: it indicates a new political reaction on the part of self-confident indigenous and local governments who take the metropolitan 'center' by its word, asking what it values more: World Heritage or cheap energy?

---

1 Germany, in spite of its 'green' reputation, was not among the significant donors.

Fig. 1: Stele at Copán, Honduras. Lithograph by Frederick Catherwood. Source: Fabio Bourbon, *The Lost Cities of the Mayas. The life, art, and discoveries of Frederick Catherwood*. New York/London: Abbeville Press, 2000.

Fig. 2: Kicksetti Totem and Sun House, Wrangell, Alaska. Sir Henry Solomon Wellcome (1853–1936). Source: Wikimedia Commons. https://commons.wikimedia.org/wiki/File:Color_post_card._Kicksetti_Totem_and_Sun_House,_Wrangell,_Alaska._-_NARA_-_297730.jpg

The conservation of the Yasuní Park is an example that confronts us with a key problematic of this volume: how to reassess the topic of cultural and natural heritage from a decolonial perspective?[2] As a number of important scholarly works have shown in the last decades, the decolonial project must not only address how 'third-world' cultures and societies are still being exploited, but also how their very 'ecologies' – and note here the plural – are being penetrated by a hegemonizing 'Western' nature in both ideological and material senses (see Escobar; Hornborg; Descola; Latour). If, since the 1960s, postmodernism and poststructur-

---

2   We prefer 'decolonial' to 'postcolonial' because the term (which originates from a Latin American response to postcolonial theory) is less burdened by some of the connotations sticking to 'postcolonial', among them a misreading of 'post' as 'after' and a neglect of indigenous and sedentary subject positions, combined with a celebratory attitude toward geographical mobility. But of course, 'decolonial', with its emphasis on the need to decolonize knowledge, has its problems, too. See the introduction to Beer/Mackenthun, *Fugitive Knowledge*.

alism destabilized and pluralized concepts such as 'civilization', 'rationality' and 'culture', they needed the addition of a postcolonial critical perspective to lay the theoretical foundations for the associated projects of, first, intellectual decolonization which critiques, among other things, the Western exclusiveness of definitions of history, heritage, and knowledge. Secondly, this convergence of three interrelated intellectual movements also set the base for the more recent ecocritical, posthumanist, and new materialist approaches that question the categorical divide between 'nature' and 'culture', subject and object, and structure and agency.

This volume, whose contributors are hailing from a wide range of disciplines, seeks to enrich these critical perspectives by adding that of the politics and poetics of 'heritage'. It aims at providing some examples of the ways in which changing conceptualizations of nature and culture intermingle in the making and commemorating of human history. More specifically, the main endeavor is to provide some particular accounts of how precisely the complex confluence of the natural and the cultural domains in the production of World Heritage sets the basis for political asymmetries. Does World Heritage continue the process of Western domination? What precisely is being preserved when we speak about the Yasuní Park in Ecuador (see the essay by Jürgen Vogt in this volume)? Or about the 'pristine' Amazonian forest? Are we referring to the cultural 'purity' of the Waorani indigenous society that dwells in this region? Or is preserving the Yasuní Park an attack against the economic prosperity of Ecuador? Does not the demand that President Correa desist from exploiting the energy resources of his country risk a setback of Ecuador's economic and political autonomy? What is then more 'decolonial', to preserve or to mine the natural wealth of Yasuní Park? The tension we address here is that of whether a stance that promotes the preservation of ecological and cultural heritage in a developing country can avoid coming into conflict with that country's demand for political and economic independence. Does an ecologically sensitive attitude to natural heritage necessarily compromise the similarly important project of decolonization? The answers to these questions are quite complex and probably depend on the scale of the analysis – regional vs. global, economic vs. ecological, short term benefits vs. long term prosperity, and so on. Far from offering a definitive response to these critical questions, we are content to show, through our contributors' particular prisms, how scholarship nowadays makes an effort to integrate scales and concepts of analysis across disciplines as part of a common effort to decolonize their own knowledge. Historical memory is a part of such knowledge, and so is heritage – an institutionalized manifestation of what shapes collective memory politically and culturally. Accordingly, we would like to regard the contributions to this volume as provocations for a more 'symmetrical' intellectual (and political) attitude toward preservation practices, in the sense that these practices involve local ecologies (natures), heritage sites (cultures), and the entangled way in which they shape collective memory. To bring *decolonial* ways of thinking about heritage into a conversation with *ecological* approaches to heritage is one of the aims of this volume.

Heritage in the Age of Geographical and Cultural Mobility

A seminal inspiration for this volume has been the work of David Lowenthal, eminent scholar of heritage politics who also edited the work of America's foremost defender of nature, George Perkins Marsh (Lowenthal, *Heritage Crusade*; Lowenthal, *George Perkins Marsh*; Lowenthal, ed., *Man and Nature*). Throughout his work, Lowenthal argues that natural and cultural heritage are in fact intimately intertwined. Historically, the awareness of the need to protect the natural environment (which Lowenthal dates, for America, to the work of George Perkins Marsh and which is also at the heart of the writings of Thoreau in the 1850s) followed on the heels of the new nation states' self-inventions in genealogies dating back to Antiquity. Since then, Lowenthal argues, the lobby groups defending cultural and natural heritage have somewhat grown apart ("Natural and Cultural Heritage" 86). While culture is predominantly protected for aesthetic reasons, that of nature follows a seemingly rational impulse to ensure the future survival of our species (87). What unites these two movements for conservation – of artifacts, of plants and animals – is a strong emotional impulse. But while this impulse is in one case directed at ensuring permanence, in the other case it is ready to accept change and adaptation (88). It is at any rate becoming increasingly futile to try to separate ecological from cultural stewardship; in fact, it often requires experts from both sides to try to solve conflicts arising from the rivalry between them, as when human settlements are endangered by the attempt to save the habitat of endangered animal species.[3]

Some time ago, the *New York Times* reported about a group of Iraqian refugees visiting the Pergamon Museum in Berlin to be introduced to Germany's cultural heritage – only to find out that the monuments forming part of Germany's 'heritage', such as the Babylonian Ishtar gate, stem from their own country (Donadio). The case illustrates the vicious ambivalence of the repatriation debate: in the light of the recent and ongoing lootings in the war-torn Middle East, even the Iraquian migrants admit that the ancient monument is better off in Berlin. In a mobilized world, they traveled hundreds of miles to escape war and persecution, to arrive unexpectedly at a place which releases strong emotional reactions in them: "Some people want to cry," the museum guide says, "When they see the colors and the shapes, they get chills" (Donadio). Thus the 'stolen' property, as it may be regarded in spite of having been removed in agreement with the Ottoman Empire, can now become a cultural-affective "bridge for immigrants." In spite of its colonial past, it can have a psychological healing effect on the deracinated refugees.

---

3   These discussions have also entered the literary field, a fact that increases their global circulation. For example, Amitav Ghosh's novel *The Hungry Tide* (2005) dramatizes such a conflict, based on a real case in the Sundarbans of Bangladesh, about habitat: between humans fighting for the preservation of their ancestral territory and an international scheme for protecting tigers confronted with extinction.

Emotional attachment to heritage is often seen as a result of global migration and a growing number of people's experience of exile. Edward Said writes of the fate of the exile that he/she has to inhabit a world "on a constantly shifting ground, where relationships are not inherited, but created. Where there is no solidity of home" ("My Right of Return" 457–58). Said's assessment of modernity's mobility is ambivalent. He is aware of the "predicaments that disfigure modernity – mass deportation, imprisonment, population transfer, collective dispossession, and forced immigration" (*Culture and Imperialism* 403). But he also identifies mobility and exile as driving forces of intellectual life. What's important is his differentiation between social relationships as being inherited (in a premodern world) and as having to be created in a globalized world. Cultural heritage offers islands of solidity and groundedness in an increasingly "liquid" cultural universe (Bauman), and in doing so it responds to an emotional need felt by refugees like the Iraqis in the example but also by all those other people who are being confronted with the many forms of displacement caused by the late capitalist economy. Within modernity's structure of feeling, heritage culture fills an emotional gap produced by individual and collective experiences of deracination and alienation. This, we suggest, in part explains its incredible cultural power.

Such attempts at explaining the heritage hype are far from new. Heritage historians David Lowenthal and Marcus Binney already reflected on the reasons for the triumphal march of the UNESCO Heritage program round the globe at the time when it had only just begun. In their early study *Our Past Before us. Why do we Save it?* (1981) they write:

> The pace of technological change, the radical modernization of the built environment, the speed of material obsolescence, an increasing propensity to migrate to new homes, and greater longevity combine to leave us in ever less familiar environments; we are remote even from our own recently remembered past. In a world grown so strange, we hunger for the sense of permanence that tangible relics can best provide. Prevailing doubts – disaffection with modern structures, pessimism about the future – add fuel to nostalgia for the past. (19)

Back in 1981, the collective pronoun "we" predominantly referred to white Westerners. Thirty years later, migrancy in search of life, work, and an escape from the effects of climate change has become a global phenomenon. Increasingly, unlike in the 1980s when we could observe the first consequences of a massive and ongoing rural depopulation (*Landflucht*), economic and political pressures drive more and more people away from their areas of origin.

Writing again on this topic in 2005, David Lowenthal suggests that the deracination from familiar areas of childhood memories contributes significantly to the influx in heritage sites:

> Because the loss of habitual environments and traditional milieus threatens our very sense of being, we treasure their surviving vestiges all the more. A deeply felt need for tangible relics of both nature and culture fuels crusades to protect and conserve them. (82)

The Iraqi immigrants' response to the Ishtar gate in Berlin's Pergamon museum, mentioned above, is a telling example of this migration-caused nostalgia for lost cultural and natural environments. Lowenthal's emphasis on tangibility seems important here; we less frequently learn of intangible things, such as sacred or literary texts, to fulfill this function, although in many cases they do provide an intellectual and emotional 'home', as George Steiner has powerfully argued in his essay "Our Homeland, the Text" (1967) and as Salman Rushdie has argued in "Imaginary Homelands" (1982).

The growing popularity of historical sites, interactive museums, theatrical reenactments and heritage websites testifies to a strong psychological need for the tangible experience of things and landscapes reminiscent of childhood homes and familiar story traditions. "Nostalgia," writes Lowenthal in his recently republished masterwork *The Past is a Foreign Country*, "transcends yearnings for lost childhoods and sciences of early life, embracing imagined pasts never experienced. From an often fatal ailment nostalgia became a benign and even healing response to dislocation, absence, and loss" (15–16). If a capitalist flip side of this emotional need is a growing market for retro products, a political flip side is its availability for rightwing nationalism promoting a "halcyon past" of "sunlit fields […] settled by peoples united by ethnicity or religion," elegantly analyzed by the UN High Commissioner Zeid Ra'ad al Hussein: a statement that received the expected slander in rightwing 'social' media.[4]

While the centrality of migration experiences for understanding the contemporary heritage hype already indicates a need to discuss heritage in the context of cultural encounters, frequent conflicts about the possession and access to heritage sites makes such an approach mandatory. The main reason for this is that the history of World Heritage is deeply implicated in the colonial history of western nations since the nineteenth century where it keeps fulfilling an ideological and sometimes even a territorial function. In this sense, the history of archaeology, the science traditionally dedicated to the salvage and conservation of heritage sites, is also a long history of acquiring cultural treasures in foreign lands in order to collect and exhibit them in the museums of Western nations (Díaz-Andreu; Aguirre). This is why presently there are discussions about repatriating many of these treasures – from human remains and moveable sacred artifacts to massive structures much more difficult to move and to return. The recent skirmish between Jordan and Israel about the national belonging of the site of the baptism of Jesus

---

4   See Hussein's speech attacking the 'bonding of demagogues' including Geert Wilders, Donald Trump and Nigel Farage on 6 September, 2016. http://www.un.org/apps/news/story.asp?NewsID=54862#.WGPw5EYzX3g (accessed 28 December 2016).

is another case in point. In 2015, the UNESCO designated Al-Maghdas on the Jordanian bank as the authentic World Heritage site, "believing" it to be the correct site because this was the view of the Christian church (Laub/McNeil). Elsewhere, ideological wars about access and stewardship of sacred sites have been waged between economic interests and indigenous groups in the media and in court rooms (Carmichael et al.).

Thus, heritage is an ambivalent and embattled ground not just for exiles driven by nostalgic longing for preserving a piece from their past but also for those who remain in their areas of origin and who see their homes encroached by economic ventures clad in the rhetoric of modernization. In both cases, heritage conflict reflects the centrality of human beings' particular emotions and attachments to place. This may seem obvious, but paradoxically individual and collective needs, and the particular interests of humans, have not always been in the focus of heritage politics – UNESCO being a program primarily oriented at abstract national concerns. However, as the entanglement of heritage with human rights is being more recently understood, the interests of people in their affective relationship to cultural and natural heritage sites is becoming more and more visible.

Especially since the beginnings of the UNESCO World Heritage programs, cultural heritage has experienced a veritable boom of conservation and at times commodification. The Italian intellectual Marco d'Eramo complained about the "murderous" effects of heritagization on Italian cities. The old parts of UNESCO-ennobled villages and cities, he writes, are deprived of all marks of modernity such as shops (except for souvenir shops where 'historical' items are being marketed). As a consequence, they are also deprived of inhabitants who do not want to live in a museum. The brand name "UNESCO World Heritage," so d'Eramo, exclusively serves the interests of the tourist infrastructure while the villages have lost their human face. Everywhere heritage is turned into theme parks with their inevitable commodification industry, while people disappear from those areas marked off as heritage sites. D'Eramo suggests the neologism "Unescocide" to capture this development.

The downplaying of current forms of human life and cultural expression caused by the foregrouding of an idealized past is a common problem for the politics of both urban sites and 'natural' heritage. Writing on the politics of national parks on different continents, Guillaume Blanc speaks of them as "territories of violence" due to the eviction and dispossession of their former inhabitants. As Blanc shows with reference to the ghost towns in the Cevennes, and as Camila del Mármol and Ferran Estrada also show in this volume, there is a certain ghostliness about many heritage sites. As with people, it seems, a heritage site, according to the traditional understanding, has to be dead in order to become embalmed in the global pantheon. The temporality of such cultural heritage sites is reminiscent of Mikhail Bakhtin's description of what he calls "castle time." Bakhtin traces the origin of this particular chronotope to the beginnings of gothic literature and the historical novel in which the castle features as an imaginary place "saturated through and through with a time that is historical in the narrow sense of the word, that is, the time of the historical past" (245–46). The castles of these literary texts have their origins in the distant past; they have an "antiquated, museum-like character." The "historical intensity" of Bakhtin's castle time is also felt at heritage sites devoid of life, frozen in a particular historical moment, yet haunted by a condensation of mnemonic energy.

Heritage Time and the Coloniality of Heritage

The instantiation of an ideal past can be observed from at least two well differentiated periods, and therefore from at least two historical 'presents'. The first one is the period to which Bakhtin refers in his comment on the invention of castle time. It happens to be the period of emerging nation states in Europe and in America and of the beginnings of archaeological expeditions to Italy, Greece, Egypt and the so-called Holy Land, as well as Latin America. The main ideological purpose of the heritage "crusades" of that period (Lowenthal) was to provide those nation-states with nation-legitimizing narratives of origins reaching back to antiquity. The second period is that of the past thirty years or so during which the invention of the culturally valuable past has undergone a significant process of expansion, caused by the process of globalization and monitored by the various UNESCO programs. These programs started off with the well-known emphasis on ancient sites: the Ramses temple at Abu Simbel, which had been removed to be salvaged from the rising waters of the Nile due to the building of the Aswan Dam in 1963–68, became the first UNESCO heritage site in 1979. Many other monuments of the distant past would follow.

It is probably no coincidence that the UNESCO program took off in the late 1970s as many European countries were in the process of salvaging past monuments both on the global and local scale – the rescue of Abu Simbel coincides with local restoration programs for preserving historical town centers. Viewed from a broader perspective, the global heritage initiative is contemporaneous with the general intensification of globalization. The accelerated global expansion of production sites and markets intensifies the significance of including as many historical periods and cultural styles as available in the global heritage museum. There is a symptomatic quality about the passion with which artifacts regarded as cultural and natural heritage – both tangible and intangible – are being set aside while the "ruination" (Stoler, see below) of less privileged places continues. While the Norwegian Aurlandsfjord with its magnificent, awe-inspiring mountains is being set aside as a celebrated natural heritage site, to name just one example, the landscape of the Osterfjord not far distant becomes ruinated as a result of mountain top removal to produce gravel for road construction. Meanwhile, many economic actors are driven by the desire to acquire as much land as possible – the prime item of colonial power. In some instances, as Charlotte Joy has shown for the case of Mali, the massive land-grabbing we can presently observe especially in Africa and in Eastern Europe coincides with the production of ancient Mali as a kind of fairy tale scenery. Heritage, as Lowenthal reminds us, is crucially about land, law, and justice ("Natural and Cultural Heritage" 81).

We can observe a remarkable concurrence, then, between the increasing musealization of the world's cultural treasures and the ongoing despoliation of places not privileged enough to join the global ark. Can the nervous amassing of World Heritage be seen as the cultural flipside – or even, with Jameson, as the 'cultural logic' – of the creation of national sacrifice areas around the globe? Ann Laura Stoler suggests as much in her recent volume *Imperial Debris*. In her introduction, Stoler describes the project of the volume as one that disentangles the complicity of the imperial nostalgia associated with World Heritage practices with the "ruination" and "petrified life" of human beings (9). While "colonialisms have been predicated on guarding natural and cultural patrimonies for populations assumed to need guidance in how to value and preserve them" (15), Stoler suggests nothing less than that the deep-felt attachment that many feel for the monuments of past civilizations – for our global heritage – is the emotional reservoir necessary for us to accept present-day despoliations around the globe as unavoidable collateral effects of globalization. Land-grabbing and forced relocations, acts of "radioactive colonialism," health-hazardous resource extraction and waste disposal in the global south, and similar 'imperial' corporate activities are thus quietly sanctioned by first world governments and populations. 'Terrorists' from Al Qaida to ISIS have understood the cultural-ideological function of these monuments whose destruction they gleefully disseminate in the World Wide Web, while turning themselves into the executioners of such historical ruination. In the twenty-first century, heritage is increasingly becoming a weapon of war.

As *Imperial Debris* and similar recent studies also demonstrate, our thinking has definitely moved beyond the ancient nature-culture dichotomy, with significant consequences for discussions of global heritage. Our initial example of the Yasuní Park in Ecuador illustrates this new direction in scholarship, as the Correa government invited the world community to respect the disputed territory for both its ecological and its cultural values, regardless of any official UNESCO status.

There is an evident tension between the planetary scope of UNESCO actions on cultural and natural preservation and the particular ways in which different peoples see what is worth being preserved and how. This, we argue, shows how deep the hook of Western coloniality goes. Despite the critical work of a few intellectual elites, it is still widely accepted that Western scientific recipes are the best to save all humans in this world from an ongoing ecological collapse. Ann Laura Stoler shows how imperialism both destroys social and natural environments and, at the same time, pretends to rescue us from the catastrophe it has itself created.

Yet leaving behind the dramatic environmental effects of the Western colonial and imperialist project, it is also possible to see that its spoil or ruination acts deep inside the bodies of humans. A well-known controversy on the blood samples of the Amazonian tribe of the Yanomami may provide a clear illustration. In 1967 a research group led by the renowned geneticist James Neel and the respected anthropologist Napoleon Chagnon extracted blood samples from Yanomami people and, without their consent, sent them to the US to be used in biomedical research. Forty years later, Yanomami people learned that their blood and the blood of their ancestors remained in freezers in North American labs, and they urged the scientific community (mainly North American geneticists and anthropologists) to return their blood where it did belong (Borofsky et al.). In 2015 diverse media and NGOs celebrated the return of Yanomami blood to the Amazon rainforest. According to Davi Kopenawa, shaman and spokesperson for the Yanomami, their blood could finally be 'put in the river upon its return'.[5]

The episode impressively shows how even anthropologists, despite their intent to take seriously native peoples all over the world, may become accomplices of scientific imperialism, disregarding for forty years the very native perspectives on how bodily substances should be used or preserved (surely not kept in a freezer!). Yet the episode also tells us about the objectification of nature, in that case of human bodies and their vital fluids. The objectification of nature is closely linked to the colonial project and the will to domesticate the newly discovered, 'wild' contexts. It is a typically Western scientific way of 'naturalization' that reinforces our divide between nature and culture, which allows to treat the former just technically, disregarding its immanent moral and political content, and which plays a crucial role in the politics of cultural and ecological preservation, as different essays in this volume illustrate.

With the Yanomami example, we aim at showing that the nature-culture divide is not shared by all, and that this should invite a rethinking of these terms in the domain of heritage politics, as Lowenthal has already noted. Such rethinking seems pretty urgent, also, because such heritage politics, managed by UNESCO and related institutions, have a global reach. So, our proposal is to turn our gaze from the planetary realm to small places, as small as a body of an indigenous person in the Amazon or elsewhere, and ask *there* what is worth being preserved, on what basis, and what we can learn from these specific perspectives in order to confront hegemonic discourses and practices of preservation.

---

5   http://www.survivalinternational.org/about/yanomami-blood-controversy (accessed 24 February 2017)

Decolonizing Heritage

That the Heritage industry is historically and causally related to the politics of territorial appropriation has already been pointed out. Aware of the entanglement between Heritage and colonial power, Helaine Silverman and Fairchild Ruggles suggest viewing the political concerns of the United Nations' commission responsible for Heritage (UNESCO) in conjunction with the work of the High Commission for Human Rights. Both the discourse on Heritage and that on human rights, they remind us, share a number of aspects, among them a strong assertion of universal values. But these assumptions become problematic in situations where the *heritage* interests of one social and cultural group get into conflict with the *human* rights interests of another group. In fact, Silverman/Ruggles argue, heritage is itself to be regarded as both an individual and a collective human right, and has been so regarded by the UNESCO itself (5). Access to certain parts of ancestral lands held sacred by a country's indigenous people – such as the "dreaming tracks" of Australia's Aboriginals – should therefore be granted as being covered by the Universal Declaration of Human Rights (7). Certainly, conflicts about access to sacred sites continue to be a source of armed clashes all over the world – from Jerusalem and Jordan to Afghanistan and Mali to Mexico, South Dakota and Tibet. The authors also point out that non-Western narratives about indigenous heritage have been systematically ignored, belittled, and erased – such as when the inhabitants encountered by the colonizers in America were not seen as descendants of the former 'higher' civilizations of the Moundbuilders or of Tiwanaku but rather as people not capable of such cultural perfection (10). Denial of a people's history has often been a preparatory step to denying its human rights as well:

> Because the denial or distortion of history/prehistory has proven to be a contributing factor in genocide, ethnic cleansing, and oppression to an extreme degree in recent centuries, history often becomes a human rights issue. Among the lessons learned is that the freedom or inability to articulate one's own cultural heritage and express one's own identity is vitally important. (11)

A major impediment for indigenous groups in having their cultural traditions and sites listed and respected as official World Heritage is that UNESCO still operates on the level of nation states and that minority groups have to file their claims through the colonial administration. By now, of course, most of their precious sites have long been ingested into the hungry maws of national heritage, their traditions overwritten with the narratives of colonial history (18).

While the decolonization of heritage will remain an important project until cultural groups have regained full control of their traditions and monuments, another recent development in heritage practice seeks to reform some of the more antiquated aspects of an older heritage industry, such as its focus on dead monuments and ghost sites mentioned above. Cornelius Holtorf and Graham Fairclough have recently diagnosed, and seek to further promote, an important shift in heritage practice – away from the conservation of national monuments and 'ghost' zones, and toward a practice of integrating heritage sites and artifacts into educational processes in multicultural learning environments. Indeed, cultural heritage has the potential of being a useful tool for conflict resolution precisely in such constellations described in the previous paragraphs – where two or more groups contend for different readings, and the possession of the same heritage items. Holtorf and Fairclough call attention to the Faro Convention of 2005 which required a redefinition of cultural heritage from its former function as static historical site to a new practical function as a vehicle for intercultural exchange and personal experience of places and objects (199–200). The Faro Convention explicitly calls for "using and exploiting all cultural heritage for high-level political, social and economic progress" including the recognition that (quoting the Faro document)

> rights relating to cultural heritage are inherent in the right to participate in cultural life, as defined in the Universal Declaration of Human Rights, that heritage is an important contributor to human development and quality of life, and that cultural heritage […] should be made to support the construction of a peaceful and democratic society. (201)

This practical aspect of heritage, Holtorf and Fairclough suggest, can be an important resource for interactive educational processes organized around storytelling and the sharing of experience. This, they emphasize, should not exclude the more painful aspects of shared history: they refer to the International Coalition of Sites of Conscience, which currently manages seventeen sites around the globe. It selects 'painful sites' as heritage sites – places that are globally representative of conflicts and divisions between communities. The aim is to use heritage for enhancing "social healing and reparation," and for promoting a sense of historical and social responsibility (204). As for the Iraqi visitors to the Ishtar Gate in Berlin, this new approach to heritage includes the possibility of a cathartic function of cultural artifacts and memories. Such interactive "heritage as action" (201), Holtorf/Fairclough write, can also enhance an understanding for the connections between human and natural environments which ought to be thought about from an anti-essentialist perspective rather than resting on the old nature-culture dichotomy (203). This contemporary form of 'Action Heritage' – somewhat reminiscent of Tax Sol's and Karl Schlesier's 'action anthroplogy' – considers the embeddedness of heritage sites in their lived cultural and ecological environments.

A crucial element in this new approach to heritage – as an ecologically aware lived and shared cultural practice – is indeed the oldest form of communication: storytelling. Holtorf/Fairclough mention an intercultural storytelling session around a Swedish stone age monument (204). To generate new respect for the cultural traditions transported by oral traditions continues to be a concern of a decolonial approach to cultural knowledge. An encounter with oral heritage also draws attention to the dynamics of cultural signification because a site or an item undergoes various transformations of meaning over the centuries and between interpretive communities. Heritage sites are essentially storied places, and it is important to know the various stories tied to them.

An extension of heritage to include intangible, immaterial elements may also invite us to consider an even more radical idea: that of the dissolution of heritage. During a former Rostock symposium, an archaeologist colleague found himself confronted with the question whether there was something called the archaeology of disappearance – the scientific observation and documentation of the gradual dissolution of monuments and other remains. He was completely flabbergasted. Our thinking about heritage demands that we cling on to every semantically resonant material scrap of ancient stuff. Only once it returns to dust does all meaning cease (Steedman).

Cultures with other practices of record keeping may think differently about this. Material things are made to disappear one day – cultural artifacts may return to nature to reenter the endless cycle of death and rebirth. Apparently, those cultures have a different source to feed individual and collective emotional needs for comfort and symbolic affinity. In 2006, the Haisla Nation in Kitamaat, British Columbia, enthusiastically celebrated the return of its ancient totem pole. The G'psgolox totem pole was a mortuary pole commemorating the spirits of its owner's departed family members. But in 1929, a Swedish diplomat, considering the pole abandoned, had it taken away to Sweden. In 1991, the Haisla rediscovered it in Stockholm's Museum of Ethnography and after long negotiations and the construction of a replica for Stockholm, the G'psgolox totem pole was returned to Haisla country – an event that received a lot of public attention. The indigenous heirs of the departed owner of the pole were deeply emotional about encountering the long-lost sculpture. The story of the pole, after all, was a story of loss and grief, both for the owner's family and for those many families which had fallen victim to colonialism and disease. Its return had cathartic and reconciliatory dimensions. Everyone knew that, had the pole remained in Haisla country, it would have rotten sixty to a hundred years after its creation in 1872. Though 'abducted' by Sweden, it had also been taken care of (see Cardinal for the full story).

Another eight years after its restitution, G'psgolox totem pole rests where it would have rested decades earlier without the transatlantic adventure: in the old graveyard in Kemano, where it now finally awaits its natural dissolution (Fig. 3).[6]

This is a rather ironical example of how the *de*colonization of heritage can work hand in hand with its *eco*logization – its return to dust. The fate of the totem pole also begs the question whether the maintenance of functioning ecotopes would not ultimately be more adequate for ensuring global survival than

---

6   The story of the G'psgolox totem pole from its creation to its return is narrated by the film *Totem. The Return of the G'psgolox Totem Pole* by Gil Cardinal (2003): https://www.nfb.ca/film/totem_the_return_of_the_gpsgolox_pole (accessed 30 December 2016).

Fig. 3: The G'psgolox totem pole at the old grave yard in Kemano, 25 April 2014.
Photo: Tony Sandin, Etnografiska museets bildarkiv 0962.0013.

the musealized preservation of dead monuments. The question at stake is whether protective measures would not have to be extended to *all* cultures and environments crucial for ensuring the survival of human and non-human life on earth. Both approaches to heritage – the decolonial and the ecological one – move the discussion of cultural heritage away from the silent monuments of high culture that dominated the discourse thirty years ago. Combined, they remind us that at the end of heritage there is not necessarily ruination and painful destruction. While heritage as an institutional hegemonic practice will only become obsolescent in a utopian future of universal peace, the impending survival of humanity on earth depends on preserving a vibrant memory of past knowledge and its human and non-human bearers.

Chapter Summaries

The volume begins with the section *Soundings: Three Approaches to the Heritage-Ecology-Coloniality Problematic*. David Lowenthal sets the stage with an up-to-date analysis of the state of cultural heritage studies, arguing that dispute is an inherent quality of cultural heritage worldwide. Caught between private and public interests, between particularist, nationalist, and cosmopolitan agendas, as well as between attempts to preserve cultural artifacts in spite of ecological concerns and attempts to protect natural sites against the ravages of industrial and touristic encroachment, heritage, one must conclude from Lowenthal's essay, is an ideological battle zone. Lowenthal gives numerous examples of how heritage – cultural, natural, and intangible – becomes entangled in political disputes whose parties are not always primarily interested in preserving the most precious achievements of natural growth and human creativity for future generations regardless of their cultural and political affinities. This situation produces its own ironies, as when tribal demands to exempt sacred artifacts from public view look deceptively similar to scientific demands for leaving artifacts in-situ and exempting them from public commodification. What's important in all of these debates, as Lowenthal shows, is the frequently massive imbalance of power between the parties involved, as when heritage interests clash with tribal demands for ecological stewardship. Within such conflicts, Indigenous nations are required to resort to culturally essentialist categories of identity to defend their interests because of an overwhelming discourse that admits legitimate claims to heritage only within the framework of homogenous, even nationalist, definitions of culture. Yet, in spite of their superficial similarity, romantic nationalistic essentialisms within Western countries differ remarkably from the strategic essentialism necessarily promoted by formerly (and continuously) colonized and indigenous groups, for whom the rhetoric of heritage is one of the few available entrance gates toward political recognition and legal protection of lifeways, environments and sacred sites. Heritage discourse, as it is framed at present, keeps intellectually outmoded concepts of cultural homogeneity in a semi-dead vegetative state. Meanwhile the "rain forest" wealth of heritage, Lowenthal asserts, has dwindled into monocultural islands – while real islands are themselves the first victims of the depletion of the environment, leaving the world with facing a growing need for a future-oriented 'living heritage', e.g. in the form of seed banks for plants (and maybe soon other species threatened with extinction).

Lowenthal's contribution is followed by *Ronnie Ellenblum's* climatological approach to a particularly crisis-ridden period in the medieval Middle East. Approaching the problematic of this volume from the perspective of ecocritical historiography, Ellenblum provokes us to pay better attention to the complex conjunctions of ecological and cultural factors in the making of history. The method of computer-based scientific reconstructions of historical climate, he asserts, will not sufficiently explain the behavior of human beings unless it is combined with the study of human cultural history, and vice versa. By triangulating data from different historical sources and periods, Ronnie Ellenblum's essay powerfully demonstrates how mass migrations and cultural destruction are frequently related to climate desasters. The essay reconstructs how the climate anomalies of the so-called Medieval Climatic Anomaly in the tenth and eleventh centuries led to disastrous effects in two areas in the eleventh-century Middle East, which suggests the precariousness of state institutions not prepared to meet such environmental hazards. The terrible events following upon the crop failures in Persia and Egypt about a thousand years ago can be read as a warning to present-day governments to remain aware of environmental change and to prepare themselves for impending disasters (such as the effects of global warming). At the same time, it offers a non-culturalist explanation for the upsurge of religious orthodoxies and fundamentalisms which, as Ellenblum suggests, may even have caused the destruction of the famous Jewish academies of Sura and Pumbeditha, located in Baghdad, in the year 1038. Ellenblum's essay thus evidences the explanatory power of combining various historiographical approaches – a combination inspired by both classical methodology dedicated to the analysis of social and cultural developments and a more recent ecologically-oriented historiography which uses climatological reconstructions of past environmental events. The essay uncannily reminds us of the mutual imbrications of climate change, religious fundamentalism, mass migration, and the wanton destruction of cultural heritage taking place in our own time and it illustrates the necessity of developing new methods for analyzing these connections in a pluricausal and non-dogmatic way.

The third approach to the heritage-ecology-decoloniality triad comes from *Karl Steel* who adds another twist to contemporary reconceptualizations of the medieval period by discussing, from a broadly postcolonial perspective, the implicit (and explicit) racialism of popular modern inventions of the Vikings. His essay magisterially dissects the racialist imagination of the Nordic mystique in the United States and beyond, presenting it as a case of "bad heritage" that stands in diametrical opposition to both what is historically known about the Norse and to the ethos of cultural heterogeneity and diversity. He pays particular attention to the construction of the myth of the Vikings as the first European settlers in North America firing the quest for national origins and celebrated throughout romantic literature and modern popular culture, e.g. 'Viking' films and heavy metal music. The ideal of white supremacy – of a rugged white-skinned and racially pure masculinity – forms the core of this mystique, Steel argues, and it serves a desire for a culturally closed, authoritarian, and intolerant society that defines itself over against an 'effeminate' Christian ethos. In doing so, it shares many features with the egomaniac and violence-admiring fascist character (in spite of the modern 'Vikings' occasional burliness and sloppiness). In addition to critically examining the 'bad' ideological content and the striking unproductivity of this image of the Vikings for solving problems of the present, Steel also produces historical evidence that shows Norse society, including the Vinland travelers, to have been culturally heterogeneous, adaptable and cosmopolitan, arguing that it is these features which ensured Norse hegemony in the pre-modern age and that qualify Norse culture as 'heritage' for our time.

The following section, *From Individual to Collective Heritage,* analyzes the influence of cultural dynamics on heritage, showing that heritage and its multiple forms do not always outlast transformations of cultural history, but also constantly initiate processes of renegotiation between individual and collective remembrance. The title of *Hans-Jürgen Lüsebrink*'s article only seemingly suggests a specifically French topic and object. It implicitly evokes the quite unknown figure of the politician and deputy during the French Revolution, Henrie Grégoire (1750–1831). However, although based on essentially French sources, in particular on the works of the abbot Grégoire, the article aims at reflecting on European and even world history: the birth and the cultural and symbolical transformations of modern states since the eighteenth century, amongst which France was a pioneering role model. National and intercultural heritage will be the key concepts for this reflection. On the one hand, the chapter focuses on the conception and realization of the *Musée national de l'histoire de l'imigration* (*Museum of the National History of Migration*) in Paris. On the other hand, it explores Grégoire's programmatic parliamentary reports on the excesses of revolutionary vandalism. Both examples are historically intermingled and closely linked to the French constitution of national heritage and intercultural memory.

Laure Lévêque's article relates to a wider cultural and literary history of the heritage concept. She analyzes Stendhal's *Voyages en France* and shows that the aesthetics of perception in the nineteenth century are, on the one hand, oriented towards and preformed by Abbot Grégoire's concept of national heritage; and that, on the other side, the understanding of heritage itself is often reduced to the dynamics of an aesthetics of perception at play in nineteenth-century travel literature. Not only the performance but also the questioning of subjectivity and authenticity challenge the potentials and limits of supra-individual conservation and the worthiness of conservation. Buildings and monuments, museums and landscapes guide Stendhal's literary voyage through France. In his literary reflections, Stendhal's fictional persona subjectively appropriates the national memory spaces that shape the collective memory and evaluates their worth as heritage. Consequently, his travel reports become an undogmatic viewpoint of a traveler on what heritage is, could be or will be, as they discuss the relation of verdiction and fiction, of localization and changing perspectives, of subjectivity and universality, appropriation and transfer.

Romeo Carabelli's chapter explores the tension between civil society, economic interests as well as national and international institutions in the process of heritagization of the Moroccan city of Casablanca. Carabelli describes the recent history of urban planning in a city whose development exemplifies some of the central cultural and social problems originating just before and after colonial emancipation. While a cultural elite named *Casamemoire* is devoted to promote and protect the cultural capital of Casablanca's oldest buildings, real-estate actors push in the direction of a quick urban modernization in order to increase prices. As mediators, national governmental institutions and UNESCO representatives seem to not have an effective recipe that may re-establish an equilibrium between collective and individual interests. Cultural capital and actual economy thus display a complex tension and a struggle for power in the management of Casablanca memory and infrastructures.

The third section, *Colonial and Decolonial Ecological Epistemologies*, explores contemporary epistemic and practical conflicts between heritage and ecological interests under the continuing conditions of a (post)colonial global order. *Peter Probst*'s chapter revisits the classic Maussian notion of the gift and uses it to analyze World Heritage logics. With his exploration of the heritagization of the Osun Sacred Grove, in the Nigerian city of Osogbo, Probst argues for the consideration of the moral aspects of heritage. Unlike the commodification of Heritage sites in the form of touristic attractions, the understanding of heritage as a global "gift" deepens not only in the moral duty of preserving the values of the human past but also the need to consider cultural and ecological values of heritage sites in terms of a collective interest. Both the case approached and the analysis employed are illustrative of the kind of decolonization of heritage logics addressed in this volume. In invoking the notion of the "gift of heritage," Probst not only critiques the neoliberal economization of sites as mere instruments of monetary exchange; he also highlights heritage sites' moral, intrinsic value, opening their definition to other, "non-Western" cultural perspectives on what needs to be preserved and why.

The coloniality of heritage is furthermore tackled in the essays by Kerstin Knopf and Jürgen Vogt. *Kerstin Knopf* addresses the issue of living Indigenous heritage in the American far North. She compares Inuit and Western knowledge systems, departing from the interesting fact that Indigenous empirical observation of the natural surroundings has produced new knowledge about astronomical and geological events independently from, but recently confirmed by, scientific calculations of such events. The example serves as an entrée for a discussion of the significance of Indigenous ways of knowing, their adaptability to the world of Western scientific knowledge, and their value as a decolonial epistemology existing alongside the classical episteme of Western science. The Arctic is a particularly well-chosen example as its contribution to global intellectual and material culture has generally been ignored, covered by a colonial prejudice that the far North had no cultural merit to speak of. As Knopf reminds us, the Arctic is presently one of the most embattled zones in the search and extraction of natural resources. It has to deal more directly than other areas with the catastrophe of melting ice, which brings it into great danger of losing its social and cultural integrity. The essay promotes a combined effort of Indigenous scholars and Western ecologists to stay the tide of this development as well as the potential of transcultural knowledge relating to the land. That knowledge, Knopf forcefully argues, should be integrated into the canon of world heritage as it may have a direct effect on future life on this earth.

Building on a general consensus about the necessity of protecting the last natural habitats on earth from destruction by resource extraction, the Ecuadorian government in 2007 offered to the world community to keep the oil in the earth provided its decision in favor of protecting Ecuador's cultural and natural heritage be remunerated by the international community. *Jürgen Vogt* describes the history of this unusual offer and of the failure of Ecuador's appeal to a cosmopolitan sense of ecological responsibility. The area in question, the Yasuní National Park in northeastern Ecuador, has now been opened for oil drilling by Chinese and Ecuadorian companies, which continues the work of US petrol companies like Chevron in Latin America. The essay illustrates the brutal choices a developing and poverty-stricken nation has to make in order to retain its relative economic independence and to stay politically afloat in the international competition for resources. Even a decolonially-minded government, the Yasuní case suggests, is ultimately condemned to become complicit with those forces it has set out to defeat, by participating in the "ruination" of life and land.

The volume ends with a section dubbed *Toward an Eco-Cultural Decolonization of Heritage*. It combines three attempts to approach the heritage problematic through the lens of a contemporary ecocritical and post-humanist theory. All chapters engage with one of the initial questions of the volume, namely what role the cosmological differentiation between nature and culture, or between humans and non-humans, plays in the constitution of heritage practices, especially in colonial and postcolonial contexts. The three contributions provide examples of how cultural analysis may also lead to crucial ecological questions of our time. The overall decolonial proposal of these final chapters aims at the 'denaturalization' of the environment, an ecopolitical gesture necessary for reinstalling a symmetry between cultural and natural human heritage.

Camila del Mármol and *Ferran Estrada* open the section with a study of how tourism is reshaping the rural landscape in the Catalan Pyrenees. The transition from rural-traditional forms of production to a tourism-oriented economy is drastically determining the development of rural areas. While tourism is indubitably opening up new possibilities of engaging in the global market, local populations and their environments are also being subject to a series of processes that reduce their existence to a monologic identity politics. The main feature of this reduction is what the authors call the "naturalization of culture," that is, the tourism-oriented economy's fostering of an image of rural societies as being fixed in an eternal past. By disguising the real economic transformations and instead staging a supposedly 'authentic' rural architecture and 'traditional' means of food production, rural communities become an attraction to tourists who wish to find in the Pyrenees not only an impressive landscape, but also the expression of 'cultures' that are so close to 'nature'. Thus, rural societies are impelled to promote the false image that for them time has not passed, or, if so, it has just gone with the slowness of natural evolution, away from urban processes of cultural acceleration.

The essay by *John Kucich* shows how such nostalgic notions of an unchanging nature is both constructed and deconstructed in colonial and nineteenth-century American texts. He introduces the concept of "panarchy" to investigate the complex and often unpredictable ways in which human and non-human forms of agency interact in the North American colonial contact zone. In approaching nineteenth-century literary and travelistic texts by the Transcendentalists Henry David Thoreau and Margaret Fuller, as well as the Ojibway-Anglo writer Jane Johnston Schoolcraft, Kucich combines postcolonial, ecocritical, actor-network theoretical and new materialist perspectives in order to elucidate a cross-cultural poetics of place in which the non-human world itself retains a certain agency. He challenges us to rethink human relations toward the non-human world in a way that regards the latter as possessing a kind of memory itself, and he invites us to rethink colonial encounters as "ecocultural encounters." The pine tree in particular – a tree that features dominantly in the cross-cultural imagination but was virtually eradicated in the lower St. Lawrence River region by 1850, can be regarded as one of many "sacraments" of that ecocultural contact zone. Kucich suggests to look more carefully at place – "not as a nostalgic category of home and folk, but as a radically decentering way of engaging with the more-than-human world." In the context of this volume's interest in the intersections between cultural encounters and heritage discourse, this essay offers a fascinating glimpse at how place can be thought of as a cultural archive and a repository of cultural energies, i.e. as 'heritage' ranging below the official categories of nationalist discourse.

In the last chapter of this volume, *Aníbal Arregui* reflects on the difference between institutionalized practices of heritage 'preservation' and the alternative route of heritage 'cultivation'. The cultivators' perspective, the essay contends, allows us to consider the entanglement of the cultural and natural aspects of human heritage. Arregui takes the example of what humans do in order to preserve the sky, that is our atmosphere, or our climatic equilibrium. He draws on the example of how a climate scientist and an Amazonian Yanomami shaman address the relation between the forest and the sky, between the human action on the biosphere and its atmospheric consequences. Despite the radical anthropological differences between these two modes of looking at the forest-sky's "ecological relations," both the shaman and the scientist share a cultivator's perspective, i.e. the vision that forest and sky do not just need to be preserved; they also need to be carefully cultivated. This cultivation has a double-sided quality, for it involves both a preservation of human-friendly natural elements and also the cultivation of those cultural or relational aspects that seem to better respond to our planet's ecological demands. Unlike heritage preservation, the cultivation of the sky offers an example of the dynamic interaction of social and ecological entities and of their mutual transformations. It furthermore focuses on how to take care not of pre-given sites, artifacts, and symbols, but of the forms of relation that will ensure their permanence.

Works Cited

Acosta, Alberto. "Erdöl oder Leben." *tageszeitung* 24 August 2013. 10 February 2017. <http://www.taz.de/!5060625/>.

Aguirre, Robert D. *Informal Empire: Mexico and Central America in Victorian Culture*. Minneapolis: University of Minnesota Press, 2005.

Bakhtin, Mikhail. *The Dialogic Imagination*. Ed. Michael Holquist. Austin: University of Texas Press, 1981.

Bauman, Zygmunt. *Liquid Modernity*. Cambridge: Polity Press, 2000.

Beer, Andreas, and Gesa Mackenthun. "Introduction." *Fugitive Knowledge. The Loss and Preservation of Knowledge in Cultural Contact Zones*. Eds. Andreas Beer and Gesa Mackenthun. Münster: Waxmann, 2015. 7–26.

Blanc, Guillaume. "Le Simien Mountains National Park (Éthiopie), un 'territoire-patrimoine' de violence." *L'aluminium et la calebasse. Patrimoines techniques, patrimoines de l'industrie en Afrique*. Eds. Anne-Françoise Garçon et al. Belfort-Montbéliard: UTBM, 2013. 133–45.

Borofsky, Robert, et al. *Yanomami: The fierce Controversy and what We can Learn from it*. Berkeley/Los Angeles/London: University of California Press, 2005.

Cardinal, Gil. *Totem: The Return of the G'psgolox Pole*. Documentary film. National Film board of Canada, 2003. 30 December 2016 <https://www.nfb.ca/film/totem_the_return_of_the_gpsgolox_pole/>.

Carmichael, David L. et al., Eds. *Sacred Sites, Sacred Places*. Abingdon/New York: Routledge, 1997.

D'Eramo, Marco. "Unescocide." *New Left Review* 88 July–August 2014. 10 February 2017 <https://newleftreview.org/II/88/marco-d-eramo-unescocide>.

Descola, Philippe. *Beyond Nature and Culture*. London: University of Chicago Press, 2013.

Díaz-Andreu, Margarita. *A World History of Nineteenth-Century Archaeology. Nationalism, Colonialism, and the Past*. Oxford: Oxford University Press, 2007.

Donadio, Rachel. "Berlin's Museum Tours in Arabic Forge a Bridge to Refugees." *New York Times* 28 February 2016. 30 December 2016 <https://www.nytimes.com/2016/02/29/arts/design/berlins-museum-tours-in-arabic-forge-a-bridge-to-refugees.html?_r=0>.

Escobar, Arturo. "After Nature: Steps to an Antiessentialist Political Ecology." *Current Anthropology* 4.1 (1911): 1–30.

Ghosh, Amitav. *The Hungry Tide*. London: Harper Collins, 2005.

Holtorf, Cornelius, and Graham Fairclough. "The New Heritage and Re-Shapings of the Past." *Reclaiming Archaeology. Beyond the Tropes of Modernity*. Eds. Alfredo González-Ruibal. London/New York: Routldege, 2013. 197–210.

Hornborg, Alf. *Global Ecology and Unequal Exchange. Fetishism in a Zero-Sum World*. London/New York: Routledge, 2011.

Hussein, Zeid Ra'ad al. Speech in front of the United Nations 6 September 2016. 28 December 2016 <http://www.un.org/apps/news/story.asp?NewsID=54862#.WGPw5EYzX3g>.

Jameson, Fredric. "Postmodernism, or the Cultural Logic of Late Capitalism." *New Left Review* I/146 (1984): 53–96.

Kopenawa, Davi. "The Blood Controversy." *Survival International* 24 February 2017. <https://www.survivalinternational.org/about/yanomami-blood-controversy>.

Latour, Bruno. *Nous n'avons jamais été modernes: Essai d'anthropologie symétrique*. París: La Découverte, 1991.

Laub, Karin, and Sam McNeil. "UNESCO backs Jordan as Jesus' baptism site as debate goes on." *AP*. 13 July 2015. 15 March 2016 <http://bigstory.ap.org/article/9441fab41e454b2db337e53503d0ecc5/unesco-backs-jordan-jesus-baptism-site-debate-goes>.

Lowenthal, David. *The Past is a Foreign Country*. Cambridge: Cambridge University Press, 1985. Reprinted 2006. (Revised Edition 2015)

—. *The Heritage Crusades and the Spoils of History*. Cambridge: Cambridge University Press, 1998.

—. *George Perkins Marsh. Prophet of Conservation*. Seattle: University of Washington Press, 2000.

—. "Natural and Cultural Heritage." *International Journal of Heritage Studies* 11,1 (2005): 81–92. Online 2006.

Lowenthal, David, and Marcus Binney, Eds. *Our Past Before Us. Why do we Save it?* London: Temple Smith, 1981.

Marsh, George Perkins. *Man and Nature*. 1864. Facsimile Reprint, Ed. David Lowenthal. Seattle: University of Washington Press, 2003.

Rushdie, Salman. "Imaginary Homelands." 1982. Reprinted in *Imaginary Homelands: Essays and Criticism 1981–1991*. London/New York: Granta/Penguin, 1991. 9–21.

Said, Edward W. *Culture and Imperialism*. London: Chatto and Windus, 1993.

—. "My Right of Return." Interview with Ari Shavit. *Ha'aretz Magazine*, Tel Aviv. 2000. Reprinted in *Power, Politics, and Culture: Interviews with Edward W. Said*. Ed. G. Viswanathan. New York: Vintage, 2002. 443–58.

Silverman, Helaine, and D. Fairchild Ruggles, Eds. *Cultural Heritage and Human Rights*. New York: Springer, 2007.

Steedman, Carolyn. *Dust*. Manchester: Manchester University Press, 2001.

Steiner, George. "Our Homeland, the Text." 1967. Reprinted in *No Passion Spent: Essays 1978–96*. London: Faber and Faber, 1996. 304–27.

Stoler, Ann Laura, Ed. *Imperial Debris. On Ruins and Ruination*. Durham: Duke University Press, 2013.

Vogt, Jürgen. "Grünes Licht für Ölbohrung im Yasuní." *tageszeitung* 24 May 2014. 10 February 2017 <http://www.taz.de/!347652/>.

Soundings:
Three Approaches to the
Heritage-Ecology-Coloniality
Problematic

CHAPTER ONE

Stewarding Disputed Heritage: Private Property, Tribal Legacy, National Patrimony, Global Commons

DAVID LOWENTHAL

Heritage is globally prized as an individual and collective good. But multiple claimants make it singularly contentious and divisive, engendering acrimonious conflict over claims to what and where it should be and by whom owned. Today's universalizing tenets are flagrantly flouted by selfish chauvinism. While international agencies such as UNESCO and the United Nations mandate global stewardship, nation states and tribal groups zealously aggrandize their own heritage against rival claimants. Only collaborative care can effectively protect global legacies of nature and culture. But universal concerns typically give way to parochial interests couched in globalist lingo. Thus Italy's repatriation of antiquities from American museums was "not nationalistic, but universal," contended culture minister Francesco Rutelli, "because all national patrimonies belong to the world" (quoted in Delaney). Given the self-serving hype of much heritage discourse, it is fair to wonder, with archaeologists Morag Kersel and Christina Luke: "Can there truly be altruistic motives behind the common goal of a protected past?" (77).

The increasingly lucrative global antiquities market exacerbates claims among competing stakeholders – private collectors, public museums, archaeologists, art historians, nations, tribes, and not least, looters, dealers, and auction houses:

- Tomb-robbers in Tuscany and Sicily, Mexico and Peru assert that their ancestors tell them where to dig for treasure, and then sell their looted ancestral heritage to feed their families.
- Mythic if not manufactured sanctity mandates secreting tribal heritage out of sight of alien curiosity, control, and corruption. Hence inscribing heritage as globally meritorious often has the paradoxical effect of rendering it not more but less accessible.
- Archaeologists deplore artifact removal and trade for destroying *in situ* heritage context and irreplaceable knowledge of the past. Yet priceless existing knowledge is largely dependent on the study of excavated and looted antiquities such as the Rosetta Stone, Assyrian cuneiform tablets, and Khmer carvings.

– Collectors are blamed by archaeologists for abetting the ill effects of the antiquities market, notably the loss of contextual knowledge consequent on illicit excavation, pillage, and export concealment. Yet collectors preen themselves as saviors of what would otherwise have succumbed to developers or iconoclasts or plain neglect; after all, they note, the vast majority of the world's museumized heritage owes its continued survival to collectors' doting stewardship.

In sum, disputants' concerns over culture, craft, context, and cash make the modern cult of antiquities a conflict-ridden minefield. As archaeologist and art historian David Scott observes of Incan artifacts, most heritage that is not looted is faked, most that is not faked is looted, and much is both looted *and* faked. The illicit antiquities market's intimate links with criminal networks in drugs, sex trafficking, and terrorist iconoclasm buttress Michael Herzfeld's take on heritage as corruption, preservation as a holy crusade against decay born of Original Sin.

Here I argue that heritage has always been fractious and divisive, by its very nature cherished as the exclusive property of competitive groups. It functions as a *casus belli* because it is an exemplary tribal bond.[1]

Heritage Stewardship is Innately Possessive

Heritage overwhelmingly reflects personal or communal self-interest. Possessions are valued as *mine* or *ours*; indeed, they constitute our very identity. "'I am what I own', whether cattle or coin, concubines or Canalettos," held collections guru John Windsor, "has been the guiding principle of the technically ignorant throughout the ages" (62). And of the cognoscenti, too. "A man's self is the sum of all he can call his," wrote psychologist William James in an era of patriarchal privilege, including "his wife and children, his ancestors and friends, his reputation and works, his lands and horses, and yacht and bank-account" (I: 291).[2] The heritage we prize is the past we possess, and we praise it *because* it is ours.

Exclusive to us, *our* past is unlike anyone else's. Its uniqueness vaunts our superiority. Heirlooms *distinguish* us from others; they get passed on only to our physical or putative descendants, to our own flesh and blood. Alien newcomers, outsiders, foreigners erode or debase group legacies. Each group's heritage is by

---

1   I initiated this argument in *The Heritage Crusade and the Spoils of History* (1998) and in "Why Sanctions Seldom Work" (2005). For subsequent elaboration, I am grateful to Marie-Louise Stig Sorensen at Oxford's archaeology seminars in 2011, to Sverker Sörlin and Libby Robin in the environmental humanities program at Stockholm's Royal Institute of Technology in 2012, and to John Henry Merryman and Lynn Meskell's heritage and cultural property programs, in law and anthropology, at Stanford University in 2015.
2   C. B. Macpherson, *The Political Theory of Possessive Individualism* (1962), traces the link between identity and ownership to early-modern European ideas of personhood. William James's articulation is expanded by Russell W. Belk, "Possessions and the Extended Self" (1988), and linked to group heritage by Richard Handler, "On Having a Culture" (1988).

definition incomparable. In treating its distinctive past as sacred, and its sacred past as distinctive, each nation becomes God's Chosen People (Anthony Smith). In celebrating their own and expunging others' heritage, nations, tribes, and faiths in fact worship themselves. And using "ancient cultural objects to affirm continuity with a glorious and powerful past," writes museum director James Cuno, is a common "way of burnishing their modern political image – Egypt with the Pharaonic era, Iran with ancient Persia, Italy with the Roman Empire" (120).

Lauding one's own legacy and excluding or discrediting those of others foments endemic rivalry. Some assert their heritage's moral or military, mental or material prowess; others lay claim to inherited traits and emblems. Both types of claim mirror stereotypes that arrogate virtue to us and deny it to others: *we* are civilized and steadfast; *they* are barbarous and fanatical, or primitive and blind. Obsession with exclusive, unique, and fiercely acquisitive identities suffuses heritage discourse with tension and conflict. Boasts of precedence and preeminence deny or clash with those of others; so do rival claims to the same valued relics and memories.

Essentialist claims based on supposed priority and innateness are untenable in historical fact and lethally divisive in practice. Yet they continue to proliferate, shaping every aspect of heritage – how it is identified, interpreted, stewarded, altered, purloined, faked, and scuttled. Such claims are embedded in traditional attachment to property, including environmental and intangible legacies. The aurora borealis has long been contested as a national find by Sweden, Norway, Russia, even by France, notes science historian Patricia Fara, on the basis that the aurora's very absence from their skies made the French more acute observers.

Pious modern affirmations of mutual respect for "the cultural heritage of all humanity" founder on the shoals of this or that ethnic, religious, linguistic, or national claim of exclusive entitlement (Silverman), buttressed by archaeologists' equally pious 1990 assertion that "indigenous cultural heritage rightfully belongs to the indigenous descendants of that heritage" (in Scarre 121–22). The self-congratulatory swamp of collective memory embracing heritage and identity now extends to today's terrain of contrition – the accusatory lineaments of museums of conscience and monumental commemorative apologia. Heritage thus becomes a doubly fearsome quagmire. Whether recalled with glory or with grief, the past is increasingly occluded in a miasma of moral self-righteousness.

Stewardship is Traditionally Parochial

Heritage remains stubbornly sectarian in essence. Invented no less than inherited tradition is jealously particularistic. Heritage stewards are mistakenly seen as selfless disinterested guardians dedicated to protecting and exhibiting the sites and objects in their care. Yet self-serving motives suffuse the whole enterprise. Heritage is mainly sought and treasured as our *own*; we strive to keep it out of the clutches of others we suspect, often with good reason, of aiming to steal it or to spoil it. Indeed, stewardship is commonly seen to require selfishness. The good steward is fiercely protective of what is in his custody. Whether on behalf of individuals or of empires, stewardship is intrinsically possessive.

But not necessarily possessive for one's own sake. The traditional steward is not an owner but a keeper for another – the guardian of sacred mysteries, the manager of a landed estate. The steward keeps vigil for someone else. For some *one*, not *everyone* else – a tribal God against rival deities, a landlord against poachers, a king against usurping nobles, a nation against foreign foes. Only those pledged to their clients' exclusive cause can be relied on as stewards. An heir must be sure his trustee acts solely on his behalf, a nation that custodians will yield no part of the domain. Stewards must be fierce watchdogs.

Dog-in-the-manger zealotry is a hallmark of national heritage, as it is of collectors' hoards. Seeing Constable paintings overseas, future British National Gallery director Nicholas Penny exclaimed: "Heritage never means more to us than when we see it inherited by someone else". Only when the English spoke of shipping ruined Norman abbeys across the Channel did the French rescue them from neglect; only when the Victoria and Albert Museum bought a seventeenth-century Dutch church fitting did the Dutch rally round their legacy; only when Americans were about to ship Tattershall Castle across the Atlantic did Parliament act to protect Britain's built heritage (Lowenthal, *Past* 416). Outrage at J. P. Morgan's transatlantic shipment of a staircase from the Casa de Miranda in Burgos prodded the Spanish into heritage protection. The Tower of London sold off two Hanoverian state crowns in 1836; for decades no one knew or cared where they were. But in 1995 word that this "purest national heritage of priceless importance" might be sold abroad roused huge dismay (Alberge, "King's"), and the crowns' ultimate 'rescue' for Britain.

Yet selfish stewardship often becomes self-defeating. Buildings about to be safeguarded as historic are allowed to decay or are even razed by their owners on the eve of being legally 'saved' from development. Legacies are sometimes destroyed to prevent anyone else from getting them. The apocryphal possessor of a unique *incunabulum* is dismayed when a second copy turns up; he at once buys it and then burns it – so his will still be the *only* copy.

Squabbling over heritage tends to cloud its authenticity. Continuing a seven-century dispute between England and Scotland, in 1950 the Stone of Scone was sundered from its accompanying Coronation chair in Westminster Abbey by Scottish Nationalists, who fashioned several sandstone copies before returning it to London. In 1996 it was formally ceded to Scotland. But no one now knows for sure which is the 'real' Stone (Rodwell). Divisive personal interests may destroy heritage integrity. Schubert's brother, after the composer's death, snipped his music scores into tiny pieces, giving favorite pupils a few bars each. Rivalry may result in some treasures being entirely withdrawn from view: Forbidden to export a Lucian Freud painting she had bought at auction, an American locked it away in a London bank vault. "If Britain's export laws could stop her hanging it in her collection, she would stop Britain's public galleries hanging it in theirs" (quoted in Alberge, "Buyer").

Bellicose xenophobia is a heritage hallmark. National anthems are full of gore. Sabre-rattling songs make it easier to cheat, fight, and kill outsiders. Anger inspirits the oppressed. From bellicose words ensue bellicose acts. "As tools of cultural identity and proof of ancestral claims to the land," lamented US/ICOMOS executive director Gustavo Araoz in the wake of Taliban iconoclasm, "heritage sites have acquired new attributes important and perverse enough to merit their obliteration and fuel war".

Heritage that conquerors cannot appropriate is apt to be expunged. As the Romans had done with Carthage, so the Nazis demolished old Warsaw as a font of Polish pride. "The intentional obliteration of any trace of cultural heritage," recognizes UNESCO's Giovanni Boccardi (in Heyman), "is part of a strategy of war." The past decade saw the archival, archaeological, and architectural legacies of Croatia, Bosnia, and Rwanda deliberately destroyed, the present decade those of Iraq, Syria, Egypt, and Algeria. As a heritage too eclectic to suit Muslim fanatics, almost everything in Afghanistan's National Museum has been stolen, sold, or smashed. Echoing Protestant iconoclasm of Catholic images during the Reformation, ISIS today 'purifies' Iraq and Syria not only of Christian but of 'infidel' Muslim religious monuments.

Biblical Origins of Heritage

Divisive and rivalrous heritage was a consequence, the Old Testament relates, of God's destruction of the Tower of Babel. In the Edenic earliest days, "the whole earth was of one language, and of one tongue." What shattered this unity after the Flood was the desire to immortalize the memory of human accomplishments – an impious hunger for heritage. The Tower of Babel elevated pride to heaven itself, "to make a name for ourselves." The tower triggered God's dispersal that sundered tribe from tribe, "scattered abroad upon the face of the whole earth" in both distance and discourse (Genesis 11.1, 4). Humanity was condemned to a babbling confusion that bred internecine misprision and strife. Each tongue's speakers spawned discordant distinctive identities out of half-remembered, half-invented legends. And these separate identities then hardened and reified into disparate factional heritages (Lowenthal, "Heritage Care"; Steiner).

The Genesis story reflects certain prehistoric actualities. Paleolithic and Neolithic migratory waves out of Africa to the ends of the habitable globe extinguished any original Ur-linguistic unity. Communication among far-flung hunter-gatherer bands dwindled more and more over time, multiplying linguistic differences. Reinforced by physical segregation, the confusion of tongues gave rise to manifold incommensurate and mutually hostile local, tribal, and eventually national cultures. To ensure communal cohesion and social solidarity, each group crafted its own exceptionalist narrative of origins, history, and destiny – a heritage, like their language, necessarily opaque to outsiders. When men on the move came into contact with one another, ruthless competition for land, for goods, and for women exacerbated differences between 'us' and 'them'. Insider identity, defined by opposition to alien others, was certified by collective tribal and national memories, first through oral recitation and later through written records.

"My Country, Right or Wrong"

Group heritage, bolstered by memory and validating identity, provides the illusion of insular havens of likeminded certitude in stormy seas of outlandish ways – even among ongoing trade contacts. Societies confront one another armored in separate identities whose likenesses they ignore or disown and whose differences they distort or invent to stress their own superior worth. Social utility requires each distinct communal heritage to be in some degree empirically false, for if it were true it could be adopted by others. Only contrived and counter-intuitive heritage can remain exclusive, literally in defiance of reality, to ensure that it is not shared by outsiders.

The sociologist Émile Durkheim explained how society succeeds by being collectively imagined, transcending and denying sensory evidence (134–38, 362, 391). Aboriginal Australian members of the Kangaroo, Cockatoo, Lizard, and Louse clans believe that they are born with a shared clan essence. Shown a photograph of himself, a member of the Kangaroo clan points to it to affirm that he resembles a kangaroo. They look alike through social contrivance. Empirical absurdity becomes social reality, as with Lewis Carroll's Red Queen. "One *can't* believe impossible things," protests Alice. "I daresay you haven't had much practice," said the Queen. "When I was your age, I always did it for half-an-hour a day. Why, sometimes I've believed as many as six impossible things before breakfast" (Ch. 6).

That society thrives on persisting error about the past has long been extolled as statecraft. Plato's *Republic* shows how such 'noble lies' instill civic loyalty. Socrates contrived a "magnificent myth that would carry conviction to our whole community." He aimed to persuade them that they had been "fashioned and reared in the depths of the earth, and Earth herself, their mother, brought them up into the light of day; so now they must think of the land in which they live as their mother and protect her if she is attacked" (Plato 181–82).

Beginning in early childhood, find psychologists Cristine Legare and Rachel Watson-Jones, the need for social inclusion and fear of ostracism unless we conform impel us to imitate daft behavior and parrot nonsensical rituals, for so doing attests our commitment to group values and makes us socially welcome. Heritage functions like empirically falsifiable taboos and ritual performances that bind those who respect them and disown those who disparage them. It strengthens group loyalty and cohesion, frequently against empirical reality. "Getting its history wrong is crucial for the creation of a nation," Ernest Renan assured French compatriots; the need for amnesia and error made naked historical truth a danger to national unity (38). "We made peace with the Middle Ages by misconstruing them," exulted the English historian Herbert Butterfield (7–8). Mistaking England's new constitution for a restoration of ancient virtues gave it a needed anachronism. Useful *because* mistaken, this fable became a pillar of national heritage in the guise of Whig History.

Every nation enhances its identity by sanctifying some mythic heritage in defiance of historical fact. Finns hold the *Kalevala* sacrosanct despite knowing it to be a counterfeit; Greeks punish deniers of the falsehood that Ottoman Turkey banned Greek schooling; Swiss chauvinists issue death threats to debunkers of William Tell's fictitious apple; Israelis ritually reenact Josephus's fable of the heroic mass suicide at Masada and idolize the heroic one-armed Trumpeldor who simultaneously wielded rifle and plow (Lowenthal, *Past* 509–11, 527–28). Error is famously commended in Joseph Roth's *Radetzky March*, whose protagonist is outraged by schoolbook puffery of his 'rescue' of Emperor Franz Josef at the battle of Solferino. "'It's a pack of lies,'" he yells. "'You're taking it too seriously,'" says a friend. "'All historical events are modified for consumption in schools, and quite right, too. Children need examples which impress them.'" The emperor agrees. "'Neither of us shows up too badly in the story. Forget it'" (16).

Were children taught what really happened, civic allegiance would wither. "Away with such skepticism!" an American magazine of 1908 denounced muckraking revision. Sacred myths were "the very soul of our history […] To take them away would now be a baneful disorganization of the national mind" (in Raphael 263). The American Legion in 1940 faulted history texts "that tried to give the child an unbiased viewpoint instead of teaching them real Americanism. We can't afford to teach them to be unbiased" (in Evans 195). British civic leaders similarly sought to proscribe history lessons that encouraged skepticism about British heroes and heroines. So too with tangible heritage – buildings, relics, artifacts of every kind are continually esteemed, manipulated, and expunged to demonstrate – or in today's penitential and apologetic mood – increasingly to disparage – the noble efforts and enduring virtues of ancestral exemplars.

Universalizing Heritage: the Modern Mission

Recent decades have seen the emergence of a globalized approach to heritage that aims to transcend tribal and abridge national interests. In this view heritage – alike the bounties of nature and the material and intangible creations of culture – is the combined legacy of humankind, held in trust for all the world's peoples, present and future. The concept of heritage as a universal good is the outgrowth of two centuries of educational and political advance that have both popularized interests in heritage and democratized notions of who is entitled to it, in line with modern visions of social equity and environmental necessity.

In the past, earthly heritage was restricted to princes and prelates, merchants and magnates; others had to be content with an uncertain legacy of an after-life. Reminded that "We are the heirs of all the ages," Ivy Compton-Burnett's lowly villager ruefully observes that "It would have been pleasant to be the heir of something besides" (159). The nineteenth and twentieth centuries expanded the remit of heritage to embrace the hoi polloi, and to enlarge its content from great monuments and genealogical entitlement to garden sheds and *genres de vie*. The poor inherited few personal goods but increasingly shared national legacies of language, landscape, and lore. Imperial museums justified their worldwide collections as educational and inspirational emporia for comparative global understanding. In the heyday of imperialism, the concept of global heritage rationalized or excused the aggrandizement of tribal and colonial cultural goods by Western conquest. The great bulk of it still remains in Western collections. But more and more 'global heritage' is taken to mean literally that everyone should be entitled to share in all of it. The end of empire in theory transformed heritage into a universal right.

Not only is heritage now seen as a global commons, it becomes ever more global in character. When people were fewer and less mobile, cultures were more isolated, heritage diffusion slow and limited. Modern communications make such diffusion swift and pervasive. Global culture of the present day is often decried as blandly uniform or spiritually vacuous. But globalization is lauded for diffusing the presumed authentically distinctive cultural legacies of *the past* – the arts and skills of classical Greece, of Confucian China, of Enlightenment Europe. As the historian André Reszler shows, Athens is now everywhere.

Universalizing Heritage: the Sober Reality

Yet the globalization of heritage in UNESCO and other international protocols, along with the worldwide deployment of similar techniques of recording, depicting, conserving, and restoring the past, aggravates rather than alleviates animus among claimants of art and antiquities, natural resources and cultural icons. Analysts of UNESCO find "more convergence in the signboards, lighting systems, management plans, […] or fencing strategies" of World Heritage sites "than in the[ir] meanings […] and social values" (Brumann and Berliner 27). For humanity's few thousands to feel and act in concert at the time of Babylon was hard enough. For their multi-billion far-flung descendants today it seems inconceivable. No all-embracing global narrative even begins to match the evocative power of tribal myths and national legends.

Indeed, the same impetus toward declaring heritage of universal value has paradoxically aggravated essentialist claims – national, tribal, ethnic, minority – to exclusive possession. Both state and subaltern restitution demands become not less but more assertive as global agencies and scholarly bodies lend them moral standing. The very protocols that proclaim heritage to be global also assert the rights of particular groups to the creations of their ancestral forebears, however far back in time. "As more nations lose the illusion of a national economic sovereignty or well being," notes Cuno, "new incentives for cultural purification" gain force, with governments "increasingly making claims of ownership of cultural property on the basis of self-proclaimed and fixed state-based identities" (119–22). Tribal, subaltern, and other minority peoples likewise use global heritage homilies to assert indigenous identity and sovereignty by means of cultural property claims, as Haidy Geismar (*Treasured Possessions*) documents for New Zealand Maori and for Vanuatu craftsmen.

Such conflicts fuel protective chauvinism, spurring nations and tribes everywhere to enact legislation aggrandizing all heritage made or found in their past or present domains, regardless of who else may have or may now live there. Tribes demand the return from museums and private collectors of skeletal remains and sacred artifacts; nations initiate lawsuits enjoining the repatriation of antiquities and works of art to their supposed homelands.

As with the Elgin Marbles (remnants of the Parthenon in the British Museum), paintings and sculpture are often anthropomorphized as living beings languishing in foreign exile (Hamilakis). "The odyssey of these objects, which started with their brutal removal from the bowels of the earth, didn't end on the shelf of some American museum," rhapsodized Rutelli about Italy's repatriation of three dozen antiquities from the United States in 2007. "With nostalgia, they have returned. These beautiful pieces have reconquered their souls" (quoted in Brodie and Apostolidis 67). Greek outrage at the British Museum's 2014 loan to Russia's Hermitage of Parthenon sculptures "torn apart" is inflamed by British Museum director Neil MacGregor's sanctimonious premise that Greece should be "very pleased that a huge new public can engage with the great achievements of ancient Greece" (quoted in Helena Smith).

Repatriation Dilemmas and Nationalist Priorities

The practical impossibility of enforcing most retention laws and repatriation claims sets up a distressing disconnect between hype and reality. Blanket export prohibition talk masks actual inability to stem the drain of cultural property. Heritage-rich nations and tribal groups *sound* bellicose in defense of heritage but are impotent to prevent its attrition. Looters in Belize outnumber and are better funded than the country's entire military. Given Italy's vaunted 40, 60, or 70 percent of the world's cultural patrimony, it is small wonder the Italian army and police force combined cannot secure from theft its relic-laden soil from *tombaroli*, its tens of thousands of museums and churches, nor can they secure its porous borders from illicit export to Swiss and overseas dealers. Draconian retention edicts encourage site destruction, and criminal plunder taints the entire international antiquities market (Smale; Brodie, "Congenial Bedfellows?"). The smuggling of looted art and antiquities to Western collectors is a major impetus for ISIS 'cultural cleansing' – and a major source of funding for ISIS armaments (Moody; Myers and Kulish).

Moreover, heritage retention and repatriation are inevitably contested among rival claimants. Should a long-buried relic be returned to where it was found, where it was made, or where it was conceived? If from an ancient provincial Roman or Incan imperial site, what modern Mediterranean or Andean state, if any, might be its rightful owner? Does a neoclassical sculpture found in Sicily 'belong' in Greece, in Rome, or in Sicily? Is Italian identity really enhanced by the repatriation from New York of an Athenian-made Etruscan vase? Does Britain suffer cultural attrition by the sale abroad of Greco-Roman antiquities, now lamented as 'lost' for having been part of a famed English collection?

National and tribal claims mask the reality that there are no 'pure' cultures; most heritage is hybrid and heterogeneous in origin and nature. Consider the disputed use of Navajo weavers' designs by mass-produced Zapotec manufacture in Mexico, which undercut the 'authentic' handcrafted Navajo tourist market in Santa Fe and elsewhere (M'Closkey; Wood). In fact, indigenous American designs and motifs derive from nineteenth-century American merchants who persuaded Navajos to copy fashionable Bukhara and other Asian rugs. The hybridity of Navajo and Zapotec rugs has today come full circle, as "traders give card models of fashionable Navajo and Zapotec rugs" to Central Asian and East European weavers:

> Navajo-style rugs are woven in Romania, Bulgaria, Ukraine, Peru, Ecuador and the Orient, where Tibetan-Nepalese and Afghan-Turkmen refugees in India and Pakistan are now imitating Navajo patterns. Thus […] in the 1890s American merchants went to the Far West to get the Navajos to copy Bukhara and other Asian rugs; in the 1990s they went to the East to get Asian weavers to copy Navajo copies of Oriental rugs (Busatta).

The Greek government insists that the Elgin Marbles' return would restore the unity of the Parthenon. But that 'unity' is a recently-contrived philhellene idealization. For most of its history the Parthenon was part of a densely built-up Hellenistic and then Ottoman town from which it could not be viewed in its entirety (St Clair 84–86). But "when it achieved its independence from the Ottomans, in 1829, Greece made the Acropolis its national symbol, then removed all non-Athenian additions to the citadel's buildings, including remnants of a Byzantine church, an Orthodox and Roman Catholic cathedral, and a mosque," notes Cuno

(122) – "all the remains of barbarity," as the German architect in charge rubbished everything that was not Classical (Leo von Klenze, quoted in Beard 100).

The Classical bias continues to demote other Greek heritage, as Ioannis Poulios recounts at the World Heritage site of Meteora monastery:

> Even after the recognition of Byzantine sites as 'heritage', the State's emphasis on the Classical past has substantially affected the overall way Byzantine sites were, and are still, approached and protected. Byzantine religious sites are looked upon from a Classical perspective, with emphasis on their artistic and art-historical significance and on the need for the preservation of their fabric, while their continuing ecclesiastical and liturgical use is largely ignored. Byzantine religious heritage was simply added to an already well-established and strict set of regulations modelled upon Western European Classical principles (41).

Conflicting Values: Nations, Tribes, and UNESCO

UNESCO inscribes a thousand-odd World Heritage sites of 'universal' value, but the manner of their selection has less to do with global standards of significance than with the heritage ambitions of UNESCO nation-state members who select, present, and profit from their designation. That only nation-states themselves can propose sites debars tribal and other minorities from meaningful participation and, they complain, relegates their own heritage to subordinate and often neglected status. "Whether one is talking about universal human rights or world heritage," concludes anthropologist Lynn Meskell, "these seemingly global elements (universal and world) remain stymied by statism" (169). In short, what is touted as a globally equalizing heritage effort turns out to be nationally opportunistic to the detriment of both global and local heritage concerns. Indigenous advocates the world over accuse UNESCO's world heritage inscriptions and state-run site managements of "human rights violations and breaches of fundamental freedoms [...] against Indigenous individuals and peoples" (Disko and Tugendhat 49).

At the same time, diktats such as the Native American Graves Protection and Repatriation Act (NAGPRA) consign much tribal heritage to demolition, to reburial, or to cloistered retention that forbids it being seen or studied by certain tribal members (women, children) and non-tribal initiates, in direct violation of universalistic Western principles (Jenkins 262–67). And tribal insistence that sacred heritage be kept secret and hidden has its uncanny counterpart among purist archaeologists who anathematize all collecting. They argue that heritage contaminated by lack of licit provenance should be locked away unseen until its rightful claimants surface, lest its allure foster yet more pillage. Indeed, such antiquities should not even be conserved, holds archaeologist Kathryn Tubb. "By rendering antiquities more aesthetically pleasing, more durable and less traceable, the conservator becomes complicit in an illicit trade that obtains the object at the expense of context, of the site, which action constitutes destruction of the past" (147). Dubious provenance thus condemns antiquities to out-of-sight neglect, as though their unhappy limbo were their own fault. Lauding stringent national laws forbidding all exports, archaeologist Neil Brodie sounds like some medieval inquisitor: "You don't just have to prove something is not guilty, but show that it is innocent" (quoted in Smale). A hundred thousand unprovenanced objects acquired long ago in good faith are barred from sale or even gift because "guilty until proven innocent," says a Chinese antiquities dealer (in Blumenthal and Mashberg).

Collectors' treasures once commonly evolved by gift into collective public heritage; now they are condemned to perpetual privacy because no museum can risk acquiring anything without an iron-clad pedigree, lest it become mired in costly repatriation litigation. Although deploring the increasing "store of antiquities, moved illegally out of their country of origin since 1970, that the country of origin may not want to reclaim and that US museums may not want to acquire," Brodie does not answer the question he poses about such orphaned heritage: "What should happen to them?" ("Unwanted" 99). Unable to find tribes to whom unaffiliated human and funerary remains could be repatriated, some American and Australian museums have had to bury them themselves.

Recent invocations of intangible heritage curtail free trade even in images and ideas. It would be ludicrous, notes cultural property authority John Merryman, to stop a Japanese 'living treasure' from emigrating to Korea, or to forbid a dwindling Canadian First Nations band from joining a thriving Minnesota tribe (26). It would be absurd for Greece to deter neoclassical architects from 'borrowing' Corinthian designs or to demand tearing down that imitative Greek temple, the British Museum. Yet peoples the world over nonetheless strive to secure everything, from deities to drumbeats and dance steps, against export. An Aboriginal tribe sued the National Aquarium in Baltimore in 2004 for replicating its sacred waterfall in a display of Australian flora and fauna; Canada cordons off its music from the US media juggernaut; Britons protect 'native' landscapes against 'alien' continental weeds and vermin; Vanuatu supports its Pentecost islanders' exclusive rights to bungee jumping (their Nagol Land Dive), including their control of tourist spectators and the ritual's artistic depiction by outsiders, and threatens to sue commercial sports copycats elsewhere (Geismar, "Reproduction" 43–45; Tabani; Cheer et al.). Foreign tattooists' use of Maori designs, "an ancestral legacy [that] should not be abused, exploited, or commodified," is censured as "pillaging the spirit of a tribal people to sate the culturally malnourished appetites of the decadent [...] West" (Te Awekotuku 248, 253). The University of Ottawa cancelled a yoga class that upset some people as a "spiritual practice appropriated from another culture" (Pavia). Prince Harry of Britain was accused of "cultural theft" in exhibiting paintings with Aboriginal motifs. "They stole our land, they stole our religion, they stole our remains," declared Tasmanian Aborigine Rodney Dillon, "and now they have stolen our images" (in Van Gelder). Against such appropriations, however, legal sanctions are generally impotent. And as attested by scores of Scottish Highland tartan pattern rights assigned to corporate entities and to fictional characters in film and fiction, intangible culture is easy prey to commercialization (Blakely).

Sanctified by global stewards, local essentialism exacerbates tribal and minority retentive zeal, further privatizing heritage. UNESCO's inscription of intangible culture aggravates matters, for the very notion of recording knowledge to save it from loss is irreconcilable with indigenous secrecy. Fearing that documenting intangible heritage furthers its exploitation, tribes opt instead for "security through obscurity," chimerically demanding the repatriation of information along with artifacts (Lowenthal, "Comment" 227).

Internationally-sanctioned local constraints encumber even *potential* heritage resources. Samoa in 2004 gained sovereign control over an as-yet-undiscovered gene of the mamala tree, *Homalanthus nutans*, whose bark contains the protein prostratin, patented in 1997 to combat HIV. The tree grows elsewhere in the Pacific, but because Samoans were the first to recognize the bark's medicinal potential, every test tube containing the gene or its product must bear a Samoan imprimatur (Cox). *All* references to tribal culture by outsiders are made subject to tribal control; a United Nations Declaration on the Rights of Indigenous Peoples (1994) certifies their "right to maintain, protect, and develop the past, present, and future manifestations of their cultures." Not only is the heritage of indigenous peoples "collective, permanent, and inalienable," held the UN in 1997; it embraces and protects "objects, knowledge and literary or artistic works *which may be created in the future*" (Niec 193, 198).

A statutory heritage safeguard can prove a two-edged sword, however. Viewing cultures as the discrete possessions of discrete groups spurs demands for official recognition to protect their "legitimacy and richness," as Oakland's school board did for Ebonics, the inner-city African-American lingo of fancied West African cum slave ship origins. But "subcultures flourish when they are just part of life, not part of the curriculum," as Louis Menand observed, "When they acquire official patronage, they're on the way to the museum" (4–5). A UNESCO imprimatur confers on "Masterpieces of the Oral and Intangible Heritage of Humanity" the fatal kiss of eternal life. Intangible things, fluid by their very nature, are ossified into factitious perpetuity. Thus we "reinforce the notion that heritage is a kind of fortress requiring constant protection," in an African rebuke, and that "every breach in its walls is one more irreversible step in losing one's culture" (Kasfir and Yai 197). Indeed, designation *promotes* loss: just as heritage commodification in general tends to alienate and dispossess local communities (Kersel and Luke 77), so the very act of cataloguing, warns a United Nations tribal protection report, may "encourage outsiders to think that the heritage of indigenous peoples can be sold" (Daes; Brown 210). The paradox of 'protecting' intangible heritage is that "we cannot consciously 'safeguard' anything before we name it, fixing it in time and, consequently, losing its dynamism" and converting it into a commodity (Kuutma 52).

In heritage's recurrent discords, lip-service to collaboration incites new conflicts. The drumbeat of dispute pervades the precincts of patrimony. Hence, international sanctions against heritage destruction and despoliation in time of war are regularly flouted by adversaries who aim to break the enemy's spirit. Hence, art and antiquities appreciation (and an insatiable global market) reinforce national and tribal insistence on the exclusive sanctity of national origins, spurring rather than stemming tomb-robbing. Hence, Euro-Mediterranean heritage 'partnership' programs intended to benefit the poorer south end up in Brussels-mandated northern hands (Schäfer). Hence, consensual non-partisan histories are jettisoned for divisive nationalist and tribalist tracts.

Dismay among presumed beneficiaries of World Heritage status mirrors discord among UNESCO's rivalrous heritage suitors. Time and again a site inscription promotes tourism at the expense of local residents forced to emigrate or to forgo modern convenience for the sake of past 'authenticity', as Charlotte Joy documents in World Heritage mud-hut Djenné, Mali. As in Djenné, so in Timbuktu, "residents are preoccupied by the challenges of crumbling houses and absent sewer systems, not the mystical desert city" (Brumann & Berliner 25). Or as in the Chinese World Heritage city of Lijiang, having to weigh the meager benefits of tourist revenue against the humiliation of feeling like museum objects, for the sake of pretended authenticity (Zhu). Time and again a living community is subverted by programs that protect an exotic past locally regarded as remote or alien to the neglect or denial of residents' own valued heritage (Ndoro; Wang; Chalcraft). Thus at Meteora heritage planners aimed "to integrate tourism within their monastic life and use tourism as a means to promote the Orthodox faith to the visitors," writes Poulios. But

> the result has been exactly opposite: the monastic communities actually saw tourism as a means to achieve financial benefits, and [...] monastic life was made to conform to the requirements of the growth of tourism. [...] The vast majority of the visitors are unable to participate in the ritual life of the monasteries, and most of the time are not even aware of it (90).

Nor is Meteora "a flourishing monastic site either. Monastic life is suppressed, under the influence of the tourism industry, and the monastic communities are increasingly restricted within their monasteries" (112).[3]

Living heritage that overlaps political boundaries engenders toxic rivalries among competing national and local UNESCO clientele. For example, the Andean *diablata,* "the dance of the Devil," a compage of pre-Columbian and Catholic ceremonies common to indigenous altiplano Quechua and Aymara peoples, is bit-

---

3   Baillie and Miura ("Conservation of a 'Living Heritage'"; "Thinking Globally") document a similar disparity between sacred aims and secular outcomes at Angkor Wat.

terly contested by Chilean, Peruvian, and Bolivian nationalists, and by hamlets and villages in each country that lay claim to the dance's origin. Bolivia accused Peru of stealing its national heritage because "Miss Peru" in the 2009 "Miss Universe" pageant wore a costume 'borrowed' from World Heritage-inscribed Oruro, Bolivia. Peru's petition to UNESCO to certify the Fiesta of the Virgen de Candelaria in Puno as Peru's own "intangible masterpiece of humanity" reignited Andean devil dance wars in 2014. Bolivia objected that Peru's fiesta 'evidence' filched Bolivian religious images, costumes, masks, and indigenous wind instruments, notably the African- or Aymara-inspired *morenada* (Dance of the Black Slaves), celebrated as "purely Bolivian" in a worldwide 2013 dance festival, "100 % Bolivian Morenada: for world peace and Bolivian Culture Respect."

Global recognition by UNESCO-sponsored heritage inscription of the *diablata*, the *morenada,* and other dances, along with their associated costumes and music, has had manifold untoward consequences. In nationalizing what had previously been trans-national altiplano ceremonial practices, it transformed ongoing living culture into inventoried heritage contested as an icon of national identity and a touristic commodity. As ethnomusicologists Michelle Bigenho and Henry Stobart point out: "If Peru names as heritage something Bolivians see as 'theirs', Bolivians lose, and vice versa. [...] Concerns of 'theft' and 'plagiarism' reflect hyperreal ideas about culture" rendered by state competition into a scarce resource to be protected by patenting and copyright. "This is my cultural identity, my Origin, my Essence, my Registered Trademark," declares a Bolivian dancer. Moreover, while celebrating the indigenous as the hearth and heart of national identities, it distances control from indigenes to mestizo-dominated state authorities. "Bolivian culture boundary vigilantes tended to be mestizos," a "far cry" from indigenous cultural performers ("Devil in Nationalism" 155–59). Indigenous identity is still expressed, however, in noisy rivalry among local dance groups. "When two music ensembles from neighboring villages meet on a path, they hardly dream of joining forces," write Bigenho and Stobart. "Rather, they [...] cacophonously confront one another [so as] to maintain ensemble identity and avoid entrainment to the rhythm of the other group":

> In festive performance in the rural Bolivian highlands, musicians representing different hamlets, neighbourhoods or *ayllus* compete with one another to dominate the soundscape [...] Each ayllu is represented by a different troupe of flute players. When they all meet in the central plaza of the village of Yura, they do not take turns playing for each other. Instead, [...] all four representative flute troupes [are] playing at once. They play for hours on end, each troupe with the year's emblematic [ayllu] tune [...] As each troupe circles, [...] the musicians [...] cling to their own tune as the other three troupes also try to do the same, all playing at full volume. ("Grasping Cacophony")

From Cosmopolitanism to Cultural Apartheid

The loss of heritage owing to resurgent national and tribal strife in the Mediterranean and the Middle East underscores the need for global oversight and control. Current ISIS iconoclasm in Iraq and Syria and heritage neglect and pillage elsewhere have their roots in the breakdown of *convivencia*, the traditional cosmopolitanism of Mediterranean ports. From Cartagena to Constantinople diverse ethnic and religious groups long lived cheek by jowl in relative harmony, an urban *convivencia* abetted and codified in the Ottoman Empire's *millet* system (Bromberger). The end of empire and the rise of nationalisms led to the ethnic and religious cleansings of the twentieth century, leaving Alexandria entirely Egyptian, Izmir and Istanbul merely Turkish, Salonika solely Greek, and so on (Driessen). Religious animus intensifies ethnic compartmentalization: Jews and Christians flee the Arab-Muslim world; jihadists behead non-purists; Jews and Palestinians, Sunnis and Shiites each ghettoize. What was once a human rain forest rich with ethnic and religious diversity has dwindled into disconnected exclusive monocultures, crippled by noxious shibboleths of purity and exclusivity (Lafi; Pelham).

On a recent visit to Israel the journalist Roger Cohen passed through the Damascus Gate into Jerusalem's Old City:

> Palestinians emerging from Al Aqsa Mosque moved toward me in a vast throng, and straight into a group of ultra-orthodox Jews headed toward the Western Wall, and at that moment, out of the Via Dolorosa, a crowd of Philippine Christians emerged, carrying a heavy wooden crucifix. It was an impossible scene, funny even, the three great monotheistic religions jostling in the alley, no way around each other.

Yet, Cohen concludes, "Nobody is going away. The peoples of the Holy Land are condemned to each other."

Each creed sees its sacred site as the "geographical point of tangency between God and man, between the eternal and history." But rival heritage claims exacerbated by religious confrontation prevent non-sectarian sharing and communication. The manifold sites of monotheistic revelation are so close to each other that they are constantly in danger of conflict and loss through destruction or conversion, mosque into church or vice versa. As the legal authority Silvio Ferrari concludes, the destruction of the Wailing Wall, the Dome of the Rock, the Church of the Holy Sepulchre, Mecca or Medina would forfeit an irreplaceable locus of sacred transcendence (4, 11–12). Their protection demands such collaborative stewardship as the current Israeli-sponsored restoration of the imperilled shrine in the Church of the Holy Sepulchre, thought to house Jesus' tomb, by Greek Orthodox, Armenian Orthodox, and Roman Catholic conservators (Hadid).

Stewarding Universal Natural Heritage

Above all what we inherit from nature urgently needs to be universally shared and stewarded. The environmental legacy is alike local *and* global. Every community owes its identity and collective well-being to familiarity with place, attachments to inhabited and domesticated landscapes. The most restlessly mobile of peoples, notably those woefully detached by diaspora, retain memories that spell 'home' and powerfully induce cohesion. But even the most settled and self-reliant peoples are increasingly dependent on the global natural 'heritage' of land, water, and air, of minerals and soils and forests, flora and fauna, of an intermeshed terrestrial ecology. "No man is an island," said John Donne four centuries ago (87); today no island is an island, all locales are bound together in a web of mutual needs. Globalization is implacably inescapable in the ecological constraints of our island-earth. "Global interdependence makes heritage universal," I wrote twenty years ago. "The legacy of nature – ecosystems and gene pools, fresh water and fossil fuels – is common to all, and requires the care of all. Exploitative technology diminishes and noxious residues despoil a natural legacy whose stewardship requires worldwide action" ("Identity" 44). The need to husband that imperiled legacy is much more urgent today.

The need to treat environmental heritage as global, to steward it for the sake of all humanity if not of all life, has become apparent only in the last century and a half. Until quite recently few took that need seriously, because the long-term consequences of gutting resources were beyond most people's comprehension and concern. Hunter-gatherer existence hardwired Paleolithic brains to ignore futures more than two generations ahead. Civilized humanity, in turn, found it difficult to sustain urbanized societies even a few centuries ahead. No millennial promise, from ancient theocracies to the Thousand-Year Reich, has lasted a tenth of its intent.

But the seven decades since the Second World War have radically transformed environmental circumstances. The bomb and nuclear fall-out unleashed awareness of risks more horrendous and more imminent than any before. And the ecological consequences of runaway population growth, resource depletion, environmental degradation, and species and habitat loss became ominously clear. Just as science lengthens memory backward into cosmic antiquity, so technology's innovations force us to focus not just on generational but geological future time-scales. Long-term precautionary thinking is already apparent in the millennial Svalbard seed bank and in the requirement, by a federal appeals court, that the US Environmental Protection Agency guard against nuclear waste leakage at Yucca Mountain *300,000 years ahead* (subsequently lengthened to a million years) (Ialenti 29–30). Future generations, should any survive, may bless us for such foresight, however belated.

Imminent climate change, notably global warming and sea-level rise, now imperils both local and global environmental heritages. Likely change may leave us estranged in unrecognizably transformed homelands or as exiled migrants to sub-polar habitats. Along with habitat loss will go much of the world's architectural heritage. The great majority of our urban fabric will be abandoned to rising seas or, with portable legacies, degraded by salinization, devastating floods, wind-driven rain, ice-to-water and salt-to-brine transitions, mold, and a host of other corrosive agents (Colette; English Heritage; Markham et al.).

Recognition of the limits of human enterprise on island-earth seems to be dawning even among the major competitors for and despoilers of heritage. Learning how to manage limited resources among a diverse and divided global community will be more difficult to achieve. There are, however, exemplars, from whose frugal and resilient traditional *genres de vie* much could be learned. Awareness of the need to cooperate in the face of collective peril has enabled several small-island societies to survive both everyday constraints and episodic disasters.

Small Island Heritage Havens

All parts of the world face ecological degradation, but small islands are particularly vulnerable because they lack biodiversity, while their wealth of endemic species makes them crucial global heritage priorities. Many island economies depend on monoculture and have little to fall back on should a particular crop or species fail. Relative powerlessness also leaves them vulnerable to foreign entrepreneurs who extract their natural resources en masse, leaving behind devastated landscapes. Deforestation and strip mining are only the most visible of these effects. No less dangerous is what is dumped on islands, including lethal residues of nuclear-bomb tests and, as exemplified by the removal of Guantánamo detainees to Palau and Bermuda, unwanted humans.

Island communities have always been vulnerable. Yet usually they have endured, attesting islanders' resilience. Social and cultural homogeneity may be advantageous in responding to new global challenges. Local leaders can rely on islanders' strength of attachment to demand sacrifices that larger, more fragmented constituencies cannot countenance.

Thanks to long experience with limited resources, islands and islanders have much to contribute to current concerns over husbanding dwindling or threatened global resources. That unlimited economic growth is not only unsustainable but ecologically catastrophic is commonplace knowledge on many small islands, where environmental constraints are abundantly apparent. Traditional island frugality teaches invaluable lessons, as do island farming and fishing techniques handed down over many generations. At a time when all coastal communities are beleaguered by diminishing fish stocks, shore erosion, and water pollution, islanders offer a wealth of conservation experience. Small islands are like the proverbial canary in the mine, providing early warnings of widespread global problems while also illumining potential solutions (Gillis and Lowenthal; Robinson and Carson; Petzold).

Of UNESCO's thousand World Heritage sites, at least one hundred are islands or parts of islands. Most are inscribed for scenic splendor or rare endemic species. Of the dozen designated for culture many are former prisons and sites of slavery or devastation – Bikini, Gorée, Robben, St. Kilda. Only a few exemplify the saving heritage traits noted above: Reichenau in Germany, Mozambique Island, Solovetsky in Russia, Pico in the Portuguese Azores.

Famed for their resilience, frugality, and sense of community are the 500 inhabitants of the Channel Island of Sark. Over four and a half centuries they have fashioned a distinctive cultural landscape on a three-square-mile plateau reachable only by sea and devoid of cars, street lights, and paved roads. Famed among astronomers as a Dark Sky site and among residents and visitors as a 'feudal' refuge from frenetic modernity, Sark has been lauded by recent major leaseholders, the billionaire Barclay brothers, for the "unspoilt, rural character, natural beauty and distinctiveness politically and constitutionally of this very beautiful, tranquil island with its roots deep in Norman and Elizabethan history."[4] Yet the Barclays vehemently opposed World Heritage status recently suggested for Sark, as it would prevent the "commercial development" they contend this "decayed lump of rock so desperately needs."[5] And they do their utmost, local residents charge, to eradicate the very ways of life, law, and landscape that they praised, sabotaging traditional heritage and "trying to ruin the governance of the island," in order to transform Sark into a Monaco-style tax-exile resort for the ultra-rich.[6]

The Sark dichotomy – heritage as integral to community identity, but if secured by UNESCO, an obstacle to equivocal 'progress' – exemplifies World Heritage conflicts everywhere. Beyond the socially disruptive consequences of gentrification and tourism engendered by UNESCO inscription, economic development is with some justification often felt as "a threat rather than a promise" to heritage, conclude Meskell and Brumann (23). And beyond contentious claims to its ownership, a certified heritage can soon become a *damnosa hereditas*, a legacy that destroys its inheritor.

---

4   Sir David and Sir Frederick Barclay, *A Manifesto for Sark*, 21 Nov 2008, point 6, quoted in Agriculture and Environment Committee of Chief Pleas, Sark.
5   Sir David Barclay to Sir Barry Cunliffe, 7 Oct. 2014. Sark Government Archives, World Heritage Site files.
6   Seigneur J. M. Beaumont, 14 Nov. 2013 (CDF 24), United Kingdom, House of Commons, Justice Committee, *Crown Dependencies: Developments since 2010. Tenth Report of Session 2013–14*, Written Evidence, 34. See Lowenthal, "Albion's Other Islets" 106–8, and Lowenthal, "Scourging of Sark.".

Works Cited

Agriculture and Environment Committee of Chief Pleas, Sark, Channel Islands, "Concerns Over the Increasing Number of Vineyards on Sark." Press Release, 1 Nov. 2012.
Alberge, Dalya. "Kings' Crowns Fall into Private Hands." *Times* [London] 4 Dec. 1995.
—. "Buyer Frustrates Art Export Laws." *Times* [London] 5 March 1996.
Araoz, Gustavo. "Heritage as Conscience." *US/ICOMOS Newsletter* No. 3 (May–June 2000): 7.
Baillie, Britt. "Conservation of the Sacred at Angkor Wat: Further Reflections on Living Heritage." *Conservation & Management of Archaeological Sites* 8 (2007): 123–31.
Beard, Mary. *The Parthenon.* London: Profile Books, 2002.
Belk, Russell W. "Possessions and the Extended Self." *Journal of Consumer Research* 15.2 (1988): 139–68.
Bigenho, Michelle, and Henry Stobart. "The Devil in Nationalism: Indigenous Heritage and the Challenges of Decolonization." *International Journal of Cultural Property* 23.2 (2016):141–66.
—. "Grasping Cacophony in Bolivian Heritage Otherwise." *Anthropological Quarterly.* In press.
Blakely, Megan Rae. "Pattern Recognition: Governmental Regulation of Tartan and Commodification of Culture." *International Journal of Cultural Property* 22.2 (2015): 487–504.
Blumenthal, Ralph, and Tom Mashberg. "The Curse of the Outcast Artifact." *New York Times* 12 July 2012.
Brodie, Neil. "Unwanted Antiquities." *Museum International* 61.1–2 (2009): 97–100.
—. "Congenial Bedfellows? The Academy and the Antiquities Trade." *Journal of Contemporary Criminal Justice* 27.4 (2011): 408–37.
Brodie, Neil, and Andreas Apostolidis. *History Lost.* Athens: Hellenic Foundation for Culture: Anemos Productions, 2007.
Bromberger, Christian. "Bridge, Wall, Mirror; Coexistence and Confrontations in the Mediterranean World." *History and Anthropology* 18 (2007): 291–307.
Brown, Michael F. *Who Owns Native Culture?* Cambridge, MA: Harvard University Press, 2003.
Brumann, Cristoph, and David Berliner. "Introduction: UNESCO World Heritage – Grounded?" *World Heritage on the Ground.* Eds. Cristoph Brumann and David Berliner. New York: Berghahn, 2016. 1–36.
Busatta, Sandra. "The Tree of Life Design: From Central Asia to Navajoland and Back (with a Mexican Detour) Part 3." *Online Journal of Anthropology* 10.1 (2014). 17 August 2016 <http://www.antrocom.net/upload/sub/antrocom/100114/05-Antrocom.pdf>.
Butterfield, Herbert. *The Englishman and His History.* Cambridge: Cambridge University Press, 1944.
Carroll, Lewis. *Through the Looking-Glass and What Alice Found There.* London: Macmillan, 1871.
Chalcraft, Jasper. "Decolonizing the Site: The Problems and Pragmatics of World Heritage in Italy, Libya and Tanzania." *World Heritage on the Ground.* Eds. Cristoph Brumann and David Berliner. New York: Berghahn, 2016. 219–46.

Cheer, Joseph M., Keir J. Reeves, and Jennifer H. Laing. "Tourism and Traditional Culture: Land Diving in Vanuatu." *Annals of Tourism Research* 43 (2013): 435–55.

Cohen, Roger. "Hope in the Abattoir." *International New York Times* 25 July 2014.

Colette, Augustin, Ed. *Climate Change and World Heritage,* World Heritage Report 22. Paris: UNESCO, 2007.

Compton-Burnett, Ivy. *Manservant and Maidservant.* London: Victor Gollancz, 1947.

Cox, Paul Alan. "Ensuring Equitable Benefits: The Falealupo Covenant and the Isolation of Anti-Viral Drug Prostratin from a Samoan Medicinal Plant." *Pharmaceutical Biology* 29 (2001): 33–40.

Cuno, James. "Culture War: The Case against Repatriating Museum Artifacts." *Foreign Affairs* 93.6 (Nov.–Dec. 2014): 119–29.

Daes, Erica-Irene. *Protection of the Heritage of Indigenous Peoples.* United Nations, Office of the High Commissioner for Human Rights, 1997.

Delaney, Sarah. "There's No Place but Home for This Stolen Italian Art." *Washington Post* 19 Dec. 2007.

Disko, Stefan, and Helen Tugendhat. *International Expert Workshop on the World Heritage Convention and Indigenous Peoples.* Copenhagen: International Work Group for Indigenous Affairs, 2013.

Donne, John. Devotion 17: "*Nunc lento sonitu dicunt, Morieris.*" 1624. *Devotions upon Emergent Occasions.* New York: Oxford University Press, 1987. 86–90.

Driessen, Henk. "Mediterranean Port Cities: Cosmopolitanism Reconsidered." *History and Anthropology* 16 (2005): 129–41.

Durkheim, Émile. *The Elementary Forms of Religious Life.* 1912. Trans. Karen Fields. New York: Free Press, 1995.

English Heritage. *Climate Change and the Historic Environment.* London, 2012.

Evans, Ronald W. *This Happened in America: Harold Rugg and the Censure of Social Studies.* Charlotte, NC: Information Age, 2007.

Fara, Patricia. "Northern Possession: Laying Claim to the Aurora Borealis." *History Workshop Journal* 42 (Autumn 1996): 37–57.

Ferrari, Silvio. "Introduction: The Legal Protection of the Sacred Places of the Mediterranean." *Between Cultural Diversity and Common Heritage: Legal and Religious Perspectives on the Sacred Places of the Mediterranean.* Eds. Silvio Ferrari and Andrea Benzo. London: Ashgate, 2014. 1–14.

Geismar, Haidy. "Reproduction, Creativity, Restriction: Material Culture and Copyright in Vanuatu." *Journal of Social Archaeology* 5.1 (2005): 25–51.

—. *Treasured Possessions: Indigenous Interventions into Cultural and Intellectual Property.* Durham, NC: Duke University Press, 2013.

Gillis, John R., and David Lowenthal. "Introduction." In "Islands." Special issue of *Geographical Review* 97.2 (April 2007): iii–vi.

Hadid, Diaa. "Rival Christians Unite to Fix Perils at Jesus' Tomb." *New York Times* 7 April 2016: A8.

Hamilakis, Yannis. *The Nation and Its Ruins: Archaeology, Antiquity and National Imagination in Modern Greece.* Oxford: Oxford University Press, 2007.

Handler, Richard. "On Having a Culture: Nationalism and the Preservation of Quebec's *Patrimoine.*" *Objects and Others: Essays on Museums and Material Culture.* Ed. George W. Stocking, Jr. Madison: University of Wisconsin Press, 1988. 192–217.

Herzfeld, Michael. "Heritage and Corruption: The Two Faces of the Nation-State." *International Journal of Heritage Studies* 21.6 (2015): 531–44.

Heyman, Stephen. "The Destruction of Syria's Cultural Patrimony." *New York Times* 17 Dec. 2014.
Ialenti, Vincent F. "Adjudicating Deep Time: Revisiting the United States' High-Level Nuclear Waste Repository Project at Yucca Mountain." *Science & Technology Studies* 27.2 (2014): 27–48.
James, William. *The Principles of Psychology*. 2 vols. New York: Henry Holt, 1890.
Jenkins, Tiffany. *Keeping Their Marbles: How the Treasures of the Past Ended Up in Museums ... and Why They Should Stay There*. Oxford: Oxford University Press, 2016.
Joy, Charlotte. *The Politics of Heritage Management in Mali: From UNESCO to Djenné*. Walnut Creek, CA: Left Coast Press, 2013.
Kasfir, Sidney Littlefield, and Labiyi Babalola Joseph Yai. "Authenticity and Diaspora." *Museum International* 56.1–2 (May 2004) [Views and Visions of the Intangible]: 190–97.
Kersel, Morag M., and Christina Luke. "Civil Societies? Heritage Diplomacy and Neo-Imperialism." *Global Heritage: A Reader*. Ed. Lynn Meskell. Malden, MA: Wiley Blackwell, 2015. 70–93.
Kuutma, Kristin. "From Folklore to Intangible Heritage." *A Companion to Heritage Studies* Eds. William Logan, Máiréad Nic Craith, and Ullrich Kockel. Oxford: Wiley, 2012. 41–54.
Lafi, Nora. "Mediterranean Cosmopolitanism and Its Contemporary Revivals: A Critical Approach." *New Geographies (Journal of the Harvard University Graduate School of Design)* 5 (2013): 325–33.
Legare, Cristine H., and Rachel E. Watson-Jones. "The Evolution and Ontogeny of Ritual." *The Handbook of Evolutionary Psychology*. 2nd. ed. Ed. David M. Buss. Hoboken, NJ: Wiley & Sons, 2015. 829–47.
Lowenthal, David. "Identity, Heritage, and History." *Commemorations: The Politics of National Identity*. Ed. John R. Gillis. Princeton: Princeton University Press, 1994. 41–57.
—. *The Heritage Crusade and the Spoils of History*. Cambridge: Cambridge University Press, 1998.
—. "Why Sanctions Seldom Work: Reflections on Cultural Property Internationalism." *International Journal of Cultural Property* 12.3 (2005): 391–421.
—. "Comment on Gwyneira Isaac, 'Whose Idea Was This? Museums, Replicas, and the Reproduction of Knowledge'." *Current Anthropology* 52.2 (April 2011): 226–27.
—. "Heritage Care: From Tower of Babel to Ivory Tower." *Change over Time* 1.1 (Spring 2011): 130–36.
—. "Albion's Other Islets: Off-shore, Overseas, and Out of Sorts." *Geographical Review* 104.1 (2014): 101–8.
—. *The Past Is a Foreign Country – Revisited*. Cambridge: Cambridge University Press, 2015.
—. "The Scourging of Sark." *Island Studies Journal* 10.2 (2015): 253–58.
Macpherson, C. B. *The Political Theory of Possessive Individualism: Hobbes to Locke*. Oxford: Clarendon Press, 1962.
Markham, Adam, et al. *World Heritage and Tourism in a Changing Climate*. Nairobi: U.N. Environment Programme, and Paris: UNESCO, 2016.
M'Closkey, Kathy. *Swept under the Rug: A Hidden History of Navajo Weaving*. Albuquerque: University of New Mexico Press, 2002.
Menand, Louis. "Johnny Be Good." *New Yorker* 13 Jan. 1997: 4–5.

Merryman, John Henry. "Cultural Property Internationalism." *International Journal of Cultural Property* 12.1 (2005): 11–39.

Meskell, Lynn. "Unesco and the Fate of the World Heritage Indigenous Peoples Council of Experts (WHIPCOE)." *International Journal of Cultural Property* 20 (2013): 155–74.

—, and Christoph Brumann. "UNESCO and New World Orders." *Global Heritage: A Reader.* Ed. Lynn Meskell. Malden, MA: Wiley Blackwell, 2015. 22–42.

Miura, Keiko. "Conservation of a 'Living Heritage Site': A contradiction in Terms? A Case Study of Angkor World Heritage Site." *Conservation & Management of Archaeological Sites* 7 (2005): 3–18.

—. "Thinking Globally and Acting Locally in Angkor." *World Heritage on the Ground.* Eds. Cristoph Brumann and David Berliner. New York: Berghahn, 2016. 15–46.

Moody, Oliver. "Isis Fills War Chest by Selling Looted Antiquities to the West." *Times* [London] 17 Dec. 2014: 14.

Myers, Steven Lee, and Nicholas Kulish. "'Broken System' Allows ISIS to Profit from Looted Antiquities." *New York Times* 9 Jan. 2016.

Ndoro, Webber. "Traditional and Customary Heritage Systems: Nostalgia or Reality? The Implications of Managing Heritage Sites in Africa." *Linking Universal and Local Values: Managing a Sustainable Future for World Heritage.* Eds. Eléonore de Merode, Rieks Smeets, and Carol Westrik. World Heritage Papers 13. Paris: UNESCO World Heritage Centre, 2004. 81–84.

Niec, Halina, Ed. *Cultural Rights and Wrongs.* Paris: Institute of Art & Law, and UNESCO, 1998.

Pavia, Will. "Student Union Takes Inflexible Approach to 'Oppressive' Yoga Class." *Times* [London] 24 Nov. 2015.

Pelham, Nicolas. *Holy Lands: Reviving Pluralism in the Middle East.* New York: Columbia Global Impacts, 2016.

Penny, Nicholas. "Constable: An English Heritage Abroad?" *Sunday Times* [London] 11 Nov. 1984: 43.

Petzold, Jan. "Limits and Opportunities of Social Capital for Adaptation to Climate Change: A Case Study on the Isles of Scilly." *Geographical Journal* 182.2 (June 2016): 123–34.

Plato. *The Republic.* 360 bc. Trans. Desmond Lee. Harmondsworth: Penguin, 1974.

Poulios, Ioannis. *The Past in the Present: A Living Heritage Approach – Meteora, Greece.* London: Ubiquity Press, 2014.

Raphael, Ray. *Founding Myths: Stories That Hide Our Patriotic Past.* New York: New Press, 2007.

Renan, Ernest. *Qu'est-ce qu'une nation?* 1882. Paris: Bordas, 1991.

Reszler, André. *Les nouvelles Athènes.* Gollion: In folio, 2004.

Robinson, Guy M., and Doris A. Carson. "Resilient Communities: Transitions, Pathways and Resourcefulness." *Geographical Journal* 182.2 (June 2016): 114–22.

Roth, Joseph. *The Radetzky March.* 1932. Trans. Eva Tucker. New York: Overlook Press, 1974.

Scarre, Geoffrey. "The Ethics of Digging." *Cultural Heritage Ethics: Between Theory and Practice.* Ed. Constantine Sandis. Cambridge: Open Book, 2014. 117–28.

Schäfer, Isabel. "The Cultural Dimension of the Euro-Mediterranean Partnership: A Critical Review of the First Decade of Intercultural Cooperation." *History and Anthropology* 18 (2007): 333–52.

Scott, David A. "Modern Antiquities: The Looted and the Faked." *International Journal of Cultural Property* 20.1 (Feb. 2013): 49–75.

Silverman, Helaine, Ed. *Contested Cultural Heritage: Religion, Nationalism, Erasure, and Exclusion.* New York: Springer, 2011.

Smale, Alison. "Growing Alarm on Cultural Theft." *International New York Times* 18 Dec. 2014: 11.

Smith, Anthony D. *Chosen Peoples: Sacred Sources of National Identity.* Oxford: Oxford University Press, 2003.

Smith, Helena. "Loan Shatters Elgin Marbles Claim, Says Athens." *Guardian* [London] 6 Dec. 2014: 10.

St Clair, William. "Looking at the Acropolis of Athens from Modern Times to Antiquity." *Cultural Heritage Ethics: Between Theory and Practice.* Ed. Constantine Sandis. Cambridge: Open Book, 2014. 57–102.

Steiner, George. *After Babel.* New York: Oxford University Press, 1975.

Tabani, Marc. "The Carnival of Custom: Land Dives, Millenarian Parades and Other Spectacular Ritualisations in Vanuatu." *Oceania* 8.3 (2010): 309–28.

Te Awekotuku, Ng. "More than Skin Deep." *Claiming the Stones, Naming the Bones: Cultural Property and the Negotiation of National and Ethnic Identity.* Eds. Elazar Barkan and Ronald Bush. Los Angeles: Getty Press, 2002. 243–54.

Tubb, Kathryn Walker. "Shifting Approaches to Unprovenanced Antiquities among Conservators." *Realising Cultural Heritage Law: Festschrift for Patrick Joseph O'Keefe.* Eds. Lyndel V. Prott, Ruth Redmond-Cooper, and Stephen Urice. Builth Wells: Institute of Art and Law, 2013. 145–62.

Van Gelder, Lawrence. "Arts Briefing." *Times* [London] 21 Aug. 2003: B2.

Wang, Shu-Li. "Civilization and the Transformation of Xiaoton Village at Yin Xu Archaeological Site, China." *World Heritage on the Ground.* Ed. Cristoph Brumann and David Berliner. New York: Berghahn, 2016. 171–92.

Windsor, John. "Identity Parade." *Cultures of Collecting.* Eds. John Elsner and Roger Cardinal. London: Reaktion, 1994. 49–67.

Wood, W. Warner. *Made in Mexico: Zapotec Weavers and the Global Ethnic Art Market.* Bloomington: Indiana University Press, 2008.

Zhu, Yujie. "Heritage Making in Lijiang: Governance, Reconstruction and Local Naxi Life." *World Heritage on the Ground.* Eds. Cristoph Brumann and David Berliner. New York: Berghahn, 2016. 78–96.

Archival Sources

Sark Government Archives, World Heritage Site files.

CHAPTER TWO

How Did Climate Change Cause the Collapse of Civilizations in the Historical Past?

RONNIE ELLENBLUM

The literate civilizations of western Asia reached one of their peaks between the middle of the tenth century CE and the end of the first quarter of the eleventh century. Chronicles written in more than half a dozen languages (Arabic, Syriac, Armenian, Coptic, Greek and Latin to name only the main languages) give annual and chronological descriptions of the political and climatic events that affected the region, as well as providing evidence for the region's economic, commercial and cultural booms. First-person letters written in direct response to the events they describe, found in the Cairo Genizah, confirm the chronicles' tales.

The region enjoyed an extended period of affluence. At the beginning of the eleventh century hundreds of thousands of people lived in cities such as Baghdad, Fustat and Qayrawan that had been founded less than three hundred years earlier by the Arab conquerors (Kennedy). The scholars of the "Shi'i Golden Age" living in Iraq, Iran and Khurasan studied the works of the Greek philosophers and their commentaries that had been translated into Arabic, and wrote their own ones. They knew the writings of Euclid, Hippocrates and Galen, and used them to add to their knowledge in the fields of philosophy, algebra and medicine (Rosenthal). At the beginning of the eleventh century, the Byzantine Empire also reached heights that it had not known since before the Arab conquests of the seventh century. Basil II (r. 976–1025 CE) is considered one of the most successful rulers of the Macedonian dynasty and of the later Byzantine Empire in general. He expanded the Byzantine realm in the east and the west, stabilized the administration and economy, and under his rule the empire enjoyed prosperity and affluence. The Fatimid dynasty, which came to power in Egypt in 969, established an efficient and competent system there. The Fatimids expanded the area of Egypt's territory and effective rule, and brought artistic and intellectual activity to new peaks.

However, despite the existence of efficient governmental systems, stable economies, and almost unprecedented cultural and intellectual blossoming, all of these Middle Eastern civilizations, in spite of being ruled by apparently competent systems, found themselves facing severe crises that began in the late 1020s and disrupted the region for several decades, reaching their peak between the mid-1050s to the early 1090s.

In 1055, the Seljuqs, a Turkmen tribe that until the late 1020s had lived a pastoral nomadic life in the steppe north of Khurasan, were able to conquer Baghdad, the capital of Islamic civilization, without a fight, and to depose the last of the Buwayhid sultans. For the next five years, they took part in a bloody civil war over the lordship of northern Iraq. The Seljuq conquest of Iran, Khurasan and Iraq, which occurred from 1029 to 1060, was the first appearance of the Turks on the historical stage of the Middle East.

Over the course of the second half of the tenth and the eleventh centuries, Fatimid Egypt underwent a long and unprecedented series of crises that comprised the collapse of the Ikhshidid dynasty, famine and plagues, internecine warfare, persecution of minorities and the abandonment of urban centers, including Fustat itself – like Baghdad, a metropolis of hundreds of thousands of inhabitants.

Byzantium also underwent similar economic crises in the same years. The crises were manifested in an unprecedented devaluation of twenty-seven percent in the real worth of the numisma within a few years (Kaplanis). This devaluation of the coinage, previously considered extremely stable in this part of the world (Lopez), occurred between 1046 and 1055 – years in which the Danube froze completely (Cedrenus II: 585). Sources tell of 800,000 nomads of Turkmen origin (like the origin of the Seljuqs) who crossed the frozen river into Byzantine territory, defeating the united Byzantine army and forcing the Empire itself to pay them heavy tribute. The crises climaxed during the mid-1050s when the previously very competent Macedonian dynasty collapsed (Charanis 197–98; Attaleiates 54–56).

Historical studies indeed provide separate political explanations for the crises that affected each of these empires – and for the events that occurred in Qayrawan and other important centers, for which there is no space to discuss here. The historical sources themselves that detail each of these crises at an annual resolution, and occasionally mentioning specific dates, refer again and again to climatic events as the direct causes of the political and economic events that followed them (see Ellenblum for a detailed description).

The many written sources describing the climatic events that occurred in the eastern Mediterranean basin and western Asia testify that at the beginning of the MCA (the Medieval Climatic Anomaly during the tenth and eleventh centuries), the region underwent a series of unusual climatic events. The climatic crises included a series of droughts, each lasting for several years, and affecting the Nile, Syria and Palestine (al-Sham), and sequences of extremely cold winters that affected the steppes, Khurasan, Iran and Mesopotamia. The sources detail both the climatic catastrophes themselves and the sequence of events emanating from them, up to their disastrous consequences.

The crises themselves are detailed in temporal and spatial sequence elsewhere (Ellenblum), but the abundant documentary evidence can be relied upon to extrapolate a model or flowchart of a typical crisis, beginning with a climatic event and ending, sometimes, with the collapse of states. The model may also explain, with the necessary adaptations, the crisis that the eastern Mediterranean basin is undergoing today (Kelley et al.).

The Length and Strength of an Affective Crisis

The crises that affected the eastern Mediterranean and western Asia during the tenth and eleventh centuries were not continuous and were composed of a long sequence of brief crises, each of which lasting a few years, or at most, two to three decades. When rains and mild weather return, or when the fierce winter cold spells are abated, life returns to normal and the extreme climatic events are gradually forgotten. Between one crisis and another, there were good years in which various parts of the region enjoyed relative affluence and stable rule. The strength of the crisis was therefore not due to its totality but rather to the power and length of short-term anomalies, and to the brief periods between one crisis and another, which stopped the authorities from being able to prepare for or prevent them.

The short-term catastrophic events, each of which lasted a decade or two, affected the availability of food and water and caused dearth and famine. Lack of food (dearth) is what put into motion social processes that eventually damaged the civilizations' resilience. The results of droughts that affected Egypt in the tenth and eleventh centuries, lasting up to six and seven years, can exemplify the significance and power of relatively "brief" crises and strengthen our claim that a decade of drought is enough to bring structural processes into play.

By way of example, Table 1 shows that the number of drought years in the Nile during the MCA (the tenth and eleventh centuries) was an order of magnitude larger than the number of similar events that had affected Egypt in previous centuries. There were several sequences of destructive droughts that lasted six and seven years; between these events of Biblical dimensions there were additional droughts lasting four years (with one good year in between), three years, and two years. Between these destructive droughts, there were periods of stability and opulence, such as between 1027–1052, when Egypt enjoyed prosperity and flourishing.

Between 283–850 AD

346	A one-year-long drought
383–85	A two-year-long drought
463	A one-year-long drought
515–16	A two-year-long drought
645	A one-year-long drought

706	A one-year-long drought
715 (?)	A one-year-long drought
745	A one-year-long drought
834	A one-year-long drought

Tenth and Eleventh Centuries

949	A one-year-long drought
954–55	A two-year-long drought
963–69	A six-year-long drought
997–98	A one-year-long drought
1004–5	A one-year-long drought
1009	A one-year-long drought
1023–26	A three-year-long drought
1052–56	A four-year-long drought
1065–72	'The great calamity' or 'destruction of Fustat'.

Table 1: Nile droughts up to and during the tenth and eleventh centuries

Is a drought lasting seven years such a rare event? It appears we have to answer this question in the affirmative. We have not even one piece of reliable historical evidence for such an extended, severe and destructive event in the Nile basin before the years 963–969 or 1054–1072 CE. The drought of the tenth and eleventh centuries are not the first documented occasions of a drought extending across several successive years: the story of Joseph (Gen. 41 and referenced also in Surah 12 of the Qur'an) refers to seven sequential years in which the Nile did

Fig. 1: The Famine Stela on Sehel Island south of Aswan, Egypt. Source: https://en.wikipedia.org/wiki/Famine_Stela

not rise, as does the Famine Stela (Figure 1), discovered by Flinders Petrie in 1887 on an island south of Aswan in Upper Egypt (Barguet).

The Famine Stela, written in Egyptian hieroglyphs, refers to seven successive years of famine and drought that ostensibly occurred during the reign of Djoser (a ruler during the first half of the 27th century BCE). The stela describes the king's concern at the extended catastrophe, and at the people's suffering and rage. The Famine Stela, however, was inscribed only at the end of the third or beginning of the second century BCE, and seems to describe a distant event that apparently occurred 2500 years earlier. Both the story of Joseph and the Famine Stela express a belief common to both the authors of Genesis and to the Hellenistic carvers of the stela, i.e. that such a disaster could befall Egypt again. These documents may refer to a real occurrence or two occurrences of famine in the distant past; however, the seven-year famine also seems to be a narrative trope used in texts of the Near East, but the first reliable historical evidence of such an extended disaster remains is that of the eleventh century.

How Does a Crisis Develop? From Climate Anomaly to Social Crisis

The flowchart below (Table 2) explains how a climate anomaly lasting no more than a decade or two can develop into a crisis that will leave its mark on society even after the original cause of the crisis no longer exists. The flowchart is based on the analysis of several social crises, each beginning with a climatic event, as described independently by various chroniclers, who saw the crisis from different locations. The conclusion to be drawn from these data is that the availability of food is the main factor through which climate affects complex societies; a scarcity of rainfalls leads to food shortage and can ultimately lead to state collapse.

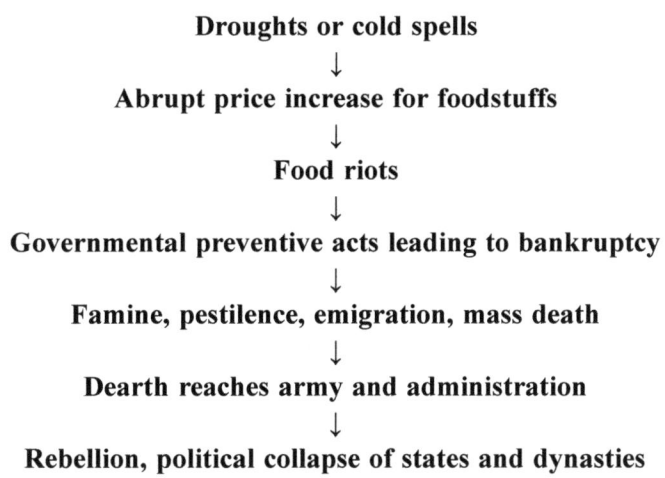

Table 2: Interconnections between Climate Catastrophes, Food Scarcity and Social Crises

Food scarcity: Based on the data we have about the connection between climate catastrophes, food shortage, and political unrest in both ancient Egypt and eleventh-century Byzantium, we can conclude that catastrophic climatic events which cause a sudden decrease in the amount of food available to the population can lead to a rapid and sharp rise in food prices. Examining a large number of cases occurring during the MCA reveals that it is food scarcity that drives the political, economic and societal processes that follow and which may cause, in extreme cases, the collapse of complex societies. This statement enables us to differentiate between climatic events that affect the availability of foodstuffs (long periods of drought, untimely rains, widespread flooding and cold spells) and therefore lead to an extended period of dearth, and dramatic one-off events, that do not affect the availability of food (such as tropical storms, non-repeating flooding etc.) and therefore have a more limited effect on societies. Cold spells are often absent from many of the scholarly debates discussing climatic changes, but in the past, they had an extreme effect on the availability of food for pastoralist societies herding their flocks in regions prone to such cold spells. Cold spells also harm crops and other forms of agriculture.

Food riots: In most historical cases, the population affected by sharp rises in food prices responded by unrest, demonstrations, and food riots. The Medieval Middle-eastern chronicles often connect the food riots and the preceding scarcity directly, explicitly and unequivocally. The populace tended to blame the rising prices on the greed of the merchants who hoarded food surpluses in their barns and warehouses, and on the corruption of the government, which cooperated with them. Governments for their part frequently attempted to subsidize foods, to set quotas and to fight against the black market.

Famine and plagues: In all the cases we looked at in which the climate anomaly that caused the crisis continued into the following year, the crisis worsened and the scarcity became actual famine, and was often accompanied by pestilence, plagues and mass death. In the absence of effective means of transporting food from one region to another, it was not possible to stop the crisis until the annual precipitation (i.e. rain and rising Nile waters) returned to average and until the extreme events were abated.

The numbers of the dead mentioned in connection to the famines that affected Fustat, Baghdad, and the cities of Khurasan or the Jazira are indeed horrifying. One source claims, for example, that during the six years of drought that occurred in Egypt between 963 and 969, in Fustat alone 600,000 people died (Yaḥyā ibn Saʿīd al-Anṭākī 129–130). The pestilence that occurred in Khurasan, Iran and Mesopotamia following the fierce cold spells of the early 1030s caused the death of 40,000 people in Isfahan during 1032–3 and a further 70,000 in the following year (Sibṭ ibn al-Jawzī 361; Matthew of Edessa I: 60: 55).

During the plague that broke out during the years of intense cold in the second half of the 1050s, the dead were buried in mass graves in Baghdad. Sources describing life in the steppe claim that in Bukhara alone there were 18,000 funerals daily and a third of the city's population died of hunger and plague (Bar Hebraeus I: 209; Ibn al-Athīr IX: 353). As in any description of plagues, the numbers are exaggerated, but they show how the crises was seen by contemporaries and are evidence of the connection between scarcity, famine, plagues and mass death.

Could the Administration Prevent the Scarcity?

The accepted belief that efficient administration could have prevented the food crises by means of correct and rational behavior, and that systemic collapse characterizes only failing states, is not supported by the medieval sources. These reveal that even a competent, talented and well-intentioned government was not able to prevent famine after long years of drought.

The fact that the rulers were aware of the need for planning but failed in accomplishing the plans is reflected in a dialogue purporting to have taken place between the Fatimid caliph al-Zahir and his muḥtasib (market inspector) at the height of one the crises, that of 1025. As the market inspector, the muḥtasib was responsible for the supply of grain and bread and had the authority to punish lawbreakers severely. Maqrīzī, who served as muḥtasib himself in a later period of Egypt's history, describes the event, and places in the caliph's mouth the claim that the muḥtasib had promised "to make sure that grain and bread were available to all" and that he had broken this promise (al-Maqrīzī, *Itti'az* II: 165). The caliph, accusing the muḥtasib of "starving the people to death and ruining the entire land," revoked the latter's authority and ordered the opening of 150 warehouses of grain and the sale of their contents to millers and bakers at a set and regulated price. He also ordered the capture of all ships bringing grain from Upper Egypt to Lower Egypt and personally took over the management of the grain stores. Yet all this was to no avail: the drought and subsequent plague intensified and spread to neighboring lands (al-Musabbiḥī I: 87–88). The army, also affected by the scarcity, looted Fustat and joined forces with the nomads, who raided the cities of Tinnin and Eshmunayn, as well as the hajj caravan. The crisis ended only after another year of drought, when the Nile finally rose once more (al-Maqrīzī, *Itti'az* II: 134–35).

This example and many others show that the governments were aware of the danger and tried to prepare as best they could. However, even the most efficient and least corrupt systems were unsuccessful and unable to prepare for a crisis that was not limited in time. None of the governmental systems existing in the Middle East at the beginning of the eleventh century had an answer for the long and severe crises buffeting them, nor to the succession of crises that prevented the food stores being replenished.

Food crises destroyed cities: Food crises caused the abandonment of some of the region's greatest urban centers, including some that had been at the height of their flowering only a short time before. A text composed in 1040 by the Khurasani writer and scholar Abu al-Fadl al-Bayhaqī while visiting Nishapur, where he had studied and worked a few years earlier, seems to best exemplify the harsh process that these cities suffered during the crises:

> Nishapur was not the city I knew from the past: it now lay in ruins with only vestiges of habitation and urban life. [...] Property owners had torn off the roofs of their houses and sold them. A great number of people [...] had died from hunger. The price of landed property had plummeted [...] the weather was bitterly cold and life was becoming hard to bear. [...] Such a famine in Nishapur could not be recalled, and large numbers of people died, soldiers and civilians alike. [T]he Turkmens did not harass or hover around us, since they too were taken up with their own welfare [...] dearth and famine had spread everywhere. (Bayhaqī II: 299)

The drought that afflicted Egypt in the mid-1050s also caused famine and mass death. One of the Arab sources claims that the drought was so severe that most of Fustat's inhabitants died of hunger or resorted to cannibalism. Dated first-person evidence of this famine can be found in a letter written by Isma'il b. Farah of Alexandria on November 6, 1056, preserved in the Cairo Genizah: "Nothing is more in demand in the city than something to eat." In another letter written a few days later, he says that "whoever leaves his house is murdered and his flesh eaten, and whoever stays at home dies of hunger" (Gil 296 no. 515b, lines 3–5). Another source reports that the famine caused a plague that spread "throughout the entire world," with 10,000 victims dying daily in Fustat alone (Ibn Taghrībirdī V: 59). At the height of the crisis, the Fatimid caliph, the ruler of Egypt that throughout history had been the granary of the Mediterranean, requested the Byzantine emperor to send shipments of grain to Egypt. The emperor, busy at the time with a struggle with his own soldiers, died before he could respond to the Egyptian request, and the empress who succeeded him discovered that she was unable to fulfil it (Ibn Muyassar 13; see Felix 119–23).

The geographer Yāqūt al-Hamawī, who wrote an important gazetteer at the beginning of the thirteenth century, attributes the "destruction" of Fustat to the seven years of drought between 1065–1072, which was probably the worst climatic disaster that hit Egypt during the eleventh century. Two quarters, the eastern and western sides of the city, he says, were ruined and deserted. People were reduced to cannibalism (Yāqūt, *Kitāb Irshād* III: 900). Archeological digs at the remains of Fustat have revealed traces of wealthy neighborhoods that were abandoned in the second half of the eleventh century, strengthening Yāqūt's claim that the eastern and southern parts of Fustat were abandoned completely during the crisis. The abandoned neighborhoods remained derelict in the crowded heart of Cairo up to the end of the twentieth century (Kubiak; Kubiak and Scanlon; Gayraud; Gayraud and Vallauri).

The crisis afflicted all the large cities in the region, including those of Syria and Palestine (al-Sham). Cities such as Tiberias, Ramla and Jerusalem contracted dramatically from the 1020s, in a short time and for no obvious political or economic reason (Avni). When the scarcity continued, and the authorities realized that spending money was of no use and only brought them to the brink of bankruptcy, they began to take steps to suppress the angry populace while attempting to preserve the army's loyalty. The rulers knew that severing ties with the military leaders would bring about their own end. When it was no longer possible to fulfill the (always many) needs of the army, the same army turned on the central government, usually leading to the flight or execution of the rulers.

The Ikhshidid dynasty, previously considered an efficient administration, collapsed after the six-year drought that afflicted Egypt between 963 and 969. The army divided into two and the fighting that broke out between the two sides only ended with the arrival of the Fatimids, who reached Egypt from North Africa. The first two things that the Fatimids did as the new rulers of Egypt was to bring shipments of grain from the western Mediterranean and to appoint a muḥtasib whose duties were to supervise the grain market, to prevent private and illegal hoarding and excessive prices, to designate spaces for grain markets, and to inflict punishment on offending millers and grain dealers (al-Maqrīzī, *Ittiʿaz al-Hunafa'* I: 117, 122; al-Maqrīzī, *Ighāthat* 13; Shoshan 181–89).

As noted above, the crisis of the 1050s was the most severe. During the harsh winter of 1054–55, when hunger and scarcity afflicted all of Mesopotamia and the government was unable to pay the salaries of the hired soldiers, Ibn al-Athīr writes that

> order broke down, and the [Turkish soldiers] robbed everyone arriving at Baghdad. Prices soared and there was a shortage of food stuffs. [... Even after] the vizier [...] settled the [soldiers'] outstanding pay from his own money [...] they continued with their disorderly and violent behavior. The Kurds and the Arabs [...] resumed their raids, their plundering and killing, so that the land became ruined and the inhabitants scattered. [Kurds ...] came down from Mosul in hope of booty. They raided the settlements [...] and plundered them. [...] The news reached Baghdad, and the people became even more fearful of the mob and the Turks. The decline in the authority of the Caliphate had become really serious. This is the dire result of dissension. (Ibn al-Athīr IX: 588–90)

On 18 December 1055, the Seljuq leader Tughril entered Baghdad at the head of his men, claiming that he wished only to spend time there on his way to make the pilgrimage to Mecca. His name was already proclaimed in the Friday prayers on 15 December 1055, three days before his solemn entry into the capital. Several days later Tughril imprisoned the last descendant of the Būyid dynasty and became, for all practical reasons, the sole ruler of Baghdad. A few days later, he arrested the last scion of the legitimate Buwayhid dynasty, and thus the nomads came to power in Baghdad, up to then the greatest and most developed metropolis in the Islamic world, without a fight.

The Social Consequences of Climate Crises

All the crises of the eleventh century were accompanied by the crumbling of society and the deepening of all social, ethnic and religious chasms, some of which had been in the open previously while others came to light when the crisis began (Table 3). In Baghdad of the 1030s and 1040s there is a correlation between winters of extreme cold and famine, and the peak years of internal conflicts. The reasons for the unrest were different, with religious riots between Sunna and Shiʻa, and between Muslims and Christians, occurring alongside 'ordinary' food riots caused by rises in prices and fights between different Sunni groups over theological questions. Hanbali leaders tried to prevent rationalist approaches and to enforce rigid orthodoxy. They persecuted sinners who dared to drink wine, sing songs, play musical instruments or even participate in the classes of teachers from rival intellectual sects. The government's ability to restrain the unrest, the persecution of Christians, and the unruliness of the ʻayyarun militias (groups of rioters who appeared in times of crisis and vanished in times of plenty), steadily decreased.

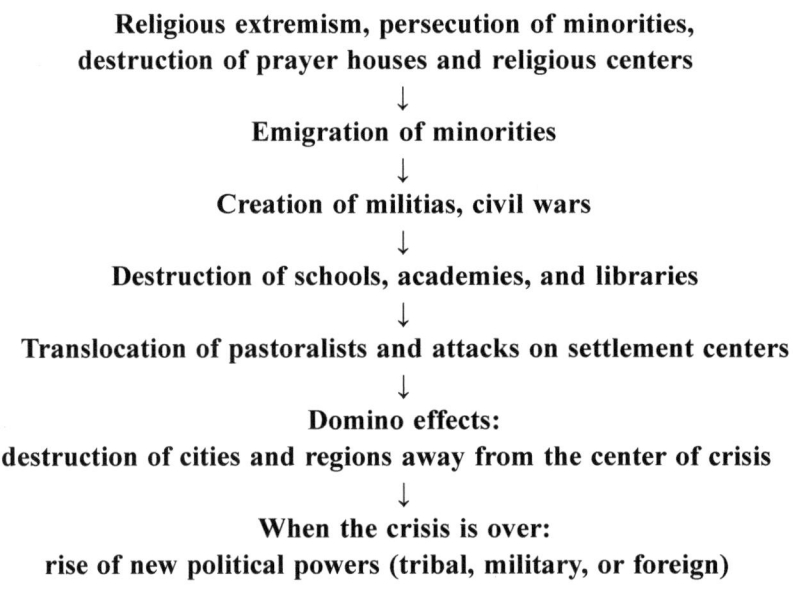

Table 3: Societal transformations and domino effects

The conflicts included religious persecution and the harassment of minorities, destruction of religious buildings, schools, libraries, academies and anything that might be considered precious to the rival group. The militias attached to the various groups spread terror and increased the feeling of insecurity.

The famous library, known as the "House of Wisdom" (Dar al-Hikmah) or the "House of Knowledge/Science" (Dar al-'Ilm) that was founded in Baghdad in the early 990s as part of the academy of Baghdad, and that contained more than 10,000 volumes, was burned twice during the 1050s. It was burned once in 1055 when the Seljuks entered into Baghdad for the first time and once again during their second takeover of the city in December 1059. The library was sacked after the fire, and the Seljuk vizier, al-Kundurī, selected the best remaining books of the collection for his own private library (Ibn al-Athīr X: 7).

The library in Baghdad was only one of many public and semi-public libraries and academies that flourished in the region during the 'Shi'i century', or the 'Islamic Golden Age' that prevailed prior to the decline of the eleventh century. Many of the libraries still operating during the first quarter of the eleventh century ceased to exist during its second quarter, and none of them survived the period of turmoil and dearth between 1027 and 1060. The libraries of Rayy (Medieval Teheran) were already destroyed in the spring of 1029 (Gardīzī 193; Ibn al-Athīr IX: 371–72) and Yāqūt asserts that the other libraries in Baghdad were also burned down during the Seljuk occupation (Yāqūt, Irshād VI: 358; see Mackensen; Eche).

The Fihrist (Catalogue) of one of these libraries gives an idea of the philosophical knowledge of that period. It included virtually the entire Aristotelian corpus and its principal Greek commentaries, many of Plato's writings, pre-Socratic texts translated into Arabic, the works of Euclid and Ptolemy, as well as medical writings ascribed to Hippocrates, and the works of Galen (Ibn al-Nadīm; Eche 315–24).

Descriptions of the climate events that occurred in 1038 can shed light on the destructive potential of climate crises: In that year, "it was bitterly cold, colder than anyone could remember in their lifetime [...] the cold there was of another degree of intensity, and snow fell continuously" (Bayhaqī II: 247–48). The freeze was severely felt in Mesopotamia when heavy snow fell in Baghdad twice and remained for days in the bazaars, "and in the month of [December] there came intense cold and the waters [in Baghdad] froze for six days" (Bar Hebraeus I: 199). In December 1038, there was a cold spell so severe that the water of the Tigris froze for six days. The Amu Darya (Oxus) river also froze in 1038, an event so rare as to almost never have happened in its recorded history. Abū al-Faẓl Bayhaqī reports a military delegation sent from Iran that reached the Dnieper region in 1038, where "the cold was greater than can be remembered, a different kind of severity. Snow fell incessantly. The army suffered in this journey more than in any other" (Bayhaqī II: 209; 247–48). During 1038, the Turks overran Nishapur and continued to conquer and loot other cities in central Iran. In Baghdad famine reigned and violence reached its peak.

In the same year of 1038, the Jewish academies (yeshivas) of Sura and Pumbeditha, the dominant scholarly centers in the Jewish world since the third century CE which had operated from Baghdad, no longer existed. We have no direct evidence of what happened to them, but it may be assumed that they were affected by or even fell victim to the violence and internal conflicts that tore apart Baghdad and the other cities of Iran and Mesopotamia in that year.

The renewed institutions of learning that emerged in Baghdād and elsewhere after the end of the crisis, no longer gave the same preference to Hellenistic traditions in philosophy and in sciences as their pre-crisis predecessors, and the intellectual shift led to the abandonment of some of the attributes of former intellectual activity. The change was described by many as a 'decline' a 'transformation' or even a 'collapse' of Hellenistic traditions in the East. In any event the new 'madrasa' institutional learning that was established in Baghdād during the 1060s, based the training of future administrators on different types of curricular knowledge.

The cadre of teachers and scholars, the curriculum, and the training of jurists were transformed, and the emphasis shifted from teaching and studying the Hellenistic tradition to Islamic law and theology. But although the term decline in this context is doubtful, it is certain that the 'Golden Age' Hellenistic tradition in this part of the world was over, to be replaced by a different intellectual agenda.

Climate Crises, Refugees, and Nomadic Migrations

The increasing violence caused migration to places outside the crisis regions. At first the affluent ones fled, but over time everyone who could escaped, although many discovered that there was nowhere to escape to, and their flight ended with the death of many refugees.

The following text refers to the events of 1079–80, which began with a drought that afflicted the Jazira and caused the mass migration of refugees from Syria to Antioch, on the southern border of present-day Turkey. The chronicler Matthew of Edessa was an eyewitness:

> At the beginning of the year 1079–80 a severe famine occurred throughout all the lands [...] [T]he blood-thirsty and ferocious Turkish nation spread over the whole country [...] Many areas became depopulated; the Oriental [Armenian] nation began to decline, and the country of the Romans became desolate; neither food nor security for the individual was to be found anywhere [...] Security of life did not exist [...] For all the peoples rose up en masse and came to these regions [...], tens of thousands deluging the various areas. [...T]he whole land was covered as if by hordes of locusts [...]. [V]ery important [...] personages [...] roamed

about begging [for food]; indeed our eyes witnessed all this. Because of the famine and the vagabonds there was a great amount of mortality [...and] it was [...] impossible to bury all those who had died. The land was filled with their corpses [...] the land stank [...] All this was the beginning of the destruction of the Oriental and Greek peoples. (Matthew of Edessa II: 72, 143–44; my emphasis, RE)

The movement of pastoral nomads from steppe and desert regions into and within the Middle East has occurred in many periods of history, but in no previous period has nomadic migration been documented in such detail. Earlier theories explaining population movements from within the Asian steppes as due to climatic reasons had nothing to rely on but intuition but the medieval sources of the MCA describe the nomads' migration in a manner that allows us to reconstruct their advance at an annual resolution and with topographic exactness.

The sources attribute the appearance of the Seljuqs in the region to the harsh winters that occurred there between 1027 and 1055: In the year 1027, writes Ibn al-Jawzī, "continuously from November to January, came a cold that no one had ever known before. Water froze solid throughout this period, including the shores of the Tigris and the wide canals" (Ibn al-Jawzī VIII: 25). Bar Hebraeus also refers to the intense cold that prevailed in Baghdad in that same year telling us that it was so great "[that] the farmers were unable to sow their crops" (Bar Hebraeus I: 191). The cold spell of 1027 was only the first of years of severe cold that hit the eastern region between 1027 and the late 1050s. In 1029, two years after the beginning of the great freeze, Ibn al-Athīr mentions the appearance of the Seljuq Turks in Khurasan for the first time. At first, he says, only a relatively small number of nomads, some "two thousand tents," arrived. The ruler of Ghazna managed to imprison their leader, to slaughter them and to banish them deeper into Khurasan. However, so many other nomads of the same Oghuz origin arrived that it was impossible to stop them: "More and more of them [...] came down from the mountains to the neighboring areas, where they looted and sowed destruction and murder" (Ibn al-Athīr IX: 377–78; I: 13). The attempt to limit these cold- and famine-driven nomads was doomed to failure. More nomads appeared every day, and the promises they made to be "loyal and behave well" were not fulfilled (Ibn al-Athīr IX: 379).

Two years later still, in 1031, Bar Hebraeus reports that "the water froze in Baghdad [...] trees were destroyed and produced no fruit at all. And there was so great a famine in the wilderness that the nomads who lived there ate their camels and their horses, and even their children [...] because of the lack of food and the scarcity of water" (Bar Hebraeus I: 193–94).

The sources continue to describe the nomads' migration south, looking for food for themselves and their herds, and how they became increasingly violent as their hopes were disappointed. The process, which involved the conquest and destruction of villages, monasteries and urban centers, can also be seen through archaeological digs of contemporary sites, which uncover layers of destruction and devastation dated to precisely these years (Eger, *The Spaces*; Eger, *The Islamic-Byzantine Frontier*; Heidemann, "Numayrid Ar-Raqqa"; Heidemann, "Settlement Patterns"; Heidemann, "The Agricultural Hinterland").

The later chroniclers tried to present the Seljuqs' movement south as the well-organized advance of regular forces headed by a charismatic leader, but the eye-witness sources show a more complex picture. Tribal groups that became violent due to the circumstances of life in the steppe each operated alone until they accepted the leadership of the charismatic Seljuq leader (and many of them were quick to abandon him when a no less charismatic rival arose). Bar Hebraeus provides us with an insightful description of such an event of joining that occurred in 1043, shedding new light on the meaning of "a new wave of nomads" and on the mechanism that enabled the Seljuks to multiply within less than a decade from a tribe of no more than two thousand tents to a confederation that was able to defeat empires. The new arrivals, he says, sat in groups of 2,000 men, at a certain distance from the sultan, not daring to approach or speak to him. They only kissed the land upon which he stood, waiting quietly for a hint that would tell them that their request to join the Seljuks was granted.

He also attributes these groups becoming violent to the lack of food in the lands to which they had migrated: "In every place where his troops meet together they plunder, and destroy and kill, and no district (or quarter) is able to support them for more than one week because of their vast number. And from sheer necessity they are compelled to depart to another quarter in order to find food for themselves and their beasts" (Bar Hebraeus I: 202; my emphasis, RE). It is clear from this description that the newly dislocated pastoralists were forced to abandon their traditional way of life and that they were looking for the protection of the charismatic leader who could have ensured their own life and the lives of their beasts.

Nomadic movement was not limited to the Seljuqs' penetration of Mesopotamia via Khurasan and Iran. Turkmen tribes of a similar background began to enter the Byzantine Empire in 1046, crossing the Danube en masse, the river having frozen in 1046 and again in 1048 (Cedrenus II: 585). The connection between the southward migration and violent behavior of previously peaceful tribes, and the almost unprecedented freezing of the Danube (it had also frozen in the fourth century CE, at the beginning of the Migration Period/Völkerwanderung) is made again and again in the written sources. The repeated attacks of the Pechenegs and western Ossetians caused the collapse of Byzantine rule in the Balkans even before the Seljuqs managed to conquer the eastern part of the Empire. The nomad conquests diminished the area under Byzantine rule to less than twenty per cent of the area that, only a few decades earlier, had been controlled by Basil II (Figure 2).

At the height of the crisis, in the mid-1050s, the Bedouin tribes of Banu Hilal and Banu Salim, documented at the beginning of the century as still in southern Arabia, arrived on the banks of the Nile. The rulers of Egypt, no doubt surprised by the strength of the migration – it was most likely the longest one documented up to then in the history of the Middle East – paid the nomads to cross the Nile and attack their neighbors and rivals, the rulers of North Africa. The nomads indeed raided the flourishing agricultural region of North Africa and turned it into a desert, destroying also the thriving capital, Qayrawan. Almost three hundred years later, Ibn Khaldun likened the migration of these tribes to a swarm of locusts and accused them of destroying North Africa and Qayrawan. But it is also possible to see them as victims of the climatic events that afflicted the region. A similar migration of the tribe of Banu Jarrah and other tribes into Sinai and Palestine was documented in annual and sometimes even dated detail (see, inter alia, Ibn al-Athīr IX: 566–70; Ibn Khaldūn I: 32–33; 36–9; Ibn 'Idari II: 441; Thiry 211–12; Brett, "Fatimid historiography" 47–59; Brett, "The Way of the Nomad" 251–69).

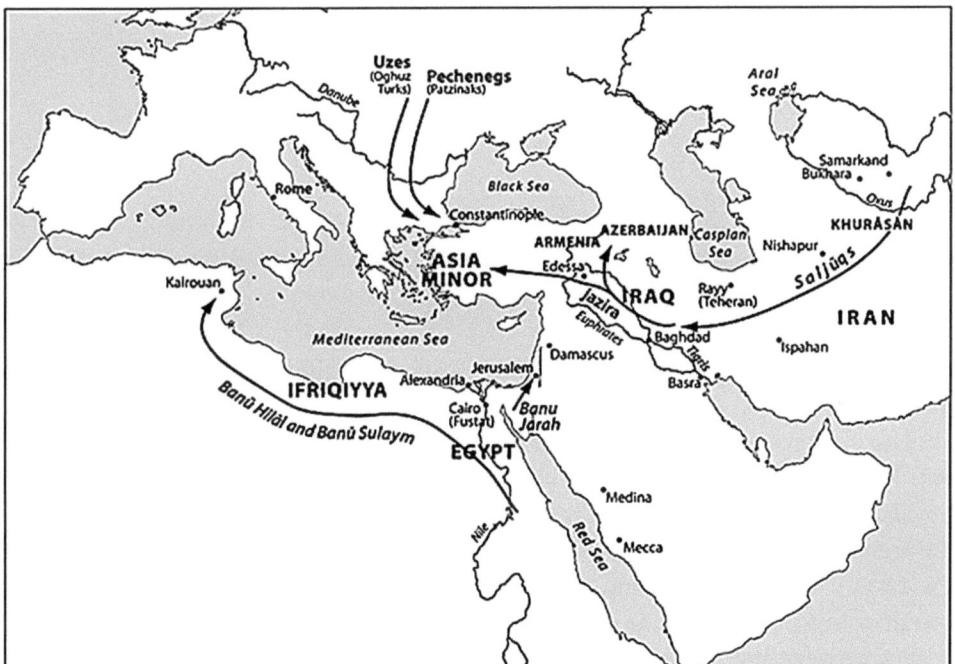

Fig. 2: Advance of the Nomadic Tribes 1029–1055. Source: Ronnie Ellenblum

The Limits of the Crisis

During the first part of the MCA, between the middle of the tenth and the end of the eleventh centuries, Western Europe enjoyed a relatively mild climate: winter temperatures were mild and above the multi-annual average, the glaciers receded, and the tree line rose. It is difficult not to see a connection between the warm anomaly and the extension of settlement in the north Atlantic (Iceland and Green-

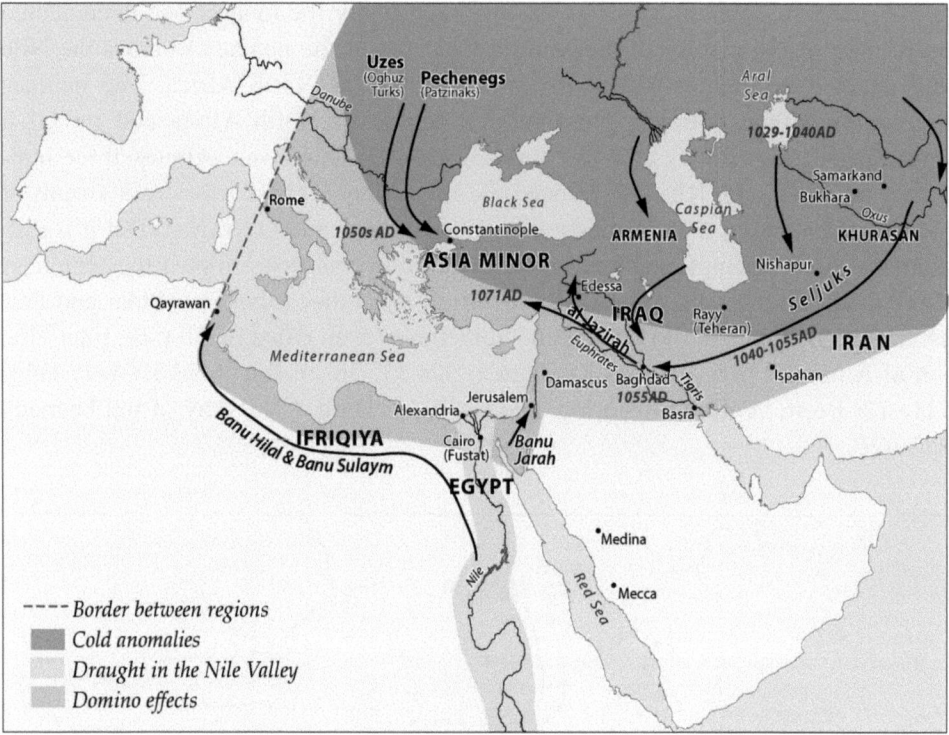

Fig. 3:   The extreme climatic events were limited to the eastern Mediterranean.
Source: Ronnie Ellenblum

land), trans-Atlantic voyages, and the general flourishing of western Europe in this period.

The circumstances of the eastern Mediterranean basin were completely different. In both east and west, there were sequences of years that diverged from it, but the general trend portrayed by the written sources is clear: a mild climate in the western Mediterranean and Western Europe, and a climate filled with crises in the eastern Mediterranean and western Asia. An imaginary line, connecting Qayrawan with Rome and the Iron Gates of the Danube, can be drawn to indicate the border between these two regions (Figure 3).

The End of the Crisis

The written sources sometimes attribute the end of the crises that disturbed the societies of the mid-eleventh century to an improvement in the climate. One of the best examples of such a connection is Ibn al-Athīr's description of the end of the civil war that tore Iraq apart, ending in December 1059. The victorious leader of the Seljuqs, Sultan Tughril Bek, escaped the final battle – in which even his wife joined his enemies – by the skin of his teeth. Ibn al-Athīr describes the rain that began to fall when Tughril Bek entered Baghdad at the head of his tattered men, and sees the rain that finally arrived as the end of the civil war: "The year," says Ibn al-Athīr, "had been one of drought, in which no rain had been seen, but that night it came and the poets congratulated the Caliph and the Sultan on that circumstance. After the Caliph's return, the rain lasted for thirty odd days. An untold number of people had perished through hunger and oppression" (IX: 648). The rain, together with Tughril Bek's entry to Baghdad, signaled the end of the crisis and the beginning of a period of affluence. Tughril continued to rule Baghdad unopposed until his death three years later, and is considered the first of the three great Seljuq sultans who amassed immense wealth and left their stamp on the entire region.

Conclusion

The understanding that significant climate changes occurred in historical periods was accepted by disciples of determinist theories, but was rejected together with those theories and is now, after an absence of many decades, returning to the center of the historiographical stage. Climatologists relied on proxies whose spatial and temporal precision was insufficient for exact description of short-term climatic anomalies that lasted less than a few decades.

I have tried to show here that it is in fact these short-term anomalies that caused structural and significant changes in the political and economic systems that impacted ethnic and religious relationships and even the curricula of schools and academies of the affected regions. The only way to identify such anomalies is through written sources – the same ones used by more classical kinds of historiography. They refer not only to the short-term anomalies themselves, but also to the causal chains connecting the climatic events to the subsequent structural changes.

The view that regards humanity as completely subservient to the powers of the natural elements prevailed for thousands of years. The list of scholars and scientists who accepted this notion, from Herodotus to Ibn Khaldun, from Pliny the Elder to Montesquieu, from Thomas Aquinas to Carl Ritter, is too long to be cited here.

This prevailing view was transformed already during the 1920s and 1930s by an equally untenable view of humanity as able to entirely control its future and even as the only agency that causes climatic changes and that could repair them. The climate change discourse that had been exciting the entire world politically, economically, and culturally since the mid-twentieth century has also rekindled the discourse on possible connections between past climatic changes and historical societal transformations. The assumption that both in the historical past and in developing societies of the present people are always autonomous and able to decide rationally about their future – that they are able to create the circumstances that will allow them to overcome the challenges of the environment – is no longer tenable and needs to be reconsidered.

The present paper presented a series of Medieval societal catastrophes that began with climatic disasters and ended with the collapse or with the decline of complex and well-established civilizations. In view of the climatic events that preceded the present crisis known as the "Arab Spring," this story may serve as a warning about the fragility of mankind and the societal upheavals that may follow as a consequence of the enormous power of nature.

Works Cited

Attaleiates, Michael. "Historia". *Corpus scriptorum historiae Byzantinae*, vol. 36. Ed. Immanuel Bekker. Bonn: Weber, 1853.
Avni, Gideon. *The Byzantine-Islamic Transition in Palestine: An Archaeological Approach*. Oxford: Oxford University Press, 2014.
Barguet, Paul. *La stèle de la famine, à Séhel*. Cairo: Impr. de l'Institut français d'archéologie orientale, 1953.
Bar Hebraeus (Abu al-Farāj). *The chronography*, translated from the Syriac by Ernest A. Wallis Budge, 2 vols. London: Oxford University Press, 1932.
Bayhaqī Abū al-Faẓl. *The History of Bayhaqi*, translated with commentary by Clifford E. Bosworth and revised by Mohsen Ashtiany, Persian Heritage Series, 3 vols. New York: Mahtab, 2009.
Brett, Michael. "Fatimid historiography: a case study – the quarrel with the Zirids, 1048–58." *Medieval historical writing in the Christian and Islamic worlds*, Ed. David O. Morgan. London: University of London, 1982. 47–59.
—. "The Way of the Nomad." *Bulletin of the School of Oriental and African Studies* 58 (1995): 251–69.
Cedrenus Georgius. *Compendium historiarum, I. Scylitzae ope*, supplemented and emended by Immanuel Bekker, 2 vols. Bonn: Impendis Ed Weberi.
Charanis, Peter. "The Byzantine Empire in the eleventh century." *A history of the Crusades*, 6 vols. General Ed. Kenneth M. Setton. Madison. *The first three hundred years*, vol. 1. Ed. Marshal W. Baldin. Madison: University of Wisconsin Press, 1955. 177–219.
Eche, Youssef. *Les bibliothèques arabes publiques et semi-publiques en Mésopotamie, en Syrie et en Égypte au Moyen Âge*. Damas: Institut français de Damas, 1967.
Eger, Asa A. *The spaces between the teeth: a gazetteer of towns on the Islamic-Byzantine – Gazetteer of towns on the Islamic-Byzantine frontier*. Istanbul: Ege Yayınları, 2012.
—. *The Islamic-Byzantine frontier: interaction and exchange among Muslim and Christian communities*. London: I.B. Tauris, 2016.
Ellenblum, Ronnie. *The collapse of the eastern Mediterranean: climate change and the decline of the East, 950–1072*. Cambridge/New York: Cambridge University Press, 2013.
Felix, Wolfgang. *Byzanz und die islamische Welt im frühen 11. Jahrhundert: Geschichte der politischen Beziehungen von 1001 bis 1055, Byzantina Vindobonensia, 14*. Vienna: Verlag der Österreichischen Akademie der Wissenschaften, 1981.

Gardīzī, ʿAbd al-Hayy. *Tārīkh-i Gardīzī ed. Abd al-Ḥayy Habībī*. Teheran: Dunyā-yi Kitāb, 1984 [1363].

Gayraud, Roland P. "Excavations at al-Fustat." *Egyptian Archaeology* 6 (1995): 34–38.

Gayraud, Roland P., and Lucy Vallauri. *Fouilles d'Isṭabl ʿAntar: céramiques d'ensembles des IXe et Xe siècles*. Cairo: Institut français d'archéologie orientale du Caire, 2017.

Gil, Moshe. *Palestine during the first Muslim period*, 3 vols. Tel Aviv: Tel Aviv University, 1983.

Heideman, Stefan. "Numayrid Ar-Raqqa: Archaeological and Historical Evidence for a 'Dimorphic State' in Bedouin Dominated Fringes of the Fatimid Empire." *Egypt and Syria in the Fatimid, Ayyubid and Mamluk eras IV*. Ed. U. Vermeulen. Leuven: Peeters, 2005. 85–110.

—. "Settlement Patterns, Economic Development and Archaeological Coin Finds in Bilad al-Sham: the Case of Diyar Mudar – The Process of Transformation from the 6th to the 10th century A.D." *Residences, Castles, Settlements: Transformation Processes from Late Antiquity to Early Islam in Bilad al-Sham* (Proceedings of the International Conference Held at Damascus, 5–9 November 2006). Eds. K. Bartl and A. al R. Moaz. Rahden: Leidorf, 2008. 493–516.

—. "The Agricultural Hinterland of Baghdad, al-Raqqa and Samarra – Settlement Patterns in the Diyar Mudar." *Le Proche-orient de Justinien aux Abbassides: Peuplement et dynamiques spatiales* (Bibliothèque de l'antiquité tardive 19). Eds. A. Borrut et al. Turnhout: Brepols Publishers, 2011.

Ibn al-Athīr. *Izz al-Dīn al-Kāmil fī al-tārīkh*. Ed. Carl J. Tornberg, 13 vols. (Leiden: E.J. Brill, 1862–1871, repr. Beirut: Dar Ṣādir 1965–1967). Eng. Translation -*The Annals of the Saljuq Turks: Selections from al-Kamil fi al-tarikh of Izz al-Din Ibn al-Athīr*, translated and annotated by Donald S. Richards. London: Routledge, 2002.

Ibn, ʿIdari. *Histoire de l'Afrique et de l'Espagne intitulée Al-Bayano'l-Mogrib*. Translated by Edmond Fagnan, 2 vols. Alger: P. Fontana, 1901–4.

Ibn, al-Jawzī. *Al-Muntaẓam fī tārīkh al-mulūk wa-al-umam*. Hyderabad: n.p., 1938–40.

Ibn, Khaldūn. *Histoire des Berbères et des dynasties musulmanes de l'Afrique septentrionale*. Translated by Baron de Slane, 4 vols. Paris: Geuthner, 1925–56.

Ibn, Muyassar. *al-Muntaqā min akhbār Miṣr* (Choix de passages de la Chronique d'Egypte d'Ibn Muyassar). Ed. Ayman Fu'ād Sayyid. *Textes Arabes et Etude Islamiques*, vol. 18. Caire: Institut Français d'archéologie orientale du Caire, 1981.

Ibn, al-Nadīm, Muḥammad ibn Isḥāq. "The Fihrist of al-Nadīm: a tenth-century survey of Muslim culture." *Records of civilization: sources and studies*, no. 83. Ed. and trans. Bayard Dodge. New York: Columbia University Press, 1970.

Ibn, Taghrībirdī, Abū al-Maḥāsin Yūsuf, *al-Nujūm al-zāhirah fī mulūk Miṣr wa-al-Qāhirah*. 16 vols. Cairo: Dār al-Kutub al-Miṣrīyah, 1919–72.

Kaplanis, Costas. "The debasement of the dollar of the Middle Ages." *Journal of Economic History* 63 (2003): 768–801.

Kelley, Colin, et al. "Climate change in the Fertile Crescent and implications of the recent Syrian drought." *PNAS* 112.11 (2015): 3241–3246.

Kennedy, Hugh. "The Feeding of the Five Hundred Thousand: Cities and Agriculture in Early Islamic Mesopotamia." *Iraq* 73 (2011): 177–199.

Kubiak, Wladyslaw B. *Al-Fustat: Its Foundations and Early Urban Development*. Cairo: American Research Center in Egypt, 1987.

Kubiak, Wladyslaw B., and George T. Scanlon. *Fusṭāṭ expedition final report*. American Research Center in Egypt Reports, 11. Winona Lake, Indiana: Eisenbrauns, 1989.
Lopez Robert S. "The dollar of the Middle Ages." *Journal of Economic History* 11 (1951): 209–34.
Mackensen, Ruth S. "Four great libraries of medieval Baghdad." *The Library Quarterly* 2/3 (July 1932): 279–99.
al-Maqrizi. *Ighāthat al-umma bi-kashf al-ghumma*. Cairo: 1957.
—. *Itti'az al-Hunafa' bi-Akhbar al-A'imma al-Fatimiyyin al-Khulafa*. Ed. Jamal al-Din Shayyal. Cario: Al-Lajnat Iḥyā' al-Turāth al-Islāmī, 1967–1973.
Matthew of Edessa. *Armenia and the crusades, tenth to twelfth Centuries: The chronicle of Matthew of Edessa*. Translated by Ara E. Dostourian. Lanham/New York/London: University Press of America, 1993.
al-Musabbihī. *Izz al-Mulk al-Juz al-arba'ūn min Akhbār Misr*. Eds. Ayman F. Sayyid and Thierry Bianquis, 2 vols. Cairo: Institut Français d'Archéologie Orientale du Caire, 1978–84.
Rosenthal, Franz. *The classical heritage in Islam*. Trans. Emile and Jenny Marmorstein. London: Routledge, 1992.
Shoshan, Boaz. "Fatimid grain policy and the post of the muĥtasib." *International Journal of Middle East Studies* 13 (1981): 181–189.
Sibṭ ibn al-Jawzī. *Mir'āt al-zamān fī tārīkh al-a'yān*. Ed. Yūsuf ibn Qizughlī. Ankara: Turkish Universities Press, 1968.
Thiry, Jacques. *Le Sahara Libyen dans l'Afrique du Nord médiévale*. Leuven: Peeters, 1995.
Yaḥyā ibn Sa'īd al-Anṭākī. *Eutychii Patriarchae Alexadtrini Annales, Corpus Scriptorum Christianorum Orientalium*. Vol. 51, Scriptores Arabici, ser. 3 vol. VII. Eds. Louis Cheikho et al., repr. Louvain: secrétariat du CSCO, 1960.
Yāqūt, al-Hamawī. "Mu'jam al-Buldān." *Jacut's geographisches Wörterbuch*. Ed. F. Wüstenfeld. Leipzig: F. A. Brockhaus, 1868.
—. *Irshād, Kitāb Irshād al-arīb ilá ma'rifat al-adīb*. (= dictionary of learned men of Yāqūt), Ed. David S. Margoliouth, 6 vols. Leiden: E. J. Brill; London: Luzac.

CHAPTER THREE

Bad Heritage:
The American Viking Fantasy,
from the Nineteenth Century to Now

KARL STEEL

The very first lines of *Historic Newfoundland* are "Come to Newfoundland! It is the cradle of white civilization in North America" (English 1). These lines, appearing in the second edition of this tourist brochure's late 1960s printing, may have been written in the mid-1950s by Leo English, its listed author. Head of the Newfoundland museum from 1947 to 1960, itself belonging to a Newfoundland that had, in 1949, just been absorbed into Canada, English obviously wants it recognized that Canadian history proper and even that of North America as a whole began in Canada's newest acquisition. Come to the east, the brochure cries out; come east and meet your ancestors!

Or, rather, meet them in the middle, as they sail west: the founding parents of the cradle of this brochure's "white civilization" were the Vikings. Its cover features a Viking ship, complete with warriors outfitted in horned helmets riding in a boat with a dragon-headed prow: the wrong helmets and the wrong kind of boat, a warship instead of the mercantile *knorr* more likely used by Newfoundland's Norse arrivals. Though L'Anse aux Meadows, the first incontrovertible evidence of a medieval Norse presence in North America, would not be discovered until 1960, Leo English still had some kind of reality in mind: *Erik the Red's Saga* and the *Greenlander's Saga*, written in thirteenth-century Iceland, speak of a "Vinland," and English followed the right hunch in promoting Newfoundland as part of this legendary land.[1] *Historic Newfoundland* is no mere historical relic. Witness, for example, a recent Newfoundland and Labrador Tourist board television commercial, featuring a set of light-skinned children frolicking amid the reconstructions of turf houses at L'Anse aux Meadows, whose voiceover concludes with "their journey ended [here]…the place your journey will begin" (*L'Anse aux Meadows*). The Vikings provide a break, starting history, but also ending it, by establishing a bond cementing past to present.

Presenting Newfoundland this way is thus not entirely a symptom of a particular historiographical fantasy but also a symptom of a particular way of thinking of history, based partially in fact and partially in a sense of what counts as a fact

---

1   For some considerations of the specifically Canadian interest in Vikings, see Mancini 892–907; and Liedl.

worth remembering. For Leo English, and for many North American enthusiasts of the Vikings before and after his time, history proper starts with the freedom of the open sea and with medieval Europe. This is 'history' because it breaks with a 'prehistoric' past hardly worth remarking on.

Historic Newfoundland devotes only its second chapter to the island's Native Americans, there before and after the Vikings, and describes their disappearance as "fate," as if neither they nor their extinction belonged to history. If history requires agency and some kind of break with the seamless and unchanging world presumed to be characteristic of the primitive, then what better agent to bring it about than a warrior sailor, arriving by surprise to literally cut the new moment from the witless past. But if history begins here, it also ends there too, because the presumptive whiteness of America's first historical visitors collapses the distinction between past and present, Europe and the Americas, and the medieval and the modern. In effect, it transforms an open-ended heritage into a closed one, in which the present, to be true to itself, must know and imitate its authentic past, without venturing into some inauthentic, muddled deviation from what is presumed to be its true core.

This chapter will be an exploration of the heritage function of Vikings in America. It will examine the whiteness so often imputed to them from the early nineteenth century to the present, through the real mania for all things Viking in the mid to late nineteenth century, and on to present day fascinations with the Norse in popular music, neo-Norse religion, and white supremacy discourse. As I will demonstrate, a fantasized whiteness is at the core of much of the American Viking fantasy. This chapter's central concern will be with how this whiteness establishes itself as both a heritage of freedom and as an obligation, a burden, or a duty – in short, as anything but freedom. Ultimately, this chapter's goal will be to complicate claims of authenticity and straightforward cultural transmission to make them useless for white supremacist heritage claims, while preserving the possibility for a culturally heterogeneous Viking heritage that might operate outside the strictures of purity.

Race and the Modern Viking

Fantasies of whiteness run through the whole of what Geraldine Barnes called the "nineteenth-century 'theatre' of Vinland" (*Viking America* 70) and through to the present day. Repeated racial signs – white skin, blue eyes, blond hair, and, very often, unusual height and strength – traverse through the entire body of Viking literature, separating the Norse from all other races, all of which were presumed to have varying combinations of swarthy skin, brown eyes, black hair, and squatness. Ralph Waldo Emerson's chapter on "Race" in his *English Traits* praised the "animal vigor" of the Norse "blonde race" (65, 72); Longfellow's poem "Skeleton in Armor" has his Norse exile love a "blue-eyed maid" (Longfellow 35), like

John Greenleaf Whittier's poem "The Norseman," which speaks of their "wild, blue eye[s]" and "yellow hair" (Whittier 39); Sarah Orne Jewett's historical survey, *The Story of the Normans*, often praises their "yellow hair," and the shine of their "blue eyes," while also faulting them for their inherent love of the sea and plunder, as they squandered the chance to dominate an America she imagines as empty and otherwise wasted (28).

We find a similar attentiveness to hair and eye color in *Canada's First Boy Baby* (who grows into a "flaxen-haired blue eyed youngster"; G. Johnson 7) and in Ottilie A. Liljencrantz's turn-of-the-century trilogy on the muscular Christianity of Nordic America, *The Thrall of Leif the Lucky*, *The Vinland Champions*, and *Randvar the Songsmith: A Romance of Norumbega*. The first of these became a Technicolor silent film, *The Viking* (1928), introduced by title cards that speak of Vikings arriving "before any [other] white man set foot on the American shore" (and whose synchronized soundtrack, comprising excerpts from *Der fliegende Holländer*, *Die Walküre*, and *Siegfried*, transitions at the film's end into a chorus singing the last couplet of the "Star-Spangled Banner," "the land of the free, and the home of the brave"; Neill). Likewise in Maurice Hewlett's *Gudrid the Fair: A Tale of the Discovery of America* (where Leif has "golden hair and beard, and blue eyes"). In 1952, a Catholic priest began a history of his state with the chapter "The First White Man in Minnesota" (Krueger 103). Champions of the Viking heritage of the Orkney Islands characterized the Vikings as tall and powerful warriors, full of vigor, and the island's original Picts as squat representatives of a transcontinental race of primitive, doomed dwarves, of which Japan's Ainu are a last set of survivors (Grydehøj). More recent examples appear in materials ranging from undisguised white supremacism to misguided professional scholarship. The 2011 film *Thor* met some small controversy when it cast the black-haired, brown-eyed Idris Elba as the Norse God Heimdall. Detractors called this particular moment nothing less than "a declar[ation] of war on Norse Mythology" ("Marvel Studios Declares War") – this in a story that represented these gods as technologically advanced space aliens. Meanwhile, a collection on Viking archaeology, published by the Smithsonian Institution, includes an article on an eleventh-century Norse penny, found in Maine in 1956, that concludes by imagining Native Americans wondering at rumors of "blond or red-haired strangers with pale skin" (Cox 207). A leading journal of medieval studies published an article on racial attitudes of medieval Iceland that uses phrases like "pure Norse" and "pure Celt," takes Tacitus's description of German homogeneity as a straightforward truth, and, astonishingly, talks about the "distinctive genes" of Celts as "produc[ing] dark features" (Jochens).

Arguably, the American version of this racial theater began with the attempts by white-identified Americans to fabricate a heritage for themselves by rooting themselves in early medieval English history (Modarelli 539). In his *Essay Towards Facilitating Instruction in the Anglo-Saxon and Modern Dialects of the English Language* (probably drafted between 1818 and 1825 and printed posthumously in 1851) Thomas Jefferson argued that "the pure Anglo-Saxon constitutes at this day the basis of our language" (8). Skipping past England's inconveniently foreign Anglo-Norman and Roman legal traditions, Jefferson identified ancient Anglo-Saxons as the core of both "the genuine structure, powers and meanings of the language we now read and speak" (23) and the American legal system.[2] The hunt for such an origin – which sometimes imagined America being settled long ago by the Phoenicians or Irish – would have seeded the ground for the reception of the Danish antiquarian Carl Christian Rafn's *Antiquitates Americanae*. This work, produced in Denmark and written in Latin, reached America in the 1830s, along with a host of excerpts, translations, paraphrases, and reviews, all of which attempted to collect every scrap of evidence of the Norse medieval presence in the Americas. The mania for Vikings catalyzed by Rafn reached its apogee in the 1890s, as counter-programming to the 400th anniversary of the landing of Columbus in the Caribbean.

In this period and even into the present day, everybody who wanted a relic of Norse exploration seemed to be able to find at least one: an armored skeleton of uncertain origin – destroyed in a fire in 1843; the Newport Tower (as it turned out, constructed not by Vikings but as part of a windmill by a seventeenth-century governor of Rhode Island); Dighton rock, a stone supposedly carved with runes, whose very illegibility, according to some early, hostile reviewers, allowed it to be read in any way the reader saw fit; New England place names, heard by amateur philologists as bastardized Norse instead of Algonquin or Iroquois; and especially several rune-carved rocks, in Oklahoma (the so-called Poteau and Shawnee runestones, 'discovered' in the 1960s) and in Minnesota. All of these provided America with the "picturesque," "gloomy" "antiquity" Nathaniel Hawthorne argued was needed to write effective "historical romances" (Hawthorne xxv) (for considerations of most of these, see Kolodny and Krueger). In an 1879 book, Albert Welles even charted George Washington's lineage back to Odin, "supreme ruler of the Scythians" and "first king of Scandinavia" (Welles 7; Krueger 180, 30). More recently, a mendacious report in 2013 of a "Viking ship" discovered in the mud of the Mississippi was immediately repeated across a host of white supremacist websites (B. Johnson; for one such reposting, Quaestor), despite the article's collection of outrageously mislabeled and misappropriated photos: its ship actually an eleventh-century longship from a Danish museum, its sword, from the Scottish Port an Eilean Mhòir ship burial, and its scholar, Nicolò Marchetti from the University of Bologna, here labelled as "James Milbury," a wholly invented professor from the University of Memphis, Tennessee. In a North America whose native historical evidence was often destroyed, unrecognized, and thought of by white-identified Americans as 'prehistoric' rather than 'historical', fabricated Norse relics provided not just the grounds for historical romance but

---

2   For the persistence of this myth of a racial and culturally homogenous medieval heritage as the authentic American self, see Flax.

for history proper, and, through this, for a strengthening of collective identity and territorial self-justification.

Even more usefully, the medieval Viking presence in America is a history of failure. The Norse had come, and then, it seemed, they had gone. Or had been made to leave. White-identified Americans could thereby imagine themselves victims, even during some of the worst periods of American white supremacy against African and Native Americans (Krueger 44–67; Mancini 888–89). Their fantasy was that the Norse had been slaughtered by the Natives or, at best, that they had been assimilated, passing on with their 'blood' whatever scraps of civilization they still possessed when the Europeans next arrived. Several nineteenth-century works, like a textbook used in South Carolina (Simms 1), dreamed up an epic past of racial tragedy, in which a Nordic or even Irish civilization, having built its mounds, was then eradicated by an influx of Asian barbarians (Kolodny 127; Krueger 34–35). Minnesota's Kensington Runestone, the most famous of the false relics, which turned up in 1898 and was almost immediately identified as an ungrammatical and anachronistic forgery, claims to be last witness to a massacre, usefully serving as a simultaneous witness of presence and absence while telling a tale of "white innocence" and martyrdom (Krueger 43). The translation of its inscription runs: "We were fishing one day. After we came home, found 10 men red from blood and dead. Ave Maria save from evil" (Kolodny 328). No wonder, then, that white-identified American readers of the so-called Vinland Sagas – *Erik the Red's Saga* and the *Greenlander's Saga* – often took particular delight in the New World death of Thorvald at the hands of Native Americans, as his blood sanctified the earth, calling out for and justifying revenge. Predictably, in 1902, his 'tomb' was turned up in New Hampshire (Robinson). One recent example of white victimization is the final scene from the Danish film *Valhalla Rising*, where its hero, a one-eyed medieval Norse warrior, an avatar of the one-eyed god Odin, catastrophically astray after an attempt to reach the crusades, lets himself be swarmed and killed by Native Americans to save his charge, a single blond boy. With works like this, we are made to hear that white America had always belonged, that it has always been embattled, and that its expansion into North America was nothing but the return of what had, in a historical sense, already been here, and that would still be here were it not for the depravations of what white-identified Americans wanted to imagine as merely false natives. This, at any rate, is the aim of the *Council of Conservative Citizen's* attempt to prove the Kennewick Man (a roughly 9000-year-old skeleton discovered in Washington State in 1996) was actually European; through these remains, whose reconstructed face looks uncannily like the actor Patrick Stewart ("who is very much white"), the article reminds white people to be wary, as their American ancestors were "wiped out by successive waves of Mongoloid invasions," and they might be again in today's multicultural America (Rogers).

Both Annette Kolodny and Geraldine Barnes present the time of Viking mania as far behind us (Barnes, *Viking America*; Barnes; "Nostalgia", Kolodny). This is true, to a degree: the great period of erecting American statues to Leif Erikson is over (at least 10 are extant, in Boston, Milwaukee, Chicago, Newport News, Duluth, St Paul, Seattle, Cleveland, and Los Angeles, erected between the beginning through the middle of the last century, with the latest one being the outlier of Minot, North Dakota, set up in 1994; Bouteleux). Kolodny sees the racial features of Viking love giving way to the love of professional sports (for example, the American Football team of Minnesota is called the Vikings) and space exploration (like the Viking landers sent by NASA to Mars) (Kolodny 332). For her part, Barnes tracks the emergence of a post-war, anti-nostalgic strain in literature about Vikings, with her key exhibits being novels by Jane Smiley, Thomas Pynchon, George Mackay Brown, and Joan Clarke. This is too optimistic.

Unconsidered by either Kolodny or Barnes, a popular strain of highly nostalgic Viking attention has solidified in the last few decades. One Viking Metal musician thinks wistfully of going out into the Norwegian woods, where his "grandfather's, father's father was standing here with his sword" (Von Helden 261). Apart from Viking Metal, the most intense form of recent amateur Viking love is the rise of modern-day "Odinists" or adherents of Asatrú (a word derived from the Aesir, the Norse pantheon). In all fairness, there is nothing inevitably racist about modern enthusiasm for Vikings. An interest in Vikings is often inspired by their reputation for vigor, their love of travel, their bravery, and their individual valor. The fascination with the bleak and indifferent cruelty of Northern environments – another frequently voiced element of this Viking mystique – is an expression of the Romantic Sublime. More recently, we can encounter this attitude in the guise of an ecological consciousness in which humans are only one element of a heterogeneous, acentric landscape. Enthusiasm of this sort, without obvious attachment to the imagined white skin or supposed ethnic 'purity' of Vikings, takes many forms: the marketing arm of Northern England promotes Vikings as the original transnational entrepreneurs (Sindbaek 84–85); sports clubs often tend to be called "Vikings" (Sindbaek 81); and Viking Metal, associated or sometimes coterminous with Pagan and Folk Metal – all subgenres of Heavy Metal music – overtly distinguishes itself from the ethnic nationalism and far-right politics of both some of the earlier strains of Scandinavian Black Metal, Viking Rock, and contemporary Heathen Metal, itself a subset of Nazi Metal.[3] Viking bands emphasize local history and culture prior to the arrival of Christianity and promote a living tradition through a modern musical form infused with heritage languages like Old Norse and Faroese, heritage instruments, and heritage song structures (notably, for Viking Metal, sea shanties; Ashby and Schofield 6). These bands collectively offer their adherents not a race fantasy, necessarily, but rather the fun of insider knowledge, amateur expertise (evident, for example, in the very proliferating categories of metal), and the naughty fun of mocking the dominant religious culture.

---

3   Many fans of Black Metal in fact scorn all political or ethnic music for being insufficiently misanthropist. See Spracklen 88. For further discussions of taxonomies of metal, see Trafford and Pluskowski; Weston.

Viking Metal shows feature historical reenactors, like the German Jomsvikings, who perform with the bands Amon Amarth and Manowar, fighting on stage, carrying out public drinking contests, and performing chant-along chorus songs in Old Norse (Heesch 75). This, plus the music's fantasies of conquest, resistance, and endurance, all have obvious and seemingly transhistorical appeals to young people, and to young men in particular.

While Viking love is far from necessarily white supremacist, white supremacy, at least in North America, nonetheless gravitates more readily towards Viking fantasies than any other ancient group. Its characteristic self-justifications are apparent even in this avowedly non-racist statement by Ivar Bjørnson, of the Viking metal band Enslaved, who explains that "his interest in his ancestral roots was aroused by his seeing himself in the wider context of the world as a whole and helps to understand other cultures instead of fearing or rejecting them" (Von Helden 260). The problem is this very language of "ancestral roots." Supported through the familiar language of cherishing cultural diversity and demands that heritage must be preserved and communal rights protected against "spiritual imperialism," defenses of Nordic heritage all too readily become a defense of a presumptive authentic whiteness that flattens out the real complexity of the ancient Norse.

The early groups of Odinists, who emerged in the first decades of the twentieth century, tended to be overtly racist, even loudly anti-semitic. *Might Is Right,* published first in 1910 and since reprinted by the white supremacist Wotansvolk, sneers at Christianity's weakness: "The Model Man of our forefathers was Odin, a War Lord, but our Ideal Man is a weeping, horsewhipped Jew. A Jew for a God!" (Redbeard 82). From material like this, beginning in the 1930s, the Australian Alexander Rud Mills renamed himself Tasman Forth and published his *Guide Book for the Anglican Church of Odin,* followed by *Hail Odin, And Fear Shall be in the Way,* and *The Call of Our Ancient Nordic Religion.* In Europe, he met with English fascists and even Hitler himself. North American Odinist documents from the 1970s and 1980s often include sentiments like "Be aware of your racial and cultural heritage and instill their values in your children" (Slauson 19); laments for the waning of the "militaristic kingdom of Prussia" (which it calls the "chief casualty" of the Second World War; Slauson 27); battle cries such as "Only by awakening the Aryan racial consciousness through the nation of Odin, can we hope to stop future bloody tragedies" (Slauson 15); and the call, by Else Christiansen (a Dane relocated to Florida and then, in her late life, deported to Canada) that Odinists must be "racial, discriminatory, self-assertive, and proud" (Klassen, "A Letter to Mrs Else Christensen"). More recently, Neo-Nazi groups calling themselves the "Vikings" were discovered twice operating within the Los Angeles County's Sheriff's Department, in 1991 and 2003 (Reynolds; Chin 43). According to the Southern Poverty Law Center (SPLC), an organization dedicated to tracking hate groups in the United States, racist skinhead and right-wing terrorist groups over the past 15 years, in and outside of prison, have banded together as the "Vinlanders Social Club" – later rebuilt as the "American Vikings" (Morlin), the "Holy Nation of Odin" (Keller), and the "Viking Youth Corps" (Jackson and Potok).[4] In 2016, a European anti-immigrant group calling itself the "Soldiers of Odin" established a chapter in Edmonton, Canada, where its members declare that they want only "sustainable immigration" and to keep "people [from] coming in and pushing any kind of agenda on Canada."

While most of these groups are, as Mattias Gardell writes, "as short-lived as daylight on northern winter skies" (Gardell, "Wolf Age Pagans" 385), and may possess only a few dozen members or even just one, the persistent return to Viking symbols attests to the persistence of this fantasy, as do the far more permanent tattoos sported by white supremacists. The SPLC's collection of white supremacist tattoos often include the Confederate Flag (which rose to prominence in the American South during the 1950s in resistance to the Civil Rights movement) but similarly frequent are mixtures of skulls, Nazi iconography, and Viking imagery, like runes, images of bearded, helmeted men carrying axes, and the very image of the tenth-century Thor's hammer whose replica is sold often at Viking Metal concerts ("A Look at Racist Skinhead Symbols and Tattoos"; Ashby and Schofield 9). Due to civil rights agitation by adherents of Asatrú, Thor's hammer is now a recognized religious symbol in a majority of American states, with several thousand self-identified members of various sects of Asatrú (Wotanfolk, for example) among white-identified prisoners.

Even those Odinist groups that either make no overt racist claims or even go so far as to actively resist their racist co-religionists still see their faith as a more authentic heritage than Christianity. For them, the Norse gods are either local, specific to a broadly Scandinavian heritage, or they are local in a wider sense, representing Europe as a whole, in its chthonic authenticity, the "native Folkway of Northern European people" (Stinson 114), according to the self-styled chieftain of "Jotun's Bane Kindrid" from the American Midwest. They establish a contrast with modernity and its presumptive values of trans- or postnationalism, emigration and immigration, all, in their minds, universal values that dissolve all ancient differences between people. Christianity, and not just Christianity, becomes the enemy. In demanding that there be "no Jew nor Greek [...] no slave nor free [...] no male and female" (Galatians 3:28), Christianity in the view of Odinists becomes a placeless religion, dedicated to uprooting local heritage that had developed for centuries or millennia. Christianity's internationalism becomes labeled as "Judeo-Christian," with all the anti-semitic force that the "Judeo" can carry: a wandering, cosmopolitan non-tradition designed to yoke its adherents into "slavish submission of Christianity" (Slauson [m]; as befits a work from 1978, the same text also praises the film *Star Wars* as the most "lucid expression of Aryan mysticism in modern times"; [n][5].

---

4 For further treatments, see Pitcavage; Gardell, *Gods of the Blood*; Gardell, "Wolf Age Pagans."
5 The document has no page numbers and instead is 'paginated' only by letters.

The first problem with so much of this new Viking enthusiasm is that it's wrong. It's not just morally wrong, and, in its belief in the transhistorical, real existence of white people, biologically wrong; it's historically wrong as well. And, as my conclusion will observe, it is also philosophically unsustainable, with an impossible combination of praise for liberty mixed with the demand to be true to a pure heritage. Dealing with the factual errors of this Viking material will be my first priority, requiring sustained exploration of how the medieval Norse lived and saw themselves.

The Heterogeneous Medieval Norse

First, the religious belief of modern Odinists tends to be based on a fixed pantheon described in thirteenth-century Christian antiquarian works like the "Gylfaginning" of Snorri Sturluson's *Prose Edda*. Recent archaeological and toponymic studies present a much different picture from this supposedly 'pure' and pre-Christian 'folkway'. Rather than the singular and sustained ancient faith imagined by Odinists, the Norse engaged in a host of varying ritual practices, with much divergence between the earliest material (from roughly 6,500 years ago) and the period of conversion (1000 years ago). Pre-Christian Scandinavian burial practices differ radically not only over time but from place to place; in some places, bodies were burnt; in others buried in pits; in others, placed in pots or kegs; some cemeteries differentiate between men, women, and children, and some do not. Far from being sealed off from the neighbors, who themselves had their own supposedly inviolate cultures, Norse religion engaged in cultural exchange with belief systems of the Celtic, Sami, Finnish, Baltic, and Slavic peoples, and anyone else the Norse came in contact with. Runes originate as an adaptation of the Roman alphabet. The Norse started to abandon outdoor shrine buildings in favor of cult houses in the fifth century of our era, likely in imitation of Roman (and especially Christian) temples, which themselves descend from Jewish and other eastern ritual practices (Andrén). The Thor's Hammer necklace becomes popular only in the ninth century, mostly in only a few areas, in some places an obvious rejoinder to the Christian cross, in some places used without reference to or perhaps alongside a heterogeneous Christianity that was practiced with an equally heterogeneous 'paganism' (Staeker; Nordeide). Despite the claims of some scholars (Gräslund 133), Thor was not a universally worshipped god among even the late 'pagan' Norse (Nordeide 221–22).

In sum, if there was a sense of shared Scandinavian identity, it emerged in the same way that the modern Scandinavian immigrants created it: through loss of and distance from what was only retroactively felt as a homeland (Gräslund). Certainly the sagas tell of violent conversions, with pagan priests and witches systematically wiped out by Christian missionaries and newly converted warriors; the modern Odinists' belief that Christianity violently destroyed the old beliefs may not be entirely mistaken, though the conversion stories of the sagas should be understood first not as mere historical records but as a literary genre with roots in the Hebrew scriptures. That said, however sudden the Norse conversion was, Christianity was far from a new arrival, and was anything but the wholesale replacement of one ancient pure faith with another. The fundamental irony here is that the very search for a faith cleansed of all impurities is a monotheistic reflex; to the degree that Odinists seek a pure Odinism, unmodifiable and intact, they remain enthralled to the very desire for purity they inherited from the Christianity that they claim to despise.

Furthermore, however the Norse thought of themselves, they didn't think of themselves as 'white', nor did they think of race, if they thought of it at all, in terms of skin color. I say this against both modern racist appropriations of the Norse and against even well-meaning modern scholarship on Norse identity, particularly the scholarship on the Norse in America. This material often follows a well-worn track: it attempts to determine if there was a Scandinavian or even 'Eurocentric' identity, and tends to describe the ways that the Norse thought of the Skrælings – which is how the Vinland sagas termed Native Americans – as 'the Other' (Williamsen) or primitives (Postema 125–29), with the somber critical moves that typically follow from these divisions. At its best, I am grateful for this scholarship's critical acuity, dedication to combating modern racism, and archival depth.

By focusing on race, however, it is hampered by the wrong framework. It is not that 'race' is a concept unique to modernity. To be sure, the myth of race, which often requires an equally mythical belief that race is visible, heritable, immutable, and a determiner of intelligence (and, by extension, full humanity), is far more developed in the modern than the medieval era, and such myths become far more elaborate, sedimented, and operate with increasingly appalling cruelty with worldwide European colonialism and the transatlantic slave trade. Yet racist hierarchies were generated in the Middle Ages, among other places, in English attitudes towards the Welsh and Irish (not incidentally during periods of conquest and colonization; Cohen 77–109) and in the attempts by late medieval Venetian slavers to differentiate themselves from the people they enslaved (McKee 38–43)[6]. Although modern engagements with the Vinland sagas and North American Vikings tend towards emphasizing the Vikings as the 'first whites' or 'first Europeans', neither of the Vinland sagas offers a homogeneous 'Eurocentric' identity. *Erik the Red's Saga* has among its Norse a German explorer, and the *Greenlander's Saga* two Scots, differentiated from the text's norm, as is common in medieval texts, through culinary and cultural differences: the German knows grapes and wine, while the Scots, wearing what the texts think of as strange Scottish clothing, are fast runners, swifter than deer. The Norse come from a heterogeneous Europe, irreducible to whiteness.

---

6   For an introduction to medieval racisms, and their distinctiveness from modern racisms, see Heng, "Invention of Race I"; Heng, "Invention of Race II."

Far from uniting the Norse into a single body, the Vinland sagas split them in two, with the pagans on one side, and Christians on the other. The sagas primarily grapple with the transition from the past to the present, when the past is at once the root of the present and separated from it by a new faith. The sagas explore this problem of history and heritage through two contrasting women: Freydis, a murderer and pagan responsible for the failure of the Vinland settlement, and Guðrid, a Christian whose descendants included bishops and other notables of thirteenth-century Iceland (Postema 121–25). The names are Dickensian in their moral significance: the wicked Freydis is named for the Norse goddess Freya, and the holy Guðrid after God himself.

The Vinland sagas' description of the Skraelings does not emphasize what is, in any obvious way, a raced difference. They describe a Skraeling leader as "tall and handsome [*vænn*]," which is precisely the same language the sagas as a whole use to describe any martial hero. The Skraelings themselves have tangled hair and enormous eyes and are – presumably apart from the leader – "ugly" [*illiligir*], and either "pale" (*folleit*) or "dark" (*svartir*), without, that is, any obvious singularly distinctive hair or skin color. The description of the Skraeling leader belongs to a medieval tradition of visible class difference, which often describes nobles as light-skinned, brave, intelligent, and beautiful, and peasants as their opposites (Pelteret). For example, the Old Norse *Rígsþula* gives an account of the origins of farmers, warrior earls, and slaves, the latter of which are "swarthy" [*svartan*], "repulsive" [*fúlligt*], and "sun-burnt" [*sólbrunnin*], while calling the earls *hvita*, white (Orchard 241–47). Differences in skin color, with all this implies about "natural" hierarchies, here justify internal social differentiation rather than dividing the Norse from other people. As for Rig himself, his name may come from the Irish for king (Orchard 337; Pelteret 83–84), making this god of human variation and hierarchy far from suitable for representing any 'pure' strain of Nordic identity.

Though many elements in the Vinland sagas attest to actual contact between the Norse and Native Americans – most notably the unmistakable description of pemmican – their descriptions of the skraelings as a whole, and even the word "skraeling" itself, belong to the medieval belief that the far reaches of the world were inhabited by monsters. A host of medieval European texts populated an almost wholly imaginary India and Ethiopia with Cyclops, Cynocephali (dog-headed humans), and Blemmyae (headless humans with faces in their chests) (Friedman and Steel). Norse texts spoke of the fearsome *blámaðr* ("Blackmen"), located either in Africa or Finland, who were, according to one text, bald and yellow-eyed, with sharp teeth and a tendency towards piglike squealing when exited (Cole 349–50). More importantly for the Vinland sagas, Pygmies were thought to inhabit the far North, as were Unipods, humans with one leg terminating in one gigantic foot: both appear on the upper edges of the early fifteenth-century Nancy map of the Danish geographer Claudius Clavus (in Danish, Claudius Claussøn Swart). In *Erik the Red's Saga*, Thorvald is killed by a Unipod's arrow, while the word "Skraeling" may simply be the Old Norse translation of the Latin *Pygmaei* (Seaver).

The still larger point is that believing in the "barbarian Viking," so common among modern Viking enthusiasts, is to take on the viewpoint of the Vikings' Christian or Muslim enemies and trading partners: the Norse did not think of themselves as rugged barbarians but as the civilized norm, who distinguished themselves, in the twelfth-century *Historiae Norwegiae*, for example, from the rough Finns and ancient Picts of the Orkneys, identified as the descendants of African Jews (Ekrem and Mortensen 59, 66). They did tend to think of the Skraelings as "other" but not as racially other in any modern sense. This is not an encounter of Nordic barbarians with noble, doomed savages, as modern literature often portrays it, but instead an encounter common in medieval travel literature between humans and dubiously human monsters, located exactly where the writers of the texts expected monsters to be. This is not a discourse of 'Eurocentrism' (contra Frakes 168–69), but rather a discourse of center and margin adaptable to a variety of contexts.[7]

Against the White Fantasy

Modern fans of the Vikings speak of them as representing the "organic unity of a race" (Else Christiansen, qtd. in Gardell, "Wolf Age Pagans" 386) and offer up "Scandinavians and the Scandinavian culture as ancient and therefore pure" (Blaagaard 11). But without a single pre-Christian Norse religion (indeed, without a pre-Christian Norse religion entirely free of Christian influences), there is no 'pure' and ancient 'folkway' that can be contrasted with Christianity, modernity, and cosmopolitanism. No single origin is available. While the medieval Norse were no less free of hierarchical categorization than any other medieval group, their chief concerns were not with the modern category of whiteness, not least of all because they did not think of skin color as the primary racial determiner. Historical claims of 'ancestral roots' lack the appreciation for heterogeneity and constantly shifting, interacting cultures, riven by internal disputes and negotiations, necessary for any truly historical analysis. Fascination with the seafaring exploits of Vikings, insofar as they are attached exclusively to the Vikings, are provincial, because they tend to take the Vikings as a unique ethnic group rather than, more accurately, as one manifestation of a global phenomenon: from the North Sea to the Indian Ocean, Norse, Croat, Swahili, Persian, and Chinese sailors all found new success in the ninth century (Sindbaek). In short, the love of Vikings tends towards being a love of a fantasized past rather than a love of history. In its more

---

7   For example, the fourteenth-century English writer of *Sir Gawain and the Green Knight*, filled Wales with monsters, not 'Eurocentrically', but to advance an English colonial project.

and less benign forms, modern amateur Viking enthusiasm should collapse when it encounters these facts.

Yet it persists, of course, which means, finally, we must examine what the Viking fantasy does for its adherents. Undoing the Viking fantasy requires more than just factual correction or mockery. In fact, since mockery was the method of white supremacist Ben Klassen, who saw the Odinists as a competitor for his Church of the Creator (Klassen, "Odinism"), mockery is clearly insufficient. What is required, rather, is undoing the fundamental logic of the Viking fantasy, which is a strange, and unsustainable, combination of agency and obligation, or, put another way, individuality and group identity. The peculiarities of this logic can be easily understood by distinguishing Viking from fascist fantasies.

In a scathing review of the attempted rehabilitation of Leni Riefenstahl, Susan Sontag characterized the fascist aesthetic as contemptuous of "all that is reflective, critical, and pluralistic," devoted to a slurry of "egomania," "servitude," and honor, "preoccup[ied] with situations of control, submissive behavior, extravagant effort, and the endurance of pain" (Sontag 89, 91). All this fits not just with Riefenstahl's films but also with Viking fantasies, particularly in those cultures, like that of the Los Angeles County's Sheriff's Department, that directly overlap with neo-Nazism, or, in earlier periods, the "grim, virile ideal of masculinity" that attracted actual Nazis to the Viking fantasy (Mees 189). But Sontag also rightly identifies the fascist aesthetic as attentive to uniforms, chrome, shininess, neatness and well-oiled and glimmering machines; it is monumental, symmetrical, idealistic, obsessed with the beautiful, and oriented around some gravitational core – the leader or some singular world-historical force. On these points, the Viking fantasy differs from fascism. The modern Viking aesthetic is sloppy, hairy, vigorous, and ravenous rather than 'healthy', certainly strong but often more 'big bodied' than 'cut'. It prefers temporary gatherings – like a metal concert or a party or initiation ceremony – to a massive, regimented party rally and the army camp. Viking aesthetics incarnate masculine populism, and a celebration of the 'maverick' individual, oriented not towards obedience to the leader but rather a celebration of a vaguely defined 'heritage', and if obedient, then obedient to an equally vague conception of 'duty', 'honor', or even 'natural law', with, behind all this, a sense of natural place and belonging.

One dominant self-characterization of the Viking fantasy is liberty. In the nineteenth century, this dream of Northern liberty defined itself against a caricature of Roman Catholicism (Kolodny 143). Promoted, among other works, by George Perkins Marsh's *Goths of New England* (1843) this prejudice "pitt[ed] Protestant, democratic, pious, hard-working Goths against Catholic, despotic, sensuous, lazy Romans" (Lowenthal 59) as part of a Nordic myth that combined "an idealized pagan past, racial determinism, militant anti-Catholicism, nativist exclusion of aliens, praise of rural virtues, [and] fear of city vices" (Lowenthal 58). Notwithstanding the actual, Roman Catholic beliefs promoted by the Vinland sagas, the American Norse were upheld as free of clerical despotism, untainted by the Inquisition, and as champions of liberty, science, and even women's rights (Mancini; Brøndal 11). The Catholic, Italian Columbus had to be pushed aside, revealed as someone who found the Americas only because he had first visited Iceland's sailors and learned the truth from them, or because he himself was *Northern* Italian. *The Viking*, the 1928 silent film, accomplishes this neatly by finishing with Leif Erikson and his sailors planting a cross on American soil, raising their swords aloft, distinguished only by their horned helmets and dragon-boat from the Columbus they either overwrite or, according to one Catholic champion, anticipate (Clarke). Champions of the Vikings emphasized how the original Icelanders – not the Irish monks who had first peopled the island, but the Norse who arrived some time later – had fled Norway's royal despotism and established the Thing, parliaments in which, it was imagined, the Icelanders managed their own government in freedom. Here Americans found the true ancestor of their own supposed love of liberty (while ignoring that the written record of Things is a history of failure, as might be expected for texts produced during the thirteenth-century collapse of Icelandic independence). Once identified with the (idealized) Thing, the politics of America could be thought of as arising from antiquity, and therefore as having an authenticating foundation, and as opening up the future, as the true inheritance of mankind, now freed from the royal and papal tyranny.

Building on this kind of work, the last century has seen Vikings in both Europe and America gradually transformed into "proto-Americans" (Sindbaek 85), representatives of industry, international trading, pragmatism, and other business-friendly virtues. Johannes V. Jensen's *Den lange rejse* (a Nobel Prize winning novel translated into English in 1923 as *The Long Journey*) upheld the Vikings as key promoters of "the essential cultural characteristics of modern Britain and North America: individual enterprise and liberal society" (Sindbaek 84). Several literary and quasi-historical works from the Orkneys, where enthusiasm for the Norse has gradually blossomed into an annual Viking festival, distinguish the lethargic, exploited Celt from the dynamic and successful Norse. In still more recent years, modern Odinists like Else Christiansen praise a natural Viking "anarchism" (Gardell, "Wolf Age Pagans" 387) or, alternately, "tribal democracy" (Gardell, *Gods of the Blood* 262) and their native "self-reliance and self-sufficiency" (Gardell, *Gods of the Blood* 278). The Asatrú Free Assembly, whose basic beliefs are collected along with many other sects in the 1978 handbook *The Religion of Odin,* asserts that "The Odinist religion places an exceptionally high value on human freedom and on individuality" and that through "heroic action" its adherents can break free of "historical forces" (Slauson 16). While it is unclear precisely what this claim means (it may be, for example, a critique of Marxism), its aim is obvious enough: it believes its adherents can act with more freedom than others.

But this praise of freedom is accompanied by an imposition of obligation. One Odinist text explains that Asatrú "religion is not noted for its belief in free will, but instead [demands that] one must follow one's fate" (Slauson 5), while another Odinist summarizes his belief as "the existence of my people is not negotiable" (Gardell, *Gods of the Blood* 283), thus loading himself with the obligation to protect an imaginary self and an imagined community. White supremacists insist that a supposedly modern cultural or ethnic integration (but see, for example, "England's Immigrants 1330–1550"), often metaphorized as a "rising tide of diversity" (Boetel), "turn[s] its back on natural law" ("Vinlanders Social Club") or fundamentally violent "natural order" (Gardell, "Wolf Age Pagans" 390). Thus on the one hand we have the demand to be free paradoxically linked to the demand to be bound to a grim, unforgiving, and unchanging 'nature'.

Coupled with a sense of nature as bleak, unforgiving, and indifferent, but also as the organic root of the authentic Nordic self, this demand is a demand to abandon creativity, skepticism, and anything but a mechanistic reproduction of what is supposed to be one's duty.[8] Such Viking enthusiasts claim a connection with medieval or the still older groups, cultures, and beliefs, whose purportedly homogeneous, traditional character offers itself to its contemporary adherents as a heritage that must be preserved. To be rendered 'authentic', lovers of the Vikings, particularly if they hold an allegiance to whiteness, must be frozen in time where they become, paradoxically, figures of perfect agency (because of their 'Viking liberty') without the true agency that would let them change. With that, the 'cradle of white civilization in the Americas' became its coffin.

This combination of mastery and freedom with stability and predictability is not unheard of: not incidentally for the Viking fantasy, dominant conventions of masculinity similarly characterize men as self-governing, inventive, and dutiful all at once. The problems here require both a sustained gender critique and a sustained critique of theories of authority and autonomy. This latter critique has its origins in feminism's preference for models of agential selves over models of the individual, autonomous self (Davies; Abrams, "From Autonomy to Agency", "A Look at Racist Skinhead Symbols"), and has, over the last decade, effloresced into the reassessments of the hierarchy of the agent/object and cause/effect binary carried out by Karen Barad, Jane Bennett, Graham Harman, Timothy Morton, and the many other thinkers loosely grouped under the rubric of speculative realism or new materialism.

The specific problem with the Viking fantasy, however, is that it dishonors the ancient Norse themselves. It is a medievalist fantasy that preserves medieval distinctiveness only as a sense of loss to be reclaimed, refusing, as Helen Young writes in a recent article on "Whiteness and Time," "the fundamental divisions between medieval and modern on which medievalism itself depends" (Young 48). The Viking fantasy's insistence on racial and religious purity and on some mixture of freedom and duty grossly misrepresents the real complexity of the medieval Norse peoples. Nor does it represent their own interests. It is not simply that the traditions the Viking enthusiasts try to recreate are irretrievably lost, as writ-

---

8 For an exemplary demand that the "Nordic ideal" be protected, see Günther 252–53; for a scholarly review, see Brøndal 14–18.

ten records say little of actual religious practice, and material cultic remains can say only so much about how they were used. Contrary to the Viking enthusiasts' dreams of a simple, patriarchal, ethnically homogeneous, organic, and geographically limited society, the actual Vikings operated in a global context characterized not by ethnic stability and cultural purity, but by migration and cultural syncretism, with the host of local practices that one would expect in a world prior to mass communication, mass production, and capitalist homogenization. A recreation of the Norse more faithful to historical facts would necessarily imagine them as hybridized, unconcerned with purity, and attentive to cultural practices at once local and interconnected rhizomatically with an everchanging host of other local contexts.[9] This recreation would require the skills of academics – textual scholars, archaeologists, historians of religion, anthropologists, sociologists, and ecologists – to generate a sense of ancient Norse ways of life with an aim of increasing accuracy and, inevitably, complexity.

The endpoint would be an abandonment of romantic nationalism and the romantic dream of unitary peoples, aimed not at some postmodern hybridity – which often simply reaffirms romantic misconceptions by inventing preexisting unities to hybridize – but at a historically careful attention to always shifting local contexts understood in an equally mobile global framework. No modern adherence to race or religious orthodoxy would be welcome in this new Viking enthusiasm. A better delight in the Norse might still be practiced, as might a sense of living heritage, and the accompanying *frisson* of being taken outside one's limited moment by connection with the deep past; but it could no longer be in the service of a politics of purity. It would be an impure modernity mingling with an equally impure past, with a people who nonetheless had a reality formed by that very impurity.[10]

Works Cited

Abrams, Kathryn. "From Autonomy to Agency: Feminist Perspectives on Self-Direction." *William & Mary Law Review* 40.3 (1999): 805–46.

Andrén, Anders. "Behind 'Heathendom': Archaeological Studies of Old Norse Religion." *Scottish Archaeological Journal* 27.2 (2005): 105–38.

Ashby, Steven P., and John Schofield. "Hold the Heathen Hammer High: Representation, Re-Enactment, and the Construction of 'Pagan' Heritage." *International Journal of Heritage Studies* (2014): 1–19.

Barnes, Geraldine. *Viking America: The First Millennium*. Cambridge: D.S. Brewer, 2001.

---

9 For one model of how to do this, concentrating on the Vinland map controversy, see Mackenthun.

10 Acknowledgements: Thank you to Michael Collins for introducing me to the *Historic Newfoundland* pamphlet, to my colleague Lauren Mancia's Late Antique-Medieval-Early Modern (LAMEM) Faculty Working Group for allowing me to present a portion of this work at Brooklyn College, CUNY, and to Alison Kinney for helping me articulate a conclusion.

—. "Nostalgia, Medievalism, and the Vínland Voyages." *postmedieval: a journal of medieval cultural studies* 2.2 (2011): 141–54.

Blaagaard, Bolette B. "Relocating Whiteness in Nordic Media Discourse." *Rethinking Nordic Colonialism*. Ed. Kuratorisk Aktion. Helsinki: Nordic Institute for Contemporary Art, 2006. 1–24.

Boetel, Karl F. (RadishMag). "@ThenTheJudgment @JohnProtevi @KarlSteel Meh. When 'you guys' stop forcing a rising tide of vibrant diversity on us, we'll stop 'obsessing.'" 6 March 2014, 1:01 a.m. Tweet.

Bouteleux, Jules. "The Many Faces of Leif Ericson." *Geometry During Wartime*. 29 November 2017: <https://geometryduringwartime.wordpress.com/2012/08/22/the-many-faces-of-leif-ericson/>.

Brøndal, Jørn. "'The Fairest among the So-Called White Races': Portrayals of Scandinavian Americans in the Filiopietistic and Nativist Literature of the Late Nineteenth and Early Twentieth Centuries." *Journal of Ethnic History* 33.3 (2014): 5–36.

Chin, William Y. "Law and Order and White Power: White Supremacist Infiltration of Law Enforcement and the Need to Eliminate Racism in the Ranks." *Journal of Law and Social Deviance* 6 (2013): 30–98.

Clarke, Richard H. "America Discovered and Christianized in the Tenth and Eleventh Centuries." *The American Catholic Quarterly Review* 13 (1888): 211–37.

Cohen, Jeffrey Jerome. *Hybridity, Identity, and Monstrosity in Medieval Britain: On Difficult Middles*. New York: Palgrave Macmillan, 2006.

Cole, Richard. "One or Several Jews? The Jewish Massed Body in Old Norse Literature." *postmedieval: a journal of medieval cultural studies* 5.3 (2014): 346–58.

Cox, Steven L. "A Norse Penny from Maine." *Vikings: The North Atlantic Saga*. Eds. William W. Fitzhugh and Elizabeth I. Ward. Washington, D.C.: Smithsonian Institution Press, 2000. 206–7.

Davies, Bronwyn. "The Concept of Agency: A Feminist Poststructuralist Analysis." *Social Analysis: The International Journal of Social and Cultural Practice* 30 (1991): 42–53.

Ekrem, Inger, and Lars Boje Mortensen, Eds. *Historia Norwegie*. Trans. Peter Fisher. Copenhagen: Museum Tusculanum Press, 2003.

Emerson, R. W. *English Traits*. Boston: Phillips, Sampson, and Co., 1856.

"England's Immigrants 1330–1550." *England's Immigrants 1330–1550. Resident Aliens in the Late Middle Ages*. 1 March 2015 <https://www.englandsimmigrants.com>.

English, L.E.F. *Historic Newfoundland*. 2nd ed. St John's: Newfoundland Tourist Development Division, 1969.

Flax, Bill. "Forget Multiculturalism: Restore the Anglo-Saxon Philosophy of Liberty." *Forbes.com* 29 Sept. 2011. 3 January 2015 <https://www.forbes.com/sites/billflax/2011/09/29/forget-multiculturalism-restore-the-anglo-saxon-philosophy-of-liberty/#73820496f81f>.

Frakes, Jerold C. "Vikings, Vínland, and the Discourse of Eurocentrism." *Journal of English and Germanic Philology* 100.2 (2001): 157–99.

Friedman, John Block. *The Monstrous Races in Medieval Art and Thought*. Syracuse, New York: Syracuse University Press, 2000.

Gardell, Mattias. *Gods of the Blood: The Pagan Revival and White Separatism*. Durham: Duke University Press, 2003.

—. "Wolf Age Pagans." *Controversial New Religions*. Eds. James R. Lewis and Jesper Aagaard Petersen. 2nd ed. New York: Oxford University Press, 2014. 383–98.

Gräslund, Anne-Sofie. "How Did the Norsemen in Greenland See Themselves? Some Reflections on 'Viking Identity.'" *Journal of the North Atlantic* 2.2 (2009): 131–37.

Grydehøj, Adam. "Ethnicity and the Origins of Local Identity in Shetland, UK – Part II: Picts, Vikings, Fairies, Finns, and Aryans." *Journal of Marine and Island Cultures* 2.1 (2013): 39–48.

Günther, Han F. K. *The Racial Element in European History*. Trans. G. G. Wheeler. London: Methuen & Co., 1927. Print.

Hawthorne, Nathaniel. *The Marble Faun*. 1860. Vol. 1. New York: Fred deFau, 1902.

Heesch, Florian. "Metal for Nordic Men? Amon Amarth's Representation of Vikings." *The Metal Void: First Gatherings*. Eds. Niall W. R. Scott and Imke Von Helden. Oxford: Inter-Disciplinary Press, 2010. 71–80.

Heng, Geraldine. "The Invention of Race in the European Middle Ages 1: Race Studies, Modernity, and the Middle Ages." *Literature Compass* 8.5 (2011): 258–74.

—. "The Invention of Race in the European Middle Ages II: Locations of Medieval Race." *Literature Compass* 8.5 (2011): 332–50.

Hewlett, Maurice. *Gudrid the Fair: A Tale of the Discovery of America*. New York: Dodd, Mead, and Company, 1918.

Jackson, Camille, and Mark Potok. "National Socialist Movement Recruits Young Children." *Southern Poverty Law Center Intelligence Report* 114 (2004). 12 February 2018 <https://www.splcenter.org/fighting-hate/intelligence-report/2004/national-socialist-movement-recruits-young-children>

Jefferson, Thomas. *An Essay Towards Facilitating Instruction in the Anglo-Saxon and Modern Dialects of the English Language, for the Use of the University of Virginia*. New York: John F. Trow, 1851.

Jewett, Sarah Orne. *The Story of the Normans, Told Chiefly in Relation to Their Conquest of England*. New York: G. P. Putnam's Sons, 1895.

Jochens, Jenny. "Race and Ethnicity in the Old Norse World." *Viator* 30 (1999): 79–104.

Johnson, Barbara. "USA: Viking Ship Discovered Near Mississippi River." *World News Daily*. 13 Aug. 2014 <http://worldnewsdailyreport.com/usa-viking-ship-discovered-near-mississipi-river/>.

Johnson, George. *Canada's First Boy Baby*. [Quebec?]: N.p., 1900.

Keller, Larry. "White Supremacist Running Odinist Network From Maximum-Security Prison." *Southern Poverty Law Center*. 20 Mar. 2009. <https://www.splcenter.org/hatewatch/2009/03/20/white-supremacist-running-odinist-network-maximum-security-prison>.

Klassen, Ben. "Odinism: A Rising Phoenix or a Dead Horse." *Racial Loyalty* 18 (1984): n.p.

—. "A Letter to Mrs Else Christensen." *Racial Loyalty* 35 (1986): n.p.

Kolodny, Annette. *In Search of First Contact: The Vikings of Vinland, the Peoples of the Dawnland, and the Anglo-American Anxiety of Discovery*. Durham, NC: Duke University Press, 2012.

Krueger, David M. *Myths of the Rune Stone: Viking Martyrs and the Birthplace of America*. Minneapolis: University of Minnesota Press, 2015.

Liedl, Janice. "A Canadian Viking in the Governor-General's Court: Medievalism in Pre-War Canada." Toronto: 2006.

Liljencrantz, Ottilie A. *The Thrall of Leif the Lucky*. Chicago: A. C. McClurg & Co., 1902.

—. *The Vinland Champions*. New York: D. Appleton & Co., 1904.

—. *Randvar the Songsmith: A Romance of Norumbega*. New York: Harper & Brothers, 1906.
Longfellow, Henry Wadsworth. *Ballads and Other Poems*. 3rd ed. Cambridge: John Owen, 1842.
Lowenthal, David. *George Perkins Marsh, Prophet of Conservation*. Seattle: University of Washington Press, 2000.
Mackenthun, Gesa. "The Vinland Map Controversy: Cartographic Imagination and Changing Cultures of Knowledge." Unpublished conference paper, Renaissance Society of America. Venice, 2010.
Mancini, J. M. "Discovering Viking America." *Critical Inquiry* 28.4 (2002): 868–907.
"Marvel Studios Declares War on Norse Mythology." *Council of Conservative Citizens*. 25 Nov. 2011. 28 February 2015 <http://conservative-headlines.com/2011/04/marval-studios-declares-war-on-norse-mythology/>.
McKee, Sally. "Inherited Status and Slavery in Late Medieval Italy and Venetian Crete." *Past & Present* 182.1 (2004): 31–53.
Mees, Bernard. "Germanische Sturmflut: From the Old Norse Twilight to the Fascist New Dawn." *Studia Neophilologica* 78 (2006): 184–98.
Modarelli, Michael. "The Struggle for Origins: Old English in Nineteenth-Century America." *Modern Language Quarterly* 73.4 (2012): 527–43.
Morlin, Bill. "Veteran Skinhead Forms New Racist Club, Peddles T-Shirts on Internet." *Southern Poverty Law Center*. 17 May 2013. <https://www.splcenter.org/hatewatch/2013/05/17/veteran-skinhead-forms-new-racist-club-peddles-t-shirts-internet>.
Neill, Roy William. *The Viking*. MGM, 1928. Film.
Newfoundland Tourism Commercial: L'anse Aux Meadows Viking Settlement. N.p. Film.
Nordeide, Sæbjørg Walaker. "Thor's Hammer in Norway: A Symbol of Reaction Against the Christian Cross?" *Old Norse Religion in Long-Term Perspectives: Origins, Changes, and Interactions*. Eds. Anders Andrén, Kristina Jennbert, and Catharina Raudvere. Lund: Nordic Academic Press, 2004. 218–23.
Orchard, Andy (Ed. and trans.). *The Elder Edda: A Book of Viking Lore*. New York: Penguin Books, 2011.
Pelteret, David. "The Image of the Slave in Some Anglo-Saxon and Norse Sources." *Slavery & Abolition* 23.2 (2002): 75–88.
Pitcavage, Mark. "Reviving Paganism." *Southern Poverty Law Center Intelligence Report* 112 (2003): n.p.
Postema, James. "First (Double) Crossing: Vikings, Christianity, and the Skraelings of North America." *North Dakota Quarterly* 76.3 (2009): 112–33.
Quaestor. "Viking Ship Discovered Near Mississippi River." *Occidental Enclave: Enthnocultural Identity and Preservation*. 17 August 2014.
Rafn, Carl Christian. *Antiquitates Americanae*. Copenhagen: Typis officinae Schultzianae, 1837.
Redbeard, Ragnar. *Might Is Right, Or, The Survival of the Fittest*. 1910. St. Maries, Idaho: Fourteen Word Press, 1999.
Refn, Nicolas Winding. *Valhalla Rising*. BBC Film, 2009. Film.
Reynolds, Matt. "Deputies Say Racist Gang Wields Power at Top of L. A. Sheriff's Dept." *Courthouse News Service*. 26 April 2013. <https://www.courthousenews.com/deputies-say-racist-gang-wieldspower-at-top-of-l-a-sheriffs-dept/>.
Robinson, J. Dennis. "Thorvald's Tombstone Is a Hoax." *SeacoastNH*. 27 Aug. 2000. 28 February 2015 <http://www.seacoastnh.com/arts/please082700.html>

Rogers, Kyle. "Kennewick Man: Who He Is and Why He Matters." *Council of Conservative Citizens*. N. p., 2003.

Seaver, Kirsten A. "'Pygmies' of the Far North." *Journal of World History* 19.1 (2008): 63–87.

Simms, William Gilmore. *The History of South Carolina from Its First European Discovery to Its Erection into a Republic*. New York: Richardon & Co., 1866.

Sindbaek, Søren M. "All in the Same Boat: The Vikings as European and Global Heritage." *Heritage Reinvents Europe: Proceedings of the International Conference Ename, Belgium, 17–19 March 2011*. Eds. Dirk Callebaut, Jan Mařík, and Jana Maříková-Kubková. Belgium: Europae Archaeologiae Consilium, 2013. 81–88.

Slauson, Irv. *The Religion of Odin*. Red Wing: Viking House, 1978.

Sontag, Susan. "Fascinating Fascism." *Under the Sign of Saturn*. New York: Farrar, Straus & Giroux, 1980. 71–105.

Southern Poverty Law Center. "A Look at Racist Skinhead Symbols and Tattoos." *Southern Poverty Law Center Intelligence Report* 123 (2006): 29 November 2017 <https://www.splcenter.org/fighting-hate/intelligence-report/2006/look-racist-skinhead-symbols-and-tattoos>.

Spracklen, Karl. "True Ayryan Black Metal: The Meaning of Leisure, Belonging and the Construction of Whiteness in Black Metal Music." *The Metal Void: First Gatherings*. Eds. Niall W. R. Scott and Imke Von Helden. Oxford: Inter-Disciplinary Press, 2010. 81–94.

Staeker, Jörn. "Thor's Hammer: Symbol of Christianization and Political Delusion." *Lund Archaeological Review* 5 (1999): 89–104.

Steel, Karl. "Centaurs, Satyrs, and Cynocephali: Medieval Scholarly Teratology and the Question of the Human." *The Ashgate Research Companion to Monsters and the Monstrous*. Eds. Asa Simon Mittman and Peter J. Dendle. Farnham: Ashgate, 2013. 257–74.

Stinson, Mark Ludwig. *Heathen Gods: A Collection of Essays Concerning the Folkway of Our People*. Liberty: Jotun's Bane Kindred, 2009.

Trafford, Simon, and Aleksander Pluskowski. "Antichrist Superstars: The Vikings in Hard Rock and Heavy Metal." *Mass Market Medieval: Essays on the Middle Ages in Popular Culture*. Ed. David W. Marshall. Jefferson: McFarland, 2007. 57–73.

"Vinlanders Social Club." *Southern Poverty Law Center*. <https://www.splcenter.org/fighting-hate/extremist-files/group/vinlanders-social-club>

Von Helden, Imke. "Barbarians and Literature: Viking Metal and Its Links to Old Norse Mythology." *The Metal Void: First Gatherings*. Eds. Niall W. R. Scott and Imke Von Helden. Oxford: Inter-Disciplinary Press, 2010. 257–65.

Welles, Albert. *The Pedigree and History of the Washington Family*. New York: Society Library, 1879.

Weston, Donna. "Basque Pagan Metal: View to a Primordial Past." *European Journal of Cultural Studies* 14.1 (2011): 102–22.

Whittier, John Greenleaf. *The Poetical Works*. Vol. 1. Boston: Houghton Mifflin, 1892. Print.

Williamsen, E. A. "Boundaries of Difference in the Vinland Sagas." *Scandinavian Studies* 77.4 (2005): 451–78.

Young, Helen. "Whiteness and Time: The Once, Present, and Future Race." *Studies in Medievalism* 24 (2015): 39–49.

From Individual to Collective Heritage

CHAPTER FOUR

Du "Patrimoine national" au "Patrimoine interculturel": Concepts et formes d'institutionnalisation, depuis la Révolution Française jusqu'au Musée National d'Histoire de l'Immigration

HANS-JÜRGEN LÜSEBRINK

Réflexions préliminaires, concepts, périodisations

Le titre de cette contribution semble renvoyer à un objet assez spécifique et très axé sur la France, et il évoque implicitement un personnage encore insuffisamment connu, l'homme politique et le député de l'époque révolutionnaire, Henri Grégoire (1750–1831). Mais cet article vise cependant, en partant d'exemples essentiellement français, en particulier de l'œuvre de l'abbé Grégoire, à éclairer des champs de réflexion historiques de dimension européenne, et même mondiale, à savoir la naissance et la transformation des dimensions culturelles et symboliques des états modernes depuis la fin du 18e siècle, parmi lesquels la France de l'époque révolutionnaire occupa un rôle de pionnier et exerça une fonction de modèle.

Le point de départ des réflexions suivantes est constitué par les concepts de "patrimoine national" et de "patrimoine interculturel." Les deux concepts sont étroitement liés à celui de "mémoire collective" et aux théories de la "mémoire collective" telles qu'elles ont été développées par Aleida et Jan Assmann en Allemagne et par Maurice Halbwachs ainsi que par Pierre Nora en France. Le terme de "patrimoine" était à l'origine, et jusqu'à l'époque actuelle, synonyme de celui d'"héritage", désignant les possessions transmises par un individu, une famille ou une dynastie, comme dans le terme de "patrimoine royal." Alors que le terme de patrimoine est un terme qui remonte étymologiquement au haut moyen-âge et même à l'antiquité romaine par ses racines latines, le concept de "patrimoine national" est, pour sa part, une construction linguistique relativement récente apparue sous la Révolution Française. La naissance de ce dernier concept et la conception d'un "patrimoine national" entre 1792 et 1794 alla de pair avec le développement d'une "conscience patrimoniale" telle qu'elle est définie par Marie-Anne Sire. Émergeant à l'époque des Lumières et mise en pratique sur le plan politique par la politique culturelle de la Révolution Française, le souci de conserver un héritage patrimonial a été confiné jusque-là au domaine strictement privé. "Jusqu'au dernier quart du XVIIIe siècle," précise M.-A. Sire,

> seuls quelques lieux et objets spécifiques échappaient à la loi de l'utilité immédiate: tel était le cas des reliques consacrées par l'Église et des *regalia*, instruments du sacre des rois de France conservés au Trésor de l'abbaye de Saint-Denis. Ces rares exemples mis à part, l'idée d'un patrimoine national n'existait pas encore: les souverains successifs considéraient alors les bâtiments qu'ils occupaient et le mobilier ou les collections qui y étaient abrités comme leurs biens personnels [...]. (Sire 13, 14)

Le concept de "patrimoine national" ainsi que la conscience collective et les visées politiques qui le sous-tendent, impliquent qu'un certain canon de monuments, d'œuvres d'art, de collections de livres et de pratiques culturelles, tel le folklore, est considéré comme constitutif pour l'identité nationale, et qu'il doit pour cette raison non seulement être conservé et restauré, mais aussi être rendu accessible au public, c'est-à-dire à tous les citoyens de la nation. Le concept et la conception du "patrimoine national" constituent ainsi un élément central de la dimension culturelle et symbolique des États-nations modernes. Ils impliquent une politique de construction, mais aussi de protection d'artefacts culturels considérés comme significatifs sur le plan national; ils impliquent également une *sémiotique de la mise en scène* du "patrimoine national" dans des musées, des expositions, des monuments, des fêtes et d'autres formes de ritualisation théâtrales; et ils demandent, enfin, une didactique de la transmission et de la popularisation ayant pour objectif de faire connaître la signification du patrimoine national à tous les membres de la communauté nationale.

La création et la construction du "patrimoine national" est ainsi à replacer dans ce processus plus large qu'Anne-Marie Thiesse a défini comme *La création des identités nationales* dans son livre ainsi intitulé, et qu'Orvar Löfgren a appelé *La nationalisation de la culture* dans un article paru en 1989. D'après la classification établie par l'historien tchèque Miroslav Hroch dans son étude intitulée *Social Preconditions of National Revival in Europe. A Comparative Analysis of the Social Composition of Patriotic Groups among the Smaller European Nations*, on peut distinguer fondamentalement trois phases différentes en ce qui concerne le processus de nationalisation dans les états et sociétés des 19e et 20e siècles.

- Une première phase de la 'découverte' et de la construction des identités nationales par les élites (écrivains, journalistes, intellectuels, artistes);
- Une deuxième phase de débats politiques conduisant à l'établissement politiquement souhaité d'institutions, de rituels collectifs et d'autres dispositifs destinés à étayer le processus de nationalisation;

– Une troisième phase de nationalisation des masses, au cours de laquelle ces dispositifs politiques et culturels étayant le processus de nationalisation font apparaître leurs conséquences sur le plan social et surtout sur celui des mentalités.

L'héritage culturel national comme construction intellectuelle et dispositif politique peut être considéré comme faisant partie de la "mémoire collective" au sens de Jan et Aleida Assmann. En tant que 'mémoire virtuelle', cet héritage culturel national englobe tous les artefacts culturels, les institutions et les pratiques devant être protégés, explicitement et sur la base de règlements politiques et juridiques, des dommages et de la destruction. La 'mémoire virtuelle' du patrimoine à protéger est ainsi à distinguer de la 'mémoire culturelle', un terme qui vise précisément la diffusion et la mise en scène publique de certains pans de la 'mémoire virtuelle' considérés comme importants, voire cruciaux pour l'identité collective d'une communauté politique et culturelle, comme celle d'un État-nation.

Le patrimoine culturel des sociétés représente ainsi un élément central de leur culture mémorielle, basée, d'après Aleida Assmann, sur des processus de sélection et visant une "durabilité culturelle" (*Erinnerungsräume* 32)[1]. Parmi les trois formes fonctionnelles de la culture de la mémoire qu'elle distingue, en reprenant les réflexions de Nietzsche y relatives, les deux premières s'avèrent d'une importance fondamentale pour la construction et les modes d'appropriation de l'héritage culturel: en premier lieu, la forme de la "mémoire monumentaire" fondée sur des grands modèles tirés de l'histoire "qui incitent à l'imitation", mais qui peuvent aussi être foncièrement manipulés; et en second lieu, la forme de la mémoire collective qui contribue, selon Assmann, à des "ancrages locaux de la mémoire et à une conscience de l'origine investie affectivement", mais qui touche à ses limites lorsque trop d'éléments du passé sont conservés et vénérés sans esprit critique. La troisième forme fonctionnelle, la "mémoire critique", susceptible de développer, selon Aleida Assmann, une force révolutionnaire en "redressant, jugeant et détruisant" (26)[2] n'occupe qu'un rang secondaire dans la construction et l'appropriation du patrimoine culturel, même si, comme le montrera l'exemple de Grégoire, elle joue cependant un rôle non négligeable.

Les concepts et catégories de "culture de la mémoire", de "mémoire collective" et de "patrimoine culturel" sont pour l'essentiel appliqués aux États nationaux, aux cultures nationales et aux espaces nationaux: on peut le constater chez Pierre Nora, dans son ouvrage magistral *Lieux de mémoire* (1984–1994), mais aussi chez Etienne François et Hagen Schulze dans leur livre sur les lieux de mémoire allemands ainsi que chez Jan et Aleida Assmann dans leur théorie de la culture mémorielle. Ceci s'explique par le fait que des concepts centraux, mais aussi des domaines et des problématiques fondamentaux dans les cultures

---

1 Assmann utilise ici les termes de "Auswahlentscheidungen" et de "kulturelle Nachhaltigkeit."
2 "revolutionäre Kraft, indem sie richtet, verurteilt und zerstört."

modernes de la mémoire, ne se sont développés que dans le sillage des nationalisations des sociétés et des cultures à partir de la fin du 18e siècle. Ce processus de nationalisation, qui, malgré la mise en cause croissante de l'État-nation, est loin d'être encore achevé, si l'on prend en considération l'ensemble des sociétés du globe et notamment les sociétés non-européennes, a modifié fondamentalement non seulement les frontières politiques, mais aussi l'univers de représentations culturelles et mentales des sociétés européennes, puis non-européennes. Cette évolution s'est réalisée essentiellement en quatre phases successives.

- Une première phase de nationalisation des sociétés européennes entre 1789 et 1818, qui a conduit à la remise en cause et la disparition des royaumes de l'histoire pré-moderne et qui a radicalement modifié la carte de l'Europe;
- Une deuxième phase de transfert des conceptions européennes de la nation, de la culture nationale de la mémoire et du patrimoine national vers l'Europe de l'Est, l'Amérique du Sud et les Caraïbes, entre 1790 et 1880, saisissable de manière exemplaire à travers la relation entretenue par l'Abbé Henri-Baptiste Grégoire avec Haïti, le premier état non-européen qui devint indépendant et fut dirigé par d'anciens esclaves;
- Une troisième phase de la constitution des États-nations – avec les nouveaux concepts et l'imaginaire mental l'accompagnant – dans le contexte de la décolonisation et de la disparition des empires coloniaux européens sur les autres continents, en particulier en Afrique et en Asie entre 1945 et 1974;
- Et enfin une quatrième phase de la naissance des États-nations et de la renaissance des cultures nationales dans le contexte de la dissolution du bloc des pays de l'Est et de la fin de l'Union soviétique, un mouvement qui a abouti à l'émergence de 25 états nationaux, depuis les Etats baltes jusqu'aux états du sud et du sud-est de l'ancienne Union soviétique, tels l'Ukraine, l'Arménie, la Géorgie ou le Kazakhstan, en passant par la Slovaquie et les républiques issues de l'ancienne Yougoslavie.

Henri-Baptiste Grégoire – Idéologue national et homme politique républicain dans le contexte de la Révolution Française

Dans ce processus esquissé de nationalisation des sociétés et cultures, la Révolution Française a joué un rôle central; elle a eu une fonction de modèle et exercé un effet catalyseur. Des responsables de la politique culturelle comme Henri Grégoire ont, en effet, repris les concepts et la terminologie du mouvement des Lumières, les ont développés et ont créé des institutions, des rituels et des dispositifs médiatiques permettant une identification des couches les plus larges possibles de la population avec le nouvel imaginaire social et ses valeurs. Comme en accéléré, on peut retrouver dans la décennie entre 1789 et 1799 chacune des trois phases évoquées précédemment, que l'historien tchèque Miroslav Hroch a qualifié de fondamentales pour les processus de nationalisation des 19e et 20e siècles, à savoir (1) la construction d'identités nationales par les élites, (2) la mise en application politique des concepts, des valeurs et des imaginaires mentaux nationaux et (3) la nationalisation des masses à travers des dispositifs médiatiques et institutionnels.

Henri-Baptiste Grégoire (1750–1831) représente un des personnages clés dans ce processus de nationalisation en France au cours de la Révolution Française. Né en 1750 dans le village de Vého en Lorraine, fils d'un tailleur de vêtements, simple curé de campagne jusqu'à la Révolution et connu par quelques publications littéraires et journalistiques ainsi que par des participations à des concours pour des prix académiques,[3] notamment son *Essai sur la régénération physique et morale des Juifs* couronné en 1788 par l'Académie de Metz, Grégoire fut élu député du Bas Clergé en 1789 à l'Assemblée Nationale Constituante où il se fit remarquer très tôt par ses positions engagées et radicales. Il plaida pour la tolérance religieuse et pour la non discrimination de la population juive, pour l'abolition de l'esclavage et de la traite des noirs, il devint un membre actif de la *Société des Amis des Noirs,* défendit en 1793 l'idée d'une déclaration des droits des gens de couleur et s'engagea, comme député à la Convention, en 1794 pour l'abolition de l'esclavage et de la traite des noirs; et enfin il soutint, en tant que membre du Comité d'Éducation Nationale de la Convention entre 1792 et 1794, une politique en faveur de la langue et de la culture nationale, qui fit de lui l'un des acteurs les plus influents de la politique culturelle pendant la période révolutionnaire. Trois domaines différents se trouvèrent au centre des conceptions politiques et des initiatives de Grégoire en matière culturelle, dont le troisième sera évoqué ci-après:

– premièrement la politique de la langue et la conception de la "langue nationale";
– deuxièmement l'engagement pour l'émancipation des minorités ethniques et religieuses, en particulier des juifs et des protestants en France, des noirs et des métis dans les colonies françaises. Son engagement pour l'abolition de l'esclavage et de la traite des noirs conduisit Grégoire à soutenir le mouvement d'indépendance en Haïti, une position qu'il fut le seul à adopter avec constance parmi tous les hommes politiques et intellectuels français, comme en témoigne sa correspondance avec le Président haïtien Pétion;
– troisièmement la conception et l'ancrage institutionnel d'un "patrimoine national".

Grégoire comptait parmi l'aile la plus radicale du Bas Clergé et occupa un rôle politique central, tout d'abord à l'Assemblée Nationale Constituante (1789–1791), puis à la Convention (1792–1795) et enfin dans le Conseil des

---

3 Voir sur la biographie de Grégoire: Necheles; Goldstein; Boulad-Ayoub

Cinq-Cents pendant le Directoire (1795–1799) (Hindie Lemay). Ses positions politiques peuvent paraître au premier abord contradictoires. Comme membre du Club des Jacobins pendant les premières années de la Révolution, il rejoignit les Girondins lorsque les Jacobins s'emparèrent du pouvoir; comme critique acerbe de l'intolérance religieuse et des structures traditionnelles du clergé, il s'engagea pendant la période de la déchristianisation des années 1793–94 pour la conservation du clergé constitutionnel; comme opposant à la monarchie, dont il avait demandé la suppression dès le 21 septembre 1792, il prit position pour un procès contre le Roi et son jugement, mais contre une condamnation à mort, une peine dont il demandait l'abolition.

> En tant que personnage solitaire non fanatique, marqué par des idéaux chrétiens et humanitaires, mais également républicains et antimonarchistes, il a survécu à la Révolution tout en restant fidèle à ses convictions religieuses et en n'hésitant pas à se montrer en costume d'Évêque de Blois à la Convention. Il s'engagea pleinement pour la défense des droits des juifs, des noirs dans les colonies et pour les autres minorités, et mena parallèlement au Comité d'Instruction publique une politique culturelle égalitaire radicale sans considération pour les pertes entraînées (Tauber 199).[4]

Les constantes de son engagement républicain et révolutionnaire sont concentrées sur deux domaines principaux: d'une part sur sa prise de position pour l'égalité, la liberté et la tolérance, fondée sur les idées du mouvement des Lumières et en particulier de Jean-Jacques Rousseau, pour l'égalité de toutes les communautés religieuses et le soutien aux classes sociales défavorisées, dont il était issu car son père était un modeste tailleur; et d'autre part sa conviction de la nécessité d'une véritable unité nationale dans des domaines comme l'administration, la politique de l'éducation, la politique culturelle et la politique de la langue, une force indispensable pour mettre en application les objectifs de la Révolution française et les idées des Lumières. De même que Rousseau, Grégoire voyait dans la politique de l'éducation – ainsi que dans la politique culturelle et la politique de la langue qui y sont étroitement liées – un levier fondamental pour opérer des transformations sociales. Cette conviction repose sur l'affirmation rousseauiste que l'homme est pour l'essentiel le produit de son éducation.

Grégoire peut être considéré comme le plus important instigateur et diffuseur des idées de la révolution culturelle des années 1789–94, qui voulaient conquérir l'ensemble de l'espace social et instaurer un ordre nouveau dans tous les

---

4 "Als nicht unfanatischer Einzelgänger mit gleichermaßen humanitär-christlichen wie republikanisch-monarchiefeindlichen Idealen überlebte er die Revolution, obwohl er seinen kirchlichen Überzeugungen treu blieb und sich gern im Gewand des konstitutionellen Bischofs von Blois im Nationalkonvent zeigte. Er setzte sich für die Rechte der Juden, der Farbigen in den Kolonien und sonstige Minderheiten ein, betrieb aber gleichzeitig im Comité d'instruction publique eine forciert-egalisierende Kulturpolitik ohne Rücksicht auf Verluste." (trad. en français par H.-J. L.)

domaines de la vie, au sens d'une culture nationale et d'une politique symbolique: "Le temps, l'espace, les mesures, le calendrier, la langue et les vêtements furent réinventés et soumis à un nouvel ordre universel afin d'uniformiser toute la nation dans l'ensemble des domaines de la vie" (220).[5] On doit ajouter, à ce vaste programme évoqué par C. Tauber, notamment la mémoire collective et son support majeur, le patrimoine national.

Grégoire parvint de façon systématique et originale, caractéristique pour son époque, à relier, dans ses nombreux rapports à la Convention et dans ses projets de loi, les nouveaux concepts radicaux en matière de langue, d'espace et de temps fondés sur la prise de conscience d'une césure révolutionnaire, avec la conception d'un "patrimoine national" intégrant également les monuments, les bibliothèques, les archives et les oeuvres d'art de l'époque prérévolutionnaire, celle de la monarchie. La conception du "patrimoine national" qui s'appuyait, pour Grégoire comme pour d'autres responsables de la politique culturelle pendant la Révolution Française, sur le terme d'"héritage," est née de façon paradoxale en 1794 dans le contexte de la remise en cause radicale de tout ce qui provenait de l'Ancien Régime, en particulier les emblèmes de la royauté, de l'aristocratie et de l'Eglise. Depuis le mois de juin 1789, mais surtout après la tentative de fuite du Roi en juin 1791 et l'abolition de la monarchie en août 1792, on assista en France à toute une série de destructions de châteaux appartenant au Roi ou à la noblesse, comme le château de Marly, à la destruction par le feu d'objets de culte et de tableaux, à la violation des tombeaux royaux comme ceux de la cathédrale Saint Denis, et à la décapitation symbolique des statues de saints. Grégoire, qui avait pris position en 1793 devant la Constituante en faveur de la destruction des symboles et emblèmes royaux, esquissa en 1794 dans ses différents rapports adressés à l'Assemblée Constituante – mais en définitive destinés aussi à l'opinion publique – et en particulier dans ses trois *Rapports sur le vandalisme*, les fondements d'une toute nouvelle politique nationale de patrimoine culturel destinée à mettre fin à la stratégie de destruction révolutionnaire.[6]

Les *Rapports sur le vandalisme* rédigés par Grégoire en 1794 destinés aux députés de la Convention, qui furent immédiatement mis en application par des décrets et projets de loi, appartiennent, comme leur nom même l'indique, au genre structurel du rapport administratif destiné à une commission parlementaire. Ils ont vu le jour après la chute de Robespierre le 31 août 1794 et constituent donc un "produit typique du discours thermidorien" (Tauber 211; voir sur le contexte: Baczko; Despois; Gautherot; Réau).[7] Comme pour de nombreux autres "rapports" de l'époque révolutionnaire, la lecture de ces rapports fait apparaître leur structure textuelle fondamentalement hybride: ils reprennent en effet, à l'in-

---

5 "Zeit, Raum, Maße, Kalender, Sprache und Kleidung wurden ‚neu' erfunden und einer universellen Neuordnung unterworfen, um so die gesamte Nation in allen entscheidenden Lebensbereichen gleichzuschalten." (trad. H.-J. L.)
6 Voir sur les *Rapports sur le vandalisme* de Grégoire: Guillaume; Marot.
7 "ein typisches Produkt des thermidorianischen Diskurses" (trad. H.-J. L.)

térieur de leur structure formelle dominante de "rapport", des éléments de la littérature pamphlétaire de l'époque, des réquisitoires judiciaires et des discours politiques oraux, destinés a priori d'abord et en premier lieu à un public physiquement présent. Dans ses *Rapports sur le vandalisme*, Grégoire se met en scène comme orateur engagé. Il a ainsi recours à des registres d'expression émotionnels, emploie le singulier collectif "Nous sommes la Nation" (Grégoire, *Premier rapport* 400), et s'adresse explicitement à certains interlocuteurs privilégiés, comme "les législateurs" et "les citoyens" (410–11). Simulant la posture d'un orateur parlant du haut de sa tribune, il exprime, avec un certain pathos, son ressenti émotionnel. Il écrit ainsi, ému par la destruction d'œuvres d'art à l'époque révolutionnaire: "les dégâts sont tels que pour les peindre l'expression manque" (405), et "il y a de quoi verser des larmes de sang" (Grégoire, *Troisième rapport* 758). Sa dénonciation des responsables de ces destructions et de leurs méfaits renoue pour sa part directement avec la rhétorique de la littérature pamphlétaire révolutionnaire. Les coupables y sont, en effet, qualifiés de "brigands," de "fripons," de "scélérats" et d'"ignorants" qui seraient animés par un "fanatisme d'un nouveau genre" et un "esprit contre-révolutionnaire,"[8] se voyant non seulement accusés, mais aussi condamnés, d'abord sur un plan purement verbal et rhétorique.

Au centre même de ces trois rapports on trouve cependant la légitimation de la conception et de l'institutionnalisation du "patrimoine national" dans le cadre d'une nouvelle politique culturelle éclairée et révolutionnaire. Grégoire y développe cinq stratégies d'argumentation différentes pour appuyer sa demande d'une protection systématique des bibliothèques, des archives, des manuscrits, des monuments et des œuvres d'art par le gouvernement révolutionnaire qui ferait abstraction de leur utilisation antérieure ainsi que de leurs propriétaires en leur attribuant une valeur intrinsèque et non-idéologique. Le "patrimoine national" devrait inclure par conséquent, selon sa demande explicite, aussi les œuvres et les documents de la période du Moyen-âge et de celle de l'Ancien Régime, des époques dont le discours de la Révolution Française cherchait à se distancer radicalement.

Le premier argument essentiel est lié à la valeur esthétique intemporelle des objets culturels et artistiques, que souligne Grégoire à l'aide de nombreux exemples et avec une terminologie très différenciée. Il ne se contente pas d'utiliser des termes se référant à l'esthétique, comme "de grande valeur," "pureté des formes," "magnifique," "précieux," ou simplement "beau";[9] mais il exprime aussi son admiration dans des passages descriptifs plus détaillés, comme celui par exemple concernant la cathédrale d'Amiens. Il la décrit comme

> un des plus beaux monuments gothiques qui soient en Europe: la magnificence, la hardiesse, et la légereté de sa construction en font une des

---

8 Voir successivement Grégoire, *Premier rapport* 411, 403; *Deuxième rapport* 63; *Premier rapport* 419; *Deuxième rapport* 69; *Premier rapport* 408, 406.
9 Voir successivement Grégoire, *Premier rapport* 403, 404; Grégoire, *Deuxième rapport* 64; Grégoire, *Premier rapport* 419, 407.

plus hardies conceptions de l'esprit humain. Les mêmes réflexions s'appliquent à celle de Strasbourg, dont la tour est la plus haute de l'Europe […]. Quand le connaisseur contemple ces basiliques, ses facultés, suspendues par l'admiration dont il est saisi, lui permettent à peine de respirer; il s'honore d'être un homme en pensant que ses semblables ont pu exécuter de tels ouvrages, et la satisfaction qu'il éprouve en les voyant sur le sol de la liberté, ajoute au bonheur d'être français. (Grégoire, *Deuxième rapport* 67)

Cette citation renvoie à deux autres modèles d'argumentation avec lesquels Grégoire légitime sa conception du patrimoine national: d'une part l'idée qu'il s'agit d'œuvres issues de la civilisation humaine, qui sont des témoins de son progrès, "des chefs-d'œuvre où le génie a déployé sa magnificence" (Grégoire, *Troisième rapport* 763) et qui représentent "le produit de plusieurs siècles de civilisation" (752). Tous les citoyens devraient pouvoir, selon Grégoire, profiter des bienfaits du progrès des arts, des sciences et du commerce, et à cette fin, il s'avère impérativement nécessaire de conserver les acquis du passé. D'autre part, Grégoire légitime sa conception du patrimoine avec celle de la gloire nationale: "Ces monuments contribuent à la splendeur d'une nation, et ajoutent à sa prépondérance politique" (Premier rapport 420; voir aussi Henri Grégoire: *Rapport fait par le Citoyen Grégoire*). "Un grand homme," souligne Grégoire, considérant la place essentielle que les artistes, les scientifiques, les écrivains devraient occuper dans la mémoire culturelle, "est une propriété nationale" (412). Pour lui, la préservation, l'encouragement et la diffusion des meilleurs talents artistiques et scientifiques doivent revêtir une signification politique et culturelle toute particulière au sein du nouvel ordre social instauré en France par la Révolution:

> La France est vraiment un nouveau monde. Sa nouvelle organisation sociale présente un phénomène unique dans l'étendue des âges, et peut-être n'a-t-on pas encore observé qu'outre le matériel des connaissances humaines, par l'effet de la révolution, elle possède exclusivement une foule d'éléments, de combinaisons nouvelles, prises dans la nature, et d'inépuisables moyens pour mettre à profit sa résurrection politique. (417)

Un quatrième modèle d'argumentation concerne les connaissances historiques et scientifiques, et par extension les 'leçons' politiques et morales, qui peuvent être tirées des monuments du passé. Ces derniers peuvent "simultanément alimenter le génie et renforcer la haine des tyrans" (408). Pour Grégoire, seule la conservation des papiers de l'inquisition – que des acteurs politiques ayant une fausse compréhension de l'action révolutionnaire voulaient détruire comme des documents provenant des tyrannies de passé – rendra possible l'écriture de leur histoire et permettra de les faire connaître aux générations futures comme un véritable avertissement. "Un jour on examinera si ces productions illégitimes et empoisonnées doivent être réservées pour compléter le tableau des aberrations humaines" (402).

L'"histoire de ces erreurs et les monuments qui les retracent ne sont pas inutiles: C'est par ses chutes que la raison se prémunit contre de nouvelles chutes et qu'elle affermit sa marche" (Grégoire, *Troisième rapport* 759).

Le cinquième modèle d'argumentation de Grégoire pour la conservation du patrimoine national est d'ordre économique. Il pose pragmatiquement la question des usages des objets patrimoniaux, c'est-à-dire "les moyens d'utiliser" (Grégoire, *Premier rapport* 415) le patrimoine culturel de la nation en prenant en considération sa valeur matérielle et marchande. Si la nation elle-même ne prenait pas en charge la protection des biens appartenant au patrimoine culturel, telle est la position défendue par Grégoire, ceux-ci seraient non seulement menacés de destruction, mais ils pourraient aussi être vendus illégalement par des personnes privées avides de profits, comme cela fut le cas pendant les premières années de la Révolution. Cela pourrait avoir pour conséquence que ces biens quittent le territoire national et soient ainsi définitivement perdus pour la nation.

Grégoire formule ainsi, pour la première fois dans l'histoire européenne, une conception cohérente de la légitimation et la préservation d'un patrimoine culturel national, pour lequel il utilise les termes de "propriété nationale" et d'"objets nationaux." Il relie cette conception et cette défense du patrimoine culturel national d'une part à une stratégie d'ancrage politique et institutionnel aboutissant à la mise en place de tout un réseau d'institutions comme la Bibliothèque Nationale, le Musée du Louvre, la Commission des Monuments ou encore le Conservatoire des Arts et Métiers dont il fut l'initiateur. Et d'autre part, il articule cette conception du patrimoine national avec une politique de l'éducation axée sur les masses populaires, qu'il présente en détail à la fin de son troisième *rapport* en précisant ses différents objectifs. Il affirme ainsi que dorénavant toutes les plus importantes collections d'art privées devront être accessibles au public. "Ces dépôts, qu'on ne voyait guère que par faveur, et dont la jouissance exclusive flattait l'orgueil et servait l'ambition de quelques individus, feront désormais la jouissance de tous: les sueurs du peuple s'étaient changées en livres, en statues, en tableaux; le peuple rentre dans sa propriété" (Grégoire, *Premier rapport* 416). Selon Grégoire, ce n'est qu'à travers une éducation artistique et politique "éclairée" du peuple, appuyée sur des institutions éducatives – telles les écoles primaires – que peut être éveillé dans le peuple un sentiment de respect pour les restes du passé. "Inspirons au peuple un sentiment de respect pour ces restes majestueux échappés à l'édacité du temps et à la fureur dévastatrice" (Grégoire, *Troisième rapport* 765).

Cet objectif montre que Grégoire connaissait la culture et les mentalités des couches sociales inférieures – surtout celles des populations rurales et des analphabètes –, peut-être mieux que tout autre dirigeant politique de la période révolutionnaire, du fait de son expérience personnelle en tant qu'ancien curé dans un village de Lorraine et aussi en tant qu'autodidacte dans de nombreux domaines de savoir. Ceci transparaît clairement dans de nombreux passages de ses rapports à l'Assemblée Nationale:

> Le mal est connu, avisons aux remèdes. Le premier est l'instruction. Répandons la abondamment. Dans cette statue, qui est un chef-d'oeuvre, l'ignorant ne voit qu'une pierre configurée; montrons lui que ce marbre respire, que cette toile est vivante, que ce livre est un arsenal propre à défendre ses droits. C'est faute de lumières sans doute qu'à Toulouse on envoyait au parc d'artillerie des ouvrages en parchemin et en vélin. (Grégoire, *Deuxième rapport* 70)

Horizons transnationaux et formes de mémoire interculturelle

Les formes de mémoire interculturelle et leurs éléments structuraux – parmi lesquels le patrimoine culturel national au sens de Grégoire constitue un élément central de la mémoire culturelle "officielle,"[10] sont en général, dans la recherche en sciences culturelles et en histoire culturelle, vus comme essentiellement monoculturels, c'est-à-dire axés sur et pensés à partir d'entités communautaires nationales. Pour Maurice Halbwachs, Pierre Nora, Jan et Aleida Assmann, "la mémoire culturelle est l'instance fondatrice d'identité d'une communauté – souvent une nation – qui fait sien un arrière plan culturel commun et qui se définit essentiellement par opposition à d'autres communautés" (Wögerbauer 203). Des termes comme "mémoire interculturelle" et "mémoire transculturelle", qui permettent sur le plan conceptuel un dépassement du cadre culturel national, ont été jusqu'ici relativement peu utilisés dans la recherche et peu développés sur le plan théorique. Michel Espagne, Matthias et Katharina Middell utilisent dans leur ouvrage collectif intitulé *Archiv und Gedächtnis* le terme de "interkulturellen Überlieferungen", "héritages interculturels", qui concerne cependant la dimension interculturelle de l'Archive et non la dimension interculturelle de sa construction discursive et de sa mise en scène publique. Gino Carmine Chiellino, éditeur de l'ouvrage collectif *Interkulturelle Literatur in Deutschland* (2007), a défini dans une interview le terme de "mémoire interculturelle" comme suit:

> Lorsque j'étudie des œuvres interculturelles en tant que scientifique, j'explique à mes étudiants que, dans ces œuvres interculturelles, on trouve une langue ou l'autre – par exemple l'allemand, l'italien, le français ou l'anglais –, mais que derrière cette langue on ne trouve pas une mémoire monoculturelle – que ce soit la culture des Allemands, des Anglais, des Italiens, etc. –, mais une mémoire interculturelle dans laquelle le protagoniste rassemble tout ce qu'il a vécu comme Italien, ou comme

---

10 Voir sur les différences entre 'mémoire de stockage' et 'mémoire fonctionnelle', entre 'mémoire culturelle' et 'mémoire communicative', entre 'mémoire officielle' et 'mémoire inofficielle', Assmann *Erinnerungsräume* 130–48; et Assmann, "Kulturelles Gedächtnis und kollektive Identität" 9–19.

Allemand, et c'est ce mélange, cette interaction, qui crée pour moi une mémoire interculturelle. (Craith 41).[11]

Les termes de "transcultural memory," "transkulturelles Gedächtnis" et "multidirectional memory" ont été proposés pour leur part par Michael Rothberg et Astrid Erll ainsi que notamment par un groupe de chercheurs luxembourgeois (Sonja Kmec, Benoît Majerus, Michel Margue, Pit Péporté), mais sans que ne soient thématisées explicitement les différences par rapport à la notion de mémoire interculturelle. Selon Astrid Erll, Rothberg critique avec son concept deux tendances de la recherche actuelle sur la mémoire culturelle: d'abord le fait que ses concepts mettent dans des conteneurs séparés la mémoire, l'identité et la culture nationale, "opening up the separate containers of memory and identity" (Erll, "Emphatische Transkulturalität" 150; Rothberg, *Multidirectional Memory* 18). En conséquence, Rothberg, comme les autres représentants des *Transcultural Memory Studies*, porte plus son attention sur les flux continus de contenus de mémoire, de médias et de pratiques entre les différentes communautés de mémoire, que sur des inventaires statiques de mémoires (Erll, "Emphatische Transkulturalität" 150). Le concept de "multidirectorial memory" utilisé par Rothberg est proche, dans sa signification, de celui de "mémoire transculturelle," mais il vise cependant à mieux cerner les articulations et les interdépendances entre différentes formes et différents lieux de mémoire:

> At the level of theory, I rethink the conceptualization of collective memory in multicultural and transnational contexts. Fully cognizant of the differentials of access and power that mark the public sphere, I nevertheless provide a framework that draws attention to the inevitable dialogical exchange between memory traditions and keeps open the possibility of a new just future of memory. (Rothberg, *Multidirectional Memory* 21)

Il semble intéressant d'essayer de distinguer aussi sur le plan de leur applicabilité empirique et heuristique ces deux concepts "transkulturelles Gedächtnis" et "interkulturelles Gedächtnis" utilisés de façon souvent synonyme dans les discussions au sein de la recherche sur la théorie de la mémoire collective. Sous le terme de "transkulturelles Gedächtnis," nous proposons de comprendre des formes de la mémoire collective (et donc du patrimoine culturel) concernant plusieurs – souvent un grand nombre – d'espaces culturels différents dépassant les frontières culturelles traditionnelles (liées aux États-nations) et mettant ainsi fon-

---

11 Texte allemand (traduit par H.-J. L.): "Wenn ich als Wissenschaftler interkulturelle Werke untersuche, dann bringe ich meinen Studenten bei, dass in den interkulturellen Werken zwar jeweils die eine oder andere Sprache geschrieben wird – zum Beispiel Deutsch, Italienisch, Französisch oder Englisch –, dass aber diese Sprache nicht etwa ein monokulturelles Gedächtnis – sei das die Kultur des Deutschen, die Kultur der Engländer, die Kultur der Italiener, und so weiter –, sondern ein interkulturelles Gedächtnis hat, in das der Protagonist all das hineinlegt, was er als Italiener erlebt hat, was er als Deutscher lebt; alles zusammen, das Zusammenspiel, macht für mich ein interkulturelles Gedächtnis aus."

damentalement en cause la notion même d'espace culturel délimité. Le concept de "mémoire interculturelle", au contraire, vise à définir des formes de mémoire collective – et donc aussi de patrimoine culturel – qui mettent en lumière à l'intérieur des frontières et des espaces culturels des phénomènes d'hybridation sociale et culturelle, ou de métissage culturel. Ces formes d'hybridation mémorielle sont indissociables de processus de perception de soi et de perception de l'autre et impliquent aussi des phénomènes d'acculturation et de conflits interculturels. Ces derniers résultent du fait que toute mémoire interculturelle est sujette à des formes de 'négociation' entre les groupes et les communautés concernés qui peuvent être conflictuelles, comme dans le cas des transformations, entre l'époque de l'Algérie française et la période postcoloniale, d'une 'mémoire interculturelle franco-algérienne'.

La question de la création et de la conception du nouveau *Musée national de l'histoire de l'immigration* à Paris, ouvert au public en 2007, mais dont l'inauguration officielle n'eut lieu qu'en 2014 du fait de dissensions politiques, dont il sera question par la suite, permet d'éclairer de façon exemplaire et de discuter les différences à la fois heuristiques et théoriques entre les concepts de "mémoire culturelle nationale," de "mémoire transculturelle" et de "mémoire interculturelle." Le *Musée national de l'histoire de l'immigration,* le premier musée national en Europe consacré à l'histoire de l'immigration, est situé à Paris dans un "lieu de mémoire" qui constitue lui-même un élément du "patrimoine national": le "Palais de la Porte Dorée," autrefois nommé "Palais des colonies," un bâtiment de style art déco construit en 1930–31 à l'occasion de l'*exposition coloniale internationale* de 1931, la plus grande exposition coloniale organisée en France avec plus de 30 millions de visiteurs. A la fin de l'exposition, il fut décidé de réunir dans un *Musée des Colonies* les nombreux objets exposés dans les sections françaises de l'Exposition. Ensuite, entre 1935 et 1961, ce bâtiment abrita le *Musée de la France d'Outre Mer*, qui reflétait les concepts politiques et les institutions développés au cours des années 1930–60, ceux de la "FrancAfrique," de l'"Union Française" (1946–1958) et de la "Communauté Française" (1958–1960). Les objets exposés orientaient le regard du visiteur vers les particularités de la France d'Outre-mer et vers ses différentes cultures et civilisations. Entre 1961 et 2003 enfin, après la fin de la période coloniale, l'ancien Palais des Colonies abrita le *Musée des Arts Africains et Océaniens.*

Entre 1931 et 1961, les objets exposés, (sculptures, cartes, objets d'art, photographies, objets d'artisanat provenant des différentes parties de l'empire colonial) et les formes de commentaires muséographiques demeurèrent en grande partie semblables et même identiques. L'objectif du musée était de mettre en scène la variété culturelle de l'empire colonial français et de glorifier le colonialisme français dans le cadre de la République Française.[12] Il s'agissait donc de mettre en scène le patrimoine culturel de la "Plus grande France" (Lüsebrink "Littéra-

---

12 Voir le texte dans le catalogue de l'exposition: "Le musée de la France d'Outre-mer se rappelle les heures de gloire de la colonisation."

ture Nationale", "Faszination und Distanznahme"), selon l'expression utilisée entre la fin de la Première Guerre Mondiale et les années 1950 marquant la fin de la période coloniale, pour évoquer la France et ses colonies dans la conception nationale de cette époque.

La fin de l'empire colonial français, entre 1960 et 1962, ne conduisit pas seulement à changer le nom du musée – qui deviendra le "Musée des Arts Africains et Océaniens" –, elle exigea également l'élaboration d'une nouvelle conception de ce musée et un élargissement de ses collections. Cette transformation d'un musée colonial en un musée ethnographique entraîna avec elle la nécessité d'effacer les traces du passé dans les commentaires muséologiques et dans les bâtiments eux-mêmes, ou de les dissimuler en grande partie. Ainsi les fresques murales du hall d'entrée et des deux salons adjacents, qui devaient mettre en avant de manière monumentale les principes fondamentaux de l'idéologie républicaine, furent-elles désormais dissimulées au regard du public et la collection d'objets fut élargie pour intégrer les civilisations africaines et celles du Pacifique, dans l'esprit d'un musée ethnographique. Les commentaires muséologiques furent réorientés pour être recentrés sur la dimension esthétique des objets présentés, dans une perspective rejoignant les conceptions d'André Malraux, le ministre de la culture de l'époque. André Malraux désirait en effet mettre en avant "la beauté des formes," en occultant pour une large part leur fonction matérielle, sociale ou spirituelle et masquant leur provenance les enracinant dans un passé colonial qu'il cherchait par tous les moyens à refouler autant que possible, en tant qu'intellectuel et homme politique résolument anticolonialiste. Un musée autrefois national a donc été remplacé par un musée transculturel consacré à l'art non européen – exposant en partie les mêmes collections dans le même bâtiment.

Les années 2003 à 2014 marquent la dernière étape jusqu'ici dans l'histoire de ce musée. En 2003, le *Musée des Arts Africains et Océaniens* fut fermé, suite à des critiques grandissantes portant sur sa conception esthétisante et dé-contextualisante, qui conduisirent à une accusation de tendances néo-colonialistes. Une large part des collections de ce musée fut transférée en 2006 dans le nouveau *Musée du quai Branly*, un musée des civilisations non européennes d'orientation transculturelle qui accorde une grande importance aux dimensions culturelles, anthropologiques et historiques des objets exposés et à leur contexte. Une petite partie de ces objets, estimée de grande valeur, fut transférée au Louvre. Parallèlement, le Président de la République de l'époque, Jacques Chirac, accompagné de son Premier Ministre, Jean-Pierre Raffarin, décidèrent de créer, dans l'ancien Palais des Colonies, la *Cité nationale de l'histoire de l'immigration* ayant pour objectif de "Faire connaître et reconnaître l'apport de l'immigration en France" (Toubon) dans les domaines sociaux, culturels et économiques, comme l'écrit dans son rapport Jacques Toubon, directeur de la commission chargée de la conception du musée. Cette *Cité nationale de l'histoire de l'immigration,* à la conception de laquelle participèrent d'éminents chercheurs sur les questions d'immigration tels Gérard Noiriel et Philippe Dewitte, fut ouverte au public en 2007, mais sans la présence de représentants du gouvernement ou du Président Nicolas Sarkozy. Cette absence s'expliquait par le fait que la conception interculturelle de ce nouveau musée ne correspondait pas aux conceptions de l'identité nationale et de la mémoire nationale du Président français, ayant crée la même année un Ministère de l'identité nationale.

Le *Musée national de l'histoire de l'immigration*, nouveau nom donné en 2012 à la *Cité Nationale,* met en scène un patrimoine interculturel, produit de l'immigration continue en France depuis 200 ans. Il est organisé selon deux sections différentes ayant en commun une même conception interculturelle: l'exposition permanente d'un côté,[13] et la Galerie des dons d'un autre côté[14] où sont regroupés et thématisés dans un cadre collectif les cadeaux et les prêts des familles d'immigrés retraçant leur destins individuels et leurs trajectoires biographiques. Les dix différentes sections qui structurent l'exposition permanente du musée abordent des thèmes comme "Les émigrés," "Face à l'État," "Terre d'accueil, France hostile," "Sport," "Religions," et "Cultures," et prennent pour base des problématiques interculturelles de l'interaction, de la perception de Soi et de l'Autre, ainsi que du transfert et de la transformation de modes de vie, de formes de conduite et de systèmes symboliques propres aux populations immigrées en les éclairant, comme dans la Galerie des dons, à travers des exemples issus de destins individuels. Le phénomène de la xénophobie par exemple, qui a caractérisé certaines phases de l'immigration en France surtout pendant des périodes de crise économiques, est illustré dans le musée non seulement à l'aide de caricatures, mais également à travers l'exemple de la physicienne Marie Curie, immigrée venue de Pologne à la fin du 19e siècle. L'intégration sociale des immigrants est présentée à travers la conception du musée comme un processus permanent entraînant des conflits, des négociations et des phénomènes d'hybridation, au sein duquel le logement, l'école, la profession et le sport constituent des contextes interculturels de socialisation et d'interaction de première importance.

La "Galerie des dons" éclaire ces processus d'intégration et de négociation interculturels dans une perspective résolument individuelle, qui remet fondamentalement en cause la dichotomie dominante entre "Nous" et "les Autres," entre "Culture d'origine" et "Culture d'accueil." Comme le montrent les nombreuses biographies individuelles et collectives présentées, les familles d'immigrants sont souvent elles-mêmes marquées par l'interculturalité et la multiculturalité. Leur hétérogénéité et leur identité plurielle sont le produit de leur parcours migratoire en plusieurs étapes à travers divers pays et cultures, à travers l'Allemagne par exemple pour les immigrants venus de Pologne.

Le *Musée National d'histoire de l'immigration* constitue ainsi un excellent exemple d'une mise en scène muséologique d'un *patrimoine interculturel* et d'une mémoire collective interculturelle. Le fait que ce musée, à cause de son implan-

---

13 Voir le catalogue de l'exposition: La Cité Nationale de l'Immigration, *Guide de l'exposition permanente* (2007).
14 Voir le catalogue: La Cité Nationale de l'immigration: *Guide de la galerie des dons* (2014).

tation dans l'ancien Palais de la Porte Dorée, constitue une sorte de palimpseste des formes du patrimoine à la fois national et transculturel, qui intègre ces formes en les transformant interculturellement; ce qui fait de cette institution, dans une perspective historique et théorique, un lieu de négociation interculturelle d'une nouvelle identité collective. 200 ans après les rapports parlementaires programmatiques d'Henri Grégoire sur les excès du vandalisme révolutionnaire, qui donnèrent naissance à une nouvelle conception du patrimoine national, sont tracés à travers ce musée les contours d'une nouvelle conception d'un patrimoine désormais *interculturel*. Paradoxalement ce musée représente en même temps, comme son nom l'indique, une institution nationale, fondée et financée par un État-nation, la France, renvoyant aux liens étroits et complexes entre le concept de 'patrimoine national' et celui de 'mémoire interculturelle', censé mettre en cause et dépasser le cadre national et ses frontières contraignantes.

Œuvres Citées

Assmann, Aleida. *Erinnerungsräume*. München: C.H. Beck, 2006.
Assmann, Jan. "Kulturelles Gedächtnis und kollektive Identität." *Kultur und Gedächtnis*. Eds. Jan Assmann et Lucian Hölscher. Frankfurt/Main: Suhrkamp, 1988. 9–19.
Baczko, Bronislaw. "Vandalisme." *Dictionnaire critique de la Révolution Française*. Eds. François Furet, Mona Ozouf. Paris: Flammarion, 1988. 903–12.
Boulad-Ayoub, Josiane. *L'Abbé Grégoire apologète de la République*. Paris: Honoré Champion, 2005.
La Cité Nationale de l'Immigration. *Guide de l'exposition permanente*. Avec une préface de Jacques Toubon. Paris: Cité Nationale de l'Histoire de l'immigration, 2007.
La Cité Nationale de l'immigration. *Guide de la galerie des dons*. Avec une introduction d'Hélène de Mazaubrun. Paris: Musée de L'Histoire de l'Immigration, 2014.
Craith, Máiréad Nic. *Narratives of Place, Belonging and Language: An Intercultural Perspective*. London: Palgrave/Macmillan, 2012.
Despois, Eugène. *Le Vandalisme révolutionnaire. Fondations littéraires, scientifiques et artistiques de la Convention*. Paris: Germere Ballière, Libraire-Éditeur 1868.
Erll, Astrid. "Emphatische Transkulturalität und die Ermöglichung kulturellen Wandels: Konzepte." *Formen kulturellen Wandels*. Eds. Stefan Deines, Daniel Martin Feige et Martin Seel. Bielefeld: Transcript, 2012. 148–58.
Espagne, Michel, Katharina Middell et Matthias Middell (éds.). *Archiv und Geschichte. Studien interkulturellen Überlieferung*. Leipzig: Leipziger Universitätsverlag, 2000.
François, Etienne et Hagen Schulze (éds.). *Deutsche Erinnerungsorte*. München: Beck Verlag, 2001.
Gautherot, Gustave. *Le Vandalisme jacobin. Destructions administratives d'archives, d'objets d'art, de monuments religieux à l'époque révolutonnaire*. Paris: Beauchesne, 1914.

Goldstein Sepinwall, Alyssa. *The Abbé Grégoire and the French Revolution. The Making of Modern Universalism.* Berkeley: University of California Press, 2005.
Gregoire, Henri. *Premier rapport sur le vandalisme.* Séance du 14 fructidor an III. Inséré dans le *Moniteur* du 9 vendémiaire an III (30 septembre 1794). Réimprimé dans: *Bulletin du Bibliophile*, 1843. 399–421.
—. *Deuxième rapport sur le vandalisme.* Séance du 8 brumaire, an III. Réimprimé dans: *Bulletin du Bibliophile*, 1851. 62–73.
—. *Troisième rapport sur le vandalisme.* Fait à la Convention nationale, au nom du Comité d'instruction publique, dans la séance du 24 frimaire, l'an troisième de la République française, une et indivisible. Réimprimé dans: *Bulletin du Bibliophile*, 1848. 751–63.
—. "Rapport fait par le Citoyen Grégoire au nom d'une Commission spéciale sur le Conservatoire des Arts et Métiers." Conseil des Cinq-Cents, Séance du 17 floréal an VI (1798). Reproduit dans *L'Abbé Grégoire apologète de la République.* Ed. Josiane Boulad-Ayoub. Paris: Honoré Champion, 2005. 211–21.
Guillaume, James. "Grégoire et le vandalisme." *La Révolution Française,* tome XLI, juillet-décembre, 1901: 155–80.
Hindie Lemay, Edna. "Grégoire, Henri-Baptiste." *Dictionnaire des Constituants, 1989–1791.* Paris: Universitas, 1991. 426–29.
Hroch, Misroslav. *Social Preconditions of Social Revival in Europe, a Comparative Analysis of the Social Composition of Patriotic Groups among the Smaller European Nations.* Cambridge: Cambridge University Press, 1985.
Löfgren, Orvar. "The nationalization of culture: constructing Swedishness." *Studia ethnologica croatica* 3.1 (1992): 101–16.
Lüsebrink, Hans-Jürgen.. "Littérature Nationale et Espace National. De la littérature hexagonale aux littératures de la Plus Grande France de l'époque coloniale (1789–1960)." *Philologiques III. Qu'est-ce qu'une littérature nationale? Approches pour une théorie interculturelle du champ littéraire.* Eds. Michel Espagne et Michael Werner. Paris: Editions de la Maison des Sciences de l'Homme, 1994. 265–86.
—. "Faszination und Distanznahme – 'La Plus Grande France' aus der Sicht der deutschen Öffentlichkeit (1781–1914)." *Visions allemandes de la France (1781–1914). Frankreich aus deutscher Sicht (1871–1914).* Eds. Helga Abret et Michel Grunewald. Basel: Peter Lang Verlag, 1995. 51–61.
Marot, Pierre. "L'Abbé Grégoire et le vandalisme révolutionnaire." *Revue de l'Art* 49 (1980): 36–39.
Necheles, Ruth F. *The Abbé Grégoire, 1787–1831. The Odyssey of an Egalitarian.* Westport: Greenwood Publishing Corporation and Negro Universities Press, 1971.
Nora, Pierre. *Lieux de mémoire.* Paris: Gallimard, 1984–1992, 7 Bde.
Réau, Louis. *Histoire du vandalisme. Les monuments détruits de l'art français.* Paris: Hachette, 1914.
Rothberg, Michael. *Multidirectional Memory: Remembering the Holocaust in the Age of Decolonization.* Stanford: Stanford University Press, 2009.
Sire, Marie-Anne. *La France du patrimoine: les choix de la mémoire.* Paris: Gallimard, 1996.
Tauber, Christiane. *Bilderstürme der Französischen Revolution. Die Vandalismus-Berichte des Abbé Grégoire.* Freiburg in Br./Berlin/Wien: Rombach, 2009.
Thiesse, Anne-Marie. *La création des identités nationales. Europe 18e–20e siècle.* Paris: Le Seuil, 1999.

Toubon, Jacques. *Mission de préfiguration du centre de ressources et de mémoire de l'immigration. Rapport au Premier Ministre.* Paris: La Documentation Française, 2004.

Wögerbauer, Christine. "An der Peripherie von Kultur und Geist. Das postmoderne kulturelle Gedächtnis bei Jorge Luis Borges." *PostModerne. DeKonstruktionen: Ethik, Politik und Kultur am Ende einer Epoche.* Eds. Susanne Kollmann et Kathrin Schödel. Münster: LIT Verlag, 2004. 201–14.

CHAPTER FIVE

Le patrimoine en question(s) : Le moment des années 1830 au prisme des "Voyages en France" de Stendhal

Laure Lévêque

Cet article envisage, à partir du cas emblématique des "Voyages en France," manière de retrouvailles avec sa patrie pour un Stendhal depuis longtemps délocalisé en Italie, ces années 1830 que Guizot devait rendre si cruciales pour l'historiographie nationale. Entre véridiction et fiction, le motif du voyage favorise un état des lieux en même temps qu'il autorise les changements de perspective qui prennent en compte les changements intervenus depuis les premières mesures prises en la matière sous la Révolution et dessine, pour l'avenir, des logiques de patrimonialisation. Et cela d'autant plus que le double point de vue d'amateur d'art et de commis voyageur qu'assume un touriste qui (re)découvre la France en Huron ouvre au maximum le prisme d'une vision dessillée, déprise de toute doxa. Une liberté qui voit Stendhal s'intéresser à ce qui doit être retenu et valorisé dans l'héritage français, où il découpe de véritables listes, mettant ainsi sous tension la notion même de patrimoine.

En France, c'est aux entours de la Révolution que le contenu que recouvre la notion de patrimoine se voit massivement questionné et investi, au moment où se pose l'épineuse question de l'identité de la nation, dont la circonscription implique, avec l'examen de la mémoire nationale, que soit spécifié ce qui, en son sein, doit être valorisé ou, *a contrario*, oblitéré. De ce point de vue, l'acte de naissance de cette problématique peut être rapporté à l'abbé Grégoire qui forge, dès 1782, la catégorie de 'patrimoine culturel', avant qu'Aubin-Louis Millin, le premier, n'en vienne, en 1790, précisément devant la représentation nationale, à évoquer la Bastille comme un 'monument historique'. Si, dans la France révolutionnaire, elle s'attache d'abord au patrimoine bâti, la patrimonialisation va progressivement étendre son domaine de compétences, préparant les voies à la Convention de l'UNESCO de 1972, qui réalise l'extension maximale du principe patrimonial, à la fois naturel et culturel.

Entre ce *terminus a quo* et ce *terminus ad quem*, les années 1830 s'avèrent déterminantes dans la négociation de la notion de patrimoine, en pleine redéfinition, entre les mesures arrêtées par la Révolution française (suivie en cela par toute la politique impériale) pour identifier un corpus identitaire dont il est décrété d'utilité publique de préserver la mémoire – ce qu'assume avec volontarisme la politique de muséalisation, entamée dès 1790, avec le catalogage des biens culturels qu'entreprend Alexandre Lenoir dans son dépôt-musée des Petits-Augustins – et les bouleversements qui s'annoncent[1] avec la révolution industrielle, porteuse d'une autre idéologie. Avant que le consensus national finalement acquis sous la Troisième République n'impose une formalisation presque cultuelle du patrimoine à honorer, dont Pierre Nora a pu recenser les principaux items dans ses *Lieux de mémoire* (1984).

Dans ce long processus d'assimilation référentielle, les années 1830 jouent un rôle moteur, marquées qu'elles sont par la recherche d'un consensus national qui réconcilie la France nouvelle, bourgeoise et libérale, consacrée par la Révolution, et la France aristocratique disparue avec l'Ancien Régime, et qui, partant, accouchent aussi d'un nouveau rapport entre passé et présent quand Guizot, revenant sur le vandalisme révolutionnaire, jetant les bases d'une gestion revue et corrigée de l'héritage, déclarait dès 1828:

> [Avoir] à cœur, tout en servant la cause actuelle, de ramener parmi nous un sentiment de justice et sympathie envers nos anciens souvenirs, envers cette ancienne société française qui a laborieusement et glorieusement vécu pendant quinze siècles pour amasser cet héritage de civilisation que nous avons recueilli. C'est un désordre grave et un grand affaiblissement chez une nation que l'oubli et le dédain de son passé (336).

Moment charnière que ce que d'aucuns ont appelé le "moment Guizot" (Poulot, "Birth"), où c'est la notion même de patrimoine qui est mise sous tension. Parvenu au pouvoir, le 10 août 1830, Guizot "fait de l'héritage culturel un enjeu de gouvernement" (Poulot, *Musée* 13), le support privilégié d'une cohésion sociale garantie par une fierté nationale puisée à la continuité des gloires et illustrations françaises, qu'il s'agit de réveiller. La création, en octobre 1830, de l'Inspection générale des Monuments historiques[2] – d'abord confiée à Ludovic Vitet puis, en 1834, à Prosper Mérimée – sera l'un des instruments de cette politique que Guizot poursuivra, de 1832 à 1837, en tant que ministre de l'Instruction publique, diligentant des recherches visant à exhumer et à publier des archives inédites de la littérature, de la philosophie, des sciences et des arts considérés dans leurs rapports avec l'histoire générale de la France qui mobilisent les meilleurs esprits: Augustin Thierry, Edgar Quinet, Jules Michelet ou Eugène Sue. Couronnement de l'édifice, Guizot est, avec Thierry et Michelet, du cartel d'historiens qui conseille Louis-Philippe dans son programme de muséalisation du palais de Versailles, entreprise de réconciliation s'il en est, arrêtée dès 1832 et mise en chantier en 1833 (Francastel), où éclate, autour de la mémoire collective, l'enjeu de

---

1 En France du moins car, en Angleterre, ils sont déjà avérés.
2 Le 21 octobre 1830, un rapport de Guizot conclut à la création d'un poste d'Inspecteur général des Monuments historiques. Il sera suivi, en 1834, par l'institution d'un Comité historique des Arts et des Monuments rebaptisé, en 1837, Commission des monuments historiques, qui recense les bâtiments méritant protection.

l'héritage, pleinement assumé dans un Versailles nationalisé devenu Musée historique dédié 'à toutes les gloires de la France'.

Parallèlement à la mise sur pied d'un étagement de services relevant de l'État chargés d'établir une nomenclature, l'idée de revue qu'implique désormais la conservation, et d'abord l'identification même, du patrimoine qui repose dorénavant sur des listes, est assumée par le principe du voyage, qui gouvernait déjà l'entreprise de recensement menée par l'un des précurseurs – sous la Révolution[3] et sous l'Empire[4] – de cette recension, Aubin-Louis Millin, mais que devait considérablement populariser la série, inaugurée en 1820, des *Voyages pittoresques et romantiques dans l'ancienne France*, dont le succès colossal[5] allait jeter sur les routes écrivains et amateurs, partie prenante d'une histoire nationale dont – signes des temps démocratiques ouverts par la Révolution – chacun entend s'emparer, générant un débat fécond qui engage, par le biais du patrimoine, la notion même d'idée nationale, que la Révolution vient de violemment secouer, imposant d'en reformuler le contenu. Et ceci pour le passé comme pour l'avenir.

C'est dire que l'examen de la question patrimoniale ne relève pas du supplément d'âme réservé à une petite communauté élitiste d'érudits mais bien d'une urgence véritablement nationale, grosse de l'image de la France, au dedans comme au dehors, urgence que manifeste aussi l'inflation de tout ce qui concourt à dresser une topographie de la France révolutionnée: gravures qui accompagnent les *Voyages pittoresques*, œuvrant à l'appropriation du territoire; statistiques, avec ce monument qu'est le grand classique de Charles Dupin, *Forces productives et commerciales de la France*, qui, en 1827 concourt à dresser un véritable Tableau de la France avant que Michelet ne donne le sien en 1833, authentique symbiose entre géographie et histoire qui acclimate l'idée d'une dialectique charnelle entre un territoire et une culture. C'est aussi là que s'origine, au-delà de la démocratisation des transports qui rend la circulation plus aisée, cette fièvre voyageuse qui saisit la librairie française, qui toujours s'accompagne d'un regard taxinomique. Tout en surfant sur la vogue, venue du XVIIIe siècle, des récits viatiques, qu'ils soient issus du grand Tour ou de *L'Itinéraire de Paris à Jérusalem* que Chateaubriand fait paraître en 1811, où l'on se promène en terre(s) reçue(s) comme incontestable(s) de culture et de patrimoine, fleurit une littérature d'un

3 Aubin-Louis Millin de Grandmaison, *Antiquités nationales ou Recueil de monumens pour servir à l'Histoire générale et particulière de l'Empire françois, tels que Tombeaux, Inscriptions, Statues, Vitraux, Fresques, etc. tirés des Abbayes, Monastères, Châteaux, et autres lieux devenus domaines nationaux. Présenté à l'Assemblée Nationale constituante, et favorablement accueillie par Elle, le 9 décembre 1790.*
4 Millin, *Voyage*, vaste synthèse des données recueillies au cours d'un voyage d'étude de deux ans (1804–1806). Il sera suivi, en 1813–1815, d'un voyage en Italie qui donnera aussi lieu à un inventaire raisonné.
5 Sous l'impulsion du baron Taylor, qui sait s'entourer de pinceaux et de plumes aux compétences éprouvées (dont Charles Nodier), 24 forts volumes, abondamment illustrés de lithographies paraissent de 1820 à 1874, balisant le territoire français: Normandie (1820, 1825, 1878), Franche-Comté (1825), Auvergne (1829, 1833), Languedoc (1833, 1834, 1835, 1837), Picardie (1835, 1837, 1840, 1845), Bretagne (1845, 1846), Dauphiné (1854), Champagne (1857), Bourgogne (1863).

type nouveau, mais dont la tonalité ironique ne doit pas masquer le sérieux, dont la série à succès d'Étienne de Jouy réalise le parangon, en promenant ses Hermites[6] jusqu'en province, enfin légitimée, dans une nation désormais une et indivisible, comme une composante du territoire, qui doit comme telle être parcourue. Une double tradition dont les textes de Stendhal que nous voudrions examiner ici nous paraissent également participer.

Inséparable de l'invention des sciences historiques qui se joue alors, dans les années 1820–1830, autour des frères Thierry, de Mignet, Quinet, Michelet, Barante, Thiers ou Guizot, qui visent à doter la France, après le cataclysme révolutionnaire et les réfections identitaires qu'il impose, d'une ontologie qui ravaude les déchirures de l'histoire et assure la permanence de soi à soi, c'est bien de cette dynamique que relève ce massif formé de trois textes de Stendhal qui composent ce qu'il est convenu d'appeler ses "Voyages en France" (les *Mémoires d'un touriste*, publiés en 1838; le *Voyage dans le Midi de la France* et le *Voyage en France*, contemporains bien que publiés à titre posthume[7]). En témoignerait, s'il en était besoin, la part que Stendhal réserve à une question qui cristallise l'identité nationale en construction, celle des races à l'origine de la nation France. Pleinement relancé par l'abbé Sieyès à la veille même de la Révolution dans son célèbre pamphlet "Qu'est-ce que le Tiers-État?", le débat, qui oppose des Gaulois rattachés à la souche indigène et populaire de la nation à des Francs qui auraient importé la féodalité de Germanie, qui a aussi fait les beaux jours de l'Académie Celtique[8], rebondit chez Stendhal, dans l'opposition qu'il admet des Kymris, des Gaëls et des Ibères (*MdT* 94–7; 298–301).

Relevant expressément de cette littérature viatique propice à l'inventaire, à la comparaison, à la hiérarchisation etc., s'ils semblent de prime abord privilé-

---

6 Étienne de Jouy, *L'Hermite de la Chaussée-d'Antin, ou observations sur les mœurs et les caractères français au commencement du XIXe siècle* (1812), *Le Franc-Parleur, suite de l'Hermite de la Chaussée-d'Antin* (1815), *L'Hermite de la Guyane* (1816); Étienne de Jouy et Antoine Jay, *L'Hermite en province* (1818), *Les Hermites en prison, ou consolation de Sainte-Pélagie* (1823), *Les Hermites en liberté* (1824).
7 Toutes nos références à ces textes, désormais abrégés *MdT*, *VMF* et *VF* iront à l'édition qu'en a donnée Victor Del Litto.
8 Au moment où, sur la scène européenne, s'affirme la singularité de la voie française, l'Académie celtique, instituée en 1804, s'emploie à lui chercher des cautions. Autour de ses fondateurs, Jacques Cambry et Jacques Le Brigant, elle rassemble 'antiquaires', érudits et savants parmi les plus éminents, dont Volney, Alexandre Lenoir, La Révellière-Lépeaux, Millin etc. qui se proposent de "retrouver le passé de la France, recueillir les vestiges archéologiques, linguistiques et coutumiers de l'ancienne civilisation gauloise", au moment où l'on suppose que le centralisme révolutionnaire va définitivement réduire les particularismes locaux. Son action passe par des enquêtes, telle celle, fameuse, de 1807, qui s'appuie sur le levier des préfectures pour diffuser un questionnaire qui dresse un état des lieux. Lorsqu'elle se rebaptise, en 1813, Société des Antiquaires de France, sa mission se voit élargie à d'autres sources, mais l'accent reste mis sur la souche gauloise, vécue comme indigène, ainsi que le précisent encore les statuts de 1829 de la Société, qui entend s'attacher aux "recherches sur les langues, la géographie, la chronologie, l'histoire, la littérature, les arts et les antiquités celtiques, grecques, romaines et du Moyen-Âge mais principalement des Gaules et de la nation française jusqu'au XVIe siècle inclusivement."

gier une réflexion égotiste[9] – "qu'est-ce qui me plairait à moi" (*MdT* 242) – les *Voyages en France* de Stendhal mènent en réalité une enquête de terrain sur ce qui est digne de retenir l'attention, réflexion d'autant plus fondée que Stendhal, fin connaisseur de l'Italie et de l'Angleterre, a également vu l'Allemagne et la Russie dans les fourgons de Napoléon et possède donc de solides éléments comparatifs. Si, au contraire de son ami Mérimée qui, attaché à l'Administration, quadrille la France pour la cause de l'Inventaire général des Monuments historiques[10], ce n'est pas une perspective de conservation qui guide Stendhal, du moins s'intéresse-t-il expressément à ce qui doit être retenu, à ce qui fait patrimoine et, au final – l'innovation est aussi là – à l'intrication organique du naturel et du culturel au sein de l'objet patrimonial si, comme le découvre le touriste, "l'intérêt du paysage ne suffit pas; à la longue, il faut un intérêt moral ou historique. Alors il y a harmonie fort agréable" (*VF* 468).

Alors que les mentalités sont loin d'avoir encore dépassé le dualisme reçu entre nature et culture, la conception des réalités patrimoniales que ces textes véhiculent, tranchant sur le tout-venant d'une production en plein essor, est d'une rare modernité.

S'y élabore même une sociologie du patrimoine, en même temps qu'une écologie du regard[11], dans le divorce – conséquence de la voie bourgeoise prise par la Révolution, que 1830 n'a fait que confirmer[12] – entre une typologie collective des vecteurs patrimoniaux sur lesquels s'appuie la mythologie nationale et leur réelle transitivité, quand le 'touriste' stendhalien marque souvent sa distance d'avec ce qu'il perçoit d'une politique de patrimonialisation qui s'appuie sur les valeurs bourgeoises et marchandes et propose un panthéon personnel qui ne dépend pas seulement de sa valeur esthétique, mais de son décalage avec l'idéologie dominante.

C'est donc un livre extrêmement complexe que Stendhal entreprend en 1837, à un moment de l'histoire de France où les impératifs de réconciliation nationale s'expriment concrètement dans la reconnaissance de marqueurs d'identité, qui s'imposent comme véritables lieux de mémoire. Au propre comme au figuré, avec le projet mûri dès 1832 par Louis-Philippe d'un Musée de l'histoire de France, musée justement inauguré en 1837 en présence du gratin des Lettres françaises,

---

9   Selon une pente que la critique est un peu trop prompte à reconnaître comme dominante chez Stendhal.
10 Il laissera une série de *Voyages* dont les premiers, *Notes d'un Voyage dans le Midi de la France* et *Notes d'un voyage dans l'Ouest de la France*, publiés avant ses propres relations, seront abondamment mis à profit par Stendhal. Mais, au-delà de cette question des sources, le rôle qui revient à Mérimée dans l'inventaire et dans la (re)découverte du patrimoine monumental, roman et gothique, est absolument décisif: ses notes de voyage et ses rapports de 1832 livrent de précieuses indications sur la situation des objets patrimoniaux dans la France d'alors.
11 Entendue dans le sens de la sensibilité aux données environnementales qu'ont récemment mise en évidence les travaux intervenus dans le champ de l'écocritique.
12 "On jouit enfin depuis 1830 des réformes introduites par Sieyès, Mirabeau, Carnot et les autres grands hommes de 1792" (*MdT* 152).

de Michelet à Dumas, Balzac et Hugo[13], preuve de la résonance que trouvent ces questions auprès des intellectuels.

C'est dans ce contexte éminemment mouvant que Stendhal imagine – au sens propre, Stendhal étant bien loin d'avoir réellement visité tous les lieux dont il parle – des *Voyages en France* qui sont à la fois un inventaire et une prospective, un geste qui solidarise passé et avenir. S'il ne tranche pas, le texte revêt une véritable valeur expérimentale, qui élabore des outils pour penser le patrimoine en même temps qu'il construit une vision. Une vision jamais arrêtée et, à l'image du voyage lui-même, découpé en étapes, sans cesse remise en branle, complétée, corrigée ou confirmée, mais toujours *in progress*. Le touriste stendhalien – dont la dénomination a tant posé problème, et pas seulement par esprit de clocher, du fait de l'origine anglo-saxonne du terme qui serait, pour la première fois acclimaté en français, mais bien aussi par sa nouveauté, indicielle d'une nouveauté qui est aussi celle du regard porté sur les objets dignes de retenir l'attention– pourrait bien signer une nouvelle relation de l'homme à son environnement, milieu naturel aussi bien que culturel. Ne serait-ce que parce que, comme l'inspecteur des monuments historiques, il classe et établit des listes, des palmarès.

Touriste, le voyageur ne l'est toutefois pas tout à fait qui, ci-devant marchand de fer que ces affaires jettent sur les routes, tient aussi du commis-voyageur. Dans ces années 1820–1840 qui sont celles de la révolution ferroviaire, le geste stendhalien, qui fait passer la partition au sein même de la figure 'héroïque', instance narrative organisatrice du point de vue, dit bien la volonté de tenir ensemble les deux France, celle du passé et celle de l'avenir.

Loin de ces guides, Baedeker ou Joanne, qui font alors les beaux jours de la librairie, le détour par la fiction sert l'auteur dissimulé derrière le touriste quand la double valence du personnage, à la fois voyageur de commerce et amateur d'art, recouvre la double voie qui s'ouvre pour l'écriture: "plate" ou "simple" et "naturelle," selon que l'on officie derrière son comptoir ou que l'on revisite pour le journal que forment ces mémoires, sensations et réflexions pour leur donner une portée généralisante (*MdT* 5). C'est en tout cas poser la question des voix et des filtres qui président à la vision et la modèlent.

Car il entre assurément dans ce touriste du Stendhal, *Arrigo Beyle, Milanese*, véritable Italien en France. Et ce d'autant plus que ses fonctions de consul le fixent en Italie – quand bien même ce n'est pas dans sa "riante Lombardie" (Pas de source précise car c'est passim que Stendhal parle de "riante Lombardie," de "pays de son cœur") – l'étrangeant un peu plus à une France que le fonctionnaire qu'il est ne fréquente plus que durant ses congés. C'est du reste l'un d'eux qu'il

---

13 Un Hugo lucide sur les enjeux de l'opération et pleinement convaincu qui, le 18 octobre 1837, écrit dans son Journal: "Ce que Louis-Philippe a fait à Versailles est bien. Avoir accompli cette œuvre, c'est avoir été grand comme roi et impartial comme philosophe; c'est avoir fait un monument national d'un monument monarchique; c'est avoir mis une idée immense dans le passé, 1789 vis à vis de 1688, l'empereur chez le roi, Napoléon chez Louis XIV, c'est avoir donné à ce livre magnifique qu'on appelle l'histoire de France cette magnifique reliure qu'on appelle Versailles" (33).

mettra à profit pour, tout ensemble, voyager et formaliser ses impressions dans ce qui deviendra *Les Mémoires d'un touriste*. Pour autant, dans cette tension entre éloignement et proximité, entre France et Italie, entre le même et l'autre, c'est bien une véritable dialectique qui joue et qui met en jeu, en même temps que l'identité nationale, l'identité stendhalienne, laquelle ne se conçoit pas en dehors de la confrontation au référent français, sans cesse mis à distance mais sans cesse interrogé. C'est paradoxalement la prise de distance avec le grand Autre stendhalien qu'est finalement la France qui annule la mise à distance et prépare des retrouvailles que tous les écrits stendhaliens portent en germe; les plus récents comme *Lucien Leuwen* ou la *Vie de Henry Brulard* comme ceux plus profondément ancrés dans l'organisation psychique: en témoignent la correspondance comme les journaux.

De fait, il y a dans cet état des lieux dressé pour la France un état des lieux de mémoire qui appartient par essence au questionnement stendhalien sur ce qui fait la civilisation et sa valeur universelle. Ce qui n'élimine pas le subjectivisme, consubstantiel à la vision stendhalienne et, paradoxalement, seule voie d'accès à l'universel.

Loin de la doxa, de la doctrine sinon de l'endoctrinement, le touriste pose comme principe d'appréhension et de compréhension du réel la nécessité de "voir par ses yeux" (*MdT* 13–4) et se récrie devant le Parisien qui "appelle beau […] ce qui est vanté dans le journal ou ce qui est fertile et produit beaucoup d'argent" (*MdT* 71), critique récurrente chez Stendhal, pas dupe de ce que les catégories esthétiques sont tissues de déterminations qui leur sont étrangères.

C'est imposer d'emblée un nouveau théâtre d'investigation, loin de ces deux aimants – Paris et l'Italie – que la critique identifie comme les pôles fertiles et tenseurs de la création stendhalienne et faire, *a contrario*, de la province une terre d'authenticité, sorte de *terra incognita*, au moins culturellement, en cohérence avec la voie française de développement, faite de centralisme.

Les *Voyages en France* de Stendhal s'intéressent au patrimoine sous toutes ses espèces:

1. Les musées, que notre 'touriste', en amateur qu'il est, ne manque pas de visiter, une fois ses affaires faites, dessinant, de Vannes à Grenoble, de Lyon à Marseille, une carte décentralisée des biens culturels, véritables bien nationaux mis à disposition de la nation entière dans ces outils à vocation pédagogique que sont les musées, qui proposent à l'appropriation des citoyens un pan du patrimoine national. Tout en œuvrant à la (ré)conciliation nationale tant, comme Napoléon, en collationnant l'ensemble du passé, le musée, même départemental, avouant tout l'héritage, peut lui aussi se dire national. On est alors, dans cette période décisive du point de vue de la gestion de l'héritage qui se caractérise par la tentative de liquider l'authenticité primitive (au sens que Benjamin donne à ce terme) des œuvres au profit d'une authenticité neuve, à laquelle le musée donne un contenu. Du moins jusqu'à la fin du XIXe, après quoi intervient une forme de réfication des œuvres, d'ailleurs présente dès l'origine, comme le sait, dès l'An VI, le *Journal de Paris* pour qui "l'Apollon ne sera plus ici un dieu mais un meuble" (Poulot, *Surveiller* 485). 'Ici', c'est-à-dire au Louvre, où l'expédie le traité de Tolentino (19 février 1797) qui organise la prédation des objets d'art italiens, lesquels viennent renforcer les fonds des musées français. C'était poser la question de l'opérativité de l'œuvre d'art au-delà de son contexte de production et, par delà, celle de modèles universels susceptibles d'œuvrer à l'édification du genre humain tout entier. C'était poser la question de l'historicité des œuvres d'art. Il est à cet égard assez significatif que le touriste ignore délibérément le Louvre, espace par excellence du triomphe où s'exhibent les "acquisitions" du peuple-roi (Poulot, *Musée* 215–6). Manière d'occulter le centre? De se séparer d'une vision totalitaire de l'outil muséal, qui a d'abord été celle des promoteurs révolutionnaires de l'idée muséale, ralliés à l'imposition d'un modèle universel d'ordre politico-esthétique depuis un musée central, parisien, qui réunirait l'ensemble des paradigmes à diffuser, vers des musées provinciaux, dont la plupart, au moins quant au projet, datent de l'An II ou de l'An III, qui devaient initialement en présenter des répliques à l'échelle du département quand bien même l'idéal démocratique qui meut ces conservateurs sent aussi la nécessité de doter les musées départementaux des mêmes missions que le musée parisien. Une difficulté d'articuler les échelles sensible chez le touriste, bien au fait de l'histoire de ces lieux de mémoire, qui rappelle, à Lyon:

> En 1807, 1808 et années suivantes, le Musée Napoléon qui était encombré de tableaux versa son trop plein dans plusieurs musées de province […] plusieurs des tableaux, fruits des victoires de 1796, sont restés dans les départements (*MdT* 116).

Il est vrai que s'il flétrit parfois les musées de province, ceux-ci ne jouissent pas toujours des moyens nécessaires à la haute politique qu'on leur confie. Celui de Rennes ne reçoit, en l'An VIII, que 150 F du département, et ses recettes ne montent qu'à 72 F en l'An IX. Mais en l'An X, c'est la manne: le département allonge 300 F qui permettent de faire encadrer des toiles et de confectionner des rampes qui maintiennent le public à distance (Poulot, *Musée* 238–9). Mais si, bien souvent, ces institutions sont réduites à vivre d'expédients, le manque de moyens n'explique pas tout et, à Vannes, pourtant directement affiliée à la culture en tant que "capitale des Vénètes qui sont allés donner leur nom à Venise" (*MdT* 311), l'aspect des monuments "n'est que triste" et manque "d'âme": la faute en incombe à la "richesse", qui corrompt jusqu'au musée même dont les "vastes salles disent bien: 'Nous appartenons à…'" (*MdT* 311). Ce musée, qui compte un Guerchin mais le laisse ronger d'humidité, bien représentatif de l'aridité du capital – "[i]l faut que l'on ait en ce pays-ci bien peu de goût pour les arts; un musée aussi pauvrement tenu fait honte à une ville aussi riche" (*MdT* 314) – vaut démonstration des vertus d'une politique culturelle, qui ne tient pas uniquement à un budget, mais bien à des valeurs. Démonstration reconduite à Marseille, dont le musée regorge de belles pièces que l'œil expert de Philippe L*** n'hésite néanmoins pas à réagencer, préconisant même de rendre à l'art toute sa portée civique en invitant à exposer dans l'espace public "un magnifique Rubens, une *Chasse au sanglier*, qui honore le musée de Marseille": "Je voudrais le placer dans une niche, à huit pieds de hauteur, sur le quai qui conduit à la Bourse. Là, il serait vu chaque jour par des milliers de promeneurs" (*VF* 529).

En cela, comme Stendhal, le touriste, que sa malice porte à vouloir rééduquer les financiers qui se rendent à la Bourse, se montre jacobin. En premier lieu pour ce qu'il se refuse à exploiter le vandalisme, topos attendu des sélections révolutionnaires, ce qui, quand l'attitude face au vandalisme sert à partager le corps des citoyens face à l'événement révolutionnaire et à sa violence, est encore une sélection, condamner le vandalisme étant le fait des tenants des nouvelles valeurs, individualistes et sentimentales. Bien plutôt, Stendhal se montre l'héritier des hommes de l'An II, de leurs principes et de leurs méthodes et reste sur la ligne de la Commission temporaire des arts[14], formée le 1er septembre 1793 pour diligenter l'Instruction sur la manière d'inventorier et de conserver, dans toute l'étendue de la République, tous les objets qui peuvent servir aux arts, aux sciences et à l'enseignement (mars 1794), prônant un changement de terminologie où les beaux-arts (ou arts libéraux) deviendraient "arts de l'histoire," manière de "montre[r] leur véritable but" (Tuetey). Au reste, lorsque, Inspecteur du Mobilier de la Couronne dirigé par son cousin Daru, Stendhal sera chargé en 1810 de l'inventaire du Musée Napoléon, il se montrera enthousiaste du savoir-faire typologique issu de ces enquêtes qui, en procédant au recensement du patrimoine, s'appuient sur des méthodes descriptives poussées au point qu'elles permettent de "décrire en une ligne un tableau quelconque, si beau qu'il soit, même la *Transfiguration*" (Del Litto 1507).

De fait, si la sécheresse synthétique ne peut que convenir à qui déclarait "pour prendre le ton, li[re] chaque matin deux ou trois pages du code civil" (Stendhal, *Correspondance* 410), reste que l'essentiel tient bien à la fonction de l'histoire, qui seule vectorise le patrimoine et lui donne son sens. Telle est la leçon reçue à Avignon, objet et d'une transfiguration et d'une transsubstantiation: "En entrant à Avignon, on se croit dans une ville d'Italie" car, d'un fleuve l'autre, on est bien "ici" comme "aux bords du Tibre" (*MdT* 156). L'évocation de la campagne d'Italie, avant que la visite du musée n'embraie sur les "tableaux de l'école italienne" (*MdT* 157) réinsère les paysages – naturels et culturels – du Midi à la fois dans la longue durée de l'histoire, matrice de la civilisation, et dans l'expérience personnelle de Stendhal. Laquelle éclate tout naturellement dans sa ville natale de Grenoble où la visite du musée, pourtant "riche de beaux tableaux italiens" – dont, plus fort encore que la Commission des arts, Philippe L*** déclare "supprime[r]

---

14 Cette Commission a une conception large du patrimoine, qui intègre la nature. Le 13 octobre 1794, elle s'élève contre les "citoyens inconsidérés" qui montent la garde à l'Arsenal où "ils se permettent de dégrader des arbres, dépouillés de leur écorce et hachés de coups de sabre" (469) et prend des mesures pour faire cesser ces dégradations.

ici la description"! (*MdT* 393) – tourne pour le touriste au 'syndrome de Stendhal' quand, profitant d'une fenêtre pour plonger son regard dans les étagements de plans du paysage dauphinois, l'œil devient véritablement fenêtre de l'âme: plus d'angle mort alors, mais l'aperture d'un champ de vision qui porte à 360 degrés quand l'ouverture de la fenêtre métaphorise la résolution de la dialectique du dedans et du dehors dans la surimpression des images abouties de la nature et de la culture.

Manière aussi, peut-être, d'ouvrir les portes du musée et de résoudre cette tension dialectique qui découle des deux voies offertes au traitement du patrimoine entre une communion privée avec les œuvres qui se donne cours au musée et une destination publique qui s'affiche dans l'investissement urbain – arcs, statues etc. – avec laquelle a renoué le programme révolutionnaire qui s'est voulu éducation pour tous, via un programme décoratif.

2. Architecture et monuments. En dépit des pétitions de principe – et de certains gestes à portée symbolique telle l'inauguration du Muséum, le 10 août 1793, date symbolique à laquelle on procède aussi à la destruction des tombeaux royaux à Saint-Denis, dont une toile fameuse d'Hubert Robert conserve le souvenir[15], manière de signaler qu'une nouvelle légitimité relaie une ancienne – loin du passé d'avoir fait table rase, son empreinte demeure partout visible, singulièrement dans la physionomie urbaine, où se donne toujours à lire un idéal de culture civique.

Une telle destination, bien davantage que les monuments conçus comme remarquables, retient un touriste qui n'abdique jamais sa qualité de citoyen. De fait, si le voyageur, de bonne composition, met un point d'honneur à se renseigner sur les curiosités locales, il court parfois le risque d'une déconvenue, ainsi qu'il le consigne dans son journal: "Nantes, le 1er juillet 1837 – Cette journée a été consacrée à la revue des monuments publics. C'est une des pires corvées imposées au pauvre voyageur arrivant pour la première fois dans un pays" (*MdT* 259). C'est qu'il faut s'accorder sur ce qu'il convient d'entendre par 'monument public': musée ou halle aux grains? Des reconversions n'étant, au reste, pas à exclure, comme à Nantes même:

> Mais comment supposer que MM. Les échevins auraient gaspillé les fonds de l'octroi pour une babiole aussi complètement improductive qu'une collection de tableaux? Il est infiniment plus probable que le bâtiment était destiné à un grenier d'abondance (*MdT* 252).

C'est que, à Nantes, comme à Lorient, sur cette façade atlantique tout entière vouée au commerce, les villes sont "bâtie[s] par la main de la raison" (*MdT* 306), entendons de la raison marchande, qui multiplie arsenaux (cf. *MdT* 243 et 308) et entrepôts, tous bâtiments rémunérateurs, loin de l'improductivité des lieux voués à la diffusion du patrimoine – "[l]es bourgeois de Lorient sont trop raison-

---

15 Hubert Robert, *La Violation des caveaux royaux à Saint-Denis*, 1793.

nables pour venir perdre leur temps à entendre de la musique" (*MdT* 308). Aussi, dans ce désert culturel[16] qui est aussi un désert humain, le touriste se montre-t-il toujours soucieux des lieux de convivialité où s'ouvrir en commun aux biens culturels. S'ils sont plutôt caractéristiques du Midi de la France, Rennes même a su investir dans une "salle de spectacle" – que, significativement, elle doit à ses "citoyens" (*MdT* 311) – et jusque dans "une sorte de promenade à couvert (première nécessité dans toute ville qui prétend à un peu de conversation)" (*MdT* 311), élément architectural qui entre plutôt dans la typologie méridionale, de Beaucaire à Orange. Aussi n'est-il nul doute pour le touriste: "Le monument vraiment social de Dol […] c'est la suite d'arcades qui bordent la grande rue marchande et donnent une promenade à couvert" (*MdT* 318).[17]

Un touriste qui se retrouve là encore sur la ligne des spéculations des années révolutionnaires ou impériales, d'accord avec Nicolas Goulet pour reconnaître différentes destinations à un monument et établir un distinguo entre monuments publics (pont, fontaine, halle etc.) et vocation triomphale, qui vise à perpétuer la mémoire d'un grand homme ou d'un événement marquant:

> "Les premiers doivent porter un caractère de simplicité et de sévérité. Les autres doivent être riches, élégans et pompeux. On ne peut donc les confondre ensemble". Et d'autant moins que "ce sera toujours l'utilité de l'objet qui frappera le vulgaire" (231–2).

De fait, si à Nantes, un arsenal symbolisait l'utile, cessant par là de participer au beau (*MdT* 243), à Marseille "aucun établissement industriel, aucune idée d'utilité, rien de petit" (*VMF* 706). Au-delà de l'antagonisme Nord/Sud, pleinement opératoire chez Stendhal, y compris en matière de politique patrimoniale, il y a chez lui une conception platonicienne qui corrèle le beau au bon. De là procède la remotivation du signe 'utile', au subjectivisme assumé. À Nantes, c'est d'entrer en système avec "l'intérêt particulier" d'une bourgeoisie égoïste qui fait fi de l'intérêt collectif qui le disqualifie quand, à Barcelone, "on prêche la vertu la plus pure, l'utilité de tous" (*VF* 565), prédication maximisante qui rend à l'utilité son emploi absolu. Il est une autre utilité que l'utilitarisme comme il est une autre civilisation que la marchande. Dans la typologie des monuments établie par Goulet, ce sont bien évidemment aux 'monuments publics' que va l'adhésion du touriste. Contristé par "une ridicule statue de Duguay-Trouin" en "culottes flottantes" à Saint-Malo (*MdT* 322), il est immédiatement transporté par ce qui réalise pour lui l'essence même de l'ouvrage d'art, le pont, agent de liaison.

Celui de Saint-Esprit est la preuve de ce qu'"on avait en ce pays une vraie passion pour le bien public" (*MdT* 155). Il est vrai que c'était en 1265. Mais il ne fait là que préparer le véritable choc, tant esthétique qu'éthique, qui attend le

---

16 Philippe L*** rapporte, scandalisé, l'affaire de ce paysan ayant exhumé quantité de parures gauloises sans pouvoir trouver à Rennes de connaisseur suffisamment éclairé pour s'en porter acquéreur au point de devoir porter les reliques à un orfèvre qui les fonde (*MdT* 314–5).
17 Et de même au Havre (*MdT* 338).

touriste au Pont-du-Gard, "simple aqueduc" sans "aucune apparence de luxe et d'ornement" "qui conduisait à Nîmes les eaux de la fontaine d'Eure," truchement d'une véritable révélation:

> L'âme est laissée tout entière à elle-même, et l'attention est ramenée forcément à cet ouvrage du peuple-roi qu'on a sous les yeux. Ce monument doit agir, ce me semble, comme une musique sublime, c'est un événement pour les cœurs d'élite, les autres rêvent avec admiration à l'argent qu'il a dû coûter (*MdT* 365).

'Arts de l'histoire', les vestiges sont aussi les dépositaires d'une morale incarnée:

> Les Romains faisaient de ces choses étonnantes, non pour inspirer l'admiration mais simplement et quand elles étaient utiles. L'idée éminemment moderne, l'arrangement pour faire de l'effet, est rejetée bien loin de l'âme du spectateur, et si l'on songe à cette manie, c'est pour la mépriser (*MdT* 365).

En dépit des apparences, Philippe L*** est loin de n'être que l'homme du passé et son rapport aux monuments historiques dit bien quels enjeux nouveaux ils recèlent: chez le touriste stendhalien, jamais un monument ne vient fossiliser l'environnement dans lequel il s'inscrit: ses leçons diffusent toujours, et c'est au présent qu'il parle. Sinon pour la réalité du présent, du moins pour son idéalité. Il acquiert ainsi une valeur d'exemplarité qui lui vient de la typologie dans laquelle il s'inscrit, au moins pour l'observateur – pour le Pont-du-Gard, l'utilité publique, à laquelle est toujours associé le monde romain, porteur d'une idée de la citoyenneté d'autant plus forte qu'elle a été réactivée par la Révolution française et qu'il y a, partant, déplacement – qui rencontre ce qu'Aloïs Riegl[18] appelle "valeur d'ancienneté" et dont Roland Recht[19] précise qu'elle est "indépendante de la beauté ou de l'exemplarité artistiques d'un monument: elle est synonyme de valeur de sentimentalité" (19). Et telle est bien l'expérience que Bourges réserve au touriste, Bourges qu'il tient en exécration jusqu'à ce qu'il avise une tour qu'il reconnaît "évidemment" pour "un ouvrage des Romains." Puissant topique: "à l'instant mon profond dégoût pour la ville a diminué de moitié," sans que le touriste se dissimule le manque d'objectivité de ses choix: "Je ne dis pas que ce sentiment soit juste, seulement, il en est ainsi" (*MdT* 196).

Toute la réflexion sur les ruines, omniprésente dans ces textes où le touriste, digne émule d'Arcisse de Caumont et d'Alexandre de Laborde, qu'il possède à fond, n'hésite jamais, comme à Autun, à prendre son bâton de pèlerin pour courir les antiques[20], entre dans ce paradigme qui se confond avec l'idée de liberté. Ainsi à Auch, ville mal bâtie que seul peut rédimer son passé romain, "Auguste"

---

18 Alois Riegl, *Le Culte moderne du monument. Son essence et sa genèse*, 1984.
19 Roland Recht, *Penser le Patrimoine*, 2008.
20 "*Autun, le 30 avril 1837* – Hier j'eus du courage, couvert de poussière et en habit de voyage, j'affrontai la curiosité et les regards hébétés des provinciaux, le tout pour aller voir des antiquités" (*MdT* 39).

y ayant "laiss[é] une colonie qui se gouverna par ses propres lois et qui nomma ses magistrats. C'est bien plus de liberté que notre constitution actuelle en accorde à Auch" (*VMF* 682–3). Stendhal reprend là un débat nourri dans lequel intervint l'antiquaire Émeric-David, pour qui les villes fortes d'un patrimoine bâti antique ont un goût plus sûr que celles qui n'en ont pas. Un tel fonctionnement devance quelque peu l'heure que lui fixe Riegl, pour qui l'assomption de la valeur d'ancienneté interviendrait dans la seconde moitié du XIXe siècle, où elle serait appropriée par ces bourgeois conquérants qui gagneraient là, au moment où il s'agit d'inventer de nouvelles sacralités, une affinité avec le passé et comme une caution historique. Mais, à en croire Riegl, la valeur d'ancienneté tiendrait du vernis et serait foncièrement anhistorique. Voire. C'est peut-être justement ce recouvrement de l'histoire et de la mémoire qu'opère le touriste stendhalien, entre valeur d'ancienneté et valeur de remémoration. Mais, il est vrai, contre le goût bourgeois dominant, lui, celui que moque férocement *Bouvard et Pécuchet* (1881), qui flétrit la vogue de l'anticomanie, celui que croque Gautier pour *La Presse*, après l'avoir flétri dans *Mademoiselle de Maupin* (1835), constamment décrié dans les "Voyages" chez ces Français qui, en musique comme en peinture ou en architecture, donnent inconsidérément leur suffrage au pompier et au rococo.[21]

De là, sans doute, les solutions hardies qu'imagine notre voyageur qui n'hésite pas à procéder à des amendements drastiques du paysage urbain. Chalon-sur-Saône est-elle morose? "[O]sons copier un temple d'Athènes ou le Panthéon de Rome, ou du moins la Maison Carrée"[22] "lorsqu'on demandera une petite église", entreprise que seul vient contrarier le fait qu'"elle serait écrasée par la hauteur de nos maisons" (*MdT* 69)! Et à Paris même, "[l]'idée d'avoir" "le Panthéon de Rome, quelques temples de Grèce, ou même la Maison Carrée […] paraîtra toute simple en 1880" (*MdT* 359). Lyon, tout Lugdunum qu'elle est, est exécutée:

> C'est le hasard tout seul qui fait faire des découvertes d'antiquités dans les environs de Lyon, ville si importante pour les Romains, que l'empereur Auguste habita trois ans, etc. Si jamais l'on cherche avec intelligence, sans doute l'on trouvera. Mais ce pays est fait pour s'occuper des métiers à la Jacquard (*MdT* 116),

rendant nécessaire que soit administré un préservatif à l'industrialisme. La destruction de la façade de l'Hôtel de Ville, restaurée par Mansart en 1674, prête à une savoureuse fantasmagorie: "je voudrais la voir rétablir de nouveau en copiant la façade d'un des beaux palais de Venise. Venise est si malheureuse et Lyon si

---

21 "Le Capitole, à Toulouse, est bien couronné par une contrebasse !" (*VMF* 607).
22 En même temps qu'est fantasmée – pendant de ce qu'Hubert Robert ou John Soane imaginent pour la grande galerie du Louvre ou pour la Banque d'Angleterre – la mise à bas des bâtiments modernes: "on bâtissait le Garde-Meuble il y a cinquante ans (cet édifice sera passable lorsqu'il sera en ruines)" (*MdT* 68).

riche, qu'il serait possible d'acheter un palais de Venise, par exemple le palais Vendramin."

Un déménagement où rien n'est laissé au hasard, jusqu'aux détails techniques: "On numéroterait les pierres de la façade et la navigation les amènerait à Lyon" (*MdT* 87). Venise dont on importerait aussi les Procuratie vecchie, dont une "copie exacte" (*VMF* 621) remplacerait avantageusement à Toulouse un Capitole "tout ce qu'il y a de plus laid" (*VMF* 620). À coups d'impératifs prescriptifs, Stendhal orchestre une véritable anamorphose, au moyen d'un processus métaphorique qui procède à des transpositions par où, par le jeu des similitudes et/ou des parentés symboliques, se transmet le sens du patrimoine.

Au-delà de l'idée, chère au tournant des XVIIIe–XIXe siècles, d'un patrimoine universel dont témoignent bien les pratiques américaines de copies en série de référents paradigmatiques – du Capitole à Venise précisément –, c'est l'essence même de l'œuvre d'art qui se voit interroger sous la copie, dont le bénéfice premier est d'en conserver l'essence. Invitation à l'émulation que formulait Lalande dans son fameux *Voyage d'un Français en Italie fait dans les années 1765 et 1766* où il posait que "[l]'entretien de ces monumens & le respect qu'on leur doit n'est point une chose de préjugé, de convention ou même d'intérêt: la philosophie & la politique doivent nous porter à conserver les monuments des hommes illustres, comme un germe pour en produire d'autres" (387). Une position qui devait puissamment œuvrer au revival du néoclassicisme, véritable style international d'alors.

Mais les réfections stendhaliennes dépassent cette doxa, qui se collètent directement avec la philosophie de l'histoire quand, après avoir rêvé après une séduisante géographie fantastique, le touriste revient sur cette tentation d'arrêter l'histoire en reproduisant des modèles esthétiques arrachés à leur milieu, Philippe L*** se félicitant finalement de ce que Colbert n'ait pas été suivi dans sa proposition de translater à Paris la Maison carrée. S'il imagine encore qu'elle puisse y être copiée[23], c'est sans illusion sur les capacités restauratrices de tels artifices: "Puisque notre triste architecture est impuissante à trouver les édifices commandés par le climat et les mœurs, elle devrait plutôt copier les constructions gothiques. Quoi de plus laid que les maisons où elle place des colonnes grecques?" (*MdT* 359).

C'est qu'il en va d'une authentique phénoménologie où, à travers un répertoire typologique, les éléments architecturaux signifient, indiciels des prises qui raccordent le sujet à l'héritage, entre permanence et solution de continuité. À Clermont, en proie à "l'épuisement moral" que procure "la vue d'un fort beau paysage", quand la nature oblitère la culture, le touriste de réclamer comme "d'un prix infini" "la colonne antique la plus insignifiante" (*MdT* 170), vœu exaucé à Nîmes où les colonnes corinthiennes sont "charmantes" (*MdT* 359) quand, à

---

23 "Ce qui serait fort simple maintenant, ce serait d'en faire une copie *exacte* à Paris" (*MdT* 358).

Auray, sous le ciel plombé de la Bretagne, "[i]l faut convenir qu'[…] une colonne corinthienne eût été un contresens" (*MdT* 286).

Partant, si les colonnes corinthiennes figurent évidemment l'aventure d'un style, elles précisent aussi un horizon ontologique, patiemment dégagé par le touriste, au fur et à mesure de ses avancées, la révélation reçue à Nîmes venant en contrepoint de l'analyse des caractères atlantiques:

> La société grossière qui inventa la mode du gothique était lasse du sentiment d'admiration et de satisfaction paisible et raisonnable que donne l'architecture grecque. Ces sentiments ne lui semblaient pas assez saisissants: c'est ainsi que, de nos jours, nous voyons les bourgeois de campagne enluminer les plus belles gravures (*MdT* 311).

Au fort des interrogations sur l'identité nationale qui caractérisent les années 1830, les monuments jouent comme une chaîne révélatrice, où le patrimoine entre dans un rapport harmonique avec sol, paysages et mœurs pour dessiner les lignes d'une axiologie qui oppose un Midi romain ou, à défaut, roman, fort de ses vertus civiques et de son amour de la culture à un Nord gothique, anglisé, bourgeois et calculateur, insensible au patrimoine, s'il n'est financier.

Dans ce moment décisif de l'histoire nationale, l'antagonisme entre ces deux systèmes axiologiques dessine les deux voies qui paraissent s'offrir à l'avenir français. Paraissent, parce qu'avec la lucidité qui le caractérise, Stendhal ne peut ignorer, au moment où il assoit ses analyses sur un principe d'historicité, que la seconde a pour elle la sanction de l'histoire. Aussi ses translations tous azimuts qui prétendent importer la culture dans la civilisation[24] relèvent-elles d'un effort désespéré pour penser ce devenir, à contre-courant des dynamiques en cours.

Reste que ce problème de l'ubiquité qu'affronte le touriste avec les déménagements qu'il envisage rencontre une question dont s'emparera Benjamin en 1935, celle de la reproductibilité de l'œuvre d'art. Questions qui a fait débat dès les prémices de la muséalisation, Quatremère de Quincy s'étant élevé avec virulence contre Lenoir et son Musée des monuments français, "réceptacle de ruines factices", "atelier de démolition," qu'il accuse de "contre-sens." "Les ruines du temps, ces monuments de la fragilité humaine, sont la leçon de l'homme, les autres en sont la honte" (56). Et de tonner contre les (re)montages que proposent les "conservatoires": "Vous y en avez transporté la matière; mais avez-vous pu transporter avec eux ce cortège de sensations, tendres, profondes, mélancoliques, sublimes, qui les environnait? […] Tous ces objets ont perdu leur effet en perdant leur motif" (57).

Avant d'asséner l'argument décisif:

> C'est trop présumer de la puissance de l'Art que de juger ses ouvrages capables de produire, en tout temps, en tout lieu, les mêmes effets;

---

24 Au sens que Kant donne à ces termes dans *Idee zu einer allgemeinen Geschichte in weltbürgerlicher Absicht* ("Idée d'une histoire universelle d'un point de vue cosmopolitique"), 1784.

comme si des sensations de la nature de celles dont il s'agit étaient des effets calculés qui dussent résulter constamment d'un principe mécanique, indépendamment de toute circonstance et de tout concours de la part des causes moralement ou matériellement environnantes (59).

Où la théorie du signe rejoint un matérialisme historique bien entendu. La violence des débats est à la hauteur des enjeux, qui tiennent à rien de moins qu'à la philosophie de l'histoire, d'une histoire en forme de Janus dont il s'agit de préciser, sous peine de se condamner à ne pouvoir habiter le présent, si elle doit regarder vers le passé ou vers l'avenir. Aussi la querelle référentielle est-elle longue, quand l'ubiquité des chefs-d'œuvre est déjà formulée par le président de Brosses, qui suggère d'établir à Versailles – déjà! Et le Musée de l'histoire de France de 1837 en comptera beaucoup – un musée des copies, où figureraient les œuvres canoniques (Guillerme 140–45). Ingres, à qui sa position de directeur de la villa Médicis confère une parole officielle, ne récusera pas cette ligne, qui soutient qu'"[i]l faut copier" et "étudier les antiques et les maîtres, non pour les imiter, mais [...] pour apprendre à voir"[25] (Delaborde 139), avant que Thiers ne pousse, aux touts premiers temps de la Troisième République, à un "musée universel," vite rebaptisé, au vu de son fonds, "musée des copies"[26] (Guillerme 286–87), inauguré le 16 avril 1873 au Palais de l'Industrie, qui composerait un musée idéal en un retour assez paradoxal chez lui au programme que s'était fixé la Révolution. Si ce n'est que, en ces temps où, avec le mouvement impressionniste, de nouvelles perspectives viennent contrarier l'académisme, l'entreprise est vite dénoncée pour ce qu'elle est: une manœuvre rétrograde que l'on doit à "un conservateur soucieux d'endiguer la montée du Modernisme" (287).

3. Les sites naturels n'échappent pas à cet horizon historiciste. On se souvient, en effet, que "l'intérêt du paysage ne suffit pas," qu'"il faut un intérêt moral ou historique" (*VF* 468) et qu'à Clermont "la vue d'un fort beau paysage" ne "conduit" qu'"au bâillement et à l'épuisement moral" (*MdT* 170), que seul pourrait conjurer l'apparition d'une colonne romaine, même insignifiante. C'est dire que l'appréciation paysagère, si elle peut être source d'éblouissement comme au Mont Blanc (cf. *MdT* 88), sur la route de Vannes (cf. *MdT* 281–2), à Marseille (cf. *VF* 489) ou dans les parages d'Avignon (cf. *MdT* 153–4), est toujours fonction d'une médiation d'ordre culturel, qui emprunte à l'axiologie déjà caractérisée, privilégiant la verticalité au plat[27], les solitudes sauvages aux campagnes densément peuplées, le naturel contre l'effet, la liberté de la broussaille à la sage agriculture rationa-

---

25 "Croyez-vous qu'en vous ordonnant de les copier je veuille faire de vous des copistes ? Non, je veux que vous preniez le suc de la plante" (139).
26 Il accueille des copies – de mauvaise facture, qui plus est, au dire de la critique – des maîtres italiens de la Renaissance, complétés par Vélasquez, Rubens et Rembrandt.
27 Comme le paysage urbain, le paysage naturel est sujet à transbordements. "Ah, si l'on pouvait transporter le mont Ventoux sur la route de Langres à Dijon" (*MdT* 58) ! Et à Paris même, "[q]uel dommage qu'une fée bienfaisante ne transporte pas [au mont Valérien] quelqu'une de ces terribles montagnes des environs de Grenoble!" (*MdT* 59).

lisée. Passe-t-on "deux heures délicieuses dans les chemins et sentiers le long de la Saône"? C'est qu'on est "absorbé dans la contemplation des temps héroïques où Mme Roland a vécu" (*MdT* 74). *A contrario*, "la belle Touraine dont parlent avec emphase les auteurs qui écrivaient il y a cent ans et ceux qui, de nos jours, les copient," ce "jardin de la France," ne peut qu'être flétri: "cette belle Touraine n'existe pas" (*MdT* 201). Et si Philippe L*** se refuse à la reconnaître, ce n'est pas seulement pour poser au paradoxe, c'est, bien plutôt, affaire de cohérence esthético-éthique: l'utile, on le sait, n'est pas beau, or, il a: "aperçu de tous les côtés beaucoup de fertilité, beaucoup de bonne et sage culture; mais en vérité, rien de beau. Quelle différence avec les bords inconnus de l'Isère!" (*MdT* 207).

Démonstration est faite de que la réception de l'héritage culturel repose sur la vision, non sur la vue, avec tout ce que cela suppose de subjectivité: fût-elle 'objectivement' belle, c'est d'être, plus qu'un jardin, un potager qui condamne la Touraine. De même que toutes les splendeurs de la nature ne peuvent racheter l'usage bourgeois qui en est fait aux abords de Lyon où, peu importe que "[l]es rives de la Saône, à deux lieues au-dessus de Lyon, so[ie]nt pittoresques, singulières, fort agréables" et, même, qu'elles "rappellent les plus jolies collines d'Italie," si

> [s]ur ces collines de la Saône, les canuts[28] de Lyon ont bâti des maisons de plaisance, ridicules comme les idées qu'ils ont de la beauté. Dans tous les genres ils en sont restés au grand goût du siècle de Louis XV; mais la beauté naturelle du pays l'emporte sur tous les pavillons chinois dont on a prétendu l'embellir (*MdT* 73–4).

Il en est de la nature comme des dépôts urbains, des jardins anglo-chinois comme des Petits-Augustins: de tous côtés, folies, au double sens du terme, quand sont pervertis et le rapport à la nature et le rapport au passé dans la juxtaposition incongrue, prétendument hors de toute conflictualité, des temporalités et des civilisations. Dans un mauvais goût assumé, se fait jour, avec les parcs à fabrique et la vogue ruiniste qui frappe toute l'Europe, un nouveau rapport au passé comme au patrimoine: à la fois méditation morbide et apprivoisement de la mort en même temps que se donne cours la tentation de l'artificiel, à laquelle sacrifiera un Viollet-le-Duc, ici dénoncée comme frelatée, sans authenticité, donc et, partant, inorganique.

Bien plutôt, dans cette attention au patrimoine dont rend compte le touriste stendhalien qui sait bien qu'analyser un objet patrimonial suppose un *connoisseurship* qui implique la longue fréquentation d'éléments qui entrent dans une série et débouche sur le découpage d'unités à la fois visuelles et sémantiques, c'est l'éducation esthétique qui est privilégiée, seule à même de retrouver avec le passé un rapport d'authenticité qui puisse ouvrir, au présent, sur une régénération. Schiller ne disait pas autre chose dans sa 9ᵉ Lettre sur l'éducation esthétique de l'homme (1794) où l'art lui apparaît comme un miroir sublime, témoin objec-

---

28 Comme le narrateur l'affirme plus loin, il faut entendre là ceux qu'on appelle alors les 'industriels', non les ouvriers de la soie: "Moi, j'étends ce nom aux négociants eux-mêmes" (*MdT* 76).

tif de la dignité perdue de l'homme, modèle prescriptif d'une possible reconquête, après catharsis: "L'humanité a perdu sa dignité, mais l'art l'a sauvée et conservée dans des pierres pleines de sens" (153). Ces pierres dont Mme de Staël éprouve l'efficace à Rome même, Ville Éternelle dont la Renaissance enferme tous les espoirs de palingénésie, dans ces "marbres antiques" qui, de Saint-Pierre aux sept collines, "en savent plus que nous sur les siècles écoulés" (105). Témoins ces statues du Palais Giustiniani, reliques sensibles du passé qui en acclimatent les vertus de même que, pour Schiller, le Romain avait conservé, sous l'Empire, les valeurs de la République depuis longtemps disparue, programme décoratif aidant.

Dépositaires de la majesté du temps et de la grandeur de la vertu, les vestiges de l'art antique, dans leur auguste simplicité et dans leur force, rendent d'autant plus sensible le triomphe du goût bourgeois, pompier, maniéré, chargé etc. sans cesse dénoncé dans la revue stendhalienne où, au final, c'est une aristocratie du goût qui s'affirme, en rien une culture pour les masses. De ce point de vue, force est de constater l'échec de la destination muséale telle que l'avaient pensée les programmes révolutionnaires qu'accuse la tension palpable, bien perceptible encore aujourd'hui, entre une visée démocratique et universaliste dont rend compte, en France, l'institution des Monuments historiques et la création des musées nationaux, et le caractère élitaire de la fréquentation réelle de ces lieux.

Dans ce contexte si particulier à la fois national de ces années 1830 caractéristiques d'une refonte de l'identité nationale travaillée par le consensus bourgeois et personnel pour un Stendhal surpris par cette France qu'il découvre, après une absence de six ans, profondément changée, ces textes accusent un clivage entre cette effusion intime qu'éprouve l'amateur devant les biens culturels qui parlent à son âme, caractéristique de la *Stimmung*, et une autre vocation du monument, appelé à faire lieu de mémoire, au sens où l'entend Nora, soit lieu de mémoire patriotique.

Car dans ce *Tableau de la France* en forme de triptyque que donne Stendhal, quasi contemporain de celui de Michelet, se joue un ralliement dont participe le patrimoine, culturel, évidemment, mais jusqu'au patrimoine naturel, quand le paysage n'a pas seulement une couleur chromatique – souvent le vert des arbres que Stendhal, écologiste avant l'heure, défend contre ceux qui n'y voient que promesse de rapport –, mais bien aussi une couleur politique. Au sens civique où il concerne le corps national tout entier si, comme l'affirme Castagnary dans le Salon de 1867, "[p]ar le paysage, l'art devient national [...] il prend possession de la France, du sol, de l'air, du ciel, du paysage français" (235). Mais bien à un sens plus partisan quand Stendhal, échouant à reconnaître en Louis-Philippe "le plus fripon des Kings"[29] qu'il vilipendait en 1835 dans La Vie de Henry Brulard

---

29 Loin des diatribes de *Lucien Leuwen*, la révision est ici totale – "où sont les abus criants? [...] Qu'y a-t-il à changer à notre constitution?" – au point que le Philippe L***, anagramme transparent de Louis-Philippe, rallié au "sage gouvernement d'un roi homme supérieur" (*MdT* 4), doit se défendre contre des accusations de palinodie: "Je ne sais où trouver des termes prudents pour peindre la prospérité croissante dont la France jouit sous le règne de Louis-Philippe. J'ai peur de passer pour un écrivain payé" (*MdT* 152).

(536), mêle désormais le blanc au rouge incendiaire que cultivait Lucien Leuwen (1834–1835) et au consensuel bleu horizon pour, finalement, avouer enfin 'les trois couleurs', emblématiques d'une histoire nationale réconciliée.

Œuvres Citées

Benjamin, Walter. *L'Œuvre d'art à l'époque de sa reproductibilité technique*. Orig. *Das Kunstwerk im Zeitalter seiner technischen Reproduzierbarkeit* [1935]. Tr. Maurice de Gandillac et Rainer Rochlitz. Paris: Allia, 2011.
Castagnary, Jules-Antoine. *Salons (1857–1870)*, vol. 1. Paris: G. Charpentier et E. Fasquelle, 1892.
Delaborde, Henri. *Ingres. Sa vie, ses travaux, sa doctrine d'après les notes manuscrites et les lettres du maître*. Paris: Plon, 1870.
Del Litto, Victor. *Une somme stendhalienne. Études et documents. 1835–2000*, vol. 2. Paris: Champion, 2002.
Francastel, Pierre. *La Création du musée historique de Versailles et la transformation du palais (1832–1848) d'après les documents inédits*. Versailles: Léon Bernard, 1930.
Goulet, Nicolas. *Observations sur les embellissemens de Paris et sur les monumens qui s'y construisent*. Paris: Leblanc, 1808.
Guillerme, Jacques. *L'Atelier du temps: essai sur l'altération des peintures*. Paris: Hermann, 1964.
Guizot, François. *Mémoires pour servir à l'histoire de mon temps [1858–67]*, I. Paris: Michel Lévy Frères, 1872.
Hugo, Victor. *Journal, 1830–1848*. Ed. Henri Guillemin. Paris: Gallimard, 1954.
Lalande, Josef Jérôme Le Français de. *Voyage d'un François en Italie fait dans les années 1765 & 1766*, t. IV. Yverdon, 1770.
Mérimée, Prosper. *Notes d'un voyage dans le Midi de la France*. Paris: Librairie De Fournier, 1835.
—. *Notes d'un voyage dans l'Ouest de la France*. Paris: Librairie De Fournier, 1836.
Michelet, Jules. *Introduction à l'Histoire universelle. Tableau de la France. Préface à l'Histoire de France*. Paris: Armand Colin, 1962.
Millin, Aubin-Louis. *Voyage dans les départemens du midi de la France*, 1–5. Paris: Imprimerie Nationale, 1807–1811.
Nora, Pierre (Ed.). *Les Lieux de mémoire*, I–III. Paris: Gallimard, 1984–1993.
Poulot, Dominique. "The birth of héritage: le moment Guizot." *Oxford Art Journal*, XI.2 (1988): 40–56.
—. *Surveiller et s'instruire: la Révolution française et l'intelligence de l'héritage historique*. Oxford: Voltaire Foundation, vol. 344, 1996.
—. *Musée, nation, patrimoine. 1789–1815*. Paris: Gallimard, 1997.
Quatremère de Quincy, Antoine. *Considérations morales sur la destination des ouvrages de l'art ou de l'influence de leur emploi sur le génie et le goût de ceux qui les produisent et qui les jugent, et sur le sentiment de ceux qui en jouissent et en reçoivent les impressions*. Paris: de Crapelet, 1815.
Recht, Roland. *Penser le patrimoine. Mise en scène et mise en ordre de l'art*. Paris: Hazan, 2008 [1999].
Riegl, Aloïs. *Le Culte moderne du monument. Son essence et sa genèse*. Paris: Seuil, 1984 [1903].

Schiller, Friedrich von. *Lettres sur l'éducation esthétique de l'homme.* Orig. Briefe über die ästhetische Erziehung des Menschen [1795]. Tr. Robert Leroux. Paris: Aubier, 1992.

Staël, Mme de. *Corinne [1807].* Ed. Simone Balayé. Paris: Gallimard, 1999.

Stendhal, M.H. *Vie de Henry Brulard [ph. 1890].* Ed. Béatrice Didier. Paris: Gallimard, 1973.

—. *Voyages en France: Mémoires d'un touriste, Voyage dans le Midi de la France, Voyage en France* [1838]. Ed. Victor Del Litto. Paris: Gallimard, 1992.

—. *Correspondance générale*, VI (1837–1842). Ed. Victor Del Litto. Paris: Champion, 1999.

Tuetey, Louis M. *Procès-Verbaux de la Comission Temporaire des Arts.* Paris: Imprimiere Nationale. 29 Novembre 2017 <http://gallica.bnf.fr/ark:/12148/bpt6k651 73086>.

CHAPTER SIX

From Town to Cultural Site: The Heritagization Paths for Casablanca

ROMEO CARABELLI

Known abroad mainly for its namesake film (Curtiz), Casablanca is the largest Moroccan town with roughly five million inhabitants, set on the Atlantic Ocean. During the twentieth century, it underwent an explosive development that has kept the town in first place in the ranking of Morocco's richest, most populous and active cities; it has become one of the most important ports and busiest metropolitan areas of Africa. As an active and cosmopolitan city, Casablanca has in recent years seen a process of cultural heritagization that is heavily linked to the colonial experience. This chapter will show the complex interaction between the actors of this town's process of heritagization. In particular, attention will be drawn to how, on the one hand, a small elite is driving the process of heritagization as part of a struggle to incorporate the city into UNESCO's World Heritage list. This struggle will also be contextualized, as it collides with the interests of other local actors who are fostering short-term initiatives of real estate development.

Imperial Development During the Protectorate

Between 1912 and 1956, Morocco was formally administered by a composite protectorate: most of the country was under French-led government while the Mediterranean Strip was under Spanish rule. A special international status was given to the Tangier area. The colonial interference began formally in Casablanca. The Algeciras Conference of 1906 tried to solve the Tangier crisis between Germany and France. The latter was establishing foreign control of the sherifian[1] country as agreed in the 1904 *Entente Cordiale* with the United Kingdom. Among the articles of this international treaty, a balance of sorts was agreed on the colonial presence in Northern Africa: the eastern part of the region would be under British control while the western part of the region would be under the control of the French.

---

1   Morocco's current royal family, the Alaoui, claim to be descendents of the prophet Muhammad; therefore, the Kingdom of Morocco is frequently referred as "Sherifian", an adjective that indicates the Royal family's claimed status.

Following the international agreement, France set about improving the Casablanca port both with a modern docks layout and by updating the commercial customs structure. In 1907, struggles in Casablanca and on the Moroccan eastern border with the French colony of Algeria heralded the entrance of the French army into Casablanca. That was the first act of a growing pressure on the Sultan Abdelaziz, which would culminate in 1912 with the Treaty of Fez. At the beginning of the last century, Casablanca was a small town on a rocky promontory with an area of less than a square kilometer. It was walled by old-design ramparts and had some 20,000 inhabitants, most of whom subsisted through fishing or through overseas commerce. The town was the catalyst for the modern development of the whole colonial state. In the first half of the twentieth century, the town's population multiplied from roughly 20,000 inhabitants in 1900 to more than 600,000 in 1950. The growth rate of the city in the latter half of the century was similarly dramatic; today, Casablanca has roughly five million inhabitants.

With the aim of coordinating the expansion, the French protectorate's Governor (*Résident Général au Maroc*, the well-known *Maréchal* Louis Hubert Lyautey) placed the urban designer Henri Prost in charge of an overall development plan for Casablanca, which had been drawn up during the First World War. Prost was the person in charge for architectural and urban plans in Morocco (his exact title was *Directeur du Service Spécial d'Architecture et des Plans des Villes*). He designed the modern plans for the most important Moroccan towns. For Casablanca, he proposed a wide urban plan stretching from the Atlantic Ocean shore to the circular boulevard, an area that had been drawn some years before, lying between the streets currently known as the *Boulevard de la Résistence* and the *Boulevard Zerktouni*. This plan was inspired by the newest theories

Fig. 1: Brendahan building: Architect: Brion, 1935. Source: RC 2009

on urban design, which had developed mainly in Germany and the United States; therefore, the plans integrated the zoning rules of these countries as well as conforming to their norms in terms of alignments and building sizes. This modernist inspiration gave Casablanca a spectacular modern urban pattern wherein architects could develop an architecture inspired by anything from the late Art Nouveau, Art Deco and the global modern styles: modern movement, ship style, functionalism and later the so-called International Style (figure 1).

By the end of the 1940s, a new plan for Casablanca had been put in motion. This one too was designed by a well-known urban planner: Michel Écochard. He started to work in Morocco in 1947 and released the new plan in 1951. Inspired by the Athens Charter on modern urban planning and applying zoning as an effective tool, the plan envisaged a linear town on the Atlantic coast, near the port of Mohammedia. At the same time, Écochard proposed a strong social housing program, including several working class quarters. Within the modern urban schemes, several architects found the chance to design and shape a large number of buildings, which became exemplar architectures of the first half of the twentieth century.

Casablanca's downtown is composed of a nucleus of buildings raised up in an urban plan implemented during the French Protectorate (1912–1956). The promoters of such an urban plan were mainly private entrepreneurs. They were acting alongside the public institutions in order to manage the town's rising demographic and economic pressures (Garret, *La Fabrique Publique* 9 and Garret, *Casablanca Confrontée*). Influencing the plans for Casablanca was the pragmatism necessary on the behalf of the public administration to develop the city in a way that would balance urban transformation without short-circuiting the economic optimism of that time. During the protectorate, this approach was entirely different from the development lines designed for historic towns such as Fez, Marrakech or Rabat. While those traditional towns were developed with a clear vision imposed by the colonial administration, in Casablanca, private entrepreneurs were heavily involved in planning activities and investment in real estate.

The Birth of a Cultural Heritage Issue

The general urban structure and the huge architectural achievements accomplished between the two world wars and in the 1950s was for a long time underestimated, mainly because of the colonial time period in which they occurred, a difficult time for local memory. Part of the knowledge we have on Casablanca's architectural history is to be found in *Casablanca: Colonial Myths and Architectural Ventures* by Jean Luis Cohen and Monique Eleb, published in 1998. The book was the result of lengthy research within the historical archives, mostly European, and became something of a heritage register. Modernity was embodied by the architecture from the colonial period and the book was written when the town was spectacularly growing and changing its image. By the end of the 20th century, the image of the town began to be no longer adequate in representing the urban dynamism its planners had been originally looking for. As in other similar cases (Abry and Carabelli 334), the current urban pressure is really high, yet the technical quality and the aesthetics of the colonial buildings allow its infrastructure to maintain an active role in the city mainly due to the architectural strength of those buildings, and not due to a heritage protection strategy (Kassou and Garret 7).

In the last quarter of the 20th century, the urban framework of Casablanca was in good condition. The core structure of the city had been maintained although its breadth was subject to systematic review. Unfortunately, the number of demolitions was increasing in a way that endangered its modernist character. The demolition of high quality buildings and other minor but frequent transformations were undermining the consistency of the urban fabric. The municipality and some investors were pushing towards a greater liberalization in the transformation of urban areas. Legal instruments did not provide effective protection of town's built heritage (Kassou 33). The Moroccan legal arsenal does not provide appropriate protection instruments for potential heritage urban areas: registration and protection of every single building is compulsory, thus denying their aggregate value and dramatically increasing the bureaucracy needed for the preservation of an area as a whole.

Many parts of the urban area reached a high level of demographic density and consequently the real estate value increased significantly. The town that had been constructed in the early 20th century was now under pressure: it was becoming a central commercial area suitable for transformation according to current economic interests. Within this atmosphere, during the 1990s the Regional Body of the Ministry of Culture (*Direction Régionale du Grand Casablanca*) and the Municipality began the registration of early 20th century buildings into the National Heritage List. Unfortunately, this positive trend progressed too slowly to safeguard the majority of the urban area.

The "Civil Society" Came into Action

Meanwhile, a new and more liberal vision of the colonial period was emerging and a part of the civil society began to gather forces to protect Casablanca's architectural and urban heritage. Such safeguarding activities were however difficult to manage, not only because of the high costs of the preservation of modern sites, but because of resistance due to the so-called cultural tradition, which was still very influential in the administration. The first sign of interest in the architectural legacy of the modern period was in the case of the Bessoneau building, also known as the Lincoln Hotel (figure 2). The building is located on the Mohammed 5th Avenue, one of the most important monumental streets in the center of Casablanca. It was abandoned for a long period and in 1989 a portion of the roof collapsed, killing several people. In the 2000s, it became the symbol of the recent heritage of Casablanca, but the building continued to fall into disrepair and to decay, culminating in its collapse at the end of 2009 (figure 3) and again in February 2015.

A second event affected another heritage building: the owner of the Villa El Mokri destroyed the house without any prior demolition authorization. This unexpectedly destructive act and the lack of preventative action awakened the determination of some of the citizens to work to ensure a better future for the safeguarding of Casablanca's modern heritage.

In 1995, an association of inhabitants devoted to architectural heritage was founded. Its name was Casamémoire, in allusion to the relation

Fig. 2: Bessoneau Building – Architect: Bride, 1917. Source: RC 2003

Fig. 3: Bessoneau Building – Architect Bride, 1917. Source: RC 2010

between the city's infrastructural inheritance and its memories. The members were both Moroccan and European; the latter predominantly French. The fact that the members of the Casamémoire belonged to the local upper classes, gave it the aspect of an elitist institution. The Association was very active and it started to put pressure on public bodies and actors, pressing them into action. While the level of protection and safeguarding did not increase significantly, the public activities of Casamémoire soon became a catalyst and platform for those who wished to be active on behalf of the preservation of the colonial quarters.

The association began to offer guided tours through the modern heritage sites of Casablanca, an activity that is permanently increasing in terms of both the number of tours and of clients, most of them foreign tourists. At the same time, Casamémoire hosted students coming from national and international schools of architecture to study the modern heritage of Casablanca. Casamémoire today offers three fundamental platforms for the dissemination of knowledge and awareness of recent cultural heritage. From 2008, Casablanca has hosted the widespread heritage activities known as "Heritage Day" (*Journées du Patrimoine*). It also took charge of the restoration of the old slaughterhouse (*Les abattoirs*) (figure 4), that were abandoned in 2000. Since 2011, it has contributed to the Popular Heritage University (*Université Populaire du Patrimoine*). These three activities may be seen as an attempt to overhaul the original elitist structure and image of the organization in order to open its activities to the entire population (Carabelli, 154).

Fig. 4:   Les Abattoirs – The Slaughterhouse – Architect: Desmarest, 1922. Source: RC 2010

The "Heritage Day", an annual event that receives increasing public favor, is what turned the Casamémoire into "The Association," the institution of note with regards to the recent heritage of the city. Heritage day began as a single-day cultural activity concerning the more representative public buildings of the city, grouped around the Mohammed 5th Square (the former *Place de France* in colonial times). Nowadays it has become a much larger event, lasting several days, involving numerous schools and multiplying the number of potential heritage sites all over the city. Year after year, the initiative gains in support and social impact, with a growing audience and a more significant presence in the media.

Some years previously, the old municipal slaughterhouse, abandoned in 2000, had been included in the list of sites that should be protected (Morocco 1). In 2008 a group of cultural associations, coordinated by Casamémoire, signed an agreement with the Municipality of Casablanca aimed at the reconversion of the old slaughterhouse in a cultural site called *Abattoirs de Casablanc: Fabrique Culturelle* (Casablanca's Slaughterhouse: A cultural Factory). With this initiative, the Association Casamémoire enabled an urban site for cultural creation, training and dissemination of artistic disciplines. Many activities are organized there and the cultural factory has become a reference point for young people interested in cultural activities. Nowadays, the collective management of the cultural factory by several associations, led by the Casamémoire, is still far from simple. The municipality has never granted a lease for longer than twelve months. Accordingly, speculative interests are always present. Furthermore, the old slaughterhouse is located near to the main railway station, the *Gare de Casablanca Voyageurs* (the Railway Station of Casablanca Travelers).

Thanks to the *Abattoirs'* activity, Casamémoire acquired wide support among the youth audience. However, its complicated management was a burden for the Association, which withdrew its responsibility in 2014, leaving room for the smaller associations, which have shown difficulties in maintaining the cultural site at its previous level.

In 2011, the French Institute of Casablanca, a cultural center well established in town, invited Casamémoire to join a Popular Heritage University oriented to heritage issues. Its aim was to present heritage issues to Casablanca's population in general, and in particular to heighten the awareness of non-experts. The Popular Heritage University recently celebrated its fifth edition and has expanded to several Moroccan cities, despite the termination of the French Institute's sponsorship. The general management of this Popular University, which integrates academics and professionals, both national and international, has contributed to increasing Casamémoire's visibility. These three major initiatives – along with the ever-increasing number of heritage tours for international tourists – have undoubtedly fostered an increased awareness of patrimonial values; they have not, however, been able to change significantly the course of the events. For instance, the financial penalty for demolition is still far lower than the capital to be gained by reconstruction; to destroy an old building and build another one in its place is still an economically productive business.

Despite its efforts, the elite interest in Casablanca's recent and modern heritage is failing to integrate a larger and more substantial part of Casablanca's residents, who still struggle with more pressing and immediate priorities related to everyday life. At the same time, the city's strong economic dynamism is reflected in investments aimed at urban transformation, such as the construction of a luxury marina and the transformation of Casa Port railway station, immediately outside of the city's historic areas.

Fig. 5: Wilaya Casablanca. Architect: Boyer, 1928/1936. Source: RC 2011

The International Path as an Incentive for Local Action

In the second half of the 2010s, Casamémoire embarked upon a complex but exciting path that has the possibility to bring about a serious transformation: they have positioned Casablanca's heritage issues on the international stage. By way of example, the publication of the book *Casablanca: Mythes et Figures d'une Aventure Urbaine* was the inspiration for an exhibition in Paris: *Casablanca Naissance d'une Ville Moderne sur le Sol Africain,* (Electra Space, 1999). Casamémoire used this chance to launch a lobbying campaign, taking advantage of the visibility the Parisian exhibition brought the area and its issues. However, the campaign was still tied to and associated with a neo-colonial agenda: an exhibition staged by French intellectuals who, used to valorizing cultural heritage, were showing the "natives" something which they supposedly were not yet able to recognize of their own accord. The exhibition was restaged in Casablanca the following year and it was the first activity carried out by Casamémoire to have a large public resonance. It was during one of the events surrounding the show that the regional branch of the Moroccan Architects' Association (the *Conseil Régional du Cen-*

tre de l'Ordre des Architectes) announced their intention to register the Bessoneau building – the Hotel Lincoln – in the national inventory. This new internationalist strategy found similar articulation in two other initiatives: Casamémoire's active participation in the regional Euro-Mediterranean project, "Mutual Heritage"[2], which provided training and knowledge surrounding the recent heritage valorization, and the identification of inclusion in UNESCO's World Heritage list as an intermediate target to safeguard the city's heritage.

The use of such internationalist strategies aimed at avoiding the neo-colonial image of precedent measures of heritage protection thus originated from a local initiative. With the first action, the participation in the international project Mutual Heritage, Casamémoire produced a guide to the twentieth-century architecture of Casablanca (Casamémoire, *Guide* 128) and a technical dossier devised as the first step towards the nomination of Casablanca for inclusion in UNESCO's World Heritage List (Casamémoire, *Casablanca*). Thus, Casamémoire proposed itself as the principal driver of the efforts to secure Casblanca's inclusion in the World Heritage List; it was a definitely "braggart" act, but, with this fascinating *coup de theatre*, Casamémoire acquired a central role in the process of the heritagization of Casablanca.

An Inescapable Corollary

The possibility of inclusion in the UNESCO World Heritage List displaced the processes of heritagization from the strictly local level to a supra-national level. In this regard, the UNESCO label stimulated local dreams of greatness. The first step was the inclusion of Casablanca sites in the *Tentative List*, the list indicating the sites on which the Member States of UNESCO intended to focus their interest in the near future. With the technical support of the Director of the Regional Delegation of the Ministry of Culture, a first document petitioning for inclusion in the *Tentative List* was sent in 2009 from Casamémoire to the headquarters of the Ministry. This was a mistake on the part of the Association; its action was perceived as an intrusion into the field of action of the Ministry (a perception which still exists). In fact, if inclusion in the World Heritage List should come to pass, it will be the first time in the Arab world that such a process can be deemed to have been driven by civil society.

The application to include Casablanca in the *Tentative List* remained a dead letter for a long time. The internal procedure of the Ministry ran aground and the request was not submitted. The reasons for this can perhaps be found in Casamémoire's proposal to include Casablanca's sites before those of the capital Rabat and in the fact of Casablanca's proposed heritage sites being of modern prove-

---

2 Mutual Heritage: from historical integration to contemporary active participation, a project co-funded by the European Union within the framework of the Euromed Heritage Programme 4.

nance. It could also have been due to the Ministry's resentment of Casamémoire's intrusion into its competence area. Alternatively, it could have been the consequence of a mere lack of initiative by the public administration.

On the other hand, during the month of Ramadan of 2010, King Mohammed's 6th visit to the kingdom was scheduled to take place in Casablanca, within its modest medina. On this occasion, the King recommended the protection of the *intramuros* district, which is the old quarter or medina. In fact, Casablanca's nineteenth-century quarter does not have any salient features from a patrimonial point of view. However, this unexpected chance made it possible to re-activate the process of its preservation. The regional executive service of the Ministry of Culture implemented a protection plan to be applied to the historic precinct. This plan identified a core urban asset, but included likewise the prospect of extending the protection program to the modern part of the built inheritance.

In 2012, UNESCO's General Assembly validated the request of Morocco and inserted Rabat among the World Heritage sites. Simultaneously, it initiated a program of the World Heritage Centre that targeted modern sites in the Arab countries (*Programme de sauvegarde du patrimoine des modernités architecturales et urbaines dans le Monde Arabe*). The second formal meeting of the UNESCO's group of experts took place in Rabat in May 2013. On that occasion, the Minister of Culture underlined the commitment of the Ministry to the cultural and architectural recognition of Casablanca on an international level. The same senior officer who had blocked the former request to include Casablanca in the Moroccan *Tentative List* required from Casamémoire the necessary documents to include their town in the list. The cooperation between the Casamémoire Association and the Ministry of Culture proceeded swiftly; the required documentation was immediately provided and, in December 2013, the first goal was achieved with Casablanca's inclusion in the *Tentative List* (UNESCO 1).

The immediate effect of this first official request was the Governor's interdiction of any building demolition inside the potentially 'heritagizable' area by the initiative of the municipal administrations. Any potential demolition would now require authorization by a commission including representatives from the Wilaya, the Ministry of Culture and the *Agence Urbaine de Casablanca* (Wilaya du Grand Casablanca 1). From an economic perspective, it seems clear that the process of heritagization has been furthered by an enlightened elite which stands for a liberal-progressive strategy of local development.

The Preparation and Management of the Casablanca's Candidature Dossier

The first UNESCO recognition had a positive boomerang effect in terms of general attention to the heritage issues in Casablanca. The "World Heritage-oriented" strategy had to continue with the implementation of the nomination dossier for Casablanca. The dossier combined complex spatial and temporal aspects that are deemed to define the elements to be valorized.

As a consequence of the complexity of the dossier and the difficulty of its practical implementation, the Ministry took the World Heritage registration project as an intrusion into its field of action. Even today, the civil society's activities, organized around Casamémoire, are putting pressure on national institutions and the Ministry is not responding well to the process. It remains fairly inflexible and does not take the pro-active role that it could.

As required by Casamémoire, and supported by the regional Prefect, on February 14th 2014 the Ministry of Culture, the Wilaya/Prefecture of Great Casablanca, the City of Casablanca and Casamémoire signed a historic agreement assigning to the latter the edition of the dossier. UNESCO supported the candidacy in identifying possible upcoming difficulties in the management of the candidature dossier. At the same time, and with the aim of improving the management of local heritage, the *Agence Urbaine de Casablanca* (the agency of the Ministry of the Interior in charge of urban management plans) launched a plan to identify potential heritage sites in order to include their preservation and enhance their cultural visibility. In order to make an effective tool of the potential candidature's dossier, Casamémoire created a working team to liaise with public local and national institutions and the candidature dossier was ready in January 2016.

With regards to the preparation of the dossier, Casamémoire had to contend with at least two sets of problems: the effective knowledge of and about the specific sites and the difficulty of producing an explicit narration that would convince of the universal value of Casablanca's heritage. The first issue required long term work by a small group of activists who struggled to organize all the available information and give it the appropriate structure and format. The second problem was more difficult because it required the binding together of all the heritage elements and provision of them with an intelligible and shareable narrative. While the first problem required long term work by a small team, the other required short bursts of activity on the behalf of a number of participants. It culminated in regular meetings where a large number of the city's technicians and heritage experts brainstormed the possibilities of the heritagization of Casablanca.

Four of those large meetings were organized in 2014. Two were open to the participation of national and international experts. Two other meetings were reserved for panel of experts directly derived from the entities involved in the dossier's implementation: representatives of the Ministry of Culture (at both national and regional level), the Wilaya/Prefecture of Grand Casablanca, the

Municipalities of Casablanca, and, of course, Casamémoire. This second group had the task of choosing, editing and validating the options proposed during the previous dossier's implementation activities. The meetings acted as a catalyst for Casablanca's heritage revalorization, and went far beyond the former proposals, which identified the town simply as a "modernity lab" or a "lab for modern architecture."

The fight for Casablanca's heritagization is a story that highlights the town's dramatic transformation between the two World Wars and immediately after the second one. During this time, local actors faced violent changes in demography, wealth, production and commercial structure. The pragmatic response to these changes was the introduction of new architectural and urban patterns, which led Casablanca into a modernity entirely unique to itself.

Lessons from Casablanca

In February 2016, Casablanca's candidature dossier was officially delivered to the World Heritage Center. At the same time, Morocco's representative at UNESCO withdrew the dossier. No official explanation for this action was given, neither by the Ministry of Culture nor by Morocco's ambassador at UNESCO. The colonial heritagization of Casablanca is an example of the need for the integration of heritage processes and the local, current way of life.

Recent colonization and the overseas expansion of Western powers during the nineteenth and twentieth centuries had a tangible effect of globalization and modernity, and they are not always made visible as part of our cultural inheritance. We know that the last two centuries had a vivid impact on current forms of 'culture', but this seems not to be recognized by a majority of Casablanca's inhabitants. The situation of Casablanca and its tangible inheritance as linked with the French Protectorate, shows how the direct and indirect actors of the local heritagization process are torn between two different kinds of local development: one is the improvement of heritage and the other one is the management of a developing economy. Of course, among property owners, increasing the value of the buildable areas is the primary concern, while for a cultural association, the prospect of immediate benefits gives way to the long-term strategy of heritagization. Within this seeming conflict of interests, local actors play their roles and manage their conflicts. Public institutions seem to be without a clear mission and are torn between the two positions: one heritage-oriented, one real estate-oriented. In fact, an active enlightened minority is trying to drive the whole town towards a high-quality tangible environment in the future. While a non-governmental team are trying to take the leadership of Casablanca's process of heritagization in order to improve the quality of urban life, civil society is pushing public institutions to deal with the hard issue of managing modernity with all of its democratic and fluctuating issues.

Works Cited

Abry, Alexandre, and Romeo Carabelli. *Reconnaître et Protéger L'architecture Récente En Méditerranée*. Paris: Maisonneuve et Larose, 2005.

Carabelli, Romeo. "Patrimoine récent et tourisme, pour une approche 'bi-partisans' – Recent heritage and tourism, for a bi-partisan approach." *Tourisme & Patrimoine récent Tourism & recent Heritage*. Eds. Rachele Borghi, Alessia Mariotti, and Nazly Safarzadeh. Tours/Casablanca: Mutual Heritage/Citeres, 2011. 17–25.

Casamémoire. *Casablanca, ville du XXe siècle, carrefour d'influences*. Casablanca: Casamémoire & Mutual Heritage, 2011.

Casamémoire. *Guide des architectures du XXe siècle de Casablanca*. Casablanca: Revue Maure & Graphely, 2011.

Cohen, Jean-Louis, and Monique Eleb. *Casablanca: mythes et figures d'une aventure urbaine*. 1998. Paris: Hazan, 2009.

Curtiz, Michael. *Casablanca (film)*. Burbank: Warner Bros., 1942.

Garret, Pascal. "La fabrique publique de l'espace public confrontée aux intérêts privés. Lyautey, Prost et les 'Bâtisseurs de Casablanca' au début du Protectorat français." *Géocarrefour* 77,3 (2002): 245–54.

—. "Casablanca confrontée à l'État colonisateur, aux colons et aux élites locales: essai de micro histoire de la construction d'une ville moderne." *Villes coloniales aux XIXè-XXè siècles, d'un sujet d'action à un objet d'histoire (Algérie, Maroc, Libye et Iran). Essais et Guide Bibliographique*. Ed. Hélène Vacher. Paris: Maisonneuve et Larose, 2005. 27–39.

Kassou, Abderrahim. "Attirail et résultats: le grand décalage." *Reconnaître et protéger l'architecture récente en Méditerranée*. Paris: Maisonneuve et Larose, 2005. 191–224.

Kassou, Abderrahim, and Pascal Garret. "La villa des Arts (une réhabilitation par défaut à Casablanca)." *Patrimoines partagés en Méditerranée*. Dir. Galila El Kadi et Sahar Attia Alexandria: Alexandria Preservation Trust, 2005. 10–17.

Morocco. Ministère de la culture. *Arrêté n° 1.301.03 (Inscription des Abattoirs Municipaux de Casablanca)*, 6/27/2003. Rabat: B. O. No. 5134, 8/14/2003.

Wilaya du Grand Casablanca. *Arreté N° 1087 concernant la protection du patrimoine bâti de Casablanca*. 2013.

Websites

Agence Urbaine de Casablanca. <http://www.auc.ma/>.
Casamémoire. <http://www.casamemoire.org/>.
Casamémoire. "Université Populaire Du Patrimoine." <http://www.casamemoire.org/index.php?id=97>.
Journées Du Patrimoine. <http://www.journeesdupatrimoine.ma/>.
Journées Du Patrimoine Casablanca. Facebook <https://www.facebook.com/journeespatrimoinecasa>.
Les Abattoirs de Casablanca. Fabrique culturelle <http://www.abattoirs-casablanca.org/>.
Les Abattoirs de Casablanca. Facebook <https://www.facebook.com/pages/La-Fabrique-Culturelle-des-Anciens-Abattoirs-de-Casablanca/337075619707162>.
Unesco 1. World Heritage Centre. <http://whc.unesco.org/>.

Unesco. World Heritage Centre. "Programme de Sauvegarde Du Patrimoine Des Modernités Architecturales et Urbaines Dans Le Monde Arabe" <http://whc.unesco.org/fr/evenements/1051/>.

Université Populaire du Patrimoine. Facebook <https://www.facebook.com/pages/Universit%C3%A9-Populaire-du-Patrimoine/123662034406254>.

COLONIAL AND DECOLONIAL ECOLOGICAL EPISTEMOLOGIES

CHAPTER SEVEN

The Gift of Heritage:
Making "Eco" Economical in Nigeria[1]

PETER PROBST

It can be assumed that the delegates of the 1972 UN Stockholm conference on the Human Environment were not aware of what was happening thousands of miles away in Nigeria when they discussed the conference agenda. At the same time they decided to take legal action to safeguard the world's natural and cultural resources, members of a local arts movement in the Nigerian city of Osogbo erected shrines in the sacred grove of the city's guardian deity Osun to save the grove's flora and fauna from destruction. Today, more than four decades later, the two developments have converged. With the implementation of the "World Heritage Convention" and the introduction of a "World Heritage List," the UN efforts have resulted in a most successful UNESCO program that has reached into practically every corner of the globe, including Nigeria. Thus, over the course of time the Osun grove has not only become Nigeria's premier "ecotourism destination" but also a "property" on UNESCO's World Heritage list.

In the following, I aim to unpack this development and explore how the notion of "World Heritage" has entered and transformed Osogbo. Before I introduce the city and its inhabitants, let me begin with a detour to Saint Petersburg in Russia. In 2012, the city hosted the thirty-sixth annual session of the UNESCO World Heritage Committee. Anthropological reports (Brumann, "Multilateral Ethnography"; Meskell) allow us to understand what happened there. Like all sessions of the World Heritage Committee, this was a massive gathering. Close to 1,000 participants from 150 states got together for eleven days to discuss and decide on matters of World Heritage. First and foremost, this included discussion and votes on proposals the individual Member States had submitted for inscription onto UNESCO's prestigious World Heritage List. The agenda was packed. Each item was accompanied with numerous files and documents. Since none of the delegates had the time to read through the thousands of pages justifying the 'outstanding value', 'integrity' and 'authenticity' of the proposed sites, a lot of information was gathered and exchanged in informal settings: over meals, in the lobby or at evening receptions. Thus, what actually informed the final vote was a mixture of different forms of decision making and informal negotiations which

---

1 A slightly different version of this article appeared in *World Heritage on the Ground*, eds. David Berliner and Christoph Brumann, Oxford: Berghahn Books, 2016. I would like to thank the editors and publisher for giving permission to republish parts of the article.

made the results difficult to predict. What seemed to be a promising proposal sometimes turned out to be a flop, and vice versa.

Perhaps that is just how decisions at big supranational conventions happen. And perhaps the belief in the rationality of these events is just naïve, and barter-like negotiations are a quite suitable model to agree on things and move forward. And yet there is a feeling of indignation. After all, the public relations campaign of the World Heritage Center invites us to understand the notion of World Heritage as a precious "legacy" that we received from our forefathers and that we need to pass on to those coming after us. Heritage then, so the argument goes, is a moral obligation and responsibility and not a matter of ordinary haggling, let alone a commodity. In other words, we expect some sense of respect towards the collective values and aesthetics of belonging that are materialized in heritage, values that cannot and should not be reduced to utilitarian ends.

The impulse of moral protest against the workings of the World Heritage Committee echoes the long debate about gifts and commodities that Marcel Mauss's seminal essay "The Gift" has triggered in the humanities and social sciences (cf. Sansi). Gifts, so the widely shared argument holds, are distinctly different from commodities. The two belong to mutually exclusive cultural worlds in which gifts stand for reciprocity, inalienability, community and sociality while commodities are associated with individualism, alienation and the profit logic of market capitalism. Seen from this binary perspective, heritage clearly falls into the category of gifts. The longer the chain of transmission and intergenerational exchanges, the more time has elapsed, the more valuable is the gift.

Clearly, the binary structure of the argument is a romanticization of the gift, a projection full of desires, nostalgias and longings that have only little to do with Mauss's original ideas and that have hence been sufficiently exposed and criticized (cf. Sigaud; Liebersohn). To engage in another round of critique would be futile then. Instead, what I want to capitalize on here is the political context of The Gift in terms of its close entanglement with the League of Nations that preceded the founding of UNESCO and the emergence of the notion of World Heritage. It is this context, so I maintain, which lends Mauss's essay a promising analytical potential for the questions this volume seeks to address.

First published in 1925, The Gift was both a political and a personal statement. As a political statement, the essay aimed to outline an ethnographically and historically grounded path for moving forward after World War I. For Mauss, the direction was clear. Already in 1919 he explained that the "most renowned moral and political act of peace, however shaky it may be, is the recognition of the principle of arbitration established by the League of Nations pact" (cited in Fournier 190). As a socialist and combat veteran, Mauss believed in the League's agenda of exchange and internationalism, to which The Gift sought to give a proper scientific basis.[2] Accordingly, his interest was not in the occasional exchange of gifts

---

2   Internationalism did not mean anticolonialism. Mauss's socialist ideals did not prevent him from questioning colonialism, just as he did not question the imperialist agenda of

between friends or individuals but in what he called "total prestations" in which "corporate personalities" such as families, clans or tribes meet in a formalized and ceremonial fashion to exchange goods, persons or services deemed necessary to preserve the social fabric. Understanding the logic of these prestations, so he argued, provided an insight into the nature of society and a way to prevent war:

> Societies have progressed in the measure in which they, their sub-groups and their members, have been able to stabilize their contracts and to give, receive and repay. In order to trade, man must first lay down his spear. When that is done he can succeed in exchanging goods and persons not only between clan and clan but between tribe and tribe and nation and nation, and above all between individuals. It is only then that people can create, can satisfy their interests mutually and define them without recourse to arms (Mauss 80).

On a personal level, The Gift was also an act of remembrance for Mauss's uncle, the sociologist Emile Durkheim, who had passed away during the war. The essay formed the centerpiece of the first number of the new series of L'Année Sociologique, the flagship publication of the sociology movement Durkheim had founded. Since Durkheim's death in 1917, the journal had ceased to appear. Using the essay to revitalize L'Année marked the importance Mauss himself lent to it. Subscribing to Durkheim's tenet that the most basic categories of human thought have their origin in social experience, Mauss situated the value of the gift not in the object or the service rendered to the receiver, but in the social relationship the gift establishes. The triad of giving, accepting and reciprocating gifts constitutes sociality; it makes or forms persons and – resulting here from – social and moral values. That is why Mauss considered gift exchanges "total social facts" or "total prestations" in that they involve and comprise all spheres of society – from economy, kinship and politics to religion, art and aesthetics.

Against the background of this original context of The Gift, the analytical potential of Mauss's essay for the understanding of heritage is both promising and problematic – "promising" because it allows us to conceive heritage as a form of "total prestation" in which the complexity of society is condensed in one single fact or phenomenon. The ample literature on heritage is a case in point. Ranging from aspects of politics and religion to aesthetics and economics, the multitude of studies not only mark the totality of heritage, they also show the limitations of approaches that try to narrow the complexity of heritage to issues of hegemony, power, and commodification/gentrification.[3] Moreover, the notion of (gift) exchange comes closest to the UNESCO wording that speaks of heritage as a "legacy" that we received from our forefathers and that we need to pass on to those coming after us as a "property." The language is telling, for it recalls

---

the League (Mazower). For works illuminating the context of Mauss's essay, see Godelier; Fournier; Hart.

3   For a similar argument, see Brumann, "Heritage Agnosticism".

Mauss's insight that properties/gifts are less about things but more about relations that things initiate and enable. Within the UNESCO framework, these relationships work both vertically, that is, as an (imagined) exchange and dialogue between generations, and horizontally, that is, as an exchange and form of mutual recognition between states and UNESCO. Accordingly, special terms and concepts like "authenticity" or "integrity," used to assess the quality of the preservation work, are less about the value of the work/object but more about the sincerity of the exchange partner offering the object to UNESCO and the willingness to honor the contract. Indeed, it is this basic moral and contractual notion of "heritage" that justifies and drives current transnational preservation campaigns as a way to foster cooperation and development, overcome conflicts and imagine a future that is worth aspiring to (De Jong and Rowlands; Basu and Modest).

But who are the exchange partners? What interests do they pursue? In whose names do they speak? It is here where the gift analogy becomes problematic, if not to say deceptive, for it risks concealing the internal dynamics of the transactions in favour of an idealized and generic picture of society. Pursuing the gift and exchange argument further in the context of heritage thus requires complicating the argument from within. Among the multitude of options available for such an exercise, I want to focus on three questions. First, if heritage is an inheritance that is passed on to the next generations, then what about the argument that gifts can change their status, i.e. that inalienable gifts can become alienable commodities, just as commodities can become gifts? Second, if heritage can be seen as a mode of exchange generating social and moral values, then how does this idea of heritage translate into and correlate with the local modes of exchange and value? And third, if the conceptualization of heritage as exchange holds true, then we need to ask who has or claims to have control over the means of exchange enabling the creation of value.

Preserving the Home of the Goddess

Let me come back then to the Nigerian city of Osogbo and its World Heritage site, the Osun Osogbo Sacred Grove (figure 1).[4] Listed as a "cultural landscape" and situated at the outskirts of the city, the grove consists of seventy-five hectares of forestland along the banks of the Osun river. Inside the grove, hunting, farming and fishing are forbidden. No permanent settlements are allowed. Instead, the area is covered with a large number of sculptures and temples of various sizes and materials.

Both the structures and the restrictions echo the religious character of the site. Osun is not only a river, but also Osogbo's guardian deity who is credited for providing wealth, fertility and protection. Every year in August, the Osun grove

---

4 The following ethnographic description is based on Probst, *Osogbo and the Art of Heritage*.

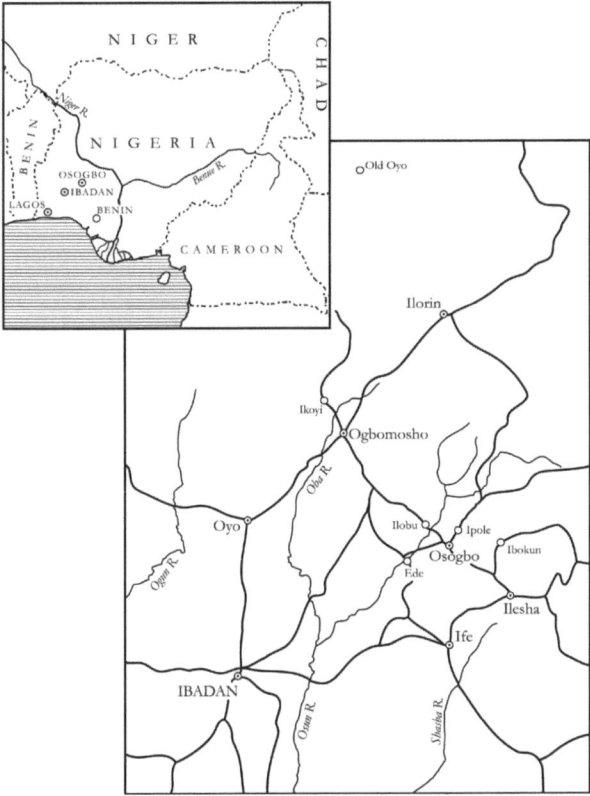

Fig. 1:   Map Of Nigeria (Peter Probst, Osogbo and the Art of Heritage, Bloomington: Indiana University Press)

Fig. 2:   Osun Osogbo Festival Pamphlet, 2016.

forms the stage of a big festival by which the people of Osogbo honor the deity (figure 2). Over the course of twelve days – from Monday through Friday of the following week – numerous small events take place all leading up to the climax of the festival: covered with a cloth and thus kept invisible for the eyes of the

Fig. 3: Reshaping the Osun grove in the late 1960s.
Photo: Ulli Beier

thousands of spectators, a ritual maiden carries sacred objects in a calabash from the palace into the Osun grove where Osun officials make a sacrifice to the deity at the river bank below the main Osun temple. The offering is said to go back to the founding of the city. According to oral tradition, the arrival of Osogbo's first king caused tensions with Osun, who felt disturbed by the newcomers. Eventually, the two parties were able to resolve the conflict by making a pact of mutual exchange and protection. Just as Osun promised to provide prosperity and protection to the king and his people, the king promised to protect Osun's homestead. The annual sacrifice not only remembers this pact, but also renews the relationship between the people and the goddess.

Over the decades, the festival has become bigger and bigger. Today visitors come from as far as Japan, Australia and Brazil, thus making the event not only important on religious grounds, but also economically. The reasons for the visit differ. While some make the journey to pay respect to the deity and reconnect with their cultural roots, others just come for the fun of it and enjoy the carnival-like atmosphere. Still others come to witness the success of an artistic rescue project that started in the late 1950s and focused on preserving and reshaping the Osun grove.

Back then the situation of the grove was precarious. The entangled forces of colonialism, Christianity and commerce had started to erode the relationship between the city and the Yoruba goddess. The cohesive force of the Osun grove declined. People began to ignore the local restrictions of hunting, fishing and farming. The grove was at risk of abandonment. In 1959, one year before Nigeria gained independence, a group of Osun ritual officials therefore approached the Austrian artist (and convert to Yoruba religion) Susanne Wenger and asked for help. Wenger agreed, and with permission of the king of Osogbo, she started to reshape the grove (figure 3). What previously was a mostly aniconic space turned into a kind of open-air gallery filled with new sculptures and architectures.

Fig. 4: Representation of the deity Iya Mapo, Susanne Wenger & Adebisi Akanji 1970s.
Photo: Peter Probst

Designed and built by Wenger and her collaborators, the works were meant to be visual gestures of evidence for the presence of the deities residing in the grove (figure 4).

In terms of media and style, the structures radically departed from conventional Yoruba aesthetics. The difference was programmatic. Wenger's vision aimed at reflecting the ruptures intrinsic to the experience of colonial modernity (1977). The general conviction was that "things fall apart" as Chinua Achebe (1958) put it in his classic novel about the effects of colonialism among Igbo villagers in Southeast Nigeria. Therefore, any return to traditional aesthetics was seen as principally and categorically void. In order to survive, the old deities had to be updated with modern aesthetics. Thus, the new shapes and forms were thought to express the fluid, open and still undetermined phase society and religion were believed to go through.[5] In a publication on the Osun reshaping project from 1977 Wenger explained the rationale clearly:

> Impatient and self-willed emancipation of the individual mind is the criterion of modern man. While the past's trust lay explicitly with the collective involvements into the transcendent forms of life, the modern individual is averse to ready-made recipes as to how to embark on the mystical adventure. Thus the Shrines, in which dwell Òrísà [Yoruba deities, PP], who himself dwells in man, have to be new and original in their concept of the enduringly divine. If not they are falsely affecting

5 The reshaping of the Osun grove was actually part of a wider project that aimed to revitalize the local arts as a kind of *Gesamtkunstwerk*. Parallel to Wenger's activities in the grove, her husband Ulli Beier collaborated with the school teacher Duro Ladipo and the British artist Georgina Beier. Sacred and profane visual and performance art all went together, resulting in the so-called Osogbo Art Movement. For a history of the events, see Beier, *Contemporary Art in Africa* and my own study (Probst "Osogbo and the Art of Heritage"; "Iconoclash in the Age of Heritage").

the spiritual flow. Their symbolism cannot persist to glorification of outlived ideals, but must encourage new interpretation, individual spontaneity and spiritual independence, which modern man needs to experience with his gods [...] Loyalty to traditional authenticity need not oppose the genius' trend towards new acquisitions and a new focus on its inner ethic. We are modern and different, but we walk the ancient grounds. (Wenger 8, 11).

Hardly surprising, Wenger's artistic intervention did not proceed without vehement critique and resistance. Members of the local Christian and Muslim communities alike were furious and tried to destroy the structures on the grounds that they promoted paganism and hindered progress. Opposition came also from the local famers and businessmen. As a commercial center with lots of immigrants, Osogbo was short of land. The Osun grove seemed to offer a solution to the problems. Besides, the revenue potential also lived up to Osun's promise to provide wealth and prosperity – at least for some members of the palace. As it turned out, members of the royal family had started to sell portions of the grove, arguing that the grove belonged to the palace. The new owners of the land brought the matter to the court where it rested for years without decision, in this way increasing local grievances. Last but not least, critique came also from Euro-American anthropologists and the international art scene. The positions varied. While some complained that Wenger's activities distorted and disturbed the study of urban/social change, others lamented about the uneasy mix of modernism, neocolonialism and egocentrism in Wenger's "metaphysical adventure."[6]

Nevertheless, Wenger's agenda proved to be successful. The revitalization project not only attracted new visitors to the city, it also protected the grove. In 1960, the grove became a national monument, and in the 1970s, a local heritage committee was formed. The 1990s saw the building of a national museum, thus turning the grove into both a public gallery and an active ritual space. The elevation correlated with the founding of the "Osun Grove Support Group" (1996) and a special Wenger Trust (1998) whose mostly European members portrayed Wenger as one of the pioneers of a "green" aesthetic and stressed the embeddedness of the grove project within the international earthworks and land art movement. Complementary to this assessment, the Support Group focused on the territorial integrity of the grove, the preservation and conservation of its biodiversity, and the support of local heritage initiatives. The most momentous boost though came in 2005 when UNESCO added the Osun grove to its prestigious list of World Heritage sites. Today the Osun grove and festival are marketed as Nigeria's biggest heritage and "ecotourism destination" and, as such, function as an important source of revenue for the local and regional government.

---

6   For a more detailed account of the critique, see Probst "Osogbo and the Art of Heritage."

From Vertical to Horizontal Politics

The modernist rescue narrative of what happened in Nigeria corresponds with the formulation of the UNESCO campaigns to safeguard heritage and preserve cultural and natural diversity. In fact, the reshaping of the Osun grove and the drafting of UNESCO conventions happened at the same time. Both shared the same sentiment of fear and concern. But what about the idea of exchange and contract which allegedly serves as the hidden charter of UNESCO's heritage politics?

A closer look at the developments reveals that the principle of exchange and contract worked more along a horizontal/spatial/national axis than on a vertical/temporal/generational one.[7] What mattered was the demand for recognition and inclusion. After all, the postcolonial insistence on recognition did not only imply eligibility in the possession of and right to nominate a "World Heritage" site. It also implied acceptance as a valid partner in the social contract that the idea of "World Heritage" signifies.

Let me explain. In 1972, when the General Conference of UNESCO discussed and eventually signed the Convention Concerning the Protection of the World Cultural and Natural Heritage, delegates quarreled over the question of how to define "World Heritage." The proposed text submitted to a committee of government experts charged with preparing a draft convention explained the matter as "heritage of universal interest." The Nigerian delegation rejected the phrase and wanted to delete the word "universal" from the text. However, the British delegation insisted on it and instead proposed to replace the phrase "universal interest" with the term "outstanding universal value," or "OUV" (Jokilehto). So-called operational guidelines justified OUV of cultural heritage by seven specific criteria: (i) masterpiece, (ii) values/influences, (iii) testimony, (iv) typology, (v) land/sea-use, (vi) beliefs/living traditions, (vii) aesthetic importance.[8]

The term "OUV" and the justifying criteria clearly echoed the prominence of Euro-American interpretations of heritage within UNESCO. As a "legacy" of the past, (cultural) heritage was conceived in the Western tradition of historic preservation – that is, in the form of buildings, churches and palaces. Accordingly, key concepts of historic preservation like "authenticity" and "integrity" were solely defined in relation to the authenticity of material, design and workmanship. As such, they contrasted markedly from many non-Euro-American cultures whose architecture often favor concepts of temporal fluidity and ephemerality (cf. Sand). Yet, a distinct shift from this stance to other conceptions of heritage hap-

---

7 Obviously, the argument is informed by Hardt and Negri's analysis of a shift from modern to postmodern forms of power. According to their argument, vertical sovereignties that structured the political world in terms of nation states have become more and more replaced by horizontal networks that are allegedly better suited to dealing with the political and economic complexities of today. While UNESCO and its World Heritage Center and Committee are certainly networks, it is debatable to what extent they can be seen as a regime (Bendix et al.), let alone an "empire."
8 On the debate about OUV, see also Labadi and the ICOMOS study compiled by Jokilehto.

pened only in the early and mid-1990s. With more and more states signing the World Heritage Convention, the criteria of definition changed and became more encompassing.[9] The more Member States signed however, the louder the critique of the World Heritage List became. The clustering of UNESCO "properties" in Europe, so the argument went, mirrored the hegemonic and postimperial character of UNESCO's World Heritage policy, which failed to give the cultural heritage of non-Western countries the same recognition as Western states. In 1994, UNESCO therefore adopted a "Global Strategy for a Representative, Balanced and Credible World Heritage List."[10]

A direct consequence of this strategy was the Africa 2009 program. Launched by UNESCO in 1998, the aim was to provide African nation states with the necessary technical and administrative support to protect and successfully nominate sites on the African continent as World Heritage.[11] Up to then, only a few African states had succeeded in inscribing a site on the list. One of them was Nigeria.[12] The new program coincided with the country's end of the military regime and the return to democracy. Moreover, Nigeria's new president was a familiar figure. Already in 1977 he had presided over the legendary FESTAC festival, which celebrated black heritage (Apter). Back in the government, Olusegun Obasanjo was eager to revive the theme of heritage as an important part of his symbolic politics. In 2000, he appointed the Yoruba priest and archaeologist Omotoso Eluyemi as new director-general of the National Commission for Museums and Monuments and Michael Omolewa, a professor of adult education at the University of Ibadan, as Nigeria's ambassador and permanent delegate to UNESCO. Later joined by Wande Abimbola, a prominent Ifa priest and "special advisor on cul-

---

9   In 1992, the World Heritage Committee introduced the term "cultural landscape", which stressed the idea of "interactions between humans and their environment" and pushed the notion of "intangible heritage" as a necessary complement to tangible heritage. Another frequently mentioned milestone in the development is the so-called Nara Document on Authenticity from 1994 (http://whc.unesco.org/archive/nara94.htm). The declaration was pushed by the Japanese delegation, whose members rejected the ICCROM definition of authenticity in terms of authenticity of material, design, workmanship and setting as defined in the Venice convention on the grounds that it did not fit local religious architecture. The intervention illustrates that UNESCO is not a monolithic block, but rather an "arena", as Brumann ("Multilateral ethnography") suggests, in which multiple actors with often competing agenda operate and struggle over issues that often come down to matters of cultural translations. For instance, in its foundational text, the *Convention Concerning the Protection of the World Cultural and Natural Heritage,* adopted in 1972, UNESCO translated the term *patrimoine naturel* as "natural heritage". From then on, "heritage" has been used in all its official texts. Its common usage explains why we have adopted it in this volume. It goes without saying, however, that the terms used in specific countries and cultures are not always equivalent to "heritage" and that their meaning varies according to different actors and historical and geographical contexts.
10 http://whc.unesco.org/en/globalstrategy, accessed 2 November 2010.
11 http://whc.unesco.org/archive/2010/whc10-34com-10De.pdf, accessed 10 October 2010.
12 In 1999, the terraced hills of Sukur in central Nigeria became the first Nigerian site inscribed onto the list on the basis of the newly introduced category of "cultural landscape".

tural affairs and traditional matters" to Obasanjo, the three pushed to enlist important features of Yoruba culture in the UNESCO program.

One of the projects was the Osun grove. Work on the nomination file had started in 1999. Four years later, in December 2003, a French UNESCO consultant met with a delegation from the National Commission of Museums and Monuments and local officials to inspect the site. The latter expressed their willingness to address the critical issues listed by the consultant but pointed to economic constraints. The consultant responded by stressing that selection as a World Heritage site would trigger economic growth in the host community by attracting tourists, therefore leading to the establishment of a viable tourist infrastructure. Among the representatives of the Osogbo palace and city council, the message was well received. A few months earlier, the Osogbo Progressive Union had launched a city website on which, under the rubric "investment opportunities," it noted:

> Given the right push, Osogbo has the natural and precedent tendency of becoming a true African "Disney World" with her God-endowed landscape, thick rain forest and above all abundance of natural artistically inclined talents. In Osogbo, notable among the many places of cultural entrancing interests are the Obafemi Awolowo University Museum at Popo Street, Nike Art Gallery, Susan Wenger's studio at Ibokun Road, the Osun grove, the Ataoja's [the king's] old and new palaces, bustling trading activities at Oja Oba or Orisunbare markets, etc. Osogbo also plays host to thousands of visitors who come from all across the globe to see and appreciate authentic African arts and also participate in the annual Osun-Osogbo Festival.[13]

Providing the "right push" was left to the new governor of Osun state, Olagunsoye Oyinlola. Oyinlola felt close to Osogbo; in the 1950s and 1960s, his father had collaborated with Wenger and her former husband, the German cultural broker Ulli Beier. The personal connection with Osogbo paid off. Shortly after Oyinlola assumed office in 2003, he gave orders to rectify the critical issues listed by the UNESCO consultant. In August 2004, the UNESCO inspection team paid a second visit to Osogbo, during which local authorities assured the team that everything possible was being done to meet their demands. Satisfied by what they saw on the ground, the team recommended that the nomination be put on the agenda for the next meeting of the World Heritage Committee in July 2005.

Meanwhile, Nigeria's President Obasanjo had been elected chairman of the Organization of the African Union, from which position he effectively pushed for Nigeria's cultural and political supremacy. The July meeting of the UNESCO World Heritage Committee in Durban, South Africa, provided the forum for these demands. It was the first time the committee had met south of the Sahara and Nigeria's ambassador and permanent delegate to UNESCO, and at that time also president of the General Conference of UNESCO, Michael Abiola Omolewa

---

13 http://www.osogbocity.com/id25.htm, accessed 7 October 2010.

in his address linked the nomination of the Osun grove to this unprecedented venue. Using the grove as an example, he stressed the uniqueness of African culture and heritage and reminded the delegates to be aware of the Western bias in UNESCO's "monumental approach" when it comes to the question of what merits preservation and what does not. The time had come, he argued, to break with the imperial structure implicit in the global heritage landscape and its peculiar distinction between nature and culture:

> You have in your hands the very delicate task to ensure the implementation of the global strategy for a more representative, balanced and credible world heritage list. While taking your decisions, I trust you will always keep in mind the uniqueness of the African heritage, which goes beyond the "monumental" approach of heritage in associating both tangible and intangible aspects, as two sides of the same coin – the forest of Osun in my country is a magnificent illustration of the combination of the tangible and intangible in one cultural manifestation. There are many other examples from different parts of our universe. It is the multiplicity of these many coins, put together that make up the diversity and the richness of humanity which we must acknowledge and justly reflect in our work and in our decisions. This is our aim. And this must be the finality of our deliberations here in the next ten days.[14]

In the end, the delegates followed Omolewa's arguments and approved Nigeria's nomination of the Osun grove on the basis of the following three features:

> (influence) The development of the movement of New Sacred Artists and the absorption of Suzanne Wenger, an Austrian artist, into the Yoruba community have proved to be a fertile exchange of ideas that revived the sacred Osun Grove.
>
> (testimony) The Osun Sacred Grove is the largest and perhaps the only remaining example of a once widespread phenomenon that used to characterize every Yoruba settlement. It now represents Yoruba sacred groves and their reflection of Yoruba cosmology.
>
> (living tradition) The Osun Sacred Grove is a tangible expression of Yoruba divinatory and cosmological systems; its annual festival is a living, thriving and evolving response to Yoruba beliefs in the bond between people, their ruler and the Osun goddess.[15]

In Osogbo, news of the UNESCO designation was met with joy and pride. As it happened, the designation coincided with Wenger's ninetieth birthday which prompted city officials to erect a huge billboard congratulating to her achieve-

---

14 http://www.unesco.org/delegates/nigeria/OmolewaWHCDurbanSpeech.html, accessed 12 October 2010.
15 For a full description, see http://whc.unesco.org/en/list/1118/documents, accessed 12 December 2014.

Fig. 5: Billboard congratulating Susanne Wenger at her ninetieth birthday, 2005. Photo: Heidi Mimra

ments (figure 5). At the center of praise though stood the city's guardian deity Osun. Officials of the Osogbo Heritage Council quickly responded that Osun had expanded her kingdom across the globe. Osun devotees performed songs praising Osun not only for her elegance and sense of beauty, but also for her wealth. Describing her as a woman with long arms and a long neck full of yellowish brass bangles, necklaces and fanciful beads, wearing precious, ornamented brass fans and a coral comb, the songs lauded Osun as a source of both fertility and prosperity; the latter alluding to the economic benefits the UNESCO award was expected to generate.

Exchange as Mediation

Let me shift the discussion and come back to the model of heritage as an imagined exchange that I introduced at the beginning of this essay. As I have argued, what lurks through the UNESCO documents regulating and safeguarding heritage is the idea of a generational transfer that resonates with Mauss's concept of gift exchange. Since preservation is seen as a moral obligation the living have vis-à-vis the dead and the unborn, i.e. future generations, heritage comes down to an imagined, intergenerational exchange in terms of property versus remembrance/preservation. The primary purpose of cherished preservation concepts like "authenticity" and "integrity" is thus to verify the sincerity of this exchange. But if "World Heritage" can really be understood as a mode of symbolic exchange generating social and moral value, then how does the idea of value and exchange work on the local level – that is, on the level of the heritage site itself?

In Osogbo, the most prominent example is the annual Osun festival. As I have noted above, the festival is conceived as a performance and re-enactment of the primordial act of exchange between the goddess Osun and the first king of Osogbo. In return for the goddess's promise to provide prosperity and protection, the king promised to respect and preserve the goddess's homestead. The pact was sealed by a sacrifice made by the king of Osogbo to the goddess, an act annually renewed during the festival.[16]

So far the picture correlates with the UNESCO model. The analogy becomes difficult, however, when one realizes that in Yoruba religious practice the exchange is not between the living and the dead but between actors of different – and often contested – ontological status. That is to say, Yoruba divinities can either be deified humans who had once achieved fame and prestige, or they can represent an independent and autonomous principle of spiritual force and power. The answer to this question is not an ontological, but a pragmatic issue. Both perspectives hold, but the question of when to opt for what depends on the context and is very often decided along political lines. After all, political legitimacy of a Yoruba kingdom requires a direct link with the divinities Olodumare, the supreme instance, is said to have sent from heaven to populate the earth. The same goes for Osun. Different genres of knowledge tell different stories and present different images of her.[17] In the ifa divination corpus, Osun is introduced as belonging to the original divinities that populated the earth. In the oriki praise songs, she is characterized as a rich merchant hailing from the Ekiti region who travelled to Osogbo where she turned into a river. Finally, in the itan local histories, she is portrayed as a powerful woman who was helped Osogbo to resist the Fulani raids.

Again, what aspect or status of Osun is invoked is very much context dependent. To understand the dynamics and motives involved in such decisions, it is helpful to go back to the 1980s, when the city was engulfed in serious social conflicts concerning the status of the Osun Osogbo festival. Muslim and Christian critics opposed the festival as a shameful demonstration of paganism. Others supported it. In an effort to alleviate tensions, the then ruling king of Osogbo, Matanmi III, officially depreciated the religious meaning of the grove and festival

---

16 What applies for the public festival holds true also for the private sacrifices. They too are thought of as mediation and exchange. In fact, the annual Osun festival entails a host of smaller festivities during which devotees gather in the grove to pay tribute to and communicate with their own individual deities, whose presence in the grove is marked by statues and/or a certain evergreen plant. The actual sacrificial items are called *ohun-ebo*, with *ebo* standing for sacrifice and *ohun* signifying sound or voice. Driven and empowered by the vital force *ase*, sound acts as a medium or apparatus enabling the mediation with the deity (Abiodun). Other media can be added as well, from food over wood to money. Practically anything can go together with *ohun*. The mediation itself is understood as a form of dialogue or visual exchange akin to Walter Benjamin's famous notion of aura and gaze: "Inherent in the gaze is the expectation that it will be returned by that on which it is bestowed" (204). Hence his legendary dictum: "To experience the aura of an object is to invest it with the ability to look back at us" (ibid.).

17 I should add that the gender of Yoruba deities is very much a subject of debate and that associations of Osun with notions of femininity and womanhood do not necessarily identify Osun as female; see Matory.

and characterized both instead as sites of commemoration and remembrance. In August 1990, in a speech delivered at the finale of the Osun Osogbo festival, he addressed the audience with the following words:

> At this point in time, it is incumbent on me to explain and educate the generality of people on the significance of Osun Osogbo festival. It has been said times without number that this festival has no religious connotations as such. The celebration of Osun does not mean the worship of it. It should be observed that the majority of the celebrants including myself, as chief celebrant, are either Muslims or Christians. As a matter of our cultural base, Osun festival stands for commemoration of founding of Osogbo as a settlement. It also stands for the remembrance of all the past monarchs, various warriors and patriots who had done a lot to make Osogbo a famous city of international repute. For example this Osun grove is the first place of settlement of my ancestors – Oba Larooye and Olutimehin who founded this ancient town about four hundred years ago…The Osun festival is a purely cultural affair of Osogbo indigenes and the celebration of which is not the sole making of the reigning Ataoja, but that of the totality of its people. (Osogbo Cultural Heritage Council 6)

When first announced, the bluntness of the statement caused an outcry in Osogbo. Members of the various religious cults were furious and insisted that the Osun festival did indeed express core religious values and beliefs. For them, the festival was not merely a matter of remembrance: homage to the goddess was central. They insisted that the reality of the powers of Osun was beyond doubt, and warned that any attempt to deny that reality would provoke the anger of the goddess and could potentially disrupt her protection of the town.

As heated and passionate as the debate was, at the heart of the matter was not the question of the ontological status of Osun but rather the specific forms or media people favored to invoke her. As I have pointed out, a characteristic feature of Yoruba society is the malleability and potential interchangeability of remembrance and religious communication. Since both options hold, the focus of interest shifts to the role of the media used to ensure and maintain an effective remembrance/communication.[18] What media qualify as effective and who owns them? The answer to that question goes right to the heart of Yoruba notions of power and authority. In the case of Osogbo, it actually defines kingship. Since Osun is considered to be the city's source of prosperity, and since prosperity can be ensured by communication with the deity, what defines authority is the control over media through which the deity can be contacted (and/or remembered).

Given the close connection with kingship, quarrels over media and religion are far from new. In fact, they are an integral part of Osogbo history. Over the

---

18 For a general debate on religion and mediation, see Belting and Morgan. For a discussion of the approach in the context of Osogbo heritage politics, see Probst "Revisiting Osogbo" and "Osogbo and the Art of Heritage" 137ff.).

last hundred years, Osogbo rulers have continuously changed religious media. Seen from this angle, the permission of the Osogbo king in the early 1960s to let Wenger reshape the Osun was part of an old and established practice. Over the last five decades, however, things have become difficult.

Property Issues

Tellingly, UNESCO refers to the entries on its World Heritage List as "properties." The respective documents are rather vague as to what the term "property" actually means. Still, what unifies the different conventions and treaties is the belief in the "thingliness" of property.[19] This tangible dimension of property, however, stands in contrast to the anthropological understanding of the term. Informed not the least by Mauss's seminal gift essay, anthropologists have long argued that property is not about things, but rather about relationships things enable and/ or initiate (Hann; Hirsch). In other words, property signifies a network of relations between actors (human and nonhuman) in which socially relevant notions of ownership, wealth, authority or identity are collectively performed and negotiated.

Admittedly, the distinction is not as clear-cut as it seems. In actual fact, both concepts go together. Not only has Osun certain properties that allow her to provide wealth and prosperity to the king and his people, the deity herself is a property in the sense that she enacts and mobilizes a network of relations that constitute the notion of Osogbo identity as a whole. At the same time, though, Osun is also a clear case for the thingliness of property and the validity of ownership. After all, Osun only exists in the material forms, for example in the media, through which she can be experienced, contacted and communicated with. That is why the media/forms are considered to be inalienable, they cannot be sold and given away, and that is why control and ownership over the media, which allow for tapping into the riches of the deity, constitute the basis for the authority of the king. The most precious media are the sacred objects the ritual maiden carries on her head to the Osun grove at the climax of the festival. As mentioned above, the objects are in a calabash covered with a cloth and thus invisible to the public, a feature which correlates with the invisibility of heritage as an abstract

---

19 Even "intangible heritage" does have a tangible expression. It is this thingliness or tangibility of property which not only allows for disputes over ownership, but also allows for the settlement of these disputes by employing a legal code and following an organized judicial procedure. The UNESCO website explains the matter as follows: "The terms cultural 'property', 'heritage', 'goods' and 'objects' are often considered as interchangeable in common parlance. Their exact definition and legal regime (alienability, exportability, etc.) are to be sought in national legislation, or in international conventions. Therefore such definitions and legal regimes vary from State legislation to State legislation, or from treaty (international convention) to treaty. Generally, the word 'property' has a legal background (linked to 'ownership'), while 'heritage' stresses conservation and transfer from generation to generation" (http://portal.unesco.org/culture/en/ev.php-URL_ID=36292&URL_DO=DO_TOPIC&URL_SECTION=201.html accessed on 2 September 2010).

value. Inside the calabash are a number of brass emblems (re)presenting Osun and Ogboni, a secret society controlling the power of the king.

In view of the above comment on the constant historical change of media in Yoruba religious politics, the argument of inalienability may surprise. A closer look at the media changes, though, reveals that old media were not discarded, but incorporated and embedded into new media, thus creating layers of media, meaning and mediation around Osun. With every new layer, however, came new tensions and conflicts. The recent introduction of "new media" in the Osun grove and the subsequent inscription of the Osun grove onto the UNESCO World Heritage List are a case in point. Much of the uneasiness revolves around questions of efficacy, ownership and value. As I have noted, with the reshaping of the Osun grove, it first became a national monument, then a public museum, and finally a World Heritage Site. This means that the grove and all its structures are now in the possession of the palace, the Nigerian state and UNESCO. The complex scenario entails numerous frictions that very much result from the ambiguous processes of exchange underlying the concept of heritage. By presenting the Osun grove to the World Heritage Committee to be nominated and accepted as "World Heritage," the Nigerian state has taken the local festival and turned it into a national "gift," as it were, to the World Heritage Committee, which reciprocated by lending the festival and the nation state recognition. As much as members of the Osun cult appreciate the global recognition, they also express concern over the effects of this development. Issues of secrecy and loss of control over access to the structures are important. Not all parts of the Osun grove are open to the public. Certain ritual places are off limits and taking pictures is not allowed. With more and more people coming, it has become difficult to restrict access to the temples and ensure the sense of secrecy and privacy that characterizes communication with the divine.

Concern about access goes together with the difficulties of remaining in control of the meaning of images that emerge in the communication with the divine. This issue is especially pertinent with regard to the flood of images generated by the rise of the Osun grove into the international heritage world. People lament that Osun does not show herself anymore; that the spirituality of the festival is decreasing as a result of uncontrolled commercialization and media coverage. In the past, so a popular argument goes, people were able to see Osun after the public sacrifice to her had been made. A catfish, one of Osun's avatars, used to jump out of the water right into the arms of the Osun priest. Nowadays, events like this don't happen anymore. Surely, complaints like this are not new.[20] But with companies like CNN and the BBC reporting on the festival, and the erection of huge LCD television screens at strategic points in the town for those who could not make it to the sacred grove, the situation seems to have reached a new crisis level. While it is tempting to understand these worries about Osun's retreat as

---

20 See Farotimi 23, who cites a complaint about photography from the 1940s.

a case of "disenchantment," to use the Weberian formulation, the real problem is not the loss and/or secularization of meaning, but its diminished controllability.

A third lament concerns the economic effects the revitalization of the Osun grove has triggered. Since Osun is a public property, as it were, there is a sense of entitlement to the benefits of exchanges and interactions taking place in and around the Osun grove (figure 6). The exchanges can be seen according to Bourdieu's (1986) classic analysis of the circuit and convertibility of different forms of capital: cultural, social and economic. Thus, the attention and prestige of the Osun grove and festival have fostered relationships between Osogbo and other cities in the Yoruba diaspora (figure 7). This relationship has not only increased the number of visitors and the amount of money they spent in the city; the influx of visitors has also changed the religious market – something members of the Osun cult do complain about. Those who are looking for answers and help from Osun now have the chance to select from a wide range of religious service providers: those who have settled in Osogbo permanently as well as others who have come in just for the duration of the annual festival. The changes fit into the franchise model the UNESCO World Heritage Center uses to propagate "World Heritage." That is to say, what UNESCO grants is basically a licensed outlet to produce and/or market highly valued and internationally recognized local culture, which can be converted into global presence and recognition, which in turn – potentially at least – can be converted into economic capital, that is, money. In contrast to the Member States, which are obliged to preserve the property, the model costs UNESCO only a little, while at the same time providing the organization with the reputation it needs to be seen as an attractive business partner. Left open are questions concerning who profits from these processes of value cre-

Fig. 6: Sponsors of the Osun festival 2015. Photo: Unknown (Source: http://globalmonitor.com.ng/photonews-pix-from-the-press-conference-on-osun-festival-that-held-at-the-institute-of-directors-in-Lagos-recently/)

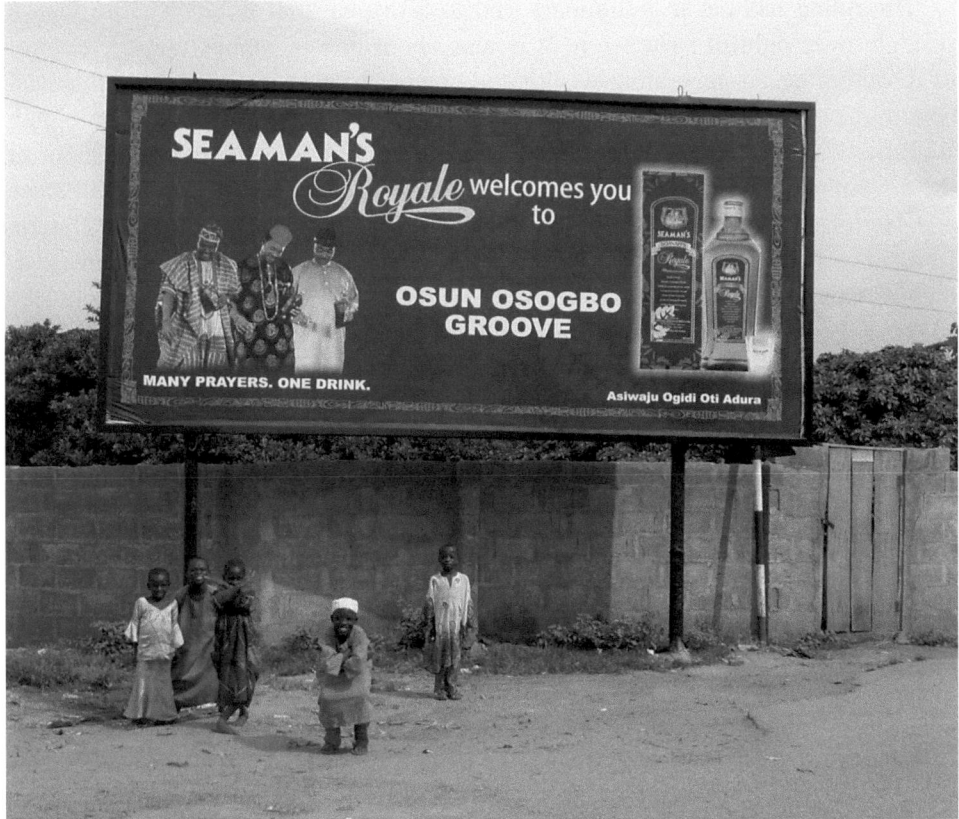

Fig. 7: Billboard on the way to the Osun Grove, 2007. Photo: Peter Probst

ation and capital conversion.[21] If Osun is a public property, should the wealth the deity is providing not be shared among all?

In Osogbo the question has aggravated old rifts and differences that recently resulted in a partial paralysis of the city's political and religious life. In 2010, the old king had died and his successor was installed. Soon after, the legitimacy of the chosen candidate was questioned. The allegations of foul play brought the matter to court, which ruled that the selection of the new king had indeed been invalid and that the incumbent of the office had to step down. The king refused to do so, however. This, in turn, enraged some high-ranking priests of the Osun cult who refused to conduct an important divination ritual at the palace. Since the ritual was/is key to the success of the festival, the priests' refusal alarmed the government, which put pressure on the players involved. In December 2011, the high court adjourned the case indefinitely pending the determination of the appeal filed by the deposed king of Osogbo.

---

21 The question is highlighted by the Ogboni emblem inside the calabash the ritual maiden carries to Osun grove at the climax of the Osun festival. Ogboni controls the king to ensure that he/she works for the public good and not for special interests.

The ruling has put a preliminary end to a dispute that is much more than a struggle over rightful succession. It is also about power, money and the control of resources/media generating wealth and power. Prior to the 2000s, the financial commitment of the government to the Osun grove and festival had been minimal. With the UNESCO nomination, this changed. Not only did the financial input of the government increase, the signs of support also encouraged the Osogbo Palace and Heritage Council to join a public/private partnership with Infogem Nigeria Limited, a Lagos-based marketing firm and event organizer. Infogem's involvement turned out to be highly effective. Contracts with high-caliber sponsors like MTN, Nigeria's leading telecommunications company, turned the annual festival into a multimillion dollar event. Given these circumstances, the Osun grove and festival are no longer in the hands of Osogbo. Instead, they have become a marketable brand, actively pushed by the neoliberal government eager to generate revenue from cultural properties.[22]

As appalling as the blatant invocation of profit is, one needs to be careful not to fall into the trap of a Euro-American modernist separation between culture and commerce, art and craft, meaningful substance and trashy kitsch. That is to say, the critique is based upon a sharp value-driven compartmentalization of objects and activities with distinctly different audiences, curatorial practices and visual ideologies. It was and still is, however, precisely the basic interconnectedness of commerce, art and festivity in Yoruba culture that enabled Osogbo to invent itself as a heritage site.[23] Surely, the meaning and consequences of this move are far from clear. Though heritage moves between the market and the nonmarket sphere, people realize that the osmosis has limits. Restrictions apply. Secrecy matters. Certain things cannot and should not be seen. Despite entering the global stage of heritage, the objects in the sacred calabash a ritual maiden carries to the Osun grove have been kept hidden. The visibility and global attention of the festival thus rests on the invisibility – and inalienability – of the festival's most valuable objects. Hardly astonishingly though, the very people who guard the cultural value of the festival feel excluded from the possibility of profiting economically from it.

---

22 The popularity has created its problems in terms of maintaining control of the 'original'. Thus in July 2014, just a few weeks before the opening of the festival, the Nigerian press cited the ruler of Osogbo commenting on his tours through the African diaspora: 'Some people even showed me a river they intend to refer to as their own Osun river but I was frank enough to let them know that Osun cannot have a duplicate anywhere in the world as only the Ataoja and top chiefs know what the festival entails each year and the spiritual process that goes with it which can only happen in Osun' (http://dailyindependent-nig.com/2014/07/organisers-unveil-plans-osun-osogbo-festival-2014/ accessed 15 November 2014).

23 For a similar argument with respect to the celebration of heritage in India, see Appadurai and Breckenridge.

Conclusion

Asked for a proper Yoruba translation of the English word "heritage," people in Osogbo sometimes referred to ogun, a term with a wide range of meanings from property and inheritance to problems and war. Personally, I found the term quite fitting. After all, if not a war, then at least a dispute characterizes also the debate about heritage in academia. Over the past two decades, scholars have argued over questions of its meaning: Does heritage signify valuable remnants of the past that require safeguarding and protection, as the preservation camp argues? Or is heritage not first and foremost a contemporary practice or discourse by which the past comes to matter in the present, as (most) anthropologists claim?

This chapter aimed to link and negotiate between these two positions by taking heritage seriously and accepting the notion of death and absence, which – willingly or unwillingly, explicitly or implicitly – informs practices and notions of heritage. Seen in this way, heritage needs to be understood as a relationship embedded in spheres of symbolic exchange that generate both social and material forms of value.

As I have shown, international preservation politics recognized and used this argument early on. Heritage worked not only as an instrument of nation building, but increasingly also as a vehicle of world making. Conventions formalized the moral obligation of exchange and turned it into treaties and contracts with the hope of generating a global consciousness and solidarity. As a result, the idea of a vertical intergenerational exchange got expanded and replaced by a horizontal politics of recognition. The necessary consequence was a proliferation of heritage sites that – in conjunction with the wave of neoliberalism and the prospect of making money with the past – led in turn to an erosion of the belief in the value of exchange/heritage. Surely, there are good reasons to maintain a critical stance vis-à-vis the official praises of heritage. Yet, viewing heritage solely as a discourse and/or construct risks the danger of failing to understand the fascination that emanates from the past. Just as property is more than ownership, value is more than a matter of money and profit. In the neoliberal age of "Ethnicity, Inc." (Comaroff and Comaroff), Mauss's reflections on gift exchange provide a useful reminder of these insights.

What makes the case of the Osun Osogbo Sacred Grove telling is the way that it allows us to comprehend the complex entanglement of different values resulting from different modes and uses of exchange. Thus, the value of exchange can be understood as a way to establish and perpetuate social relationships in terms of sociality, as a means of achieving fame as an end in itself or as a form of recognition in terms of acceptance as a worthy partner of exchange. Accordingly, the spectrum of exchange partners varies, ranging from exchange between states, between individuals or between human and non-/semihuman actors, like the goddess Osun and her liquid body, the Osun river.

Taken together, heritage does indeed qualify as a "total social fact," to invoke Mauss one more time. It is both a medium and a symbol of sociality, albeit not for all. As such, heritage is also a prominent target for all those who reject the model of sociality that the exchange processes of heritage constitute – or rather are thought to constitute. Iconoclastic attacks on World Heritage sites, such as the destruction of the Buddha statues in Bamiyan or the demolition of the tombs of Islamic saints in Timbuktu are powerful political demonstrations of disinterest and rejection of the models of sociality upon which these sites are built. To understand this message not only means to take the values of heritage seriously and to recognize the entangled processes of exchange that generate them. It also means to realize the struggle people engage in to remain in control of the means of exchange.

Works Cited

Abiodun, Rowland. "Understanding Yoruba Art and Aesthetics: The Concept of Ase." *African Arts* 27.3 (1994): 78–91.

Achebe, Chinua. *Things Fall Apart.* London: Heineman, 1958.

Appadurai, Arjun, and Carol A. Breckenridge. "Museums are Good to Think. Heritage on View in India." *Representing the Nation.* Eds. David Boswell and Jessica Evans. London: Routledge, 2002. 404–20.

Apter, Andrew. *The Pan-African Nation: Oil and the Spectacle of Culture in Nigeria.* Chicago: University of Chicago Press, 2005.

Basu, Paul, and Wayne Modest (Eds.). *Museums, Heritage and International Development.* London: Routledge, 2015.

Beier, Ulli. *Contemporary Art in Africa.* London: Praeger, 1968.

Belting, Hans. *Das echte Bild: Bilderfragen als Glaubensfragen.* Munich: CH Beck, 2005.

Bendix, Regina, Adyita Eggert, and Arnika Peselmann (Eds.). *Heritage Regimes and the State.* Göttingen: Göttingen University Press, 2012.

Benjamin, Walter. *The Writer of Modern Life: Essays on Charles Baudelaire.* Cambridge, MA: Harvard University Press, 2006.

Bourdieu, Pierre. "The Forms of Capital." *Handbook of Theory and Research for the Sociology of Education.* Ed. J. Richardson. New York: Greenwood, 1986. 241–58.

Brumann, Chris. "Multilateral Ethnography: Entering the World Heritage Arena." *Max Planck Institute for Social Anthropology Working Papers* 136, 2012. 2 September 2012 <http://www.eth.mpg.de/cms/en/publications/working_papers/pdf/mpi-eth-working-paper-0136.pdf>.

—. "Heritage Agnosticism: A Third Path for the Study of Heritage." *Social Anthropology* 22,2 (2014): 173–88.

Comaroff, Jean, and John Comaroff. *Ethnicity, Inc.* Chicago: University of Chicago Press, 2009.

De Jong, Ferdinand, and Michael Rowlands (Eds). Special Issue on "Postconflict Heritage." *Journal of Material Culture* 13,2 (2008).

Farotimi, David. *The Osun Festival in the History of Osogbo.* Lagos: Facelift. 1990.

Fournier, Michel. *Marcel Mauss: A Biography.* Princeton, NJ: Princeton University Press, 2005.
Godelier, Maurice. "Some Things You Give, Some Things You Sell, but Some Things You Must Keep for Yourselves: What Mauss Did Not Say about Sacred Objects." *The Enigma of Gift and Sacrifice.* Eds. Edith Wyschogrod, Jean-Joseph Goux and Eric Boyton. New York: Fordham University Press, 2002. 19–35.
Hann, Chris M. "Introduction: The Embeddedness of Property." *Property Relations: Renewing the Anthropological Tradition.* Ed. Chris M. Hann. Cambridge: Cambridge University Press, 1998. 1–47.
Hardt, Michael, and Antonio Negri. *Empire.* Cambridge, MA: Harvard University Press, 2002.
Hart, Keith. "In Pursuit of the Whole." *Comparative Studies in History and Society* 49,2 (2011): 473–85.
Hirsch, Eric. "Property and Persons: New Forms and Contests in the Era of Neo-Liberalism." *Annual Review of Anthropology* 39 (2010): 347–60.
Jokilehto, Jukka. *What is OUV? Defining the Outstanding Cultural Value of Cultural World Heritage Properties.* Paris: ICOMOS, 2008.
Labadi, Sophia. *UNESCO, Cultural Heritage, and Outstanding Universal Values.* Lanham, MD: Altamira Press, 2012.
Liebersohn, Harry. *The Return of the Gift. European History of a Global Idea.* Cambridge: Cambridge University Press, 2010.
Matory, Lorand. "Is there Gender in Yoruba Culture?" *Orisa Devotion as World Religion.* Eds. Jacob K. Olupona, and Terry Rey. Madison: University of Wisconsin Press, 2008. 513–58.
Mauss, Marcel. *The Gift: Forms and Functions of Exchange in Archaic Societies.* London: Cohen & West, 1966 [1925].
Mazower, Mark. *No Enchanted Palace: The End of Empire and the Ideological Origins of the United Nations.* Princeton, NJ: Princeton University Press, 2009.
Meskell, Lynn. "The Rush to Inscribe: Reflections on the 35th Session of the World Heritage Committee, UNESCO Paris, 2011." *Journal of Field Archaeology* 37 (2012): 145–51.
Morgan, David. "Mediation or Mediatization: The History of Media in the Study of Religion." *Culture and Religion* 12,2 (2011): 137–52.
Osogbo Cultural Heritage Council. *Annual Festival Program.* Osogbo: Government Printer, 1990.
Probst, Peter. "Revisiting Osogbo: Religion, Media, and Control in a Nigerian World Heritage Site." *Critical Interventions: Journal of African Art History and Visual Culture* 7 (2010): 65–83.
—. *Osogbo and the Art of Heritage: Monuments, Deities, and Money.* Bloomington: Indiana University Press, 2011.
—. "Iconoclash in the Age of Heritage." *African Arts* 45.3 (2012): 10–13.
Sand, Jordan. "Japan's Monument Problem. Ise Shrine as Metaphor." *Heritage in the Modern World.* Eds. Paul Betts and Corey Ross, Past and Present Supplement No. 15 (2014): 126–57.
Sansi, Roger. *Art, Anthropology and the Gift.* London: Bloomsbury, 2014.
Sigaud, Lygia. "The Vicissitudes of the Gift." *Social Anthropology* 10.3 (2002): 335–38.
Wenger, Susanne. *The Timeless Mind of the Sacred: Its New Manifestation in the Osun Grove.* Ibadan: Ibadan University Press, 1977.

Chapter Eight

Indigenous Knowledges, Ecology, and Living Heritage in North America

Kerstin Knopf

Climate change and global warming have become buzzwords in today's public discourse. Most people are aware of these natural phenomena; scientists are alarmed, continuously warn the world about the effects, and their research results influence international politics. But Western scientists and international politics have little interest in Indigenous knowledges that can contribute to solutions to this global problem. In 2010, the much-acclaimed Inuit director Zacharias Kunuk[1] released his film *Qapirangajuq: Inuit Knowledge and Climate Change*, co-directed with the Canadian environmental scientist Ian Mauro (University of Winnipeg).[2] This film is a first step to counter this neglect as the filmmakers ask Inuit elders from different Arctic regions to speak about the changes they observe in the Arctic as a result of climate change, Western industrialism, and Western research. The film makes clear that Indigenous knowledge needs to be accepted as an equal scientific contribution to Western science if we even want to come close to solving global ecological problems. This article will take the documentary film as entry point for presenting some thoughts on Indigenous and Western ecologies and knowledge systems as well as their relationships in the power matrixes of our globalized world. The article employs the terms 'Western' and 'Eurocentric' as denoting political, cultural, economic, and intellectual thought and practice with roots in European societies and knowledge traditions that spread throughout the world during the colonial era, and 'non-Western' and 'non-European' as denoting thoughts and practices generated in cultures, societies, and knowledge traditions that were understood as 'other' to centralized European traditions. Yet, these concepts cannot be clearly defined and become increasingly blurred through transcul-

---

1   Zacharias Kunuk is most known for his film *Atanarjuat: The Fast Runner* (2001), which won the Golden Camera in Cannes 2001, *The Journals of Knud Rasmussen* (2006), co-directed with Norman Cohn, and *Maliglutit* (Searchers) (2016), an adaptation of John Ford's *The Searchers* to Inuit culture and Arctic landscape.
2   The film was screened in parts at the Climate Summit in Copenhagen in 2009 as a Canadian/Inuit contribution to the discussions. The filmmakers made it a point not to fly to Copenhagen and thus cause kerosene emission, but to have the film screened and participate in discussions via skype. The film had its world premiere at the ImagineNATIVE Film and Media Arts Festival in Toronto in 2010 with a following discussion with Kunuk and Mauro that interacted with the world through skype. The film can be watched online or downloaded from the Isuma television website: http://www.isuma.tv/hi/en/inuit-knowledge-and-climate-change/movie.

tural and transnational dynamics in present societies. Likewise, it is not assumed that there are unified or homogenous 'Western', 'European' or 'non-Western' and 'non-European' understandings of knowledge and knowledge practices. It will then discuss Indigenous knowledges as living knowledges and intangible cultural heritage vis-à-vis issues appearing in the development of the heritage discourse and the problems that David Lowenthal has formulated as the 'discontents' of 'minority heritage' (The Heritage Crusade 84–87). Indigenous knowledges, the article argues, constantly adapt to changing influences and conditions, engage with Eurocentric knowledges, and produce new decolonized knowledges.

Introduction

The climate change, caused by unrelenting capitalist growth and the explosive increase in energy production and consumption as well as industrial wastes, creates a global situation where local, often Indigenous, people and poorer nations with less political clout than the G20 states bear the brunt of the environmental consequences. For example, floods in Bangladesh, droughts in Western Africa, and oil spills in Nigeria wreck harvests and pollute landscapes that are necessary for local food production and survival. This often results in catastrophic hunger epidemics and mass migrations to the countries of the global North. Likewise, systematic harvesting of lumber and toxic pollution of river systems and landscapes in Canada, for example through the Mount Polley mine disaster in August 2014, the Kalamazoo River oil spill, tar sand tailing spills in Alberta, and open pit uranium mining in Northern Saskatchewan (Notzke, *Oil Sand Truths*), extremely limit additional low-economy means of sustenance like fishing and hunting that are necessary for many impoverished Aboriginal and Inuit families. For example, clear cutting in British Columbia and Northern Ontario causes soil erosion, devastated fish populations in adjacent river systems, and the loss of wildlife habitats, and Inuit in the Arctic are advised not to eat caribou and sea mammal meat because of increased mercury levels in the animals (Dietz, Outridge, and Hobson 6121; Rachel Walker n. p.). All this happens in acquiescence with Western nations who are the beneficiaries of such environmentally discriminatory politics and business practices as well as with governments of affected Indigenous and other local peoples, who often feel pressed to weigh the desire to retain territorial privileges up against the need to react upon the material precarity of their communities. Even if individual Western people will critique such politics and practices, it is difficult to withdraw from a world where massive coal, oil, and gas extraction and production destroys landscapes and livelihoods, where cell phones contain precious metals for the extraction of which Indigenous people, for example in India, are displaced from their homelands, and where the world's hunger for beef, soy, sugar, and wood still causes nations like the Guaraní in Brazil to be removed from their traditional lands in order to make room for big scale farming (Lewis Evans n. p.). Environmental pollution is the continuation of colonial regimes and the side effect of global neocolonial business practices condoned by the IMF and the World Bank.

The increasing efforts to battle global warming and environmental destruction, too, are concentrated in the hands and minds of mostly Western scientists and politicians. Hardly are Western scientists and international politics interested in which ways Indigenous people and their knowledges can help in the scientific study of the critical environmental situation the world is confronted with, as well as providing possible solutions. There is no understanding yet that Indigenous knowledge about the earth and its flora and fauna, that elders' observations about changes in nature and the climate, are as important for an understanding of what is happening to the globe as the research of Western scientists. Already in 1992, the Arctic researcher George Hobson holds in his article "Traditional Knowledge *Is* Science": "Western scientists have a tendency to reject the traditional knowledge of native peoples as anecdotal, non-quantitative, without method, and unscientific [...] From our scientific ivory towers we tend to ignore basic knowledge that is available to us" (Hobson n. p.). Likewise, in Kunuk and Mauro's film the Inuit elder Rita Nashook says: "Southerners don't want to understand Inuit ways. They are ignorant about our culture, don't consider our opinion, and treat us like we know nothing" (Kunuk and Mauro n. p.). By ignoring Inuit knowledge in these areas, Western scientists waste valuable input that would definitely facilitate their research and generate better results, or I dare say, results that are closer to the realities and circumstances they try to penetrate.

Such ignorance and neglect of Indigenous knowledges, I argue, is a legacy of colonial and neocolonial relations and a colonial epistemology that regards Indigenous social structures, religions, values, ways of living, and knowledges as inferior, insignificant, and even barbaric. Decolonizing scientific discourses and acknowledging Indigenous knowledges is necessary lest we continue to foreclose valuable knowledge that will help dealing with global conflicts and environmental problems. The Mi'kmaw scholar Marie Battiste stresses that the well-being of ecologies and environments depends on the people "who either cultivate it for good or extract it for goods" (*Decolonizing Education* 98). She says that the world's Indigenous people continue to cultivate 80 percent of the world's natural biodiversity, which goes hand in hand with drawing from and preserving their cultural knowledge (98). This, according to her, references the linkages between biological and cultural diversity that David Harmon has described (2002). Battiste suggests: "The potential benefit of Indigenous knowledge for all societies [...] is to draw on the vitality of Indigenous knowledge and its dynamic capacities to solve contemporary problems as well" (*Decolonizing Education* 97). In this line of thought, Angela Cavender Wilson notes that Indigenous linguistic and ecological knowledge teems with valuable information about the unique North American homelands and ecosystems (81, 83). And in the documentary *Qapirangajuq* Rita Nashook holds: "Inuit culture is oral and we keep knowledge in our minds. Even

Fig. 1: Rita Nashook Speaking about Inuit Knowledge and Arctic Animals. Source: Igloolik Isuma Productions & Kunuk Cohn Productions 2010.

without text, our culture is full of wisdom. We have knowledge about animals, their birth cycles, when they shed fur, when they mate, and when animals gather" (Kunuk and Mauro n. p.) (Fig. 1).

Another speaker says that Western biologists do not have generations of experience of interacting with arctic animals. And in the same vein, Sheila Watt-Cloutier, former International Chair of the Inuit Circumpolar Council (ICC) and recent Right Livelihood Award winner, explains: "Scientists don't realize the knowledge of our hunters. Hunter knowledge is rich in information and must be included. Southerners often have a narrow perspective, based only on studies. This has to change. Especially with respect to polar bears and marine mammals" (quoted in Kunuk and Mauro n. p.).

It is essential to understand Indigenous knowledges and practices not as static, solely traditional, and directed at a precolonial past, but as dynamic, innovative, and changing according to neo/colonial influences, new technologies, and political developments (Grenier 6). It is likewise important to insist on an understanding that traditional *and* contemporary Inuit knowledge is invaluable, because certainly Inuit have adapted to Western influences and changes in climate and their environments, and it is this contemporary knowledge, or "living knowledge," as Ian Mauro says (ImagineNATIVE n. p.), – interpreting land and ice, water, weather and sky, wildlife signs and fixing snowmobiles and such things with simple means – that is similarly important as traditional knowledge. Inuit may not state this clearly, but they know the old *and* changed Arctic like no one else. Likewise, I propose that the often-used term 'traditional knowledge' in itself is inappropriate and patronizing, because it locates Indigenous knowledge in the archaic and primordial and disallows Indigenous modernity. Thus, I suggest using the term 'Indigenous knowledge/s' with the understanding that it includes traditional *and* contemporary Indigenous knowledges.

Fig. 2: Low Altitude Refraction. Source: Igloolik Isuma Productions & Kunuk Cohn Productions 2010.

The Documentary Film[3]

The film *Qapirangajuq: Inuit Knowledge and Climate Change* is a conventional documentary, employing interviews, footage of interviewees and every-day Inuit activities, archival footage, and sound matching the content, here Inuit ajaja songs and songs by the Inuit artist Lucie Idlout. As in Kunuk's other documentaries,[4] the filmmakers refrain from using an authorial voice-over that explains the background of the presented issues and provides extra information – a documentary style inherited from Griersonian filmmaking that many other Indigenous documentary makers employ. In Kunuk's documentaries one has to watch and listen carefully; he nearly never explains anything but lets the interviewees speak; he provides images that comment on what is said, or simply images that relate to Inuit life – these images, then, also speak. In fact, the whole film is a string of interview parts grouped according to the respective aspect of Inuit observations and illustrated with matching footage. Conspicuously, the introductory and closing shot of a sun seemingly going up and down on the horizon is not explained. This is the phenomenon of low altitude astronomical refraction (LAAR), the bending of light from celestial sources that are close to the horizon, depending on the surface temperatures (Sampson, Lozowski and Machel 5652). Higher surface temperatures in the Arctic seem to impact upon this phenomenon, which the film indicates but does not explain. Only an attentive viewer will wonder and inquire about such an image (Fig. 2).[5]

---

3 I have further written about this film in *Indigenizing Science*.
4 For example *Exile* (2008) about the forced relocation of several Inuit families into the high Arctic in 1953, 1500 kilometers north of their home in northern Quebec, as part of Canada's policy to maintain Arctic sovereignty and land claims to the northern Arctic.
5 Neither in the film nor during the discussion after the Toronto premiere do Kunuk and Mauro specify whether these images are taken from a sunrise or sunset; they might deliberately leave this question unanswered. Mauro explains low altitude refraction in the discussion after the premiere: "Hot air is sitting above this very cold surface of ice, permafrost, snow. And […] you have […] an inversion layer: hot above cold. And right at the inter-

At the beginning, elders talk about their childhood and their traditional way of living, a filmic example of self-locating that is necessary according to Indigenous discourse practices and research (Kovach 110–13). Instead of archival footage of the times the elders talk about, Kunuk and Mauro provide images of contemporary hunting and fishing camps with modern equipment, where whole families temporarily live and children play. The visuals counterpoint the content of the narrated information, a subtle device to draw attention to either visual or audio content. The images, moreover, communicate that hunting and fishing have adapted to modern times, and that the custom of setting up such camps and children learning through play and by helping the adults has prevailed. In one shot a boy of about twelve years of age nonchalantly walks into camp with a gun and a shot bird – the image clearly articulates that although hunting and youth activities have adapted to modernity, the custom of hunting will be continued by the young. Such comment could be made by a narrative voice, but the filmmakers avoid such top-down educational style. Similarly, when the elders speak about the ice sheet becoming increasingly thinner, Kunuk and Mauro juxtapose footage from a film shot by the anthropologist Bernard Saladin d'Anglure presumably in 1956 with their own contemporary footage. In the former we see men digging a hole in the ice for fishing that is five to six feet deep, in the latter we see that the ice is not even a foot deep, indicating that global warming has caused the thickness of the ice to decrease. Again, no commentary; viewers have to draw their own conclusions.

Another important fact about Kunuk's filmmaking is certainly that his interviewees speak Inuktitut, usually accompanied by English subtitles. Besides supporting language preservation,[6] he transmits a sense that Inuit life to a large extent happens in Inuktitut and not in English. He knows that the elders have to speak in their familiar surroundings and contexts and in their first language Inuktitut in order for these cultural testimonies and scientific observations not to lose any meaning in translation. Mauro said in the skype discussion after the screening premiere that only Kunuk was able to make such a film, since he is an accomplished filmmaker, he has knowledge of the land, Inuktitut is his first language, and since he is able to understand the five different dialects of Inuktitut that the elders speak in the film (ImagineNATIVE n. p.).

As well, the film consistently employs an Inuit perspective; it gives voice only to the Inuit elders and politicians, with no Western scientist or 'expert' commenting on what they explain. This is certainly a metafilmic and critical reference to the colonial and neocolonial politics of representing Indigenous people from a supremacist, and supposedly more knowledgeable, Western position in travel

---

face of this very complex air profile the light bends differently and it refracts […] like light going through a prism. The sun appears to have shifted in the horizon and it's an optical shift" (ImagineNATIVE n. p.).

6 On the positive impact of Indigenous language broadcasting (TV and radio) see David 45–50.

reports, notebooks, historical and anthropological texts, novels as well as in film and other electronic media that we encounter throughout Western discourses from the sixteenth century onwards. One should distinguish between rather dominant-supremacist and more self-reflective Western texts aware of neo/colonial practices of representation and their own participation in this practice. But one must keep in mind that also well-intended and well-done non-Indigenous documentaries or historiographic books, for example, about Indigenous cultures and issues are made from a Western perspective, are part of Western representations of the Indigenous, and support the idea that Western knowledge is more legitimate because assumedly more objective, based on empirical evidence, and generated in logo-centric rationalism. Not including a single Western voice and employing an Inuit perspective throughout the film counters Western politics of representation and lends the necessary importance and authority to Inuit voices and knowledge. Mauro stated that the filmmakers did not feel the need to include Western scientists, adding that "elders should be able to express their view without scientists having to validate it" (ImagineNATIVE n. p.).

What the elders actually say in the film is worrisome, to put it mildly. The masses of the world population are not aware of these drastic changes that happen first and more seriously in the Arctic. Because of its unique position and climate, the Arctic is more vulnerable to pollution and the effects of climate change as the film makes clear. The consequences of warmer arctic waters and melting glaciers, multiyear-layered ice, and permafrost soil for polar animals and for the Inuit are serious and often devastating. Both animals and people have to adapt to changes in their environment for which they are not responsible, and in some aspects, this means a decrease of life quality or simply danger. Some of these consequences are summarized in the following: the melting of the ice interferes with the animals' life cycles and sustenance; overland and -ice navigation has become more difficult for Inuit; the ice is much thinner and hunting more dangerous; the fur of seals has become thinner and of inferior quality; the melting of the permafrost ground causes instabilities of the soil, there are more and more serious floods in waterways close to and in communities, indeed whole communities stand on unstable ground that threatens to collapse; melting ice floes and the closer edge of the ice drive polar bears closer to communities to hunt; because of the wind changes, Inuit weathermen can no longer provide reliable forecasts; because the south wind brings acid rain and because of mines in the Arctic and Subarctic, caribous and other animals have drastically increased mercury and other pollution levels – this is actually meat that the Inuit consume, because they still depend upon hunting for sustenance.

Watt-Cloutier has termed global warming a "human rights violation" for the Inuit, when, as chair of the Inuit Circumpolar Conference, she filed a petition to the Inter-American Commission on Human Rights in 2005 and requested relief from human rights violations due to climate change (Inuit Circumpolar Council Canada n. p.). Mauro pointedly said that the Arctic becomes the dumping ground for Western industrial waste; and termed the poisoning and warming of the Arctic "environmental racism" – another form of discrimination against Indigenous peoples in our globalized world. In a global perspective, I suggest, it makes more sense to speak of 'environmental discrimination' as whole regions inhabited by Indigenous *and* non-Indigenous local people suffer from changes and pollution of their environments due to industrial production, its wastes, and emanating dangers. Examples are the environmental consequences of the extraction of the Athabascan tar sands, of deep sea oil drilling in the Gulf of Mexico, of open-pit uranium mining and storage in Canada and in the US, of mineral mining in India, Chile, and Africa, and the nuclear catastrophes in the Ukraine and Japan (Dewar n.p.; Notzke *Oil Sands Truth* n.p.; Metha n.p., SDSG n.p.; Mapani and Kribek). If we take the concerns raised in the film as an example and apply them to a global perspective it becomes more than obvious that Indigenous and regional life and concerns are dominated by multinational corporations and centralized governments, political bodies and knowledge centers. In other words, the regions often do not have a voice in matters concerning themselves, predominantly when they harbor coveted natural resources whose exploitation is driven by national and multinational business interests. Indigenous and local voices are overridden at higher levels; it is a regular political practice that governments are lobbied by national and global business players. What is more, the local population is most often split over the Faustian dilemma whether to participate or protest against natural resource extraction. Some fervently oppose such projects and warn against consequences for humans and the environment and some are convinced they will bring needed economic development, jobs, and profit shares for the communities.[7]

Some of the elders' observations and conclusions may sound quite unbelievable to Western viewers. For example, the observations that the sun now sets at a different place, nineteen kilometers across the horizon, which is a spatial shift of forty-four degrees; that earlier there was only one hour day light for hunting in winter, now there are two hours; that the "daylight" (meaning the sun) is higher up in the sky and more intense; and that the star constellations have shifted their positions in the sky. Yet these observations were made by Inuit in five different Arctic regions (Fig. 3).

The Inuit elders believe that all these phenomena are caused because the axis of the earth has tilted, as they state in the film. NASA, the ultimate scientific authority on such issues, had rejected such deviations as not measurable until recently, as Mauro states (ImagineNATIVE n.p.). Trying to account for these observations, Mauro argued that, in all probability, the phenomenon was caused by low altitude refraction. He says:

---

7   See Warren Cariou and Neil McArthur's documentaries *Land of Oil and Water* (2008) and *Overburden* (2008) about the effects for communities and the environment of the Athabascan tar sand extraction.

Fig. 3: Ludy Pudluk Speaking about Changed Daylight and Sun Set. Source: Igloolik Isuma Productions & Kunuk Cohn Productions 2010.

By linking different ways of knowing, we discovered that a warming atmosphere is actually changing the refraction index of the sky, which dramatically alters the visual landscape of the Arctic. [...] Understandably, the elders attribute the visual change to a tilting earth, but it's actually an optical shift caused by a complex interplay between the wind, atmosphere, earth and ice. (SSHRC n. p.)

A recent NASA study (2016) confirms this assumption: it found that there is a measurable polar motion and, indeed, a shift of the earth's spin axis; and "that all of the main features of polar motion are explained by global-scale continent-ocean mass transport. [...i.e.], the spatiotemporal variability in the transport of water mass between the continents and the oceans" (Adhikari and Ivins 1; see also Borenstein n. p.). This means that because of climate change and melting ice masses on both poles, there is more water in the oceans and, in turn, its changing flow causes massive weight shifts on the earth. It seems that the elders' hypothesis of the axis tilt was rather close to what Western scientists found out a few years later.

Life in the Arctic has been inhibited in further ways. Research of biologists, so obviously necessary and justified to us Westerners, has serious consequences for the animals and the Inuit: for example, the use of helicopters for reconnaissance surveys in order to assess bear populations is destructive to their sense of hearing, and because of tracking collars polar bears are inhibited in their hunting and starve. Drugging and tagging of polar bears means that Inuit are advised not to eat their meat and that the bears' sense of smell and relation to human beings has changed; they are now frequently seen close to and in Inuit settlements, endangering the people – this is seemingly a result of climate change and biological research. In Western science, data acquired through population assessment is compared to the collected data from recent years. Inuit, however, have observed bears for whole generations and have kept this data as oral knowledge. Such different views could easily be reconciled if scientists and Inuit were at the same table communicating with readiness to view the issue also from the other's point of view and with the necessary respect for the other's cultural traditions. But this open approach requires tolerance and persistence as well as willingness to critically assess one's own perspective, not only the perspective of the other.

Indigenous Knowledge in Western Environments[8]

Marie Battiste is one of the most determined researchers on Indigenous knowledges and education. She explains:

> Indigenous knowledge comprises the complex set of technologies developed and sustained by Indigenous civilizations. Often oral and symbolic, it is transmitted through the structure of Indigenous languages and passed on to the next generation through modeling, practice, and animation, rather than through the written word. [...] It is a knowledge system in its own right with its own internal consistency and ways of knowing, and there are limits to how far it can be comprehended from a Eurocentric point of view. [...] Indigenous knowledge is an adaptable, dynamic system based on skills, abilities, and problem-solving techniques that change over time depending on environmental conditions. ("Indigenous Knowledge and Pedagogy" 2, 11)

Battiste thus understands Indigenous knowledge as a knowledge system, cultural practices and technologies that are not fixed, as is often assumed in Western thought, but that continuously adapt to environments, changing cultural influences and political practices. Its premises are grounded in holism and relational world views, it defies categorization, and it operates, if we borrow Western categories, in an interdisciplinary and transcultural mode ("Indigenous Knowledge: Foundations" n. p.). But, according to a Western logocentric and Cartesian understanding of science, Indigenous knowledge has been viewed as primitive, folkloric, unscientific, and insignificant. The Western academy assigns primacy to knowledge based on reason, logic, science, and empirical proof and tends to exclude knowledge based on observation, oral tradition and narratives, non-linear thinking, and even the spiritual. Indigenous epistemologies are associated with the latter categories. Therefore, as a Western-based logic suggests, Indigenous knowledges cannot belong to the legitimate materialistic worldview of true science, reason, and logic. Battiste says that Western educational institutions have disclaimed Indigenous knowledges and nurtured the belief that non-Western cultures "contribute nothing to the development of knowledge, humanities, arts, science, and technology." She refers to this rejection as a manifestation of what she terms "cognitive imperialism" ("Indigenous Knowledge: Foundations" n. p.; see also Grenier 9). This same Eurocentric notion has been applied in other parts of the world as well.

---

8   This part has strong overlaps with Knopf "The Turn Toward the Indigenous."

The Sami scholar Rauna Kuokkanen says: "the academy [...] has ignored, overlooked, and dismissed [Indigenous] ontologies – in fact, the academy's structures and discourses are built on the assumption that there only is one episteme, one ontology, one intellectual tradition on which to rely and from which to draw" (3). Similarly, Gloria Emeagwali, professor of African Studies, holds:

> Several strategies have been used to reinforce the myth that regions outside Europe contributed nothing to the development of science and technology either in terms of hardware or software – the view that historically the majority of the world have been passive recipients of a so-called Western science and technology. (n. p.)

Thus, as Cree scholar Margaret Kovach and many others make clear, prioritized Western-based research practices and policies reproduce colonial relationships in the academy:

> It manifests itself in a variety of ways, [...] most noticeably through Western-based policies and practices that govern research, and less explicitly through the cultural capital necessary to survive there. [...] Indigenous communities are being examined by non-Indigenous academics who pursue Western research on Western terms. (28)

As a consequence, Indigenous academics around the world[9] call for decolonizing and 'Indigenizing the academy', meaning including Indigenous knowledges into our academic and scientific discourses on an equal basis. They do not ask to privilege but rather to equally include Indigenous epistemes, discourses, practices, and methodologies and interweave Indigenous and Western knowledges, education, cultural beliefs, and values in order to combine their respective competences. At the same time, these academics have examined the conditions and practicability of this decolonizing endeavor. They warn that including Indigenous knowledge into Western-dominated academies will transform oral-based into print-based knowledge systems (Kovach 12) and risk validating Indigenous knowledges and methodologies solely according to Western standards. Such process might further subject Indigenous knowledge to Western control (Grenier 13, 55), and, moreover, potentially appropriate, tokenize, and exploit it as it is already happening in the pharmaceutical industry.[10] Leslie King describes such practice as follows:

> One response [to the loss of biodiversity and knowledge about biodiversity] is the tendency for scientists attempting to "integrate" western

---

9   Such calls are contained in the research and books for example by the Canadians Margaret Kovach and Shawn Wilson, the Sami Rauna Kuokkanen, the Maori Linda Tuhiwai Smith, Ulia Popova-Gosart (Udmurt) from Russia, and the Native Americans Devon Abbot Mihesuah and Angela Cavender Wilson.
10 Cultural Survival Canada states in 1995 that the "world market value of pharmaceuticals derived from plants used in traditional medicine had an estimated value of 43 billion United States dollars [USD] in 1985. Less than 0.001% of the profits have gone to the original holders of that knowledge" (qtd. in Grenier 16). See also Tuhiwai Smith 118–19.

science with traditional ecological knowledge, to abstract the knowledge from the culture and attempt to classify, codify, record, and use that knowledge (for instance in research on climate change) without reference, and often without credit, to the culture from whence it came. ("Competing Knowledge Systems" 166)

The movement to create intellectual property rights including means of compensation for knowledge, though, runs the risk of devaluating the knowledges by commodifying them and making them more vulnerable for exploitation (Leslie King 166). Likewise, Cavender Wilson pinpoints such practices in the humanities: "Often, the university has accepted only what it can appropriate for colonial purposes (the field of anthropology alone, notorious for their Indigenous data collecting, offers endless examples of this) and dismissed any knowledge that challenges the status quo and Western ways of knowing" (73). The integration of Indigenous knowledges, of course, needs to spare out and respect knowledge and materials that are restricted tribal-specific knowledge and materials, not meant for the study by the larger world, e.g. sacred objects, sacred knowledge and practices, and human remains (73). Indigenizing the academy must thus proceed along the principles of respect, recognition, reciprocity, and responsibility that have been outlined by several Indigenous and non-Indigenous scholars.[11]

As Kovach and others note, one major dissimilarity between both knowledge systems is that Western research usually compartmentalizes the world and problems to be studied, breaks down natural systems into the smallest or simplest manageable parts, isolates problems from their interlinkages with others, while Indigenous knowledge sees them holistically and as a set of relationships (Kovach 1; Atleo, *Tsawalk* xii; Grenier 11; Shawn Wilson 127; see also Kuokkanen 157). Furthermore, Milton Freeman observes that Western scientists are concerned with linear causality, assuming that one can predict future developments if one understands the causes or effects of past and present phenomena. Indigenous people, in contrast, most often see themselves and their environment as "constantly reforming multidimensional interacting cycles, where nothing is simply a cause or an effect, but all factors are influences impacting other elements of the system-as-a-whole" (Freeman n.p.). Freeman thus suggests understanding these ecosystems on the basis of systemic relationships, or better, not studying what phenomena are but the influences they have on other phenomena. Another difference between the two knowledge systems concerns the value they attach to quantitative and qualitative information. Western scientists predominantly use quantitative data to generate mathematical models of animal population dynamics, which are in turn employed to calculate sustainable yields of the resource and to establish hunting or fishing regulations. Dené people, for example, are more concerned with general qualitative conditions and development trends of species than

---

11 See Grenier 42; Mike Evans et al. 5; Kovach 67; Kuokkanen 144–55; 157; Shawn Wilson 77.

with exact numbers (Johnson n. p.).¹² Nevertheless, when concerned with similar objectives – for example environmental protection – both knowledge systems share many similarities; spotlighting such similarities instead of differences is a useful place to start educational reform, as Battiste proposes ("Indigenous Knowledge: Foundations" n. p.). Dené researcher Martha Johnson holds that

> both knowledge systems require thoughtful and systematic observation to understand ecological processes and that both seek to utilize resources in an ecologically sustainable manner. The main difference between the two systems appears to be in the different types of information gathered, how this information is interpreted and expressed, and the approaches to resource management. (n. p.)

Possibly most rational suspicions arise about the Indigenous validity of belief and a spiritually-based moral code that regulates the interaction with and usage of the environment. Western natural scientists usually eschew or deny belief in creation, in accordance with Enlightenment ideas centered on reason that dominate contemporary scientific thought, and clearly distinguish between myth and reality and between earth, animals, and humans. Indigenous knowledge systems interweave these supposed 'oppositions' and 'differences', and see the natural environments, flora, fauna, and humans as equal co-existing beings. Western scientists likely seek a rationalist scientific explanation of natural phenomena, based on developing and testing hypotheses, theories, and laws (Johnson n. p.) – which are themselves sometimes closer to belief than we would like to admit.¹³ At the same time they seem to be indisposed to accept Indigenous spiritual explanations of such phenomena. Johnson explains:

> What they often fail to recognize, however, is that the spiritual explanation conceals conservation strategies and does not necessarily detract from the reality of a situation and the making of appropriate decisions about the wise use of resources. It merely indicates that the system exists within an entirely different cultural experience and set of values, one

---

12 See Ellen Bielawski, who confirms that Inuit did not increase their interest in accuracy in measurement of phenomena but were rather interested in their general character. Grenier also makes this point: "the scientific community prefers to deal with quantitative data, rather than with the interview or qualitative data that characterize IK" (39).
13 See, for example, Bruno Latour who, speaking about violence triggered by fundamentalist 'belief' questions the established dichotomy between belief and information/communication/science. He argues that both are different templates, have different objectives and are not comparable, hence should not compete on the same level of human thought or cancel each other out. The idea here is, moreover, that science has a strong relationship with belief when scientists study phenomena, encounter contradictions, enigmas, and problems, and envision explanations and solutions by hypothesizing and going through a long research and testing process. Belief in the appropriateness of their understanding of the issue and of possible solutions is necessary in order to justify dedicated research time and to convince colleagues and funding agencies of the sound approach to the issue. This belief in one's knowledge and vision seems similar to Indigenous belief in the protocols of land use and the appropriate approach to contradictions, enigmas, and problems.

which paints no more and no less valid a picture of reality than the one which provides their own frame of reference. (n. p.)

Indigenous people, on the other hand, are often critical of Western science and technology because in their perception they tend to control and interfere with nature, and sometimes have a socially and ecologically destructive impact,[14] although some Western techniques of measurement provide data that Indigenous knowledge cannot acquire and that can prove to be beneficial (Johnson n. p.).

Indigenous and Western Concepts of Ecology

Western environmental science and philosophy, and also public discourse, have come a long way and have, possibly as a late reaction to climate change, accepted views of 'ecocentrism' or 'biocentrism'. They battle the pervasive belief in anthropocentrism, which assumes that the natural world exists exclusively for humans, serves their needs and should be protected for use by humanity (Rowe 106). Ecocentrism and biocentrism are nature-centered approaches as opposed to human-centered approaches. They reject a division between the human and non-human world, deny that human life is of higher value than non-human life, and believe in a general interrelatedness and interdependence between all natural life. Christopher Manes reminds us:

> If fungus, one of the 'lowliest' of forms on a humanistic scale of values, were to go extinct tomorrow, the effect on the rest of the biosphere would be catastrophic, since the health of the forests depends on *Mycorrhyzal* fungus, and the disappearance of forests would upset hydrology, atmosphere, and temperature of the entire globe. In contrast, if *Homo sapiens* disappeared, the event would go virtually unnoticed by the vast majority of Earth's life forms. As hominids, we dwell at the outermost fringes of important ecological processes such as photosynthesis and the conversion of biomass into usable nutrients. No lofty language about being the paragon of animals or the torchbearer of evolution can change this ecological fact. (24)

Indigenous views on ecology and sustenance have much importance for environmental science. Jeannette Armstrong, professor at UBC Okanagan, international consultant to UNESCO, Judge of the First Nations Court of Justice, speaker for the land, and traditional knowledge keeper in her nation, introduces the Okanagan concept of *tmixʷcentrism* into ecology discourse. According to the Okanagan [Syilx] world view, human beings are "intricately woven into the very fabric of the life force of the land" (Armstrong, "Kwtlakin?" 31). This view is well demonstrated with the Syilx word for 'land', *tmxwulaxw*, translated as "from nothing,

---

14 See the statements of Inuit elders in the documentary *Qapirangajuq: Inuit Knowledge and Climate Change*.

the life force spreading outward, is here in continuous cycles. [...], spreading outward in many individual strands" (30). The Okanagan people see themselves as one of those strands, "which are continuously being bound with others to form one strong thread coiling year after year into the future as the life force of the land" (31). Armstrong explains:

> the *tmixw* [life force of the land] are Chiefs ['people' in animal and plant forms] in the Syilx meaning of the word – that is they represent a role – in being duty-bound to twining/coiling the many strands. They are meeting to find a collectively agreed-upon way for the "People-to-be" [human beings] to survive, and at the same time to maintain the grand imperative of twining/coiling the many strands into a unity of direction and existence. ("Constructing Indigeneity" 158)

The Okanagan, she says, practiced an environmental ethic with the foundational principle of an intentional regeneration of *tmix^w* [life-force], meaning that all life forms, including human beings who are also *tmix^w*, must be seen as unique and equally important for the life-force, must be provided with the means for regeneration but also have the obligation to regenerate (160–62): "Humans have the ability to kill *tmix^w* as a life-force and so they are duty bound to respect all life forms equally within the concept of *k'wulncutn*. They also have a natural duty, like all life forms, to survive within nature's law that [conditions that] they have nothing else to eat but *tmix^w*" (161–62). The Okanagan concept of

> *tmix^{w}centrism* is a human system to protect the rights [...] of each *tmix^w* to full regeneration, full aliveness and existence in their own identity through knowledgeable practice. [...] The Syilx view is that the other *tmix^w* already are 'wise' in that they are bound by their own process for full regeneration and already practice it to great efficiency and reciprocity, it is the human which does not. [...] The Syilx *tmix^{w}centricity* as a principle binds the human as social beings to moral obligations towards all *tmix^w* in the duty to synchronize human behavior with the regenerative order of the physical environment, as good practice based first on moral reasoning. ("Constructing Indigeneity" 299–301)

Armstrong proposes *tmix^{w}centrism* as an alternative environmental theory and argues that it shares presuppositions with Western environmental ethics, e.g. J. Baird Callicot's 'ecocentrism', Paul Taylor's 'biocentric egalitarianism', Daniel Berthold-Bond's 'ethics of place', and Herman Daly's 'economics of sustainable development'. These concepts have much in common with the Syilx environmental ethic but also show fundamental differences in the notions of life forms and land, their value and 'personhood', and their relations and duties as well as notions of sustainability and sharing.[15] But more important is, according to Arm-

---

15 For the extensive discussion of such commonalities and differences in presuppositions and views see Armstrong, "Constructing Indigeneity" 221–74.

strong, that such Indigenous and Western concepts can converge to create an ecological and ethical framework directed at sustainable practice (291–92).

The Nuu-chah-nulth philosopher Richard Atleo (Umeek) also introduces Indigenous conceptualizations of the world and its beings into discourses of environmentalism in his books. He explains that creation is a unity; the meaning of *heshook-ish tsawalk* is 'everything is one'. *Tsawalk* is a theoretical approach that assumes reality and the universe to be one network of relationships, a unity of the physical and metaphysical aspects of existence (*Tsawalk* xi, 117–18). He says:

> In the Nuu-chah-nulth worldview every life form is of one *thli-muhk-sti* (spirit), of one essence. Contrary to the classical Western view, the Nuu-chah-nulth do not assume that humans have one type of life essence or spirit and the bear another. Both, in the beginning, were of the same essence, of the same *thli-muhk-sti*. Observed differences between the human form and other life forms are products of transformations that resulted in the adoption of different types of outward "clothing" by each. (*Tsawalk* 61–62)

In the same manner, the Gitksan and Wet'suwet'en believe that human beings "are part of an interacting continuum that includes animals and spirits. Animals and fish are viewed as members of societies that have intelligence and power, and can influence the course of events in terms of their relationship with human beings" (Gisday Wa and Delgam Uukw qtd. in Atleo, *Tsawalk* 62). While Armstrong explains Syilx *tmix^{w}centrism* with reference to the "Four Chiefs Story," Atleo also uses several stories to explain Nuu-chah-nulth concepts and beliefs, or better, to illustrate how they are essentially transmitted. The "Aint-tin-mit" story explains how biodiversity was created as in the beginning all beings were people and were transformed by Aint-tin-mit into different beings (59–61). The story of "Bear" tells how the people came to share the salmon with the bears; it demonstrates how sustainability, sharing, helpfulness, and protocols of behavior can be developed (*Principles of Tsawalk* 100-1). Such protocols include protocols of human "predation" upon any plant and animal (122) and are necessary to maintain "humans, animals, and spirits in an equitable, or balanced, relationship" (*Tsawalk* 63).

A mature eco-system, according to Atleo, is a system where diverse life forms live in balance and harmony (*Principles of Tsawalk* 100-1). He explains how agreements over protocols between life forms were achieved in order to ensure balance and harmony – they are not easy to continue as current environmental problems are an expression of or result of violation of agreements and protocols (102). 'Protocols of *Tsawalk*' are "a system of life management, […] agreements or treaties between life forms that must compete for resources on one planet" (156). They "move competitive relationships away from conflict and towards harmony until all the constitutional principles of life – mutual recognition, mutual consent, and mutual respect – allow for the continuity of all life forms" (156), making it unconstitutional for one species to make decisions for other life forms and to take unilateral action. Oppositions and conflicts were resolved through the *haḥuuḷic* principles of recognition, consent, and respect by ancient Nuu-chah-nulth that then ensured continuity of all beings (143). Traditional Nuu-chah-nulth decision-making and conflict-solving was a long process that enabled every council member to speak on the particular issue, ensuring recognition and respect for all [life forms]. Each must understand the issue and arguments; a probable solution was again addressed by all indicating dissent or agreement (*Tsawalk* 88–90). Even if members disagreed, they would support the final solution simply because they understood the overall concerns and arguments and were involved in achieving the resolution – a process so unfamiliar to our democratic systems and respective practices that usually alienate the outvoted minority and exclude it from the resolution of the majority.

Atleo proposes the concept of *Haḥuuḷism*, a synthesis of Indigenous and Western worldviews that seeks to make possible "an equitable and harmonious working relationship between the two ways of life" (*Principles of Tsawalk* 140). *Haḥuuḷism* is a neologism derived from *haḥuuḷi*,[16] meaning land and its resources owned by a Chief, and the ending *ism*, indicating an ideology or philosophy (139, 153).[17] The principles of the land-centered approach *haḥuuḷism*, much like the Okanagan *tmix^{w}centrism*, "are taken from ancient beliefs and practices that sought constantly to strengthen life through emphasizing relationships between all life forms [...and] a necessary struggle for balance and harmony" – a difficult struggle and state as difficult to maintain (139, 155). The logical consequence of Atleo's thought and his grounding principle of *tsawalk*, then, is that responsibility for current ecological problems and environmental protection lies with all humans, colonizing and colonized peoples alike (*Tsawalk* 58). Respecting and taking serious Indigenous ways of knowing, philosophical knowledges and their environmental ethics are first steps for settler colonial nations and groups of people that benefit from contemporary neo-colonial global relations and exploitive business practices to share responsibility for planetary crises.

Indigenous Knowledges as Living Heritages

David Lowenthal describes 'heritage' as that with which groups of people individually or collectively identify as their shared legacy and connection to the past ("Identity, Heritage" 41). Heritage means a link to the past beside history, tradition, memory, myth, and memoir, the core of collective identity and self-respect, "a nutriment as necessary as food and drink" (*The Heritage Crusade* 3, 5). He assigns to it an "essential role in husbanding community, identity, continuity, indeed history itself" (xv). Because its link to manifold aspects of the

---

16 Pronounce *ha-hoolth-ee* (*Principles of Tsawalk* x).
17 *Ḥahuuḷi* may also mean the link between the physical and non-physical realms (153).

near and remote pasts – e.g. "family history, buildings and landmarks, prehistory and antiques, music and paintings, plants and animals, language and folklore" – heritage defies distinct definition ("Identity, Heritage" 42). Since it produces collective identities, heritage has advanced as a defining trait of ethnic and territorial groups, and nation states (43). At the same time, Lowenthal warns, non-Western collectivities increasingly adopt Western concepts of personalized and national identities, individual grandness, and sovereignty; likewise, architectural and other material manifestations of heritage now supersede other forms (45–46). Thus, Richard Handler holds, imperialist and colonized cultures "have agreed to a world view in which culture has come to be represented as and by 'things'" (qtd. in Lowenthal, "Identity, Heritage" 46).

It is not surprising, then, that Indigenous heritage as protected by the UNESCO was for a long time material- and place-based (Alivizatou 45–47). The International Work Group for Indigenous Affairs states "[t]he World Heritage Convention governs the identification and protection of tangible, immovable world heritage (i.e. 'sites') considered to be of 'outstanding universal value', much of which is located on Indigenous territories" (IWGIA n.p.).[18] UNESCO's expanded definition of intangible cultural heritage after the 2003 "Convention for the Safeguarding of Intangible Cultural Heritage" reads:

> "intangible cultural heritage" means the practices, representations, expressions, knowledge, skills – as well as the instruments, objects, artefacts and cultural spaces associated therewith – that communities, groups and, in some cases, individuals recognize as part of their cultural heritage. This intangible cultural heritage, transmitted from generation to generation, is constantly recreated by communities and groups in response to their environment, their interaction with nature and their history, and provides them with a sense of identity and continuity, thus promoting respect for cultural diversity and human creativity (UNESCO "Text of the Convention", n.p.).

After the "International Expert Workshop on the World Heritage Convention and Indigenous Peoples" in 2012, the UNESCO formulated as one preamble in its "World Heritage and Indigenous Peoples – A Call to Action": "Recognizing the vibrant contribution that Indigenous peoples make to the maintenance of the common heritage of humankind through their *world perspectives, knowledge, cultures, laws, customs, practices, lives, and institutions*" (UNESCO "World Heritage and Indigenous Peoples", n.p.; emphasis added). While the UNESCO respects non-material aspects of culture as heritage, it employs a Western logic to its denomination of heritage. Even in the same document Indigenous heritage is mentioned as heritage sites and not as knowledge, tradition, practices and the like. Accord-

---

18 Indigenous management or Indigenous participation in the management of Indigenous World Heritage Sites is an important issue that requires much discussion which cannot be offered here. See Susemihl.

ing to this Western logic, Indigenous heritage is preserved in sites, in material places, as the range of Indigenous heritage sites also makes clear, whether we think of the Uluṟu-Kata Tjuṯa National Park and Kakadu National Park in Australia, the Head-Smashed-In Buffalo Jump and S'Gang Gwaay in Canada, or the Cahokia Mounds State Historic Site and Chaco Culture National Historical Park in the United States. Indeed, because it still distinguishes between tangible and intangible cultural heritage, the UNESCO concept of 'heritage' is a Eurocentric concept of heritage imposed upon Indigenous peoples that is in need of a more holistic understanding of heritage without institutional compartmentalization and polarization that the dichotomy entails (Alivizatou 47–48). Now also many Indigenous people share this Western view of cultural heritage. Idealizing individual creativity and innovation in writers, scientists, statesmen and such people, who become thus transformed into grand national personalities, is a Western normative tradition that builds heritage as Lowenthal states; this concept is as well more and more internalized among non-Western cultures ("Identity, Heritage" 46).[19] Although Lowenthal, like the UNESCO, employs a Eurocentric perspective on heritage (the keywords he uses, such as buildings and landmarks, prehistory and antiques, music and paintings, and folklore, speak to his European understanding of heritage), he also thinks of non-European concepts of history: while Western cultures treasure material- and place-based heritage, artifacts, texts, and archives, "[m]any other cultures long dwelt more on orally transmitted memories and ritual processes than on tangible and archival heritage" ("Archives, Heritage" 193).

Inuit knowledge of the Arctic landscape, its flora and fauna, climate and weather, and changes of these environments and their own ways of life in the past century, as well as Inuit cultural and historical knowledge, is heritage according to this concept of non-European intangible cultural heritage. From an Inuit perspective, the conservationist UNESCO approach to safeguard intangible cultural heritage for the people and to involve local communities in the process (Alivizatou 46) might even appear patronizing. The concepts of 'protection' and 'conservation' might be questionable to begin with. Inuit communities are able to take care of their knowledge themselves and would likely not understand it as 'heritage'. They are the ones that constantly adapt and reproduce cultural knowledge, and thus ensure its continuity. The responsibility of the settler colonial nation, and indeed the rest of the world, is to make sure that favorable conditions for such

---

19 The number of famous Indigenous leaders in oral and print discourses appears to trouble Lowenthal's statement. However, Lowenthal speaks of a Western individualistic tradition in terms of creativity, i. e. art, literature, music, theater among other things, whereas famous Indigenous personalities of the eighteenth and nineteenth centuries were mostly political and military leaders. An exception is for example Se-quo-ya, who invented the Cherokee syllabary. Most often, Indigenous traditions comparable to Western understandings of the arts are collective traditions, such as oral, performance, boat-building, mask-making or pottery traditions of certain nations. Nevertheless, it seems appropriate to think of Western individualistic and Indigenous collective traditions as tendencies within cultural frameworks with clear-cut differences slowly disintegrating, specifically so in hindsight of the many well-known Indigenous scholars, writers, artists, and filmmakers.

knowledge (re)production are maintained, i. e. access to land, respect for self-government models, and reduction of global warming and environmental pollution. Furthermore, a dynamic understanding of knowledge and heritage is necessary, including, in the Arctic for example, knowledge about how to hunt, skin, and eat a seal, how to fix a snowmobile motor with such thing as an empty bag of chips, or how to repair a government house roof under Arctic conditions.

Shirley Tagalik explains that *Inuit qaujimajatuqangit* – Inuit epistemology or the Indigenous knowledge of the Inuit – is based on three continuums: knowledge continuum, time continuum, and relationship continuum. *Inuit qaujimajatuqangit* is "knowledge embedded in process" and "reliant on the cultural expectation of *iqqaqqaukkaringniq* (deep thinking that leads to innovation). This is a dynamic process of knowing, applying, experiencing, evaluating, and creating new knowledge grounded in a continuum of knowing and continually improving" (2). This adapting and creating new knowledge is and has always been necessary to ensure survival. Likewise, the time continuum means that deep understandings of views and values of the past influence and support success in the future. And finally, building of relationships is central to *Inuit qaujimajatuqangit* and "is a consistently applied life building process aimed at establishing self-reliant, wise individuals who can cope successfully and actively contribute to the wellbeing of others and to the continual improvement of society" (2–3). Since Inuit knowledge includes traditional and contemporary knowledges constantly changing and adapting to neo/colonial, climatic, and industrial influences, it can be seen as 'living heritage' as suggested in the 'memorial' heritage discourse, which understands cultural heritage "as a corpus of processes and practices that are constantly recreated and renewed by present generations effecting a connection with the past" (Alivizatou 48).

But there are warnings against homogenization and commodification of living Indigenous knowlegdes in our capitalist and globalized world. The 'discontents' of such 'minority heritage' due to colonization and Westernization of non-European cultures, as Lowenthal argues, are manifold: diverse tribal views on aspects and content of heritage might be homogenized into pan-tribal or even pan-Indigenous views vis-à-vis other tribal or mainstream government concerns and political clout; diverse distinct ethnic and regional legacies might become more alike. Generalized abstractions of specific forms of religion and shamanism might become vehicles of cultural nationalism and political struggles. Indeed, even religious concepts and practices might be 'Westernized', popularized, and commodified by Indigenous sellers and New Age buyers of initiation seminars and ceremonies. Confrontation with the mainstream and Western cultures erodes distinctiveness, as Lowenthal explains: "The more minorities negotiate with sovereign powers and exchange views and tactics among themselves, the more all heritage takes on a similar Western tinge" (*The Heritage Crusade* 84–85). Western mainstream trivializes Indigenous legacies by reducing and formularizing their diversity into omnipresent and retrievable icons of Indigeneity, like profiles of famous chiefs, their speeches, historic sites, wise proverbs, traditions, and skills – many of which slip into the realm of stereotypes. Mainstream expectation of 'unsullied heritage' and economic pressure, in fact, compel Indigenous groups into participating in such tendencies of cultural homogenization, reduction, stereotyping, and locating Indigenous cultures in a 'primitive' and 'authentic' past (*The Heritage Crusade* 85–86; 197–98).[20]

Although, indeed, all these tendencies are noticeable and continue to shift Indigenous heritages and concepts of pasts and legacies, it seems as if Lowenthal's premise itself is an idea of more or less static cultures that somehow lose their 'authentic' make-up through continuous contact with other cultures and influences. Postcolonial, hybrid, and transcultural approaches would certainly see Westernizing and homogenizing tendencies as part of the very transformation processes that apply to all cultures in different ways and intensities. Based on the discussed documentary, I would like to argue that Inuit knowledge indeed is changing and adapting to Western influences, technical developments, and climate change; and that this change is part and parcel of a living culture and its knowledge that should be understood as living heritage. Mary Simon, former president of Inuit Tapiriit Kanatami and Canada's first Ambassador for Circumpolar Affairs, says that being on the frontline of environmental change and struggles does not make Inuit "hostile to new forms of development or locked into a kind of paralyzing nostalgia for the days of old" (889). She does not rule out non-renewable resource development for Inuit in order to become economically self-sufficient if done with "best practices from around the world" (890).

Indeed, the idea of intangible cultural knowledge being heritage is not new. Written concurrently with Lowenthal's influential book *The Heritage Crusade and the Spoils of History* (1998), Darrell Posey and Graham Dutfield in their book *Beyond Intellectual Property* understand Indigenous cultural knowledge as 'heritage' (85, 122; see also Battiste and Henderson, *Protecting*; Ermine "The Ethical Space" 200). The Pueblo writer Simon Ortiz describes Indigenous oral traditions as 'heritage'. He introduces the idea of *participation* in oral tradition which unites tellers and listeners in building responsibility for the information transmitted (86, 90, 94). George Sefa Dei describes African anti-colonial knowledge as 'heritage knowledge' and its recovery as African scholarship and knowledge production (102, 105). Applied to the situations of shooting and screening the film *Qapirangajuq*, we can see the filmmakers and the world audience as participants of this knowledge transmission. The information contained in the film, when it is taken into consideration, processed, and responsibly treated by other Inuit or Arctic people, Western scientists and the world audience, can also be seen as knowledge production – it acquires a character of living heritage.

The integration of Indigenous knowledges into the academy, called for by many scholars such as Margaret Kovach, Rauna Kuokkanen, Devon Abbot

---

20 Another example of this invention of a usable heritage is discussed by Karl Steel in this volume.

Mihesuah and Angela Cavender Wilson, Ulia Popova-Gosart, Linda Tuhiwai Smith, and Shawn Wilson, goes hand in hand with the decolonization of the academy, its Eurocentric premises, assumptions, frameworks of thoughts, guidelines, and practices, and with "a consciously critical assessment of how the historical process of colonization has systematically devalued our Indigenous ways" (Cavender Wilson 72; see also Battiste, *Decolonizing Education* 69, 72). Such integration requires a fundamental rethinking of Western logocentrism and the Cartesian split of mind and body, or at least respect for deviating views. In this way, it can produce new and needed knowledge. Applying Indigenous holistic thinking to science and education, meaning to see all beings, things, and phenomena in relation to each other, acknowledging the unity of the physical and spiritual world (Battiste, *Decolonizing Education* 76), and understanding all knowledge as context-based and community-based, not (solely) text-based, will ensure what Fyre Jean Graveline has called "In-Relation pedagogy" (quoted in Battiste 74). Holistic thinking, in this line of thought, is one further aspect of Indigenous living heritages. In the same way Dei has described African holistic perspectives:

> Both Indigenous and traditional/local knowledge work with the nexus of society-culture-interface, as well as the interrelations of the body, mind and soul. […] Indigenous knowledge affirms spirituality as a site of knowing and further argues that knowledge and resistance go hand in hand. For African peoples such knowing is a form of 'heritage knowledge' (Joyce King, ["A transformative vision"] 2005). This heritage knowledge is characterized by a philosophy of 'worldsense', i.e., systems of thought and ontologies speaking to the realities and workings of the cosmos, and the nexus of nature, society and culture. (111–12)

Recovery, integration, and decolonization produce new and modified knowledges with a hybrid Indigenous and Western base; this process of knowledge production involves continuous adapting and updating according to varying influences and conditions – also in this sense can Indigenous knowledge be seen as living heritage that could benefit the larger world. "The potential benefit of Indigenous knowledge for all societies," Battiste writes, "is to draw on the vitality of Indigenous knowledge and its dynamic capacities to solve contemporary problems as well" (*Decolonizing Education* 97). It is in this sense that Atleo presents *Haḥuuɫism* as a Nuu-chah-nulth perspective that "requires the addition of other perspectives [including Western ones] in order to be more complete" – a concept of being together that has the potential to help solving global crises (*Principles of Tsawalk* 169).

Battiste speaks of necessary 'trans-systemic' analyses and methods that go beyond the distinctive Indigenous and Eurocentric knowledge systems and ensure a regeneration of new relationships between both systems, because neither the Indigenous nor the Eurocentric one alone can facilitate needed academic decolonizing reforms (*Decolonizing Education* 103). Thinking along these lines, the Cree scholar Willie Ermine applied the concept of 'ethical space' developed by

Roger Poole to the in-between space that is created when Indigenous and Western knowledges are connected:

> the idea of the ethical space, produced by contrasting perspectives of the world, entertains the notion of a meeting place, or initial thinking about a neutral zone between entities or cultures. The space offers a venue to step out of our allegiances, to detach from the cages of our mental worlds and assume a position where human-to-human dialogue can occur. The ethical space offers itself as the theatre for cross-cultural conversation in pursuit of ethically engaging diversity and disperses claims to the human order. (202)

Of course, this concept involves the notions of 'engagement' and 'dialogue' aiming at interacting that is "modeled on appropriate, ethical and human principles" and at "shifting the status quo of an asymmetrical social order to a partnership model between world communities" (202–3). Battiste believes that "[i]t is not a merge or a clash, but a space that is new, electrifying, and even contentious, but ultimately has the potential for an interchange or dialogue of the assumptions, values, and interests each holds" (*Decolonizing Education* 105). We could possibly imagine this in-between space along the lines of Homi Bhabha's 'third space'. In this enabling space, so Battiste, Indigenous and non-Indigenous people can begin to truthfully speak about the predicaments and issues that face us (105), or, as Ermine says, about how to construct a society that is based on our humanness and not on prescriptions from systems and institutions that try to run our lives. Such thinking helps us recognizing each other as humans and finding common ground (Ermine, Interview n. p.). This in-between ethical space of thinking and acting, I suggest, is the space for living knowledges to operate in.

Indigenous and Eurocentric knowledges and methodologies have been integrated in the academy and empirical projects in manifold ways. For example, Taiaiake Alfred describes the land-based and Mohawk language-infused 'Akwesasne Cultural Restoration' program as a reaction to a normative monoculture in Canada, Eurocentric dominance of education, and environmental pollution of Mohawk environments. The program thus seeks to provide youth with the necessary skills, knowledge, and experience in land, language, and culture in order for Akwesasne people to retain and regenerate land-based practices in the community. Similarly, the Mi'kmaw of Potlotek in Cape Breton reacted to a crisis of education caused by colonial and neocolonial regimes of education with the development of a bilingual band-operated school in the community. The objective was to provide a community-based model of education that would recognize the students' Mi'kmaw culture and language and include what elders and parents desired to be part of the education beside the provincial curriculum. This education drew upon holistic thinking and the rich oral cultural knowledges and traditions and was done in Mi'kmaw (Battiste, *Decolonizing Education* 87–89). Another example: In order to develop a workable management program for the restoration of native vegetation on the Hawaiian island of Kaho'olawe, which is now "largely denuded and highly disturbed by alien weeds," Samuel Gon III and others undertook a review of Hawaiian traditional ecological knowledge, land management and restoration practices (Gon III 5). And Polly Walker explores the possibilities of integrating several Indigenous and Eurocentric ways of conflict resolution (Walker 2004). All these are examples of Battiste's 'trans-systemic' approaches and integration of Indigenous and Eurocentric knowledges and practices in Ermine's 'ethical space' that facilitates new or modified decolonized knowledge production. They speak to the continuing use and adaptation of Indigenous knowledges that is dynamic and in flux and is thus living knowledge. With an extended idea of 'heritage', detached from sites and things, we can see this dynamic traditional and contemporary Indigenous knowledge and the new decolonized knowledge as living heritage that will benefit the world.

Works Cited

Adhikari, Surendra, and Erik R. Ivins. "Climate-driven polar motion: 2003–2015." *Science Advances* 2016. 10 October 2016 <http://advances.sciencemag.org/content/advances/2/4/e1501693.full.pdf>.

Alfred, Taiaiake. "The Akwesasne cultural restoration program: A Mohawk approach to land-based education." *Decolonization: Indigeneity, Education & Society* 3.4 (2014): 134–44.

Alivizatou, Marilena. "Contextualizing Intangible Cultural Heritage in Heritage Studies and Museology." *International Journal of Intangible Heritage* 3 (2008): 44–54.

Armstrong, Jeannette. "Kwtlakin? What is Your Place?" *What is Your Place? Indigeneity and Immigration in Canada.* Ed. Hartmut Lutz with Thomas Rafico Ruiz. Augsburg: Wissner, 2007. 29–33.

—. "Constructing Indigeneity: Syilx Okanagan Oraliture and tmix^{w}centrism." PhD Diss. University of Greifswald, 2009. 1 October 2010 <http://ub-ed.ub.uni-greifswald.de/opus/volltexte/2012/1322/>.

Atleo, Richard E. *Tsawalk: A Nuu-chah-nulth Worldview.* Vancouver: University of British Columbia Press, 2004.

—. *Principles of Tsawalk: An Indigenous Approach to Global Crisis.* Vancouver: University of British Columbia Press, 2011.

Battiste, Marie. "Indigenous Knowledge and Pedagogy in First Nations Education: A Literature Review With Recommendations." Prepared for the National Working Group on Education and the Minister of Indian Affairs, Indian and Northern Affairs Canada (INAC), Ottawa, ON. 2002. 10 October 2016 <http://www.afn.ca/uploads/files/education/24._2002_oct_marie_battiste_indigenousknowledgeandpedagogy_lit_review_for_min_working_group.pdf>.

—. "Indigenous Knowledge: Foundations for First Nations." 2005. 15 August 2012 <http://www.win-hec.org/docs/pdfs/Journal/Marie%20Battiste%20copy.pdf>.

—. *Decolonizing Education: Nourishing the Learning Spirit.* Saskatoon: Purich, 2013

—. and James (Sákéj) Youngblood Henderson. *Protecting Indigenous Knowledge and Heritage: A Global Challenge.* Saskatoon: Purich, 2000.

Bielawski, Ellen. "Inuit Indigenous Knowledge and Science in the Arctic." *Canadian Arctic Resources Committee* 20.1 (1992). 28 April 2016 <http://www.carc.org/pubs/v20no1/inuit.htm>.

Borenstein, Seth. "NASA: Global warming is now changing how Earth wobbles." *Phys.org*. 8 April 2016. 10 October 2016 <http://phys.org/news/2016-04-nasa-global-earth.html>.

Cavender Wilson, Angela. "Reclaiming our Humanity: Decolonization and the Recovery of Indigenous Knowledge." *Indigenizing the Academy: Transforming Scholarship and Empowering Communities*. Eds. Devon Abbot Mihesuah and Angela Cavender Wilson. Lincoln and London: University of Nebraska Press, 2004. 69–87.

David, Jennifer. "Clear Signals: Learning and Maintaining Aboriginal Languages through Television." *Indigenous Screen Cultures*. Eds. Marian Bredin and Sigurjon Baldur Hafsteinsson. Winnipeg: University of Manitoba Press, 2010. 35–51.

Dei, George Sefa. "Indigenous anti-colonial knowledge as 'heritage knowledge' for promoting Black/African education in diasporic contexts." *Decolonization: Indigeneity, Education & Society* 1.1 (2012): 102–19.

Dewar, Dale. "Uranium mining and health." *Can Fam Physician* 59.5 (May 2013): 469–471. 10 October 2016 <https://www.ncbi.nlm.nih.gov/pmc/articles/PMC3653646/>.

Dietz, Rune, Peter M. Outridge, and Keith A. Hobson. "Anthropogenic contributions to mercury levels in present-day Arctic animals – A review." *Science of the Total Environment* 407 (2009): 6120–6131.

Emeagwali, Gloria. "Eurocentrism and the History of Science and Technology." 20 March 2014 <http://www.africahistory.net/eurocentrism.htm>.

Ermine, Willie. "The Ethical Space of Engagement." *Indigenous Law Journal* 6.1 (2007): 193–203.

—. Interview with Daniel Coleman. 1 September 2015 <https://www.youtube.com/watch?v=85PPdUE8Mb0>.

Evans, Lewis. "The 'slow genocide' of Brazil's Guarani people must stop." *Ecologist*, 3 June 2016. 10 October 2016 <http://www.theecologist.org/News/news_analysis/2987751/the_slow_genocide_of_brazils_guarani_people_must_stop.html>.

Evans, Mike, et al. "Common Insights, Differing Methodologies: Towards a Fusion of Indigenous Methodologies, Participatory Action Research, and White Studies in an Urban Aboriginal Research Agenda." n. l.: Okanagan Urban Aboriginal Health Research Collective, n. d.

Freeman, Milton M.R. "The Nature and Utility of Traditional Ecological Knowledge." *Canadian Arctic Resources Committee* 20.1 (1992). 28 April 2011 <http://www.carc.org/pubs/v20no1/utility.htm>.

Gisday Wa, and Delgam Uukw. *The Spirit in the Land: Statements of the Gitksan and Wet'suwet'en Hereditary Chiefs in the Supreme Court of British Columbia, 1987–1990*. Gabriola, BC: Reflections, 1992.

Gon III, Samuel M. "Application of Traditional Ecological Knowledge and Practices of Indigenous Hawaiians to the Revegetation of Kaho'olawe." *Ethnobotany Research & Applications* 1 (2003): 5–20.

Grenier, Louise. *Working with Indigenous Knowledge: A Guide for Researchers*. Ottawa et al.: International Development Research Centre, 1998.

Handler, Richard. *Nationalism and the Politics of Culture in Quebec*. Madison: University of Wisconsin Press, 1988.

Harmon, David. *In Light of Our Differences: How Diversity in Nature and Culture Makes Us Human*. Washington D.C.: Smithsonian Institution Scholarly Press, 2002.
Hobson, George. "Traditional Knowledge *Is* Science." *Canadian Arctic Resources Committee* 20.1 (1992). 28 April 2011 <http://www.carc.org/pubs/v20no1/science.htm>.
ImagineNATIVE. Interactive event and live webcast of global skype discussion after film premiere *Qapirangajuq: Inuit Knowledge and Climate Change*. 1 November 2010. 28 April 2011 <http://www.isuma.tv/hi/en/inuit-knowledge-and-climate-change/imaginenative-live>.
Inuit Circumpolar Council Canada. "Inuit Petition Inter-American Commission On Human Rights To Oppose Climate Change Caused By The United States Of America." 7 December 2005. 28 April 2011 <http://www.inuitcircumpolar.com/inuit-petition-inter-american-commission-on-human-rights-to-oppose-climate-change-caused-by-the-united-states-of-america.html>.
IWGIA. "World Heritage Sites and indigenous peoples." 19 September 2015 <http://www.iwgia.org/culture-and-identity/world-heritage-sites-and-indigenous-peoples>.
Johnson, Martha. "Dené Traditional Knowledge." *Canadian Arctic Resources Committee* 20.1 (1992). 28 April 2011 <http://www.carc.org/pubs/v20no1/Dené.htm>.
King, Joyce E. "A transformative vision of Black education for human freedom." *Black Education: A Transformative Research and Action Agenda for the New Century*. Ed. Joyce E. King. New Jersey: Lawrence Erlbaum Associates Publishers, 2005. 3–17.
King, Leslie. "Competing Knowledge Systems in the Management of Fish and Forests in the Pacific Northwest." *International Environmental Agreements: Politics, Law and Economics* 4 (2004): 161–77.
Knopf, Kerstin. "The Turn Toward the Indigenous: Knowledge Systems and Practices in the Academy." *Amerikastudien/American Studies* 60.2/3 (2015): 179–200.
—. "Indigenizing Science?! Global Warming, Inuit Knowledge, and Western Scientific Discourse." *Reflections on the Far North of Canada in the Twenty-First Century – Interdisciplinary Perspectives*. Eds. Stephan-Alexander Ditze and Jana Nittel. Bochum: Universitätsverlag Dr. N. Brockmeyer, Diversitas Linguarum. Forthcoming.
Kovach, Margaret. *Indigenous Methodologies: Characteristics, Conversations, and Contexts*, 2009. Toronto: University of Toronto Press, 2010.
Kuokkanen, Rauna. *Reshaping the University: Responsibility, Indigenous Epistemes, and the Logic of the Gift*. Vancouver: University of British Columbia Press, 2007.
Latour, Bruno. "Beyond Belief: On the Forms of Knowledge Proper to Religious Beings." Lecture at University of Groningen, 12 May 2014. 13 October 2016 <http://sggroningen.nl/nl/evenement/beyond-belief>.
Lowenthal, David. "Identity, Heritage, and History." *Commemorations: The Politics of National Identity*. Ed. John R. Gillis. Princeton, NJ: Princeton University Press, 1994. 41–57.
—. *The Heritage Crusade and the Spoils of History*. 1998. Cambridge: Cambridge University Press, 2003.
—. "Archives, Heritage, and History." *Archives, Documentation, and the Institutions of Social Memory: Essays from the Sawyer Seminar*. Eds. Francis X. Blouin

Jr. and William G. Rosenberg. Ann Arbor: University of Michigan Press, 2006. 193–206.

Manes, Christopher. "Nature and Silence." *The Ecocriticism Reader: Landmarks in Literary Ecology*. Eds. Cheryll Glotfelty and Harold Fromm. Athens and London: University of Georgia Press, 1996. 15–29.

Mapani, Benjamin, and Bohdan Kribek, Eds. *Environmental and Health Impacts of Mining in Africa*. Proceedings of the Annual Workshop IGCP/SIDA No. 594, Windhoek, Namibia, 5–6 July 2012. 10 October 2016 <http://www.unesco.org/new/fileadmin/MULTIMEDIA/HQ/SC/pdf/IGCP594-Proceedings_Windhoek_12-Part1.pdf>.

Metha, Pradeep S. "The Indian Mining Sector: Effects on the Environment and FDI Inflows." OECD Conference on Foreign Direct Investment and the Environment. 2002. 10 October 2016 <https://www.oecd.org/env/1830307.pdf>.

Mihesuah, Devon Abbot, and Angela Cavender Wilson, Eds. *Indigenizing the Academy: Transforming Scholarship and Empowering Communities*. Lincoln and London: University of Nebraska Press, 2004.

Notzke, Claudia. *Aboriginal Peoples and Natural Resources in Canada*. Concord, ON: Captus, 1994.

—. *Oil Sands Truth*. 10 October 2016 <http://oilsandstruth.org/>.

Ortiz, Simon. "Native Heritage: A Tradition of Participation." *Simon Ortiz: A Poetic Legacy of Indigenous Continuance*. Eds. Susan Berry Brill de Ramírez and Evelina Zuni Lucero. Albuquerque: University of New Mexico Press, 2009. 86–94.

Popova-Gosart, Ulia, Ed. *Traditional Knowledge and Indigenous Peoples*. n.l.: L'auravetl'an Information and Education Network of Indigenous Peoples (LIEN-IP) and World Intellectual Property Organization (WIPO), 2009.

Posey, Darrell A., and Graham Dutfield. *Beyond Intellectual Property: Toward Traditional Resource Rights for Indigenous Peoples and Local Communities*. Ottawa: International Development Research Center, 1996.

Rowe, Stan J. "Ecocentrism: the Chord that Harmonizes Humans and Earth." *The Trumpeter* 11.2 (1994): 106–107.

Sampson, Russell D., Edward P. Lozowski, and Hans G. Machel. "Variability of observed low-altitude astronomical refraction (LAAR) from different geographical locations: progress toward a global map of LAAR variability." *Applied Optics* 44.27 (20 September 2005): 5652–57.

Simon, Mary. "Canadian Inuit: Where we have been and where we are going." *International Journal*. Special Issue: *The Arctic is Hot*. Part II. Guest Eds. John Eric Fossum and Stéphane Roussel. LXVI.4 (Autumn 2011): 879–91.

Social Sciences and Humanities Research Council (SSHRC). "Altered perspectives: Inuit knowledge provides scientific insight into climate change." *SSHRC Newsletter* 2010. 10 October 2016 <http://www.isuma.tv/fr/inuit-knowledge-and-climate-change/wwwsshrcca-altered-perspectives-inuit-knowledge-provides>.

Susemihl, Geneviève. "Cultural World Heritage and Indigenous Empowerment: The Sites of S'Gang Gwaay and Head-Smashed-In Buffalo Jump." *Zeitschrift für Kanada-Studien* 33.1 (2013): 51–77.

Sustainable Development Strategies Group (SDSG). "Report: Current Issues in the Chilean Mining Sector." 10 October 2016 <http://www.sdsg.org/wp-content/uploads/2010/02/10-10-08-CHILE-REPORT.pdf>.

Tagalik, Shirley. "*Inuit Qaujimajatuqangit*: The Role of Indigenous Knowledge in Supporting Wellness in Inuit Communities in Nunavut." National Collaborating Centre for Aboriginal Health, University of Northern British Columbia, 2009–

2010. 2 May 2016 <http://www.nccah-ccnsa.ca/docs/child%20and%20youth/In
digenous%20Knowledge%20in%20Inuit%20Communities%20%28English%20
-%20web%29.pdf>.
Tuhiwai Smith, Linda. *Decolonizing Methodologies: Research and Indigenous Peoples*. 1999. London and New York: Zed Books, 2002.
UNESCO. "Text of the Convention for the Safeguarding of the Intangible Cultural Heritage." 10 October 2016 <http://www.unesco.org/culture/ich/en/convention>.
—. "World Heritage and Indigenous Peoples – A Call To Action." 13 February 2017 <whc.unesco.org/document/120074>.
Walker, Polly O. "Decolonizing Conflict Resolution: Addressing the Ontological Violence of Westernization." *American Indian Quarterly* 28.3/4 (2004): 527–49.
Walker, Rachel. "The Arctic Food Chain: Mercury and Polar Bears." 10 October 2016 <http://polarfield.com/blog/the-arctic-food-chain-mercury-and-polar-bears/>.
Wilson, Shawn. *Research Is Ceremony: Indigenous Research Methods*. Halifax and Winnipeg: Fernwood, 2008.

Filmography

Cariou, Warren, and Neil McArthur, dirs. *Land of Oil and Water*. Canada, 2008. 44 min.
—. dirs. *Overburden*. Canada, 2008. 15 min.
Kunuk, Zacharias, dir. *Exile*. Igloolik Isuma Productions. Canada, 2008. 48 min.
—. and Norman Cohn, dirs. *The Journals of Knud Rasmussen*. Igloolik Isuma Productions and Bartok Film. Canada and Denmark, 2006. 112 min.
—. and Ian Mauro, dirs. *Qapirangajuq: Inuit Knowledge and Climate Change*. Igloolik Isuma Productions and Kunuk Cohn Productions. Canada, 2010. 54 min. <http://www.isuma.tv/hi/en/inuit-knowledge-and-climate-change/movie>.

CHAPTER NINE

Ecological Conservation vs. Big Oil: The Case of Yasuní in Ecuador

JÜRGEN VOGT

The Western Amazon is one of the last large continuous natural forest areas. It stretches over Peru, Colombia, Ecuador and Southern Venezuela. Part of this region is the Yasuní, in Ecuador. It is one of the areas in the world with the highest biodiversity. The Yasuní National Park was established by Ecuador in 1979, and in 1989 the UNESCO declared it a Biosphere Reserve. It has a great variety of plant species, especially many sorts of trees, but it is primarily the amphibians – frogs, toads, turtles and snakes – that enhance its biological value. Some of the indigenous communities that live here have very little contact with the outside world and were able to preserve some of their unique cultural traits.

However, the Yasuní is not only rich in animals and plants. Its underground stores huge oil reserves. For a long time, the area has been mapped and divided into regions, and the concessions and drilling permits have long ago been given to national and international oil companies. The beginning of the actual extraction of oil was only a matter of time. This essay will trace the conflict between the interests of an international extraction industry and the interests of cultural and ecological preservation in the Yasuní.

UNESCO Biosphere Reserve

A biosphere reserve is initiated by the UNESCO in a region in order to support sustainable environmental, economic and social development. The so called "Man and the Biosphere" program ensures its further development, evaluation, and links the most important ecosystems on a global scale. That does not mean classic nature conservation in a strict sense. Citizen participation is at the core of the program. The overall objectives are to maintain biodiversity and ecosystem functions:

– to develop cultural landscapes and
– to promote climate protection, as well as
– to develop the social, economic and cultural conditions for environmental sustainability.

In the UNESCO's own description "Biosphere reserves are 'Science for Sustainability support sites' – special places for testing interdisciplinary approaches to understanding and managing changes and interactions between social and ecological systems, including conflict prevention and management of biodiversity." They are "nominated by national governments and remain under the sovereign jurisdiction of the states where they are located. Their status is internationally recognized" (UNESCO, "Biosphere Reserves").

Each biosphere reserve has a protective function, a development function and a research and education function. Biosphere reserves are divided into three zones:

– a core area, geared towards the conservation of nature,
– a buffer zone for sustainable use of nature, and
– a socio-economically oriented transition zone.

In June 2014, the UNESCO counted 631 biosphere reserves in 119 countries. The major part with 290 reserves is in Europe and North America. Followed by 130 reserves in Asia and the Pacific, 120 in Latin America and the Caribbean, 64 in Africa and 27 in the Arab States (UNESCO, "Biosphere Reserves").

Ecuador

Ecuador is located in north-western South America. With approximately 284.000 square kilometers it is slightly larger than, for example, the United Kingdom (some 244.140 square kilometers). It has about 15 million inhabitants, and is one of the most diverse countries on earth in geographic, topographic, climate and ethnic terms.

In the west, the Pacific coast region extends with alluvial land and low coastal mountains. In the center is the Andean region with its volcanoes. In the east are the Amazon lowlands. And some 1000 km off the coast there are the Galápagos Islands in the Pacific.

The proportion of the indigenous population is estimated at 40 percent (mainly Kichwa), the mestizo are a further 40 percent, the people with European ancestry ten to fifteen percent, and African Americans five to ten percent.

Ecuador hosts nearly 50 national parks and protected areas of different categories all over the country. The UNESCO has declared six of these areas as biosphere reserves: The most popular and oldest ones are the Galápagos Islands in the Pacific Ocean (65.000 ha, biosphere reserve since 1984). The largest one is the Yasuní National Park in eastern Oriente (980.000 ha, since 1989). Other protected areas are the Sumaco Biosphere Reserve, in the west of Ecuador in the Province of Napo (about 205.000 ha, since 2000); the Podocarpus-El Condor Biosphere Reserve, in the south of Ecuador in the province of Loja (since 2007); the

Macizo del Cajas Biosphere Reserve in the southwest of Ecuador in the provinces of Azuay and El Oro (976.600 ha, since 2013); and the Bosque Seco Biosphere Reserve in the southwest of Ecuador in the provinces of Loja and El Oro (500.000 ha, since 2014) (UNESCO, "Latin America and the Caribbean").

Economic and Political Surroundings

Ecuador lives from the export of raw materials. Oil, bananas, cocoa, flowers and shrimp are the main export products. The oil production now accounts for 60 percent of total exports and contributes to the state budget with up to 35 percent. This was also the case when the mid-left-wing candidate Rafael Correa won the presidential election in November 2006. Correa was supported not only by his own party, the social democratic Movimiento PAÍS, but in the final ballot he was also elected by the indigenous party Pachakutik and the left party Movimiento Popular Democrático. In 2008, after an intensive debate, Ecuador's citizens voted for a new constitution which included – for the first time in history – the Rights of Nature which are mainly based on the indigenous concept of "good living" (Buen Vivir – sumak kawsay). But since the beginning of Correa's first presidency Ecuador's policy is dominated by the question of how to divide up power and political responsibility between the central government and non-governmental organizations and movements. While Correa wants to be present with a strong state in all areas, the trade unions and the indigenous movements are striking for the autonomy of their organizations and demands.

In April 2009 and in February 2013, Correa was re-elected as President. His popularity rests primarily on his government's spending policy. Never before did a president in Ecuador tap so many sources from which to distribute money among Ecuadorians. According to the Ecuadorian Ministry of Finance, Correa's government was able to make public investments of about 25.5 billion US dollars in the years from 2007 to the end of 2012. This is four times the amount spent by the four previous presidents together in the years 1998 to 2006.

One reason for this generosity was the high price of oil. Ecuador benefited from the rising commodity and raw material prices on the world markets. Even the international financial crisis of 2008 was relatively harmless, thanks to the immense demand from China and India. While the official unemployment rate is 5 percent, 55 percent of the workforce are underemployed. 25 percent of the population is considered poor and the number has not gone back for years. In order to combat this calamity, Correa relies on the further exploitation of mineral resources.

The Constitution and the Concept of a Good Living

One of the reasons Correa won the support of the indigenous, left and social movements was his promise to lead Ecuador to a new Constitution. And indeed, in 2007 President Correa made way for a referendum on the convening of a Constituent Assembly. In November 2007, the Constituent Assembly convened for the first time. Nine months later a draft constitution, with 494 articles, was worked out. Finally, in September 2008, Ecuador's citizens voted in a referendum – mainly for – the new constitution.

One of the highest principles of the constitution is the concept of "buen vivir" – good living, or, in the Kichwa language, *sumak kawsay*. Buen vivir is inscribed in the preamble of the constitution and thus declared a constitutional right where the founding fathers and mothers write: "Decidimos construir una nueva forma de convivencia ciudadana, en diversidad y armonía con la naturaleza, para alcanzar el buen vivir, el sumak kawsay" ("We decided to build a new way of living together as citizens, in diversity and harmony with nature, to achieve the good living, the sumak kawsay") (Constitución 15; translation JV). Buen vivir is not about the good life of the individual in the modern western sense, but about a respectful relationship between the different cultural and social groups of Ecuador's population and a responsible relationship to nature. As Alberto Acosta, the former president of the Constituent Assembly, writes: "The good living has to do with a different way of living, with many social, economic and environmental rights and guarantees" (Acosta 220; translation JV). In the constitution this concept is named more than 20 times.

Acosta describes the approach of the good living as

> more than a constitutional declaration. The good living presents itself as a way to create together a new development regime and therefore a new way of life. It is therefore an important qualitative step from "sustainable" development towards a different vision that is much richer and more complex in content. The proposal of the good living can, whenever it is actively absorbed by the society, be introduced with much emphasis in global debates on transformations (220).

Equally remarkable is the fact that in the constitution nature is recognized as a legal entity. Article 72 says:

> Nature is entitled to restoration. This restoration is independent of the obligation of the State and natural or legal persons for compensation to individuals and groups who depend on affected natural systems. In cases of severe or permanent environmental impact, including those linked to the exploitation of non-renewable natural resources, the State shall establish the most effective mechanisms in achieving the restoration and take appropriate measures to eliminate or mitigate adverse environmental consequences.

It is amazing that a country like Ecuador, which depends to such a large extent on the exploitation of natural resources, has been able to vote for such an ecologically-minded constitution, showing respect for nature and aiming at the protection of nature. The constitution provides the background for the tug of war between the continuation of an extractive oil policy and the changes towards a post-extractive policy. And, as we will see, the extractive policy will keep the upper hand in spite of the constitutional text.

Yasuní National Park and the Yasuní Biosphere Reserve

The Yasuní National Park was created in November 1979. The park covers 9820 square kilometers. It is not only the largest protected area in Ecuador, but also the country's only Amazonian national park. Two scientific research stations, the Yasuní Research Station and the Tiputini Biodiversity Station, were established in the Yasuní National Park area in 1994. Research from these two stations has revealed that it is one of the most biodiverse places on the planet. It is uncertain why Yasuní is so diverse but one likely factor is the region's high rainfall and relatively steady non-seasonal climate. It is ever-wet and ever-warm.

In 1989, the area in and around the original limits of Yasuní National Park was designated as a Biosphere Reserve by the UNESCO. The Yasuní Biosphere Reserve covers 16.820 square kilometers.

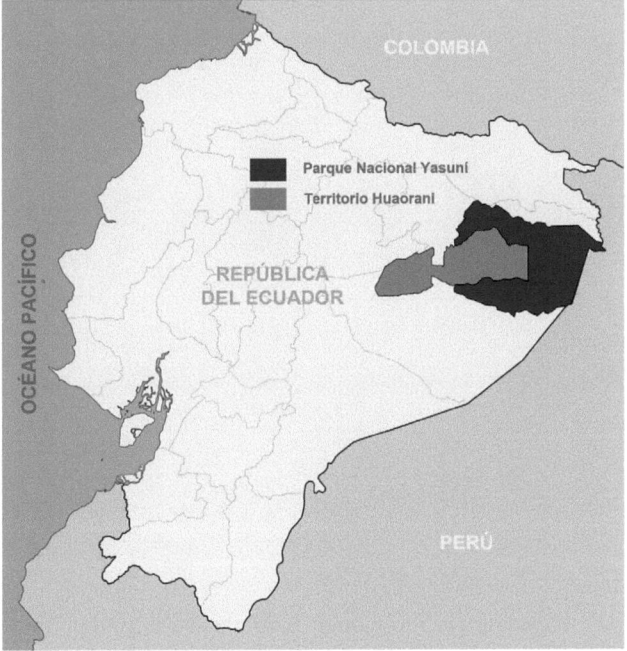

Fig. 1: State of Ecuador with Yasuní National Park. Source: Wikimedia Commons. https://en.wikipedia.org/wiki/Yasuni_National_Park

Along the guidelines of the UNESCO "Man and the Biosphere" Program, the Yasuní Biosphere Reserve (figure 1) includes a core area of 5000 square kilometers, a buffer zone of 7000 square kilometers, and a transition zone of 4820 square kilometers. The most impressive aspect of Yasuní National Park's biodiversity is the number of species packed into small areas. 150 species of amphibians and over 120 species of reptiles is the highest documented biodiversity in the world. The diversity of birds (around 600 species) and mammals (around 200 species) in that area is also extremely high. For plants, the Yasuní region is one of the few places on earth with at least 4000 species per 10000 square kilometers. The Yasuní Research Station holds the world record of tree species in just one hectare. The whole region extends beyond the traditional tribal lands of indigenous communities such as the Kichwa and Woarani. Here are also two indigenous peoples living in voluntary isolation.

However, the Yasuní is not only rich in animals and plants. Its underground stores huge oil reserves (figure 2). For a long time the area has been mapped and divided into blocks, and the concessions and drilling permits have long ago been given to national and international oil companies.

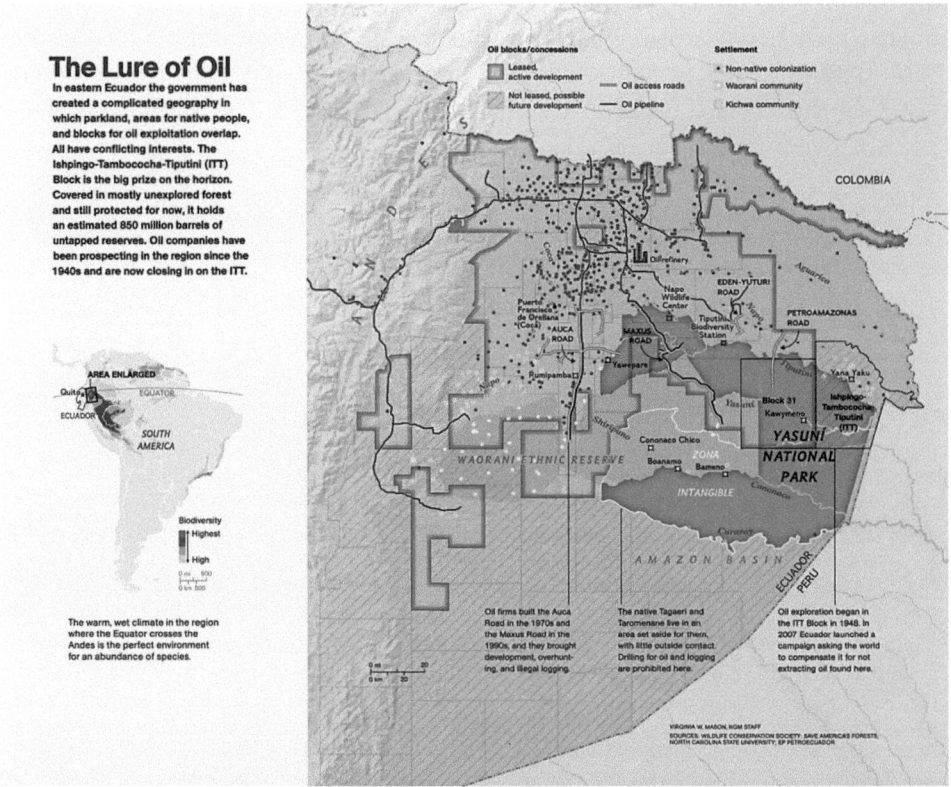

Fig. 2:   The oil fields, including (in the eastern part) the Ishpingo-Tambococha-Tiputini (ITT) oil exploration fields intersecting with the UNESCO biosphere reserve.
Source: National Geographic. https://natgeoeducationblog.files.wordpress.com/2013/08/yasunimap.jpg

In July 2010 the blocks were rearranged. Each block now covers 200.000 hectares. In and around the National Park there are eight blocks. The blocks 16, 31 and 43 (ITT) spread mostly over the northeast of the Yasuní. The area of the block 43 (ITT) was previously divided into the three oil fields: Ishpingo, Tambococha and Tiputini. Since the reorganization, they have been combined into one block with the number 43 (also called ITT). It is estimated that they may contain 846 million barrels of oil, which means 20 percent of the country's oil reserves. Since 2012 the state-owned Ecuadorian company Petroamazonas holds the majority of concessions in the Yasuní.

The Ishpingo-Tambococha-Tiputini Initiative

After Ecuador's President Rafael Correa was sworn into office in 2007, a unique initiative – which gave rise to much hope – became part of the national policy: The Ishpingo-Tambococha-Tiputini Initiative (short ITT Initiative) was personally announced by President Correa in 2007. Correa declared that his government wanted to protect the unique biodiversity of that region and the territories inhabited by the indigenous people.

The ITT Initiative is based on the proposals of the local population to leave the suspected oil reserves of 846 million barrels in the Yasuní untouched and in this way avoid risks to the environment. Although the ITT Initiative is only about a small part of the territory of the Yasuní region, it is estimated that some 20 percent of the oil reserves of the country are located there.

But the idea of the ITT Initiative goes beyond the prevention of the extraction of oil. If the initiative were successful in preventing the burning of oil, it would also prevent over 400 million tons of carbon dioxide from being released into the atmosphere. Therefore, the proposal of the ITT Initiative includes an approach with an appeal to the international community. As future carbon dioxide emissions are to be avoided, the Ecuadorian government requested the international community to pay half of the estimated export value of 7.2 billion US Dollars to a trust fund of the United Nations over the next 13 years.

But even before Correa announced the ITT Initiative, he reassured the oil companies that there would be a "Plan B," which meant the possibility that the oil might be explored after all because it would be irresponsible to abandon the petrodollars and not use them for fighting poverty and improving health and education.

Until today there has been no great oil accident in the region of Yasuní of which we know. But what happened in the neighbouring province of Sucumbios is well known. There, the US oil company Texaco was leading a consortium which was awarded the oil concession in 1964. Texaco left poisoned drinking water, dead rivers and lagoons. More than 114 billion gallons of toxic wastewater and crude oil leaked into the ground. The rate of poisoning and cancer in the province is well above the national average. It was one of the biggest oil disasters worldwide. After Texaco had left the country in 1992, former workers and residents of the region ranged a class action. The trial lasted almost two decades and Texaco was eventually taken over by Chevron. In August 2012, the Court of Sucumbios sentenced Chevron to pay 9.5 billion US dollars in damages. The company refused to accept the verdict. And in March 2014, a US federal judge in New York ruled in favor of Chevron. But this is not the end of the story. In March 2015, the International Court of Justice in The Hague, Netherlands, not only rejected a complaint of Chevron but also confirmed the legitimacy of the legal action taken by the Ecuadorian government in 2012. It is a model case for the competition between the interests of a resource extraction company protected by the government of a hegemonic industrial nation with a government of the so-called global south seeking to assert its social and ecological rights granted by international agreements.

The Failure of the ITT Initiative

Together with Sweden and a few other northern countries, Germany had at first been an important supporter of the ITT Initiative. In 2008, under the red-green government, the German Bundestag voted – across all parties – to contribute to the Ecuadorian trust fund of the United Nations. However, after the change of government in 2009, the new Federal Minister for Economic Cooperation and Development, Dirk Niebel, withdrew support for the initiative. The cancellation strengthened not only the Ecuadorian oil lobby; it was a devastating signal to other potential donors.

In August 2013, Correa declared the end of the initiative. Of the expected 3.5 billion US Dollars, only 13.3 million US Dollars had – according to Correa – been paid until then. Therefore, Correa blamed the international community for the failure. "The world has let us down," he said in August 2013 (Andrianova). One reason for the failure of the initiative may have been the effects of the global economic and financial crisis after 2008, but primarily it is the hypocrisy of precisely those very states that are releasing most of the greenhouse gases. "The main factor of the project's failure is that the world is a great hypocrite," Correa said (Andrianova).

Alberto Acosta, the former president of the Constituent Assembly and Correa's first Minister for Energy and Mining in 2007, somewhat contradicted this view and made Correa himself responsible for the failure. "The indecision of the President was the greatest hindrance to the initiative," said Acosta (personal communication). Correa's indecision did not offer enough reassurance to convince the decision makers and get the international financial resources.

China's Impact on the Yasuní

The growing influence of China in Latin America is well known. The already and steadily growing demand of the Chinese economy for commodities and raw materials is the motor for an aggressive search after these goods (Hill). Today China is one of the largest creditors of Ecuador. According to official numbers during the year 2011 the credit sum increased to around 7.2 billion US dollars, or 11.7 percent of Ecuador's GDP. "Much of this debt is part of 'commercial operations' with Petroecuador [the state owned oil company]. The guarantee would be oil, and loans at astonishingly high interest rates" (Martínez 6).

In Ecuador, the presence of Chinese state-owned companies in the oil sector is very strong. This includes not only the blocks 16 and 31 but also block 43 (ITT) in the Yasuní region. The first agreement between China and Ecuador, which included the Yasuní, was signed in 2007. The Chinese oil and gas company SINOPEC, together with the Brazilian Petrobras and the Chilean ENAP, signed a memorandum of understanding with the Ecuadorian government on the exploitation of the oilfields Ishpingo, Tambococha and Tiputini. It seemed that with the official announcement of the ITT Initiative this agreement would have become obsolete. Another explanation is that Correa had been playing two games at once right from the beginning. As David Hill writes in *The Guardian* in February 2014, "The Ecuadorian government was negotiating a secret 1 billion US Dollar deal with a Chinese bank to drill for oil under the Yasuní national park in the Amazon while pursuing a high-profile scheme to keep the oil under the ground in return for international donations."

According to Hill the first negotiating summit took place in May 2009, long before President Correa declared the end of the ITT Initiative:

> The document, entitled "China Development Bank Credit Proposal," bears the name of Ecuador's Ministry of Economic Policy Co-ordination on every page. Under the heading Results of the 1st Negotiating Round: preliminary agreements, which took place from the 13–23 May 2009, it states: "Last minute clause: The Ecuadorian party has said it will do all it can to help PetroChina and Andes Petroleum explore ITT and Block 31." (Hill)

In a letter to the Guardian the Ecuadorian Ambassador to the UK, Juan Falconi Puig, denied that Ecuador ever agreed to this last minute clause (Hill).

PetroChina and Andes Petroleum belong to the Chinese state. Alexandra Almeida, from the Ecuadorian Environmental NGO Acción Ecologica, concludes: "The document shows that in 2009 Ecuador's government negotiated with China to do all it could so Chinese oil companies can explore in ITT and Block 31, contradicting the Yasuní-ITT Initiative that was in effect at the time" (quoted in Hill). In Ecuador, it may be concluded, Chinese companies have contributed significantly to the expansion of the mining frontier, mainly in the Yasuní, showing little or no interest for the consequences this will bring about to the peoples that are hidden in the forest, and to their environment. The companies have also evidenced little interest in improving working conditions and responsibility to workers and former workers. However, environmental activists claim that the Ecuadorian government bears a joint responsibility for the failure of protecting Ecuador's natural heritage against the interests of the extraction industry.

Protest Against Oil Drilling from Inside and Outside the ITT

In Ecuador, the oil is state property, but the resident communities must give their permission for any form of seismic analysis or drilling. According to the Constitution, the indigenous communities must be involved in every government decision affecting the environment.

The community of Llanchama is the only remaining indigenous community that refuses to enter into an agreement with the oil companies concerning 3-D seismic studies on their land. 26 families live in the community, which means more than 150 residents. 65 of them are entitled to vote. They make their political decisions together, as a group. The territory of the community of Llanchama covers 26,000 hectares, 80 percent of which lies in block 31 and 20 percent in block ITT. Their settlement area is considered an untouchable-honored possession.

As the Yasuní National Park was established, no one outside the forest dwellers had realized that communities had been settled there for centuries. In 1979, when the Ecuadorian government set up the Yasuní National Park, more than 20,000 hectares of the community were included as part of the park. Ten years later, the community realized what had happened, what had been done to them. The same happened in 1989 when the area was designated a Biosphere Reserve by the UNESCO. Only in 1995 did the community of Llanchama receive official recognition. They possess no land title, however, but a licensed agreement for their traditional homeland. This means that nothing can be done on their territory without the community's consent

After Correa's decision, a civil movement started up in Ecuadorian society. Nationwide opinion polls reflected that nearly 65 percent of the citizens were against oil drilling in the ITT, and that over 70 percent wanted to be consulted additionally on this matter. The so-called "Consulta Popular" (a citizens' referendum) is made possible by the Ecuadorian Constitution, in case of the exploitation of non-renewable resources in a protected zone. The result of such a "Consulta Popular" is binding.

In 2014, the Environmental Alliance "YASunidos" collected – within the legally stipulated period of 180 days – 760,000 signatures to demand a referendum law. The Constitution provides 5 percent (585,000) of the signatures of the voting population as a valid quorum. However, in May 2014, the competent National Electoral Council decided, after a controversial examination procedure, that over half of those signatures were invalid. In this way it was possible for the Ecuadorian government to circumvent the convening of the referendum.

The Falling Oil Price – a New Chance for the ITT?

Oil is being extracted in Ecuador since 1972. The country achieved a new record in 2014, when around 203 million barrels were extracted, that is 5 percent more than in 2013. Nevertheless, the government revenues between the months of January and October have reached the same amount of 11 billion US dollars during the years 2013 and 2014. The reason is the decline in oil prices on the world market since mid-2014. In the last five months of 2014, the price for Ecuadorian oil fell from 92 US dollars to 47 US dollars per barrel. This also reduces the revenues estimated by the government from the ITT region. Even in August 2013 Correa had estimated a value of more than 18 billion US dollars. The basis for his calculation was an oil price of 70 US dollars per barrel.

In February 2015, however, the figure had dropped, according to the state oil company Petroecuador, to nearly 43 US dollars per barrel – that is 27 US dollars less for every barrel extracted. The value of the suspected ITT oil reserves has thus been reduced by around 7 billion to 11 billion US dollars.

However, Alberto Acosta saw no chance that the government could renounce the promotion of oil extraction in the ITT region for lack of profitability. Instead Acosta warned that "there may be a temptation to reduce environmental, labor and social standards in order to reduce the cost of oil extraction, with a greater environmental and social impact" (Araujo). In any case, for Acosta the Yasuní is not to be measured by the rising or falling value of oil. He views "the preservation of Yasuní" to be "more than an economic issue because it seeks the protection of life, biodiversity, peoples in voluntary isolation, the decrease of CO^2 emissions and the conservation of water sources" (Araujo).

Green Light for Oil Drilling Inside the Yasuní

The preparations for the oil extraction continued to advance, and despite national and international protests, the Ministry of Environment in Quito gave green light for the exploitation of the oil fields of Tiputini and Tambacocha in May 2014, giving the state oil company Petroamazonas the necessary environmental license.

The entire Amazon region had already been studied with the 2-D seismic system. Seismic investigations provide a fairly detailed picture of what is stored in the soil and all the Yasuní region has been explored in this way. There are already eight drill holes. They are closed with valves in different places in and around the park. The valve of Tiputini is over 40 years old. The local people call it 'la muneca', the puppet (figure 3). But if it should be opened, oil will still come out;

Fig. 3: 'La Muneca': the more than 40 year old valve of the Tiputini drill hole. Photo: Jürgen Vogt.

Fig. 4: Oil-asphalt chunk in the surface soil of Tiputini. Photo: Jürgen Vogt.

and half a meter in the ground there are still black chunks of oil-asphalt (figure 4).

In many areas the next step is a so called seismological, three-dimensional exploration. This means every 200 or 300 meters a little explosion will be detonated in the ground, to determine the presence of oil from the reflection of the detonation waves. Only after these measurements are completed will it be possible to decide where new holes are to be drilled. And this is still uncertain, especially in the blocks 31 and ITT.

While Tiputini is outside the National Park, Tambacocha is part of it. The oil field Ishpingo is still not affected. "We want to avoid engaging in this field, to keep it as an untouchable zone of Yasuní park," explained Environment Minister Tapia while the building of the exploration camps and the extraction of crude oil in Tiputini and Tambacocha was on the way. In September 2016, Ecuador started with the production of 20,000 barrels of oil per day on a platform in Tiputini, which is only 1,500 meters outside of the tabooed zone. Following the will of the government the daily output will rise up to 300,000 barrels in the next six years.

Conclusion

The economic dependence of many countries of the southern hemisphere on commodity exportations is truly not a new phenomenon, and their reduction to the role of mere suppliers of raw material has continued for decades.

A change, however, has occurred among the actors. With the takeover of the government by center-left or leftwing politicians and parties in various countries in South America, the state has entered the stage as an active and strong player in the distribution of wealth. This can be seen as an instance of the Global South resisting the dictates of the industrialized countries of the First World. The most prominent examples for this counterhegemonic attitude are the former presidency of Hugo Chávez in Venezuela and the actual presidency of Evo Morales in Bolivia and Rafael Correa in Ecuador. They stand for a policy of nationalizing the exploitation of natural resources, especially in ores, oil and gas.

Ideologically, their policy is also directed against the centuries-long dominance of the great northern neighbor, the United States, as US oil companies like Chevron and Texaco dominated the extraction of resources in Latin America until the entrance of new imperial players like China. The anti-imperial, or decolonial, governments are concurrent with the economic rise of the financially strong People's Republic of China whose desire for new raw material resources and suppliers can hardly be quenched. Previously, mainly international corporations had been criticized for the ruthless exploitation of natural resources and local governments for their submissiveness. Yet, today it is often the center-left or leftwing governments of those Latin American countries that are also under criticism, and which have to struggle to legitimize the ongoing extractive policies and their consequences.

The dispute over the oil in the Yasuní is just one example of this struggle about the benefits and the negative effects for nature and society. It also shows that despite the most progressive of constitutions, not to mention the international protection measures, such as the designation as a UNESCO Biosphere Reserve, there will be no structural change towards a post-extractive society without the political will of the political leadership.[21]

---

21 In January, 2018, drilling began in the first production site inside Yasuní National Park. With its newly erected platform Tambococha-2, the state-run oil company Petroamazonas intends to tap the 287 million barrels of oil it reckons to lie in 1,800 meters depth. The Moreno government decided to reduce the size of the section within Yasuní sacrificed for drilling from about 1,000 to 300 acres while adding another 50,000 acres to the protected area of the national park altogether – clearly a compromise between economic and conservation interests. On February 4, 2018, seventy percent of the citizens of Ecuador endorsed this policy in a popular referendum.

Works Cited

Acosta, Alberto. "Das 'Buen Vivir'. Die Schaffung einer Utopie." *Juridikum. Zeitschrift für Kritik, Recht, Gesellschaft* 4 (2009): 219–23.
Andrianova, Anna. "The new Chavez? Oil trumps rain forest in Ecuador." CNBC 26 August 2013. 23 February 2017 <http://www.cnbc.com/id/100978260>.
Araujo, Alberto. "La caída del precio del crudo reduce rentabilidad del Yasuní-ITT." *El Comercio* 6 March, 2015. 19 August 2016 <http://www.elcomercio.com/actualidad/yasuni-itt-rentabilidad-precio-petroleo.html>.
Constitución de la República del Ecuador. 2008. 19 August 2016 <http://www.asambleanacional.gov.ec/documentos/constitucion_de_bolsillo.pdf>.
Hill, David. "Ecuador pursued China oil deal while pledging to protect Yasuní, papers show." *The Guardian* 19 February, 2014. 19 August 2016 <http://www.theguardian.com/environment/2014/feb/19/ecuador-oil-china-yasuni>.
Martínez, Omar Bonilla. "La geopolítica petrolera China en Ecuador y el área andina." *Tensões Mundiais, Revista do Observatório das Nacionalidades* 10.18–19 (Jan./Dec. 2014): 257–75.
UNESCO. "Biosphere Reserves – Learning Sites for Sustainable Development." 19 August 2016 <http://unesco.org/new/en/natural-sciences/environment/ecological-sciences/biosphere-reserves/>.
—. "Latin America and the Caribbean: 125 biosphere reserves in 21 countries." 19 August 2016 <http://www.unesco.org/new/en/natural-sciences/environment/ecological-sciences/biosphere-reserves/latin-america-and-the-caribbean/>.

TOWARD AN ECO-CULTURAL DECOLONIZATION OF HERITAGE

CHAPTER TEN

Naturalizing Culture in the Pyrenees: Heritage Processes and the Eternalization of Rural Societies

Camila del Mármol and Ferran Estrada

Introduction

The analysis of heritage processes in the Catalan Pyrenees allows us to discuss the 'naturalization of culture' in rural contexts. These phenomena refer to the displacement of the concept of culture onto an idealized field of 'nature', allowing for the disguise of the underlying conditions of heritage politics. In these processes we find a particular intertwining of local ideas of authenticity, nature and the past; concepts that are fundamental for the making of heritage. From an ethnographical perspective, we focus our study on specific processes of naturalization of culture within rural contexts and in particular the fields of heritage production, rural architecture and food production.[1]

By 'naturalization of culture' we understand a historical and social process by which the conception of culture moves towards an idealized representation of nature. Building on a critical tradition stemming from Marx's analysis of the eternalization of the relations of production, we analyze the mechanisms through which culture, and hence cultural heritage, becomes naturalized in the making of heritage. The understanding of heritage as an objectifying process by which some elements are reinterpreted and isolated from their original relations of production has already been denounced by several authors (Guillaume). Of course, we understand that this process is not exclusive to rural contexts.

Rural contexts are likely to be understood as the optimal scenarios in which nature and culture appear to be ideally integrated, enabling a naturalization of rural culture and cultural heritage processes. This situation allows for the concealing of the political, economical and historical intermingled logics that are inherent to heritage practices. In this article we focus on the specific fields of rural architecture and food production in order to explore the processes by which

---

[1] This research is based on long-term ethnographic fieldwork in the Catalan Pyrenees developed by the two authors in different periods (especially between 2006 and 2011). This work was supported by the Spanish Ministry of Education and Science and the FEDER Program under Grant ['*Patrimonialización y redefinición de la ruralidad. Nuevos usos del patrimonio local*' (CSO2011-29413)].

they become 'naturalized'. Our analysis shows some of the sociopolitical consequences that the naturalization of culture brings about, highlighting its ability to preclude dissent and debate.

In the next section we introduce some characteristics of the territory in which research has been carried out: Heritage, and more specifically heritage processes, are a crucial aspect of its current economic development. Following this, we discuss the naturalization of heritage in rural contexts and analyze the mechanisms by which present rural culture gradually becomes defined as belonging to the fields of 'nature', reminiscent of the past and of authenticity. Finally, we delve into certain domains of heritagization in the Catalan Pyrenees, namely rural architecture and the so-called *productes de la terra* (regional food products), to explore how the naturalization of culture is shaped within heritage processes.

Heritage in the Catalan Pyrenees

The Catalan Pyrenees, in northwest Spain, have experienced a complex set of transformations during the last century; these have brought about a new organization of social, economic and political structures that offer new ways of conceiving the territory and new uses of the existing resources (Vaccaro and Beltran; Roigé and Frigolé; López i Gelat et al.). Our research was conducted in different areas of the Pyrenees and the adjacent mountainous areas of Catalonia, such as the Alt Urgell, Val d'Aran, Alta Ribagorça and the Montseny Massive. Analogous processes to those observed in this territory can be found in other areas of Europe: a changing rural economy and occupational structures that have allowed for a diversified and uneven developing of the land, which has brought about new activities and services (see Lowe et al.). However, these processes should not be understood as a sudden change; ie as the sudden abandonment of traditional agriculture in favor of a tourist based economy; but rather as a progressive transformation that owes much to the dynamics of depopulation, to the local effects of the global economy and to the development of new values and uses of the territory towards a new rural modernity (Collantes).

During the 20th century, the progressive weakening of traditional subsistence livelihoods based on small-scale agro-ranching activities and forest uses was a common feature of the Pyrenees' regional economy. These processes came together with the implementation of new economic activities such as mining, large scale timber extraction, hydropower plants, and factories of all types (Vaccaro; Campillo et al.). In some areas an important dairy industry developed, changing the previous patterns of traditional activities (Tulla; Gascón). These changes, together with the impact arising from the economic interactions with the industrialized lowland areas, resulted in profound social transformations, including an acute dynamic of rural depopulation (Ayuda and Pinilla; Molina).

The successive transformations experienced during the 20th century ended up reorienting the use of the territory towards new conceptualizations of the territory. Landscape, nature, and culture became new commodities for urban consumption, giving rise to a leisure economy based on the heritagization of nature and culture (Vaccaro and Beltran; Frigolé, *Producció cultural de lloc*). By heritagization we refer to a series of processes that affect the local uses of the past, adapting them to the standardized models of representation and interpretation of the past within heritage hegemonic discourses (Smith, *Uses of Heritage*). Heritage products are one result of these processes, ready for consumption by a widely urban population. The expansion of heritage as a hegemonic idiom worldwide has been largely discussed by several authors (Herzfeld; Franquesa; Collins, among others). In the past decades, heritage processes have developed in mountain areas together with the restructuring of the productive model. The progressive disarticulation of traditional agro-ranching activities, together with the impacts of global capitalism and European policies, have enhanced the intensity of the restructuring of these territories' profitability in the face of the new demands and needs of the contemporary economy, thus fostering the emergence of new postindustrial landscapes (Sivaramakrishnan and Vaccaro).

We understand heritagization as a process that alters the significance of an array of elements from the past within a specific, present social and economic context, resulting in new products which are labelled as 'heritage'. By outlining it as a "mode of cultural production", heritage is understood as a process of meaning-generation which produces new categories and acts as a device that re-signifies territories, resources and people (Kirshenblatt-Gimblett 7). Nature, landscape and local culture have been thus transformed and redefined within these new discourses, allowing for a reconceptualization of both the material contexts and the local imaginaries. Different authors have referred to the ever-increasing array of elements that are considered heritage (Heinich; Bendix), thus fostering an inflationary dynamic by which almost everything can be turned into the legitimate heritage of a certain society (Hartog). In the following pages we provide a characterization of the ways in which these general processes of heritagization materialize; in particular, heritage politics within specific rural areas of the Catalan Pyrenees.

Rural areas in Europe share common features in relation to demographic, economic and social patterns. Though not identical, they have been considered from a generalist perspective by some government bodies, for example the European Union. In the framework of the EU structural funds, and especially regarding some documents such as the report The Future of Rural Society (European Commission 32) which is seen as the first step towards rural development in Europe, tourism has been identified as a strategic development sector for rural and mountainous areas. This document analyses the characteristics of European rural areas and their evolution over the past decades, stating a situation of "structural backwardness" especially in the Mediterranean regions (European Commission 22–23). The aim of the European Commission seems here to define a policy framework that deals with the standard problems confronting these areas, one of them being the "protection of the environment and development of the countryside", in order to promote the development of areas "providing recreation and leisure for the city-dwellers" (European Commission 32). This document also stresses the need to defend "the cultural heritage (architecture, folklore, etc.) [...] not only in its own right but also because in many areas it is the key to the development of tourism" (European Commission 40). The concept of heritage appears as a tool that underlies the wider process of creating new tourism destinations.

Incentives to develop tourism in the Catalan Pyrenees were part of local government plans and measures and EU structural development funds, mostly from the 1980s onwards (Del Mármol, "Through other Times"). The conversion of the Pyrenees into a tourist destination originated in the 19th century and was influenced by similar processes to those occurring in the Alps (Briffaud). However, it was not until the 20th century that the tourist development infiltrated the whole area. From the 1980s onwards, the tragic reality of depopulation has been turned into an idyllic representation of seclusion that is thought to be attractive to visiting urban dwellers. Many actions have been implemented, including the creation of natural parks, a series of town planning measures to preserve the landscape, the improvement of transport infrastructure, the recovery of old paths, the creation of ethnographic heritage sites such as ethnographic museums, an increase in the appreciation of local festivals and celebrations, and the restoration of churches and monuments that are considered to be of historical interest (see Frigolé, *Producció cultural de lloc*; Roigé and Frigolé; Roigé and Estrada; Vaccaro and Beltran). The discourses transforming the Pyrenees into a tourist attraction responded to the strategic objectives defined within different developmental plans, as with the afore-mentioned approach put forward by the European Commission as well as similar documents stemming from national and Catalan governments. Considered together, it could be said that these development plans place the region within a political agenda that integrates a series of common directives for the future of European rural areas (Vaccaro and Beltran). At the same time, the outcome of this integration of the regions into a major social representational model is to promote a unified Europe that finds in its rural areas the remnant of its traditions and the roots of its immanent identities. These new ways of considering the territory have resulted in new sociopolitical and economical uses of the past that are a fundamental aspect of the heritagization of the Pyrenees.

Naturalizing Culture

We contend that the naturalization of culture is a characteristic of heritage processes in rural areas. By 'naturalization of culture' we mean a historical and social process by which the conception of culture moves towards an idealized representation of nature. In his *Grundrisse*, Marx unfolds the processes by which production is presented "as encased in eternal natural laws independent of history, at which opportunity bourgeois relations are then quietly smuggled in as the inviolable natural laws on which society in the abstract is founded" (37). This critical tradition paves the way for an analysis oriented to restoring the historic and social processes that allow for the naturalization of the social as an eternal and universal abstraction. Bourdieu argues along these lines when analyzing the historical mechanisms responsible for the relative dehistorization and eternalization of the structure of the sexual division. In this sense, he reminds us that "what appears, in history, as being eternal is merely the product of a labor of eternalization performed by interconnected institutions such as the family, the church, the state, the educational system" (viii). Following his claim of "combating these historical forces of dehistorization" (viii), we propose to analyze the mechanism by which culture is being naturalized within certain heritage processes, turning it into an element detached from history; an abstraction, eternal and absolute and devoid of its historical meanings.

The 'naturalization of culture' as a social process works by projecting qualities associated with the realm of nature into sociocultural elements. If 'nature' is regarded as "trans-historic, trans-social and trans-cultural" and it "builds a consensus in relation to its safeguarding" (Jeudy 5),[2] the naturalization of culture would imply the transference of this array of attributes to the domain of culture. Marc Guillaume has already denounced the 'naturalization' of conservation politics that gives rise to a naturalized vision of heritage both natural and cultural.

In order to understand these processes, we examine the various meanings of the concept of nature in our societies. This topic has been discussed thoroughly by different authors (Descola; Strathern; Williams). Williams long ago stated that an analysis of the different ideas of nature, its changes and historic transformations, would be far beyond the scope of a single piece of writing (68). We do not pretend to delve into the complex characteristics and meanings of the dichotomy of nature-culture within the Western tradition, since Strathern has already argued that "nature and culture cannot be resolved into a single dichotomy" (178). We will leave aside the debate around the contending interpretations concerning the different ontological settings for the idea of "nature" or the "environment", such as those positions defended by well-known contemporary scholars (e. g. Latour, Descola, Viveiros de Castro, Ingold, Escobar). Instead, we will focus on three main aspects of the meaning of nature in a local context that we place within the consciously overgeneralized pool of "Western-capitalist" societies.[3] What we will try to do therefore is to explore general assumptions about the concept of nature,

---

2   In French in the original: "appelle un consensus autour de sa sauvagarde malgré toutes les formes de destruction qu'elle peut subir."

3   For these ideas we are building on common definitions of the term 'nature' in English, Catalan and Spanish (see *Oxford Dictionary*, *Diccionari de la Llengua Catalana* de l'Institut d'Estudis Catalans and *Diccionario de la Lengua Española* de la Real Academia Española).

and to understand what we have come to call the naturalization of culture in the Pyrenees as:

1. The understanding of the phenomena of the physical world as a reality external to humans.
2. An idealized image of the environment, unscathed by human activities.
3. The basic, essential, innate or inherent features, character, or qualities of something or someone, carrying within this a sense of inevitability.

Building upon these meanings, the naturalization of culture would imply:

1. On the one hand, a conceptualization of culture as a reality external to humans, that is, an abstraction with a life of its own, emulating the process by which nature is understood as external to humans. In this sense, culture is represented as an isolated and reified concept; uprooted from the uncertainties of social relations from which it emerges.
2. On the other hand, the naturalization of culture involves casting certain idealized attributes and essential qualities associated with nature over sociocultural realities. These realities, or a part of them, are therefore thought of as being close to nature; this would mean that certain elements of the social and cultural life of people share attributes with an idealized and rather fixed idea of nature that escapes the social process of becoming.
3. Finally, and related to the second point, naturalizing culture supposes perceiving some elements of the social and cultural realm as essential features of society; in the sense that they are (or should be) what they are on the basis of a natural imperative. It is 'natural' that they are like this.

Authenticity, Past and Nature

Diverse authors (Poulot; Lowenthal; Heinich; among others) have pointed to the role of concepts such as 'authenticity' and the 'past' as central categories for understanding heritage processes. In order to analyze the naturalization of culture within heritage we should also attend to the intertwining of these categories with the idea of nature. Accordingly, we will follow the meanings of these concepts as a way of disclosing the constituting relationships that underpin some of the ideological foundations of what we call the naturalization of culture.

'Authentic' can be split into two basic meanings: the first is related to the undisputed origin or authorship of an element; its genuine character; its legitimacy to represent a significant feature of something. The second definition is related to the idea of being true or loyal to the original, or to its principles or origin. Thus, an important aspect of 'authenticity' is its relation with origin. Benjamin states that "the authenticity of a thing is the essence of all that is transmissible from its beginning, ranging from its substantive duration to its testimony to the history which it has experienced" (221). This origin means also a relation to the past; that is, to the history of the object in the sense of its tradition. In fact, what is at risk in the era of mechanical reproduction is the 'aura' of the work of art, since "the technique of reproduction detaches the reproduced object from the domain of tradition" (221). MacCannell has long followed a similar line of thinking:

> For moderns, reality and authenticity are thought to be elsewhere: in other historical periods and other cultures, in purer, simpler life-styles. In other words, the concern of moderns with 'naturalness', their nostalgia and their search for authenticity are not merely casual and somewhat decadent, though harmless, attachments to the souvenirs of destroyed cultures and dead epochs. They are also components of the conquering spirit of modernity – the grounds of its unifying consciousness. (3)

A nostalgic approach to the past is a common feature in the search for authenticity and in heritage politics. The further away something is considered to be, in temporal or spatial terms, the more authentic it is perceived as being. The idea of origin is developed within an evolutionary approach in which 'older' works are also considered to be 'more authentic'. García Canclini posits that "the idea of authenticity idealized some moment of the past as a sociocultural paradigm; thus throwing into oblivion the fact that every culture is the result of selection processes" (187).[4]

There is indeed a certain correlation between ideas of past and authenticity and the concept of nature as understood in our societies. On the one hand, the different meanings of authenticity are closely linked to the meaning of nature explored above. 'Authentic' in its sense of 'trustworthy' is close to the idea of 'nature' as referring to the essential features of something or someone (a person, an element or institution) that has not been transformed or 'denaturalized' but has remained authentic. On the other hand, 'authentic' is related to the meaning of 'nature', as we have seen, in the form of an idealization of the environment.

As for the concept of the 'past', it is also closely related to assumptions regarding ideas about nature and culture. We have already referred to a conception of nature and culture as opposed and differentiated entities prevailing in our society (Descola; Strathern; Yanagisako and Delaney). Nature is usually conceived as being prior to culture: an entity that is preexistent and independent from human development (see Fabian).[5] The tendency to assimilate the 'natural' with an a priori has already been denounced by Strathern as being a consequence of a specific intellectual tradition within our own culture. The basic conception under-

---

4 In Spanish in the original: "la idea de autenticidad idealiza algún momento del pasado como paradigma sociocultural, y olvida que toda cultura es resultado de una selección."
5 Yanagisako and Delaney (4) explore the transition from a 'God-given' nature in the biblical worldview to a "rule-governed Nature, stripped off it cosmological moorings and therefore presumably generalizable to all peoples."

lying these ideas is that humanity, in the course of its evolution, grew progressively apart from nature due to the development of culture. From this stems the idea that the older a cultural element, the more 'natural' it is. Furthermore, one could say that in heritage processes the reverse relation is likewise important: the more 'natural' an element is considered to be, the older it is. In this sense, those sociocultural elements that are thought of as being closer to nature are also deemed more ancient. This would be the case in the practice of transhumance, for instance, which is seen, analyzed and valorized as a millenary practice that has not changed since Neolithic times (see Estrada, Nadal and Iglesias); such logic however ignores the contemporary context of transhumance and the actual ways it has been practiced up until the last decades of the past century.

This kind of local, ethnohistorical observations can be framed within more general analyses concerned with the uses of the past and its values in contemporary societies (Appadurai; Lowenthal; Jameson; Bensa and Fabre; Kaneef). Frigolé (*Patrimonialization and the mercantilization of the authentic*, 28) contends that the production of heritage also entails the production of the past, allowing for the emergence of a new multiplicity of conceptions and uses of it. He argues that an important conception of the past, as it works within heritage processes, is the one related to the origins. These "origins", as a special vision of the past, are widely spread within heritage discourses. It is usually referred to as an original state of elements; these elements are considered aside of any logic of transformation that could eventually 'denaturalize' them.

As we have seen, both the concept of 'authenticity' and the 'past' are closely related to idealized conceptions of nature, especially within heritage processes. As we will see in the next section, we can also find these concepts to be central ideas of the discourses that configure the new values and practices of heritagization in rural contexts.

Approaching Culture to Nature in Rural Contexts

In our field research, we observed that the Pyrenees have undergone a specific process that has shaped the place as a tourist attraction, especially over the last thirty years. We have referred to this as a process of enchantment, in which negative considerations have been transformed into attractions that feed from romantic traditions and bucolic perspectives to entice visitors (Del Mármol, "Through other Times"). Nature has been an important aspect of this process and it is still considered an essential feature of the tourist attraction. Natural parks and protected areas have long existed in the Pyrenees but they proliferated particularly from the 1980s onwards due to the new legislative framework that emerged after the Franco dictatorship and with the influence of the European Union environmental programs (Vaccaro and Beltran). As an example: 46,6 % of the Alt Pirineu and the region of Aran (encompassing most of the Catalan Pyrenees territory) is currently located within some type of natural protection area.⁶ Nowadays, this area is described in tourist brochures as:

> A place where you and nature are in perfect harmony, making you feel beautiful and good inside. A land marked by soaring mountains, a rich cultural heritage and exceptional cuisine. Unspoiled nature surrounds you as you enjoy sports activities, visits to natural parks and a culture stretching back to ancient times. A cradle of cultures where ancient customs and traditions have been preserved. Calmly savour the essence of a life that retains its authenticity.⁷

Bruner and Salazar, among others, have studied the multiple links between tourism and imagination, offering a critical analysis of some social representations of such links. For Bruner (21) "Metanarratives are the largest conceptual frame within which tourism operates." Salazar, in turn, understands imaginaries as "socially transmitted representational assemblages that interact with people's personal imaginings and are used as meaning-making and world-shaping devices" (864). Salazar focuses on tourist imaginaries to understand the way in which tourism (re)invents and (re)shapes identities and destinations. The 'natural' character of rural areas must be thus thought of as part of these imaginative devices that support tourist discourses. Salazar calls for us to understand such imaginaries not as fixed meanings; rather, we must remain alert to new forms of meaning-making and their circulation, as this is what currently shapes many parts of the rural world.

Heritage processes in rural areas are therefore mediated by specific imaginaries that have historically shaped social representations of place. The Catalan Pyrenees have for a long time been represented by a romantic vision under the auspices of famous writers and intellectuals close to the *Renaixença* (Jimenez and Prats).⁸ From the perspective of this movement, the Pyrenees are seen as the cradle of Catalan identity. The mountains are understood as a place of purity, where nature is expressed in all its majesty. Thus, the Pyrenees were represented as a refuge of old values and ancient traditions. In the same vein, the way the inhabitants were regarded changed from close-minded and unpleasant people to a new image which is closer to that of the 'noble savage' (see Roma). An idealized image of nature in its pristine form has ever since been a structural component in the shaping of the Pyrenean imaginaries. Vaccaro and Beltran (17) have already referred to a recent 'naturalization of rural landscape' in the form of an environmental recovery occurring after the decrease in agricultural pressure on the land. To this we must add the naturalization of culture and cultural heritage that finds in the rural context an idealized scenario in which culture and nature appears to

---

6   Source: Departament de Territori i Sostenibilitat, Generalitat de Catalunya. Idescat, 2013.
7   Visit Pirineus, Generalitat de Catalunya. Available from: <http://www.visitpirineus.com/ca/pirineus> Last accessed 13/08/2014.
8   The *Renaixença* is a romantic literary movement interested in the revival of Catalan language and culture that developed in Catalonia at the beginning of the nineteenth century.

converge. They are a direct consequence of the idealization of the rural world, believed to be more 'natural' than the urban contexts. Within this idealization, fields became nature (Acosta). Agricultural and mountain areas where industrialization had an uneven impact have been turned into representations of an alleged pristine nature detached from the urban and modern world. This comes hand in hand with representations of traditional ways of life, purer environments, natural and healthy productions, etc. Acosta argues that these areas work nowadays as reservoirs of cultural and natural meanings (91).

In the following examples we will emphasize the hegemonic character of heritage processes in order to follow the impact of discourses oriented towards the naturalization of culture. As we will show, the stress on the hegemonic character of developmental plans and policies is important to understand the evolution of the area.[9]

Architecture

Architecture in the Catalan Pyrenees has undergone a process of heritagization in the past decades. Old images from the towns can be seen in different contexts. They illustrate tourist pamphlets and brochures and decorate walls in bars, restaurants and private houses. What is noteworthy when observing these pictures from the past is the similarly outward appearance that some hamlets seem to conserve. At first sight, ochre hues and earthy color tones prevail, and in some cases the size of towns remains rather similar to what it was in the past. These features can lead the distracted observer to believe that continuity with the past is a natural result of a traditional way of construction that remains alive in the present. A closer analysis however, confronts us with the strategic aims of a rural architecture that in recent times has become a touristic attraction of the Catalan Pyrenees (Roigé, Estrada and Beltran).

Local architecture in these areas has been subject to a strict selection of features that shape an idealized 'traditional style'. Adherence to such features has been ensured through specific measures such as legal documents on urban planning that define and apply these new conceptions of traditional style to the Pyrenean towns. Interestingly, these external representations of the 'local style' have been largely accepted by local populations, changing the representations and values of what is considered 'appropriate' and 'beautiful' regarding architecture.

---

9 Nonetheless, we do not ignore the counterhegemonic power embedded in heritage discourses, which has been thoroughly analysed in recent works (Collins; Breglia; Franquesa; De Cesari; Smith et al.). We have elsewhere analysed the production of heritage discourses on a local level, unpacking the competing definitions that must be contextualized in broader processes of debate and opposition (Roigé and Estrada; Del Mármol, *Pasados Locales*). Though the growing interest of those working on heritage studies in the complex implications of heritage processes that go beyond simplistic top-down approaches, the hegemonic character of heritage discourses cannot be ignored.

Building techniques and styles have become a common topic of conversation, through which to discuss changing values and conflicting visions of the territory. Both the analysis of the legislation on urban planning, rules and documents[10] as well as our ethnographic research reveal a novel definition of a legitimate "rural architecture", referred to as the "traditional way of construction" of the area. In this regard, we contend that heritage processes outlining the architectural "tradition" of the Catalan Pyrenees have led to a naturalization of certain styles and building techniques.

As a result, a somewhat homogenized style can be observed across the mountains, a clear dominance of stonewalls and red or grey slate roofs and wooden doors and windows. It is not just the materials that are strictly determined by urban and construction regulation (mostly stemming from local and regional authorities); the heights of the buildings, the degree of inclination for rooftops, openings and designs are also regulated. Recent depopulation and the isolated character of some villages have helped in many cases to prevent the excesses of the construction bubble that have been the norm in Spain in recent decades. Other areas more related to tourism and secondary house development[11] in the past years have also implemented specific measures to preserve the idyllic appearance of rural traditional construction. This style, defined as traditional and rural, is understood as an inheritance of ancient ways of life that are recalled as being "embedded nature." An example can be found in the type of materials used for the exterior of buildings in the area. Houses are usually built of stone, wood, grey or red slate: these materials are deemed as being "local" and they reinforce the image of natural constructions, using elements extracted directly from nature without being previously transformed. There is an extended idea that this traditional style responds to a functional way of building, adapted to the natural conditions of the environment and to the needs of its dwellers. In this sense, it is con-

---

10 Llei 4/1980, de 16 de desembre, de creació de l'Institut Catalá del Sol; Llei 9/1981, de 18 de novembre, sobre protecció de la legalitat urbanística; Llei 37/1984, del 9 de gener, de mesures d'adecuació de l'ordenament urbanístic de Catalunya; Projecte de Delimitació de Sòl Urbà dels Municipis de Fígols-Alinyà, la Vansa-Fórnols y Josa-Tuixent; Llei 2/2002 de 14 de març, d'urbanisme (DOGC 3600, de 21/03/2002) modificada per la Llei 10/2004 d'urbanisme (DOGC 4291, de 30/12/2004), i definida pel Decret Legislatiu 1/2005 de 26 de juliol (DOGC 4436, de 28/07/2005); El Pla Territorial Parcial de l'Alt Pirineu i Aran (DOGC 4714, de 07/09/2006) deriva de la Llei 23/1983 de Política Territorial (DOGC 385, de 30/11/1983) i del Pla Territorial General (LLei 1/1995, de 16 març).
11 Population patterns are an important aspect of the recent transformations in the Catalan Pyrenees. After several waves of depopulation during the 20th century, this tendency stagnated at the end of the past century. The villages in the upper valleys usually present very low population indexes that is composed of mainly older local residents and some younger inhabitants that could be both locally born or neo-rurals, as they have come to be called. Another important category of local population, especially in the most depopulated villages, are second residents owning a summer or weekend house. They could be both emigrants that have always kept their family houses, or just outsiders (normally originating from other areas of the Catalan territory) that felt attracted by the area. Bigger cities should be excluded from this rough draft that corresponds to small villages and hamlets situated mostly in the upper valleys.

ceived as a 'natural architecture', in opposition to artificial and modern types of construction. Traditional architecture would thus "emanate from the territory."[12]

The documents referred to above clearly define a new "traditional typology" that must be adhered to, which includes guidelines about permitted materials and even the colors of the outside walls. This new typology, based on alleged traditional practices, will outline the current and future appearance of most villages and buildings in the area. These processes have been shaped by associating local architecture with traditional methods of construction that are supposedly 'more natural', since they are understood as being a result of traditional knowledge that has been passed down from rural societies from the past. Thus, the new architectural parameters have been shaped under the influence of specific images of rusticity that give rise to an 'aesthetics of nature'. 'Natural' materials and construction techniques are prioritized, as well as chromatic tones using natural pigments that mimic the nuances of the local landscape.

The bucolic ambience that these normative features would appear to give to the villages and hamlets obscures a strict regulation that has prevented many valleys from attempting alternative avenues of economic development. Following traditional patterns of construction and prioritizing specific materials often results in an increase in building prices. The obligation to respect the traditional volumetric parameters of construction also makes it difficult to open small enterprises that would need bigger units to be able to operate. These regulations become stiffer when referring to hamlets that are within or close to the natural parks. In this regard, many local inhabitants criticize the current legislation on urban planning on the basis that it limits the diversity of possible uses of the territory. The emphasis these norms and legislations put on the decorative and aesthetic aspects of construction in the area ignore other negative impacts on the territory and its people. For example, the growing residential areas oriented towards secondary residences in different areas of the Pyrenees require urban services such as drinking water, sewage systems and garbage collection; such services will be required for only a few days every year and are not economically sustainable by local councils out of the peak season. Moreover, this construction model generates speculative dynamics that prioritize building activities over agricultural and ranching practices, which are forced to compete for scarce land in mountain areas. These processes have an important effect on the depopulation indexes in these territories, since the increased prices of land and houses push the younger generation to emigrate.

---

12 *Plan Nacional de Salvaguarda de la Arquitectura Tradicional*, 2014.

Productes de la Terra

The concept of *productes de la terra* (regional produce) has similar connotations in Spanish, French and Catalan speaking regions, usually alluding to the link between some products (ideally manufactured) with the land and the territory (Bérard and Marcheney; Grasseni, "Packaging skills"). Regional food products are an excellent example of an element that integrates ideas of nature and culture, authenticity and the past, in the complex process of its heritagization.

Several examples from the Catalan Pyrenees and adjacent areas exemplify the heritagization of the *productes de la terra* (Espeitx, Massanés and Cáceres). These processes can be framed against the backdrop of the notion of 'risk' projected towards the production of food under the industrial condition of global capitalism (Medina). According to Medina, this is expressed in the increasing alienation of the production processes involved in the food industry. A prevalent idea is that 'traditional processes of production' are directly controlled by people, in contrast to the industrial modes of production, that are perceived as escaping human control. The result is an increasing nostalgic desire to consume 'traditional products' that are deemed 'purer and more natural'. Traditional forms of production are being shaped and revalorized within complex processes of evaluation and meaning that include the production of 'traditional practices' that must however match current regulations and markets.

The label of heritage is applied to food products in the form of certificates of origin (for example PDO – protected designation of origin – and PGI – protected geographical indication – within the EU). One example is the cheese production of the Alt Urgell, in the Catalan Pyrenees. Building on a long tradition of milk and dairy industry developing from the beginning of the 20th century, the region has more recently struggled to reach new markets with its artisanal cheese. This transformation of meanings and products is built on two separate local traditions that nowadays have merged into a single narrative. The first tradition in question is the region's long history of milk and dairy industry that has prompted an important transformation of the local productive patterns both in relation to agricultural uses and industry development (see Del Mármol and Vaccaro). From the 1950s onwards, the local dairy industry developed a specialization in cheese and butter, to be sold mostly in urban areas. The second local tradition is relatively more recent, first appearing in the 1980s, but is symbolically connected with older traditions. New inhabitants attracted by the material and social conditions of the territory settled in at a time when the area was strongly depopulated; inspired by an ideal of self-sufficiency these new categories of the local population came to be known as 'hippies'. Many of these new residents developed new handicraft activities, targeting the new markets opened by a growing tourist economy. Many of them specialized in the artisanal manufacturing of cheese. Besides the technical developments in these modes of production, an important symbolic work has been undertaken in order to explicitly relate these contemporary artisanal activities with past practices developed within peasant households in the context of the subsistence economies. Part of the new artisanal activities were imported practices and know-how from different contexts, as we can infer from the fact that many producers of artisanal cheese traveled to France in order to learn the local methods and knowledge of cheese production.

These separate histories were presented as being convergent within the new narratives that tried to position the Alt Urgell area as a cheese production center for the Pyrenees. Accordingly, an important trade fair of artisanal cheese products has been organized in the capital of the region every year since 1999, and several certificates of origin within the European Union regulations have been obtained. These certificates work as legitimating devices, adding value and meaning to forms of production that are reminiscent of the natural territory and traditional and vernacular ways of subsistence in which they originated. Despite the clear discontinuities in the history of the milk and cheese production in the area during the past century, the efforts to present a discourse of continuity reveals the inner-workings of heritage processes. The discourses of continuity within an imagined past are key to understanding the production of value (both economic and symbolic) and the legitimatization of current practices of production.

This example illustrates how the association of contemporary practices with specific values related to 'nature' and 'rural culture' is fundamental for the production of heritage processes in rural areas such as the Catalan Pyrenees. The positive connotations of concepts related to nature and rural culture work as instruments of the politics of heritage. Certificates of origin are part of this process, by which ideas of authenticity of origins, tradition and closeness to nature are used to promote new products. The emphasis on an idealized past both conceals the complexity of the relations of production that is a constitutive part of the new products and obscures the contradictory relations that these practices have with global and national regulations (Bérard and Marchenay; Paxson). Patterns of hygiene and environmental restrictions are in this regard an important aspect of the contemporary economy of ecologic and certified productions, sometimes overshadowing their disciplinary consequences over products, places and local forms of social organization (see Grasseni, "Packaging skills", as an example).

Conclusions

In this essay we have explored the 'naturalization of culture' as a driver of logics within heritage processes in rural contexts. Exploring the specific context of heritagization in the Catalan Pyrenees, we have reflected on the current dynamics of heritage politics. As a result, we have shown how 'nature' can work as a powerful device, creating symbolic values that can be transformed into economic values in the market. Authenticity and antiquity have also been examined as powerful domains of social imagination mobilized within these processes. Nature can be idealized as a collective good, but also, through the process of its heritagization, transformed into a commodity ready to be consumed (Vaccaro and Beltran). In this sense, the naturalization of culture seems to involve the revalorization of certain cultural elements. We have argued that this revalorization aims at commercializing some "authentic" natural-cultural elements that are made salient within the logics of heritagization.

Despite our specific ethnographic context, we think that our case study can contribute to a rethinking of the politics of heritage in rural contexts in general. We have stressed the role that the perception of the 'naturalness' of certain cultural elements plays in the process of their heritagization and argued that in some cases those elements considered to be closer to nature may become the ideological and material drivers of some heritage processes.

Within the domain of rural architecture, we have seen how traditional methods of construction that are allegedly more natural have been identified as being "the local architecture," both by governmental bodies and from the perspective of the local population. To a great extent, the heritagization of rural architechture is sustained by the hegemonic understanding that local architectural forms stem from the traditional knowledge of rural societies from the past.

The example of Regional Food Products illustrates how the association of contemporary practices with specific values related to 'nature' and 'rural culture' is fundamental in order to understand the production of heritage in rural areas. In the light of our example, we have shown how the perception of the 'naturalness' of cultural elements as the *productes de la terra* plays a key part in the construction of local identities in rural contexts.

Works Cited

Acosta, Rufino. "Ruralidad, agricultura y transacciones entre imaginarios." *PH Cuadernos* 26 (2010): 81–93.

Appadurai, Arjun. "The past as a scarce resource." *Man, New Series* 16,2 (1981): 201–19.

Ayuda, María Isabel, and Vicente Pinilla. "El proceso de desertización demográfica en la montaña Pirenaica el largo plazo: Aragón." *Ager: Revista de Estudios de Despoblación y Desarrollo Rural* 2 (2002): 1001–138.

Bendix, Regina. "Heritage between economy and politics. An assessment from the perspective of cultural anthropology." *Intangible heritage*. Eds. Laurajane Smith and Natsuko Akagawa. New York: Routledge, 2009. 253–69.

Benjamin, Walter. "The work of art in the age of mechanical reproduction." *Illuminations. Essays and reflections*. Walter Benjamin. 1955. New York: Schocken Books, 2007.

Bensa, Alban and Daniel Fabre (Eds.). *Une histoire à soi. Figurations du passé et localités*. Paris: Éditions de la Maison des sciences de l'homme, 2001.

Bérard, Laurence, and Philippe Marchenay. *Les produits de terroir. Entre cultures et réglementes*. París: CNRS Éditions, 2004.

Bourdieu, Pierre. *Masculine domination.* Stanford: Stanford University Press, 2001.
Breglia, Lisa. *Monumental Ambivalence: The Politics of Heritage.* Austin: University of Texas, 2006.
Briffaud, Serge. *Naissance d'un paysage.* Toulouse: Université de Toulouse, 1994.
Bruner, Edward. *Culture on Tour: Ethnographies of Travel.* Chicago: University of Chicago Press, 2005.
Campillo, Xavier, Rosa Ganyet, Francesc López, and Rosa Majoral. *L'Alt Urgell. Estructura territorial, recursos i activitat econòmica.* Barcelona: Caixa de Catalunya, 1992.
Cesari, Chiara de. "Creativeheritage: Palestinian heritage NGOs and defiant arts of government." *American Anthropologist* 112,4 (2010): 625–37.
Collantes, Fernando. "Rural Europe reshaped: the economic transformation of upland regions, 1850–2001." *Economic History Review* 62,2 (2009): 306–23.
Collins, John. "'But what if I should need to defecate in your neighborhood, Madame?': Empire, Redemption, and the 'Tradition of the Oppressed' in a Brazilian World Heritage Site." *Cultural Anthropology* 23,2 (2008): 279–328.
Descola, Philippe. "Beyond Nature and Culture." *Proceedings of the British Academy* 139 (2006): 137–55.
Escobar, Arturo. "After Nature: steps to an antiessentialist polititical ecology." *Current Anthropology* 41,1 (1999): 1–30.
Espeitx, Elena, Toni Massanés, and Juan Cáceres. *Com a la llosa, res: transformacions alimentàries al Pallars Sobirà i a l'Alt Urgell.* Barcelona: Departament de Cultura, 2001.
Estrada, Ferran, Elisabet Nadal, and Juan Ramón Iglesias. "21st Century Transhumans. Transhumance in the Context of Social and Economic Change in the Alta Ribagorça". *Social and Ecological History of the Pyrenees State, Market, and Landscape.* Ed. in Ismael Vaccaro and Oriol Beltran. Walnut Creek: Left Coast Press, 2010. 105–26.
European Comission. "The Future of Rural Society." *Commission communication transmitted to the Council and to the European Parliament on 29 July 1988.* COM(88) 501 final 1988. Bulletin of the European Communities Supplement 4/88.
Fabian, Johannes. *Time and the Other. How Anthropology Makes its Object.* New York: Columbia University Press, 2002.
Franquesa, Jaume. "On keeping and selling: The political economy of heritage making in contemporary Spain." *Current Anthropology* 54,3 (2003): 346–69.
Frigolé, Joan. "Producció cultural de lloc, memòria i terciarització de l'economia en una vall del Prepirineu." *Revista d'Etnologia de Catalunya* 30 (2007): 70–80.
—. "Patrimonialization and the mercantilization of the authentic. Two fundamental strategies in a tertiary economy." *Constructing Cultural And Natural Heritage. Parks, Museums and Rural Heritage.* Eds. Xavier Roigé and Joan Frigolé. Girona: ICRPC Llibres (4), 2010: 27–38.
García Canclini, Nestor. *Culturas híbridas. Estrategias para entrar y salir de la modernidad.* Mexico D. F.: Grijalbo, 1989.
Gascón, Carles. *Comarques oblidades. Josep Zulueta i el Pirineu l'any 1890.* La Seu d'Urgell: Edicions Salòria, 2010.
Grasseni, Cristina. "Packaging skills: calibrating Italian cheese to the global market." *Commodifying Everything: Consumption and Capitalist Enterprise.* Ed. Susan Strasser. New York: Taylor and Francis, 2003. 341–81.

—. *Developing Skill, Developing Vision: Practices of Locality at the Foot of the Alps.* Oxford: Berghahn Books, 2009.

Guillaume, Marc. "Invention et stratégies du patrimoine". *Patrimoines en folie.* Dir. Henri-Pierre Jeudy. Paris: Éditions de la Maison des sciences de l'homme, 1990. 13–20.

Hartog, François. *Régimes d'historicité: Présentisme et expérience du temps.* Paris: Éditions du Seuil, 2003.

Heinich, Nathalie. *La fabrique du patrimoine: De la cathédrale à la petite cuillère.* Paris: Éditions de la Maison des sciences de l'homme, 2009.

Herzfeld, Michael. "Engagement, gentrification, and the neoliberal hijacking of history." *Current Anthropology* 51.2 (2010): 259–268.

Ingold, Tim. *The perception of the environment: essays on livelihood, dwelling and skill.* London: Routledge, 2000.

Jameson, Fredric. *The cultural turn: Selected writings on the Postmodern 1983–1998.* London: Verso, 1988.

Jeudy, Henry (dir.). *Patrimoines en folie.* Paris: Éditions de la Maison des Sciences de L'Homme. 1990.

Jiménez, Sole and Llorenç Prats. "El turismo en Catalunya: evolución histórica y retos de futuro." Pasos. *Revista de Turismo y Patrimonio Cultural* 4,2 (2006): 153–74.

Kaneef, Deema. *Who owns the past? The Politics of Time in a 'Model' Bulgarian Village.* New York: Berghahn Books, 2004.

Kirshenblatt-Gimblett, Barbara. *Destination Culture. Tourism, Museums, and Heritage.* Berkeley: University of California Press, 1998.

Latour, Bruno *Nous n'avons jamais été modernes. Essai d'anthropologie symétrique.* Paris: La Découverte, 1993.

López i Gelat, Feliu, Jordi Tàbara, and Joan Bartolomé. "The rural in dispute: Discourses of rurality in the Pyrenees." *Geoforum* 40 (2008): 602–12.

Lowe, Philippe, Jonathan Murdoch, Terry Marsden, Richard Munton and Andrew Flynn. "Regulating the new rural spaces: the uneven development of land." *Journal of Rural Studies* 9 (1993): 205–22.

Lowenthal, David. *The Past is a Foreign Country.* Cambridge: Cambridge University Press, 1985.

MacCannell, Dean. *The Tourist: a New Theory of the Leisure Class.* Berkeley: University of California Press, 1999.

Mármol, Camila del. *Pasados locales, políticas globales. Procesos de patrimonialización en un valle del Pirineo catalán.* Valencia: Germanias, 2012.

—. "Through Other Times: The Politics of Heritage and the Past in the Catalan Pyrenees." *Tourism and the Power of Otherness: Seduction of Difference.* Eds. David Picard and Michael Di Giovine. Bristol: Channel View Publications, 2014. 31–51.

—., and Ismael Vaccaro. "Changing Ruralities: between Abandonment and Redefinition in the Catalan Pyrenees." *Anthropological Forum* (2015). DOI: 10.1080/00664677.2014.991377.

Marx, Karl. *Introducción General a la Crítica de la Economía Política.* 1857. México: Siglo XXI Editores, 1989.

Medina, Francesc. *Reflexions sobre les alimentacions contemporànies. De les biotecnologies als productes ecològics.* Barcelona: Editorial UOC, 2010.

Molina, David. "El proceso de desertización demográfica de la montaña pirenaica en el largo plazo: Cataluña. Ager." *Revista de Estudios sobre Despoblación y Desarrollo Rural* 2 (2002): 81–99.
Paxson, Heather. "Post-Pasteurian Cultures: the Microbiopolitics of Raw Milk Cheese in the US." *Cultural Anthropology* 23,1 (2008): 15–17.
Poulot, Dominique. *Une histoire de patrimoine en Occident, XVIIIe–XXIe*. Paris: Presses Universitaires de France, 2006.
Roigé, Xavier, and Ferran Estrada. "Socio-economic use of cultural heritage in a natural park: The Montseny mountains." *Constructing Cultural and Natural Heritage. Parks, Museums and Rural Heritage*. Eds. Xavier Roigé and Joan Frigolé. Girona: ICRPC Llibres, 2010. 77–90.
—., Ferran Estrada and Oriol Beltran. *La casa aranesa. Antropologia de l'arquitectura a la Val d'Aran*. Tremp: Garsineu edicions, 1997.
—., and Joan Frigolé (Eds.). *Constructing Cultural and Natural Heritage. Parks, Museums and Rural Heritage*. Girona: ICRPC Llibres, 2010.
Roma, Francesc. *Del Paradís a la Nació. La muntanya a Catalunya*. Valls: Cossetania, 2004.
Salazar, Noel. "Tourism imaginaries: a conceptual approach." *Annals of Tourism Research* 39,2 (2012): 863–82.
Sivaramakrishnan, Kalyanakrishna, and Ismael Vaccaro. "Postindustrial Natures: Hyper-mobility and Place Attachments." *Journal of Social Anthropology* 14,3 (2006): 301–17.
Smith, Laurajane. *Uses of Heritage*. London: Routledge, 2006.
—., Paul Shackel, and Gary Campbell. *Heritage, Labour and the Working Classes*. New York: Routledge, 2011.
Strathern, Marilyn. "No nature, no culture: the Hagen case." *Nature, Culture and Gender*. Eds. Carol MacCormack and Marilyn Strathern. Cambridge: Cambridge University Press, 1980. 174–223.
Tulla, Antoni. *Procés de transformació agrària en àrees de muntanya. Les explotacions de producció lletera com a motor de canvi a les comarques de la Cerdanya, el Capcir, l'Alt Urgell i el Principat d'Andorra*. Barcelona: Institut Cartogràfic de Catalunya, 1984.
Vaccaro, Ismael. "Post-industrial valleys: the Pyrenees as a reinvented landscape." *Journal of Social Anthropology* 14,3 (2006): 361–76.
—., and Oriol Beltran. *Social and Ecological History of the Pyrenees: State, Market, and Landscape*. Walnut Creek, CA: Left Coast Press, 2010.
Viveiros de Castro, Eduardo. "Cosmological deixis and Amerindian perspectivism." *Journal of the Royal Anthropological Institute* 4,3 (1998): 469–88.
Williams, Raymond. "Ideas of Nature." *Problems in materialism and culture*. London: Verso, 1980.
Yanagisako, Sylvia, and Carol Delaney. "Naturalizing Power." *Naturalizing Power: Essays in Feminist Cultural Analysis*. Eds. Sylvia Yanagisako and Carol Delaney. New York: Routledge, 1995. 1–24.

CHAPTER ELEVEN

Panarchy and the Cross-Cultural Dynamics of Place in Nineteenth-Century America

JOHN J. KUCICH

I have lived in New England for almost all of my life, but it wasn't until I was in my twenties that I began thinking about the groundnut, or hopniss, more formally known as *apios Americana*. It's a plant native to the region, a modest twining vine that flowers in mid-summer along stream banks and sandy woodland soil. Little noticed today, it was a staple of the Indian diet before contact – the plant has a series of tubers the size of a small potato. Henry David Thoreau had read about it and was fascinated by this relic of colonial and pre-contact times, but it took him years of botanizing before he began to see the plant in his native Concord (*Walden* 512–13). I'm no botanist, and I searched in vain for years. A couple of years ago, however, I was on a canoe trip in Maine that included several members of the Penobscot tribe. We camped one evening on an island in the Penobscot river, and the moment we stepped ashore, one of them, Jenny Neptune, pointed out the groundnuts growing everywhere in the sandy soil. There they were – walnut-sized bulbs half-exposed by recent floods (figure 1). We gathered a bowlful, peeled and sliced them, then fried them for dinner. They were nutty and crisp, firm-fleshed, with a faint savor of the sandy earth. I haven't tasted them since.

Fig. 1: Johann Wilhelm Weinmann, "Apis Americana, Ischas, Erdbirne." *Phytanthoza-Iconographia. Silve Conspectus Aliquot Millium, tam Indigenarum quam Exoticarum, ex quatuor mundi paribus ...* Regensburg: Lentz, Seutter, Ridinger, Haid, 1737. 4 Vols. Vol. 1. Plate 149.
Source: Rostock University Library. Photo: Gesa Mackenthun.

I offer this story not as an invitation to foraging wild food but as an example of a certain kind of contact that's worth more attention in studying literature and culture. Most of my work has involved the fields of multiculturalism and ecocriticism, and both fields tend to be structured by binaries – the interplay between a dominant and subordinate culture in the former, and the relationship between the human and natural world in the latter. My relationship with the groundnut, I suggest, offers a richer model, one structured around at least three coordinates: European American culture, Algonquian culture, and the environment both of these cultures share. The interplay among these elements, I argue, offers a far more nuanced, complex and dynamic picture of our world than critical approaches that focus only on one or two of them – a picture that captures the complexity of place as it is shaped by competing stories of the people who claim it, a picture that traces how the features of a given environment work to shape the multiform human world that enters into its web, a picture that traces how the human power dynamics that shape cultural interaction, of exchange, conquest, settler colonialism and survivance, are inflected by an ecological dynamic infused with its own agency. The groundnut, in its humble way, offers both history and presence. It is, after all, not a fixed cultural artifact but a living part of a dynamic ecosystem, a plant struggling for sun and nutrients, deeply woven into the woodland ecology. But we see it because of our cultural memory. Thoreau barely remembered digging the roots in his childhood, and he came to know the plant best in the accounts of early European settlers that he read systematically. Jenny Neptune drew on her own Penobscot cultural memory when she stepped onto that island – a memory that had overlapped with Europeans who learned from their Native hosts how to read the local landscape and how it might feed them. But these stories, though they crossed paths over centuries of contact, remained distinct. Neptune and I saw the same plant, but differently, situated as we were at a nexus of relationships that fixed our tangled histories to a living root exposed by spring floods to an early summer sun.

Panarchy, which joins the organic chaos of anarchy with an all-encompassing inclusivity and the fertile energy of the Greek god Pan, is a good term for describing the complexity of this dynamic, with its nested ecologies, its strange feedback loops and its surprising resilience (figure 2).

Another good term comes from Thoreau himself – the *wild*, the endless capacity of the more-than-human world to humble one particular species

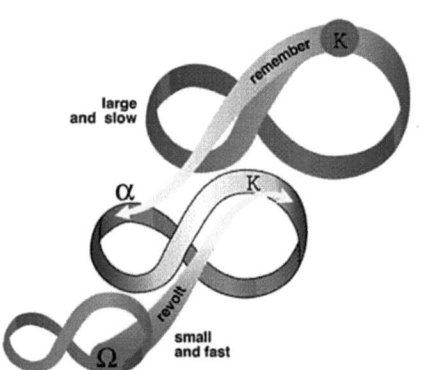

Fig. 2: Panarchy.
Source: Resilience Alliance.
https://www.resalliance.org/panarchy

of large mammal and to renew itself in ways that we humans can never fully control nor predict. I'm writing at a time, of course, when our particular strain of human culture threatens the very ecological web upon which we depend. Our culture needs to change, and fast, and looking carefully at moments in the past when writers found themselves transformed by moments of ecocultural contact, when they tapped into these panarchic patterns and energies, may help us do so.

Points of ecocultural contact have not received much attention by recent scholarship more focused on tracing the contours of settler colonialism or mapping the many strategies by which native peoples worked to preserve their sovereignty. The physical and cultural violence in these colonial settings was staggering, and it's crucial both to trace the workings of an ideology that is still very much with us and to recognize the myriad forms of resistance used to blunt its force. Yet, as Mary Louise Pratt argued in her definition of the contact zone, focusing solely on these separate stories misses how these distinct cultures were transformed by their encounters. And I suggest that while these encounters were shaped in part by global forces with metropolitan origins, they were also profoundly local in nature. Much recent scholarship of native sovereignty has emphasized how deeply interwoven native political and cultural life were with a specific land base; settler colonialism, too, unfurled along the contours of the land Europeans seized. There are, thus, many moments when European and Native American writers have engaged in a tangled process of cultural exchange shaped by their common reliance and dependency on the environment. Such exchanges may be purposeful or oblique, friendly or hostile, marked by sudden understanding or shot through with mistrust, mixed messages or missed connections. On one level, these are cultural encounters in which people bring their distinct histories, stories and practices together, and a careful reader can watch how these archives overlap, intertwine and, like two coils of cultural DNA, make something new. Yet these moments are not strictly cultural. All, I argue, are shaped profoundly by the more-than-human world, by human and non-human actants, to use Bruno Latour's term, who have their own agendas, histories and stories to tell, and these moments of contact help us see the vast web of relations that tie this mesh together and trace the direction of its becoming.

I will focus on two of these transcultural stories in this essay. Margaret Fuller, traveling in the Great Lakes region in 1843 on the trail of the Anglo-Ojibway poet Jane Johnston Schoolcraft, sees an oak tree as a model for a new kind of environmental and cultural synthesis. And Henry David Thoreau, journeying through the Maine Woods with his Indian guides, Joe Attean and Joe Polis, catches glimpses of the Penobscot world that helps him formulate a vision for a reenchanted universe. All these actants came away from these encounters transformed, in large part because the usual circuits of colonial encounter were run through the enormously complicated mesh of the material world.

Place, Materiality, and Ecocultural Contact

This project draws on a variety of critical perspectives. One strand centers on the dynamics of place, from Martin Heidegger's notion of dwelling to Henri Lefebvre's and Yi-Fu Tuan's Marxist and postmodernist geographies of space. Lefebvre reminds us that the human construction of space – the cultural meanings and material conditions that texture and shape our ideologies – are economic in nature, and hence our dwelling reproduces, wittingly or not, structures of power that are too often defined by exploitation and class struggle. The rustic farmhouse and bridge Heidegger dwells on in his essay "Building Dwelling Thinking" are not, after all, entirely innocent. Yet more recent postmodern geographers like Tuan and Edward Soja show that the ideological forces that shape our experience of place are never singular nor uncontested: cities like Los Angeles, for example, have a life of their own that reflects the dynamic diversity of the many human and environmental forces that interact with anarchic energy, creating what Soja calls a "third space" between the dominant ideology of place and the material conditions of existence where a kind of spatial justice can grow.

Postmodern geographers have focused mostly on diverse and dynamic urban environments, and in working to free human societies from a narrow economic determinism, they have mapped primarily the dynamics among human groups that share a contested space. Another strand of place-based theory (and poetics) grew out of the environmental movement in the 1980s and took as its starting point distinct landforms – a watershed or distinct geological regions – and then imagined how human societies might be more responsibly integrated within them. Different bioregionalist writers – most famously Gary Snyder – have mixed the elements of ecology, conservation, mysticism, anarchy and local activism in different proportions, but all have sought to develop a vision and a very practical roadmap to living sustainably in a given place, grounded in a sense of responsibility that runs from the myriad activities of everyday life to a global politics informed by local knowledge.[1] While Ursula Heise and Wai-Chee Dimock have lead the call for planetary consciousness in cultural studies, the tension between these approaches is one of emphasis rather than kind – almost all writers who focus on a given bioregion acknowledge that the boundaries of any ecosystem are fluid, and that any given example of living responsibly in a local environment is, in part, a global, even a cosmopolitan gesture. As Snyder himself argues, applying the lesson of one of his Buddhist teachers, "You sit, and you sweep your garden. It doesn't matter how big your garden is" ("The 'East West' Interview" 111).

---

1   Bioregionalism has roots in the place-based land ethic articulated by Aldo Leopold. Gary Snyder was a prominent spokesman and theorist for the movement as it took shape in California in the 1980s; see his essays collected in *The Practice of the Wild* (1990). A good recent collection of ecocritical essays is *The Bioregionalist Imagination* (2012), edited by Tom Lynch, Cheryll Glotfelty and Karla Armbruster.

This process of tending one's garden – this mutuality of human groups and their environment – has been the focus of scholars working under the headings of the new materialism, object-oriented ontology and material ecocriticism. With roots in the monism of Baruch Spinoza and the vitalism of Henri Bergson, theorists such as Bruno Latour, Jane Bennett and Timothy Morton have steadily eroded the human-nature divide and set about rethinking ontology, hermeneutics and ethics in a manner that replaces the human subject with the shifting field of relationships that structure a material world that is animate, ever-evolving and full of surprises. For Latour, individual subjects and facts are better understood as "actants," temporary intersections in the vast web of matter and energy that make up our universe, whether stone, plant or human; each shimmers into being with its own story, its own interest, and its own force on the beings around it. Such a view, for Bennett, allows for the reenchantment of the world, a possibility to reset the human-nature dichotomy and rethink notions of identity and sympathy. Her work tends to circle around examples of the quotidian – a plastic bag in a gutter, a tree alongside a railroad – that, from her perspective, blossom into life. Morton in particular focuses on how this approach might transform the conditions that have led to our current ecological crisis, seeking to recover a deeper, animistic, "archelithic" relationship that structured the relationship between humans and the more-than-human world before the advent of what he terms "agrilogistics" some 5,000 years ago. Farming and its ideational counterparts, from Genesis and the expulsion from the garden to Plato's idealism to Enlightenment rationalism, set humans apart from their environment, but, Morton argues, the archelithic was never fully suppressed. Others, particularly Serenalla Iovino and Serpil Opperman, have attacked one keystone of that wall of separation, arguing that the more-than-human world is structured by semiotics and storytelling no less than the human one. All matter, they argue, is storied matter.

Yet in this effort to develop a material ecocriticism that breaks down the human/nature binary, there is a pronounced tendency to see the human side of the equation in monolithic terms. Human cultures are, of course, always shifting and evolving in response to changing environmental conditions, intercultural conflict and, more typically, both. Older accounts of the contact zone by, for example, Mary Louise Pratt, and the more recent focus on settler colonialism by Patrick Wolfe and Mark Rifkin, among many others, have emphasized how this dynamic has been structured by a very specific geopolitical condition: the wave of European colonization that began in the early modern era, with a remarkably long half-life. This focus on the transformations of settler societies offers a useful balance between the broad forces that shaped the encounters between European and indigenous peoples in colonies across the globe, along with the particulars of cultural form as they clashed in very specific environments. In exploring these charged moments of interaction, I also draw heavily on the work of Keith Basso on the Western Apache and Lisa Brooks on the southern Algonquian in examining the complexity of Native American 'place-worlds'. Their recent studies have traced how fully imbricated Native cultures are with the specific geographies of their homeland – connections that undergird the intense relationality (marked out in story, ontology and ethics) of tribal groups and their more-than-human kin. Basso and Brooks both stress that the environment is not merely a backdrop for tribal tradition, a passive setting for rich but essentially distinct archives of history, but a fully active author of those traditions. The whole ecosytem – its geology, hydrology, flora and fauna – speaks, and the rich traditions of indigenous peoples are best understood not as records of human activity but rather as ongoing conversations among members of the more-than-human community. A key insight for both critics is that this process has been both dynamic and multivalent. Native communities, European-American society and the ecosystems that framed their struggle all had a role and a voice in shaping this emerging world we continue to share.

Panarchy is a term that helps capture the tentative and contingent nature of this process. It was formulated by the ecologist Buzz Hollings in 2002 to capture the complexity of ecosystems and their resilience in the face of change – even the human-induced catastrophes that shape our world. It replaces the notion of a single ecosystem with a model of nested ecologies that overlap and extend outward in ways that defy categorization. These interconnected systems, further, have a kind of memory, a flow of material and energy that responds to and reinforces past events in a manner that ensures stability. And finally, these systems have the capacity to revolt. When one feedback mechanism breaks down for any variety of reasons, new patterns emerge in unpredictable ways with unpredictable consequences – strange loops that cross boundaries and remake systems. Hollings' work on resilience has transformed ecology. But the term "panarchy" has deeper roots as well. It was used in 1860 by the Belgian botanist, writer and political theorist Paul Emil de Puydt to describe a form of government that included all forms of government – individuals would choose the system they preferred, with different citizens following different regimes. His work has attracted recent attention from political theorists interested in anarchism and the open and flexible democratic possibilities of the internet.[2]

My interest is more descriptive than predictive. Panarchy is a particularly useful term to capture the immense variety of regimes individuals use to engage with the world around them. One lesson from reading literature from a variety of times and perspectives is that while state (and non-state) power is real, it is never complete. Different peoples and communities map out their own networks of obedi-

---

2   I'm indebted to Laura Dassow Walls for introducing me to this field; see her review essay "Beyond Representation: Deliberate Reading in a Panarchic World." Much of the recent work on panarchy as systems theory comes from the Resilience Alliance, an academic society that builds on the pioneering work of ecologist C. S. Holling. Panarchy has a more tangled history in political theory, with the nineteenth-century botanist and theorist Paul-Emile de Puyd inspiring followers among internet activists, anarchists and a former Dartmouth College fraternity. The website Panarchy.org gathers a comprehensive list of panarchist writing.

ence and resistance, with innumerable ideologies that capture these shades of difference. Extend this map to vast networks of the more-than-human world, and the overlapping systems of power, of agency, resistance, and resilience grow dizzying. We live, I argue, in a panarchic world, and we need to learn to see it.

Talking Trees: Jane Johnston Schoolcraft and Margaret Fuller

No one was more alive to the beauty of the Great Lakes region than the Ojibwe-Anglo-Irish writer Jane Johnston Schoolcraft, or Bamewawagezhikaquay. The daughter of an influential Ojibwe mother and an Anglo-Irish father who settled in Sault Ste. Marie, just below Lake Superior, in 1792 to trade fur, Schoolcraft was raised in traditional Ojibwe culture and given a highly literate English education, both in her father's extensive library and, for a short time, in an Irish boarding school. Deeply versed and firmly positioned in both cultures, Schoolcraft chose to remain in her Ojibwe homeland, where she married the U.S. Indian Agent and pioneering ethnographer Henry Rowe Schoolcraft, who gained international fame by retelling traditional Ojibwe stories he heard from Jane, her mother, Ozhaguscodaywayquay (Susan Johnston) and her extended family.[3] It was on her return home from her unhappy sojourn in Ireland that she had the experience described in one of her most important poems, "To a Pine Tree." The poem captures a moment of aesthetic power described above, a shudder of recognition shot through with difference; it is, I suggest, a good example of ecocultural contact, an interweaving of cultural attitudes and power differentials that have, as their focal point, a key feature of a specific environment.

The poem records the young narrator's delight at seeing a landscape she recognizes as home; Henry Schoolcraft notes that Jane wrote it at his prompting at some point in their courtship or marriage. Here is the first stanza, in Ojibwe and English; the rest of the poem follows in English:

> Shing wauk! Shing wauk! Nin ge ik id,
> Waish kee wau bum ug, singh wauk
> Tuh quish in aun nau aub, ain dak nuk I yaun
> Shing wauk, shing wauk No sa
> Si e gwuh ke do dis au naun
> Kau gega way zhau wus co zid

---

3 Scholarship on Jane Johnston Schoolcraft owes a huge debt to Robert Dale Parker's excellent edition of her work, which includes a thorough introduction. Among the recent essays on her work, Bethany Schneider's "Not for Citation: Jane Johnston Schoolcraft's Synchronic Studies" has been particularly influential in my own reading of Schoolcraft's work.

Translation

The pine! the pine! I eager cried,
The pine, my father! See it stand,
As first that cherished tree I spied
Returning to my native land.
The pine! the pine! oh lovely scene!
The pine that is forever green.

Ah beauteous tree! ah happy sight!
That greets me on my native strand
And hails me, with a friend's delight,
To my own dear bright mother land
Oh 'tis to me a heart-sweet scene,
The pine – the pine! that's ever green.

Not all the trees of England bright,
Not Erin's lawns of green and light
Are half so sweet to memory's eye,
As this dear type of northern sky
Oh 'tis to me a heart-sweet scene,
The pine – the pine! that ever green. (89–90)

It's unclear whether the translation is Jane's or Henry's – a frequent question in Schoolcraft's work, since much of her writing was unpublished and survives in Henry's manuscripts.[4] We don't have an independent translation of the poem, though the two versions track closely – both have eighteen lines, and the Ojibwe version, unusual for traditional songs, uses a loose rhyme scheme. The English version is tightly metered and rhymed; it is not a literal transliteration of the Ojibwe as much as a poetic translation, an effort to capture the meaning and impact of the poem by drawing on the culturally distinct norms of English literature. Thus the look of the text – the Ojibwe and English versions side-by-side, highlighting both the transferability of the poem across this linguistic divide and offering a clear sense of what gets lost in that transfer – underscores the complexity of contact that the poem both describes and embodies.

The story of this particular pine was clearly part of the Johnston family lore, retold to help reaffirm Jane's – and the broader family's – ties to the Ojibwe homeland. The poet calls her father to see the tree "that greets me on my native strand / And hails me with a friend's delight, / To my own dear bright mother land" (lines 8–10). Schoolcraft explicitly defines her motherland against her father's landscape of England and Ireland; while his inheritance is evident in

---

4 Robert Dale Parker discusses the context of the poem and issue of translation in his introduction to Schoolcraft's work (50–52) and in his notes to the poem (90).

the language and form of the poem, she clearly defines herself in the matrilineal terms of traditional Ojibwe culture. Most strikingly, this matrilineal heritage flows through the environment of her native land. The pine greets her, hails her – summons her with a mark of Althusserian recognition to which the poet eagerly responds, fitting herself into a culture and environment that blend seamlessly once she crosses its threshold. Once across this strand, she recognizes herself as native, a status granted by a totemic tree. In English, this personified tree has a playful register, a figurative gesture common in the eighteenth-century nature poetry Schoolcraft might have read in her father's library. In Ojibwe, a language that marks almost all the elements of the natural world with animate personhood and a culture shaped by stories of transformation and a spirit-saturated environment, the personified pine tree is anything but a figure of speech. This small poem is a testament to the power inherent in the Ojibwe environment and the difficulties inherent in translating it into English. Thus what reads in English as mere literary device, a fairy-tale world where the very objects of home welcome the speaker into their circle, signifies quite differently in an Ojibwe world, where a rich tradition of story and ceremony establishes the reciprocal relationship between humans, trees, and all the members of the more-than-human world – a relationship reestablished by songs like this one. Schoolcraft's poem is a ceremony that binds her and the pine tree together into an Ojibwe place-world.[5] Yet the doubled nature of the poem – its juxtaposition of the English and Ojibwe worlds – produces a dark undercurrent. Motherland is pitted against the world of her father, and the final stanza records her distance from her father, as the "dear type of northern sky" (line 16) speaks to her but, conspicuously, not to him. Though England and Ireland have their own trees, their own green landscapes, they do not speak to her, and thus this moment marks her inability to cross this cultural and environmental, this colonial, border.

When read with its initial audience in mind, a promising young U.S. Indian agent, the poem takes on political overtones. "To a Pine Tree" in this context highlights the poet's ties to an American landscape defined against that of England, though its version of American, sketched in lines of Ojibwe and located on a border that straddles the line between the U.S. and Canada, offers a version of cultural and political identity quite different from that flowing from Washington. The pine tree becomes available as a symbol of American identity alongside many others drawn from the natural environment in the early national era, a message underscored when, as Robert Dale Parker notes, references to Upper Canada were crossed out on the manuscript. The presence of the Ojibwe text, however, works against this effort to subsume the poem into a nascent U.S. cultural identity, preserving an unassimilable Ojibwe difference rooted in a more fluid, borderless environment. What Jane intended by giving the poem to her suitor/hus-

---

5   The literature on Ojibwe culture is extensive. For a good introduction to the interrelations of language and story, see Anton Treuer, *Living our Language: Ojibwe Tales and Oral Histories* (2001).

band we can only guess – the gesture may have been an effort to help him master the Ojibwe language, or a means of welcoming him into her family circle, or an attempt to explain one of her life-defining choices, or to explain in delicate terms that her deeply held ties to her homeland might conflict with Henry's own identity and political ambition. That Henry preserved this poem, and later sent it to the Anglo-Irish writer Anna Jameson, who visited and befriended the family on her tour of Canada before returning to her career in England, underscores the complexity and reach of this modest lyric about a common tree.

I don't have space to trace this world here, and Schoolcraft's point is, in part, that I never fully could – the web of this community, of people, trees and the stories that connect them, makes them recognizable to each other, allows them to speak, and is as localized as it is thick. The translation of the poem underscores the nonequivalence of the two versions. The Ojibwe pine – *shing wauk* – is not the English pine, though their proximity allows us to look across this border. For a poem written for her prospective husband, it stands as a telling gesture – an effort at once to reach across a cultural border and affirm its inviolability. Her husband – her readers – can enter into this place-world to the extent that they can read across this border, recognize the pine tree as part of the more-than-human world, and have that recognition returned. The pine tree stands as the sacrament of this cross-cultural marriage. And while Henry Schoolcraft cherished the poem, keeping it preserved among his papers long after Jane's death, it seems clear that the pine never spoke to him as it did to her.

Other European American writers, however, listened. The Transcendentalist writer Margaret Fuller traveled to the Great Lakes region in 1843, a few years after Jane Schoolcraft's death; she had read Henry Schoolcraft's *Algic Researches* (1839) and knew of Jane's poetry and prose from Anna Jameson's memoir, which included a long account of the Schoolcraft and Johnston families. Fuller appreciated Schoolcraft's importance as a writer uniquely situated to transform an American sense of place. "By the premature death of Mrs. Schoolcraft," she wrote, "was lost a mine of poesy, to which few had access. […] We might have known in clear outline, as now we shall not, the growths of religion and philosophy, under the influence of climate and scenery, from such suggestions as nature and the teachings of the inward mind presented" (124). Fuller's language plays here on the economics of resource extraction that would soon transform the small but important trading village of Sault Ste. Marie into a major port for shipping the copper and other mineral wealth of Lake Superior to eastern cities; she herself marveled at the economic explosion of Chicago and Milwaukee that were in 1843 just beginning to spill beyond the borders of their early forts and settlements. Ojibwe stories about the land were, from one perspective, an equally valuable raw material for the new American nation – one that Henry Rowe Schoolcraft was eager to exploit.

Fuller had a different goal in mind here. She sees in Schoolcraft the possibility of framing an organic, authentic understanding of a culture deeply rooted in a specific environment. The book that Fuller wrote about her travels, *Summer on the Lakes in 1843*, highlights Fuller's own sense of homelessness, and her travels are, in one sense, an effort to place herself in the Great Lakes environment. In doing so, she certainly takes part in the discursive dynamic of settler colonialism. She celebrates the efforts of settler families to build new lives, notes the haunting presence of an Indian past and bemoans the fate of a few scattered Pottawatomie families who remain on land that has inevitably passed to white settlers. She notes, too, how the Manitou Islands, where her steamship stops to take on fuel, have been denuded of pine trees. "The old landmarks are broken down, and the land, for a season, bears none, except the rudeness of conquest" (18). Indeed, this comment offers a clue about why Jane Schoolcraft's poem was set near Niagara Falls – by the early 1800s, the white pine had been eradicated from the lower reaches of the St. Lawrence. Fuller recognizes that pine trees are not merely fuel, and that their demise marks a profound shift in an ecocultural world.

Yet towards the end of her travels, Fuller offers another tree as a model for how to adapt to this environment. After long, digressive stories about women who are remarkably disconnected from their material surroundings – Marianne and Frederika von Haufe – she returns to the land before her:

> Do not blame me that I have written so much about Germany and Hades, while you were looking for news of the West. Here, on the pier, I see disembarking the Germans, the Norwegians, the Swedes, the Swiss. Who knows how much of the old legendary lore, of modern wonder, they have already planted amid the Wisconsin forests? Soon their tales of the origins of things, and the Providence which rules them, will be so mingled with those of the Indian, that the very oak trees will not know them apart – will not know whether itself be a Runic, or Druid, or Winnebago oak. (102)

This mingling of cosmopolitan stories allows Fuller to imagine a West no longer defined by cultural succession but instead by a certain kind of coexistence located in the environment itself. The oak tree, rather than city or settlement, holds together different cultures with overlapping ties to the land. Fuller's language uses the rhetoric of settler colonialism, of Europeans planting their own stories on land wrested away from native peoples, their transplanted lore an ideological affirmation of political violence. Yet Fuller subtly undercuts this rhetoric as well. These Germanic stories, for one, grow not on a clear-cut environment but amid the native forests, suggesting an argument for valuing the forest based not on resource extraction or agriculture but instead on a cultural value that reaches across the Atlantic. The woods of Wisconsin help a new people take root in the land. Crucially, though, their stories don't supplant an earlier culture but mingle with them in a hybrid crop of cosmopolitan nativism. Fuller sketches how a place-world transforms, as immigrants allow their own stories to settle into the contours of a new ecosystem and listen as the land offers up stories of its own.

The oak is significant here – a storied tree in both northern European and Algonquian cultures, it is a shared emblem, a signifier open enough to weave together distinct cultural strands into a cohesive fabric. For Schoolcraft, the white pine is a mark of environmental, and hence cultural, distinctiveness between her Anglo-Irish and Ojibwe identities; in Schoolcraft's poem, too, the pine has agency, hailing poem's speaker and doing the work of weaving her into the land. For Fuller, the oak is the vehicle of story, an overwritten page. Yet this mingled text is not unreadable – the oak is still an oak, and if no single story will now define it – whether Runic, Druid or Winnebago – Fuller leaves a final term for the reader to fill in: *American*. If the pine tree, for Schoolcraft, anchors an unassimilable Ojibwe world, the oak tree, for Fuller, is the mark of American's multi-cultural promise. The oak is, moreover, not merely a passive signifier. The nexus of competing cultures and mingling stories jolts the tree into a kind of self-awareness. This is a different dynamic from the one that allowed Schoolcraft to recognize the hail of the Ojibwe pine. If for Schoolcraft, the pine spoke of the richly textured place-world of her Ojibwe motherland, a voice her Anglo-Irish father cannot hear, for Fuller, it is the multiplied layers of cultural resonance that animate the oak, providing a thickness of reference that leads to a crucial moment of not-knowing. The tree itself, and the people whose lives and stories are bound together in this landscape, becomes aware of its new self only when confronted by the strangeness of conflicting stories in a contested environment.

Thus the oak represents a story-saturated landscape that contains the record of human diversity and the key to its fundamental unity. The passage is open to a series of familiar critiques. It subsumes cultural identity into vague diversity that diminishes the meaning and power of separate traditions and communities. It focuses on the dynamics of identity rather than political conflict and physical oppression, with no attention to the often brutal forces that brought these settlers to a Midwest emptied of its native people. It deflects attention away from native communities and their ongoing struggle for sovereignty – indeed, Fuller seems more concerned with Winnebago stories than with the people who tell them. Yet the tree marks a shift in Fuller's approach to the landscape away from a narrative of Indian vanishing and towards one of cosmopolitan presence. This storied and baffled oak tree also sets up Fuller's far richer and more reciprocal encounters with Native people and space later in the book. What is most striking about the passage is the status of the oak. In the strange mixture of stories that cohere around this tree, it shimmers into life, a landmark that is not erased by the succession of cultures but enchanted by the strange loops of story. The tree gains its power because, in this mingling of traditions, it cannot be finally known, but instead leads its readers deeper into the mesh that weaves together a landscape in the process of becoming. The oak tree becomes, in a word, panarchic.

Spirits of the Woods: Henry Thoreau and Joseph Nicolar

Strange trees appear elsewhere in the literature of the nineteenth century. In "Chesuncook," the middle essay in Henry Thoreau's *The Maine Woods* (1864), a pine tree shimmers into a life beyond the reach of the lumberman's saw: "It is not their bones or hide or tallow that I love. It is the living spirit of the tree, not its spirit of turpentine, and with which I sympathize, and which heals my cuts. It is as immortal as I am, and perchance will go to as high a heaven, there to tower over me still" (685). In reaching for a way to place a value on the pine tree that stands against commodity or aesthetics, Thoreau here stretches beyond Judeo-Christian ontology to a version of pantheism that would have been quite familiar to Schoolcraft. It was too strange for the editor of *The Atlantic Monthly*, James Russell Lowell, who deleted the passage when he published the article, over Thoreau's strong objections. It was not the first time he ran into trouble for blurring the lines between the human and natural world. In a letter to Horace Greeley in 1853, who had similar objections, Thoreau wrote "I was born to be a pantheist – if that be the name of me, and I do the deeds of one" (*Correspondence* 294). His caginess is striking here. He claims to come by this ontology on his own, through his own interactions with the natural world, living a creed that comes not from the world of ideas but from deeds, from the myriad physical interactions that define his life in nature. His pantheism, he suggests, springs from the mesh itself.

Or does it? Thoreau, even more than most of his mid-nineteenth century cadre of writers, long immersed himself in classical Greek culture; he also immersed himself in the newly available Hindu scriptures, imaginatively bathing himself in the sacred waters of the Ganges after returning from his morning ablutions in Walden Pond. A more controversial source of Thoreau's pantheism is the Native American culture he studied throughout his life. The letter to Greeley was written six months before Thoreau visited Chesuncook, but it comes several years after Thoreau began gathering his Indian Notebooks. Scholars are divided on what to make of this extensive interest, with some, like Richard Fleck, arguing that Thoreau's engagement with Native cultures was sensitive and highly sympathetic, while others, notably Joshua Bellin, respond that Thoreau's attitude was more typically in line with an ideology that saw Indians as child-like primitives at best and degraded savages at worst, and in either case fated to soon vanish in the natural succession of races. All of these attitudes are in full display in the Maine Woods essays, where Thoreau toggles back and forth between a landscape of relentless settlement and untamable wildness, between a chronology of succession characterized by Indian vanishing and an eternal present in which Native people and their cultural forms survive intact, and between treating the Penobscot guides who lead him through this landscape with patronizing contempt and deeply felt respect.

It is crucial to note how deeply invested Thoreau's guides were in this process. Both of the Penobscot Thoreau traveled with – Joseph Attean (which Thoreau spells "Aitteon") and Joe Polis – were important tribal leaders, deeply versed in tribal traditions and fully involved in helping the tribe adapt to the colonial pressures that shaped Penobscot life in the nineteenth century; they are best understood, as I've argued elsewhere (Kucich, *Lost in the Maine Woods*), as cultural diplomats rather than as wilderness guides, not props for Thoreau's encounter with the wild but savvy negotiators carefully assessing how this writer might serve the cause of Penobscot sovereignty. Their efforts to help Thoreau see the Maine Woods in a new way was part of their strategy.

What were Attean and Polis thinking? We have only Thoreau's account to go on for their reactions to these journeys. We know that Attean and especially Polis were respected political leaders as well as keepers of tribal tradition. We also know that these traditions were kept intensely private in the nineteenth century, a way of preserving tribal cultural sovereignty in an era of intense colonization. The best sense we have of this Penobscot world comes from Joseph Nicolar, a tribal leader from the end of the nineteenth century who was a young man when Thoreau visited Maine. Towards the end of his life, he gathered the traditional stories he had heard from his youth and wrote them down in English in a remarkable book, *The Life and Traditions of the Red Man*, in 1893, for an audience of both a rapidly modernizing Penobscot nation and whites who had plenty to learn from their Indian neighbors. The book focuses on the creation of the Penobscot culture hero Klose-kur-beh and his early deeds as he sets the pattern for the Penobscot world, defeating monsters, inventing the skills that would allow the people to live, and establishing the rituals of respect and reciprocity that would guarantee the relationship between humans and their more-than-human relatives. Klose-kur-beh's central message: "there was a living spirit in all things, and the spirit of all things has power over all […] the Great Spirit was in the sun – moon – stars – clouds of heaven – mountains, and even in the trees of the earth" (102). This doctrine of immanence was reiterated in every Klose-kur-beh story Nicolar retold. One offers a particularly interesting context for Thoreau's "Chesuncook" pine noted above:

> When night came this same lonely feeling was upon him, he prepared a place for his night's rest. After the darkness had come and before laying down to sleep, to cheer himself, Klose-kur-beh did sing. When this was done, the seven trees that stood nearest bent their tops and listened to the singing of Klose-kur-beh, and when the singing was over, the largest of the seven straightened its body up and said, "How grateful the heart of man ought to be when he can bring cheer to himself by singing when lonely. When my kind and I sing, we sing in distress; when the fury of the winds shake our limbs we sing in wailing, – our roots are many and strong and cannot move to avoid the fury of the heavens. Because you can move at your pleasure do not linger here, but on the morrow when the sun rises take your canoe, and with your companion go forth toward the sun and keep the same course seven days and seven nights. […]

When you find land it will be like this land and the trees the same as we. Your work will then be complete because you will have found that there is spirit in all things, and where there is spirit there is power, and as there is knowledge in us, we, the seven trees, will show you the power that is in us and will smooth the way for the whole time of your journey." (123–24)

The key insight of this story – that there is spirit in all things, and that power comes from understanding and respecting this – occurs again and again in Nicolar's book; it is the lynchpin of the Penobscot connection to their environment, the key to their cultural sovereignty. This sensibility is entirely at odds with the extractive economy most evident in the saw mills around Old Town – an economy that employed many members of the Penobscot tribe, including both Attean and Polis. Nicolar's story, then, is an important cultural counterweight to an emergent capitalism, one that had far deeper roots in Penobscot traditions than Thoreau's plea for the "living spirit" of the pine. Klose-kur-beh's message was crucial both for the whites who came in increasing numbers to the Maine Woods and for the Penobscot themselves.

How much of this message Thoreau heard from his Penobscot guides is difficult to say. His last journey, with Joe Polis, was his most sustained encounter with the Penobscot world and his best chance to learn something of the tribe's sacred traditions. Traveling across Moosehead Lake, Polis retells a central Penobscot story about Klose-kur-beh's originary hunt. Thoreau proves a poor listener – he dismisses the story as rather long-winded, told by Polis with "dumb wonder, which he hopes will be contagious" (725). It clearly isn't, and it's the last traditional Penobscot story Polis will tell. Yet Polis continues to initiate Thoreau into the Penobscot world in other ways, sharing lore about plants and animals, geography and place names, until Thoreau begins to get a sense of the vast scope of what he termed, in "Natural History of Massachusetts," "a more perfect Indian wisdom" (41). Indeed, the very evening after he dismisses the story about Klose-kur-beh's hunt, he is struck with wonder at finding phosphorescent wood – something he had read about but never seen. The Penobscot were long familiar with the phenomenon, and with Thoreau in a more receptive mood, Polis is happy to convey the Penobscot word – *Aroosoqu'* – and a brief story. Thoreau experiences what Adorno calls a shudder. "Nature must have made a thousand revelations to them which are still secrets to us," Thoreau writes, and it jolts him out of a scientific register, out of hermeneutic certainty into a mythic world of unknowing rooted in the strangeness of the environment. In Timothy Morton's rendering of Adorno, the shudder is an aesthetic expression of being touched by the otherness of the world – of being ecological (142). Thoreau surrenders to it: "I let science slide, and rejoiced in the light as if it had been a fellow-creature. […] I believed that the woods were not tenantless, but choke-full of honest spirits as good as myself any day" (731–32). This encounter with the Penobscot world –

and more particularly with its more-than-human elements – leaves Thoreau, in a word, enchanted.

This enchantment lingers throughout the rest of the journey and, I suggest, through the rest of Thoreau's life. In the mid-1850s, Thoreau turned increasingly to the systematic study of the ecosystem around Concord, devoting careful, scientific scrutiny to phenology (the study of plant and animal life cycles) and forest succession. Yet this shift in focus was not a turn away from the transcendentalism of his early writings as much as an effort to better understand its wellsprings. In his final months, as he gradually succumbed to tuberculosis, Thoreau worked to pull together several of his lectures into finished essays; one of the last became "Walking," which culminates in a curious epiphany at Spaulding's Farm, on the edge of Concord. Walking through a pine wood at sunset, he half-glimpses, half-imagines a family of ethereal beings who live on the edges of the material world, amidst the golden afternoon rays that illuminate a pine grove behind an ordinary farm.

> I was impressed as if some ancient and altogether admirable and shining family had seated there in that part of Concord, unknown to me; to whom the sun was servant; who had not gone into society in the village; who had not been called on. […] The pines furnished them with gables as they grew. Their house was not obvious to vision; the trees grew through it. I do not know whether I heard the sounds of a suppressed hilarity or not. They seemed to recline on sunbeams. They have sons and daughters. They are quite well. […] Nothing can equal the serenity of their lives. (252)

The passage radiates a warmth and wisdom that make it a keystone in his understanding of Nature and his own place within it. The wisdom these mysterious beings they offer is hard won, and elusive:

> But I find it difficult to remember them. They fade irrevocably out of my mind even now while I speak and endeavor to recall them, and recollect myself. It is only after a long and serious effort to recollect my best thoughts that I become again aware of their cohabitancy. (253)

This passage has long puzzled commentators, in part, I argue, because of its ambiguous provenance. These beings have a tangled ancestry. One branch leads back through German Idealism to the monism of Baruch Spinoza, Lucretius and pre-Socratic Greeks. Another springs from the ancient British folklore of spirits, little people, and faeries – a world very much intact in nineteenth-century Concord, an example of what Morton calls the archelithic, the pre-agricultural cultural forms that survive in the shadows beyond the sharp corners of modernity. Another, I suggest, traces its roots to the Indian world that had long fascinated Thoreau, to the "honest spirits" Polis helped him name. And still another is the pine wood itself – a vitality and presence Thoreau has taught himself to see by his long practice of close observation, until the woods themselves shimmer into life.

The key insight of Spaulding Farm and its curiously unnamed inhabitants is not any single thread of ancestry but their hopeless commingling. Thoreau's word, "cohabitancy," is significant – this passage is the only one cited for the word in the Oxford English Dictionary; more broadly, "to cohabit" suggests dwelling in one place together. In reference to animals or things, this suggests a passive and discrete co-existence; ecologists use the term for different species who share the same territory. In reference to people, the word means a couple living together without the sanction of marriage, a sexual relationship that is at once recognized and extra-legal. It's not clear which meaning Thoreau has in mind here, or indeed whether this family is even human, but the liminal quality of these beings is key – they are co-present but almost invisible, part of the generative fabric of the Concord woods, but outside the channels of human authority. Spaulding is unaware of who shares his woods, but for Thoreau, these moments of recognition are dream-like states tinged with eros. These beings represent the perceptual frisson of seeing around corners towards surprising connections. And they are vessels of wonder. For in the Maine Woods and Spaulding Farm, Thoreau finds not the cold science that was too often the water-bearer of colonial capitalism but the awe and mystery of seeing the world's unity through the eyes of difference.

Panarchy and Ecocultural Contact

I will end with a few comments about my approach to what I've been calling ecocultural contact. In the broadest terms, I've tried to weave together the two main dualisms that have settled over U.S. cultural studies in recent years – the effort to unpack the dynamics of cultural contact, almost always in context of vastly asymmetric power, at the heart of race studies and settler colonialism, on the one hand, and the effort to critique the unfolding relationship between humans and their environment in a range of settings that make up the growing body of ecocriticism. Putting these approaches in conversation, I argue, enriches both. Studies focused on racial and cultural difference need to recognize that these encounters are shaped in profound ways by their setting, by the more-than-human actants that are very much part of the story. Schoolcraft's pine shapes the *metis* world as much as her response to it is shaped by the cultural conflict she embodies; Fuller's oak tree, similarly, speaks for a Great Lakes landscape shaped by settler colonialism, giving voice to the trees cut for fuel on Manitou Island. Similarly, the pines in the Maine Woods are not, for Thoreau and Nicolar, mere symbols, but real beings with their own histories and stories that shape the interactions of their human relations.

Tracing these lines of influence offers a more complex map, one that follows panarchic connections and unexpected loops. Such an approach asks us to look more carefully at place – not as a nostalgic category of home and folk, but as a radically decentering way of engaging with the more-than-human world. By looking at conflicting stories of place, for one, we get a better sense of how unstable a category it is. Jane Schoolcraft was lost during her trip to Ireland; a pine tree helps her rediscover where – and who – she is. Fuller saw a Wisconsin oak, the focal point for the several cultures mingling in the Great Lakes region, as suddenly unsure of what it was, and in the uncertainty saw the promise of a more just future. Thoreau followed the best maps he had into the Maine Woods, but once he began to read the Penobscot map, he realized how lost he really was. This moment of loss, of finding a familiar environment suddenly grown strange, is crucial in an ecocultural approach – these are moments when ideologies fracture and new stories begin to emerge, to cross the barriers that, according to the colonial episteme, divide culture from culture, human from nature. New connections, new patterns of interaction and agency emerge, as separate fields in the vast web that connects us all begin to flow into each other. The new materialism, with its vitalist monism that works to reenchant the material world by returning to a very old ontology, is useful in theorizing these moments of exchange, the hermeneutics that shape communication in the mesh.

And panarchy, too, is a term that helps capture the complex, unpredictable, daunting, dizzying and exhilarating nature of these moments of cultural contact. These strange loops have, after all, unforeseeable results. Any history of the contact between native peoples and European American settlers in the Maine Woods or the Great Lakes will tell a long story of cultural and environmental devastation. Yet it's important to keep in mind that this is not the only story. In August of 2016, a new national monument, Katahdin Woods and Waters, was established in the Maine Woods, a forest preserve that has its roots in the spirit of the pine Thoreau learned to see, thanks to his Penobscot guides, a century and a half ago. There the white pine – elevated to the status of common ecocultural heritage – will grow to tell its story. And I should note, too, that walking to my class one day along a small stream choked with multiflora rose and a few straggling grape vines, I noticed a small twining vine with pinnate leaves. There it was – the groundnut, or hopniss, I had first seen through the eyes of my Penobscot guide. I brought my class outside to look – none of them had seen it before, though a few had heard of it. It was now part of their story. We left the tubers in the ground, to sprout anew next year.

Works Cited

Basso, Keith. *Wisdom Sits in Places: Landscape and Language Among the Western Apache.* Albuquerque: University of New Mexico Press, 1996. Print.

Bellin, Joshua. "In the Company of Savagists: Thoreau's Indian Books and Antebellum Ethnology." *The Concord Saunterer* 16 (January 2008). Online: MLA International Bibliography.

Bennett, Jane. *Vibrant Matter: A Political Ecology of Things.* Durham, N.C.: Duke University Press, 2010.

Brooks, Lisa. *The Common Pot: The Recovery of Native Space in the Northeast.* Minneapolis: University of Minnesota Press, 2008.

De Puydt, Paul Emile. "Panarchy." *Revue Trimestrielle* July (1860): 222–45.

Dimock, Wai-Chee. *Through Other Continents: American Literature across Deep Time.* Princeton, NJ: Princeton University Press, 2008.

Fleck, Richard. *Henry Thoreau and John Muir Among the Indians.* Hamded, CT: Archon Books, 1985.

Fuller, Margaret. *Summer on the Lakes in 1843.* Urbana, IL: University of Illinois Press, 1990.

Heidegger, Martin. "Building, Dwelling, Thinking." *Poetry, Language, Thought.* Alfred Hofstadter, trans. New York: Harper Colophon Books, 1971.

Heise, Ursula. *Sense of Place and Sense of Planet: The Environmental Imagination of the Global.* New York: Oxford University Press, 2008.

Holling, C. S., and Lance H. Gunderson. *Panarchy: Understanding Transformations in Human and Natural Systems.* Washington, DC: Island Press, 2001.

Iovino, Serenella, and Serpil Oppermann. *Material Ecocriticism.* Bloomington, IN: Indiana University Press, 2014.

Kucich, John J. "Lost in the Maine Woods: Henry Thoreau, Joseph Nicolar and the Penobscot World." *The Concord Saunterer* 19/20 (2011): 22–52.

Latour, Bruno. *Politics of Nature: How to Bring the Sciences into Democracy.* Cambridge, MA: Harvard University Press, 2004.

Lefebvre, Henri. *The Production of Space.* Donald Nicholson-Smith, trans. Cambridge, MA: Blackwell Publishers, 1991.

Lynch, Tom, Cheryll Glotfelty, and Karla Armbruster. Eds. *The Bioregionalist Imagination.* Athens: University of Georgia Press, 2012.

Morton, Timothy. *Dark Ecology: For a Logic of Future Coexistence.* New York: Columbia University Press, 2016.

Nicolar, Joseph. *The Life and Traditions of the Red Man: A Rediscovered Treasure of Native American Literature.* Ed. Annette Kolodny. Durham: Duke University Press, 2007.

Pratt, Mary Louise. *Imperial Eyes: Travel Writing and Transculturation.* 2nd Edition. Routledge, 2007.

Resilience Alliance. <http://www.resalliance.org>.

Rifkin, Mark. *Manifesting America: The Imperial Construction of U.S. National Space.* New York: Oxford University Press, 2009.

Schneider, Bethany. "Not for Citation: The Synchronic Strategies of Jane Johnston Schoolcraft." *ESQ: A Journal of the American Renaissance* 54 (2008): 111–44.

Schoolcraft, Jane Johnston. *The Sound the Stars Make Rushing Through the Sky: The Writings of Jane Johnston Schoolcraft.* Ed. Robert Dale Parker. Philadelphia: University of Pennsylvania Press, 2008.

Snyder, Gary. "The 'East West' Interview." *The Gary Snyder Reader.* Washington, DC: Counterpoint, 1999.

—. *The Practice of the Wild.* San Francisco: North Point Press, 1990.

Soja, Edward. *Thirdspace: Journeys to Los Angeles and Other Real-and-Imagined Places.* Cambridge, MA: Blackwell, 1996.

Thoreau, Henry David. *The Correspondence of Henry David Thoreau.* Eds. Walter Harding and Carl Bode. New York: New York University Press, 1958.

—. *The Maine Woods.* New York: Library of America, 1985.

—. "A Natural History of Massachusetts." *Collected Essays and Poems.* New York: Library of America, 2001.

—. *Walden.* New York: Library of America, 1985.

—. "Walking." *Collected Essays and Poems.* New York: Library of America, 2001.

Treuer, Anton. *Living our Language: Ojibwe Tales and Oral Histories.* St. Paul, MN: Minnesota Historical Society Press, 2001.

Tuan, Yi-Fu. *Topophilia: A Study of Environmental Perception, Attitudes, and Values.* New York: Columbia University Press, 1990.

Walls, Laura Dassow. "Beyond Representation: Deliberate Reading in a Panarchic World." Ebr [electronic book review], "Critical Ecologies" thread, posted. 9 July 2009 <http://www.electronicbookreview.com/thread/criticalecologies/deliberative>.

CHAPTER TWELVE

Cultivating the Sky

Aníbal Arregui

Newton's apple did not fall solely due to gravity. Despite the mathematics describing the trajectory and acceleration of a falling apple, equations alone do not explain the forces that put the apple up there in the first place. Indeed, an apple tree had been planted in the garden of Newton's family home, in Lincolnshire, years before that particular apple was gently released one peaceful day in 1666. While the young mathematician was hit (so the legend goes) on his brilliant head by the unexpected apple, if it had been his mother sitting under the tree, she would likely have looked upwards, contemplating the beauty of her agricultural artifact, wondering about the mysterious physiochemical forces that make life appear and grow… and probably, therefore, avoiding an unnecessary accident. 350 years later, the world is still persuaded that the smartest person in that Lincolnshire garden was Sir Isaac Newton; however, it was obviously his mother.

The anecdote is notorious since, proceeding from that apple, the whole human sky has started to fall down upon us, as the ancient Gallic proverb has it. Today some still calculate the physics of the fall, as Newton did, while others apparently remain oblivious to the possibility of any fall, with the current U.S. president Donald Trump serving as a good example.[1] Meanwhile the intelligence of our mothers has been indecently downplayed, and now we humans just don't know why in the world we abandoned the caring cultivation of a garden that is becoming too wild and too violent for us to remain in.

In this chapter I will present a very general anthropological diagnosis of what has led *some* human cultures to abandon the caring cultivation of their gardens, that is, their biosphere. But the problem I want to outline is not limited to the cultivation of the surface on which human life rests. The core *cultural* problem I shall address here is precisely the impact that human action on the biosphere has on the atmospheric dynamics. This means looking not so much at how or why things fall apart, but rather looking at what we did or did not do on the ground to ensure the beauty and stability of the space above our heads. It is the very sky itself that has been left uncultivated ever since Newton's findings.

---

1   On June 1, 2017, Trump pulled the U.S. out of the 2015 Paris Agreement on climate change mitigation, with the argument that this step would help the U.S. economy, in particular its fossil fuel industry. Shear, Michael D. "Trump Will Withdraw U.S. From Paris Climate Agreement." *New York Times* 1 June 2017. 26 July 2017 <https://www.nytimes.com/2017/06/01/climate/trump-paris-climate-agreement.html>.

Parallel to the apple anecdote – with its far-reaching consequences for the development of modern thinking – anthropology has ever since struggled to gain a place among the sciences of Newtonian cosmology; but anthropology still remains, paradoxically, much closer to Newton's mother's way of knowing the world. From Newton's mother's perspective, the falling apple equation is a cultural problem and not a physical or mathematical one, for at least two reasons. Firstly, because falling apples have been, in great part, previously cultivated: they fall from trees that have been put there by humans. It is not by chance that all the research inspired by the Anthropocene paradigm has in the last years demonstrated that human cultures, and in particular industrial capitalism, have become the main impact factor on the Earth system's ecology (Crutzen). Human 'culture', from the Latin *colere* and *culturare*, has not only to do with symbols but also with very specific actions on the environment; actions that may at first seem oriented to the preparation of the ground for social life, but which will dramatically affect and be affected by what happens 'up there'.

This leads us to the second reason as to why the current rebellion of our sky is a cultural problem. Only some cultures, especially Euro-American and scientifically-driven ones, have introduced this separation between the biosphere and the atmosphere, the earth and sky. While inverting the power relation between Above and Below to the benefit of the latter, modern science retained Judeo-Christian theology's strict division of the world into these two zones. It could be argued that scientific emancipation from Godly forces thus involved certain loss of sight of the actual relationship between earthly and celestial beings. The problem is then a cultural one and it should be addressed in its cultural specificity. This means asking why scientific rationales, with their tendency to self-enclosing specialization within their particular fields of expertise, have led us to think in terms of a neat separation of levels of existence – namely, atmosphere and biosphere – while for instance animistic cultures, with their much less compartmentalized fields of knowledge, have preserved a profound notion of the relation between the earth and the sky.

This is of course a rough generalization of both Western science and animistic ways of dividing the world in which humans live. Besides abstract analytical comparisons, animism and (Western) science are often more complexly enmeshed than it may seem at a first glance. Where should we place Newton's mother, for instance? Her views were, in some ways, modern, while still leaving room for a wonderment as to how life is generated. Many details, exceptions, personal particularities, contradictions and anthropological continuities should be likewise part of the description of the epistemic field extending from 'science' to 'animism'. There is probably no other way to decolonize our thinking than to question the very limits we have always taken for granted.

As an anthropologist interested in both conceptual systems – in their differences as well as in their affinities – I will in this chapter resort to a particularly illustrative example of how 'science' and 'animism' respectively conceive of the relation between the earth and the sky. After introducing some theoretical background, I will present the case of a climatologist and an Amazonian shaman who have in the last years been involved in a public dialogue about the relation between forest trees and rainfall patterns. I shall argue that the interest of the case lies in the fact that these spokespersons not only identify their radically different takes on the trees-rain relation; they have also tried to navigate that anthropological gap in their pursuit of a common ecopolitical goal: the protection of the Amazonian forest and its sky. The overall proposal of this chapter is to approach the potential convergence of (a particular form of) climate science and (a particular form of) animism in terms of their shared perspective on the 'cultivation' of the sky: a generative/relational ecopolitical attitude that contrasts with the idea of 'preservation' of a previously given heritage.

Inheriting an Atmosphere

This is the final chapter of a volume on the often latently colonial logics of World Heritage and the practices of heritagization. As different contributors to the volume show, the domination and political asymmetries involved in heritage practices are not always self-evident. On the contrary, the practices of preservation or conservation of landscapes, artifacts and symbols are presented as forms of human salvation. Cultural and natural niches are institutionally and legally detached from previous social and natural dynamics, and a new dynamics are set for them, so that these niches remain 'untouchable' yet economically productive.

The motivation inspiring heritage culture is *a priori* well-intended, but one can ask what is being swept away in the gesture of preservation; in other words: one can consider the possibility that to institutionally preserve something means that something else is not deemed worthy of being preserved. Heritage gestures may in this regard be seen as culturally selective, often deeply colonial, for the criteria of preservation still come from the cultural settings that have championed the violent expansion and exploitation of alien peoples and territories in human history. The Heritage logic follows a typically Euro-American mode of thought, a Cartesian tradition full of dichotomies that points not only to the earth-sky separation but also to other problematic dualisms such as nature/culture, matter/symbols, mind/body, etc. (Hornborg). However, the hegemonic mode of being in the world constituted by Cartesian and Newtonian ideas is not the only option that should be considered as socially plausible, culturally fit and ecologically desirable.

I would argue that current heritage logics are still dominated by the young Newton's focus on the properties of an actual, physical world; perhaps we need to collectively be hit once more on the head by a falling apple, as it were, before we reconsider the point of view of Newton's mother, that is, the perspective of the cultivator who looks toward the future. One may wonder what sort of sky we want for our future generations, and what we should do *now* in order to preserve what is good in our current atmosphere. Patrimonialization or musealization of the air we breathe is surely not the smartest solution – since it needs to flow free from institutional constraints; nor is its financialization, in the form of carbon credits that give the wealthiest economies license to pollute the atmosphere of all (Layfield).

However, attention to the inner workings of heritage processes may aid us in considering what the world's dominant institutions are currently doing in order to preserve certain artifacts, landscapes and symbols. And from the successes and pitfalls of World Heritage politics one might perhaps extract some ideas as to what to do in order to also preserve the valuable entities that flow above us. This is why this essay will engage with the question of how to recover a cultural, or even agricultural perspective on our sky. The example of the dialogue between the shaman and the climatologist will illustrate the gestures that some people concerned with the earth's environmental degradation are performing in order to show us that humans, as cultivators, should care about their sky. Earthly gestures have celestial consequences. Animists never forgot this and scientists are now apparently getting back to this point. Meanwhile, the sky has started to show a reaction against us, careless gardeners, who might now seek to tame this growing violence, and ensure that a livable atmosphere will be inherited by future generations.

Forest-Sky Relation as Tensional Space

> I'm lost in a forest / All alone / The girl was never there /
> It's always the same / I am running towards nothing /
> Again and again and again and again…
>
> *A Forest,* The Cure, 1987

Robert Smith gave a modern voice to two related questions that have for a long time troubled classic philosophy and the natural sciences respectively: on the one hand, the metaphysical discussion around contour-limits vs. tension limits, and on the other hand the ecological depth of the forest. The French philosopher Gilles Deleuze brilliantly combined both problems in his *Spinoza* lecture at the *College de France* (1981). There, Deleuze elaborated on the dramatic watershed that Stoic philosophers inflected on metaphysics, when they contended that the limits of the world's entities should not be thought of in terms of geometrical *contours,* as suggested in the Platonic-Euclidean tradition, but in terms of *tensions,* that is, putting the emphasis not on the form but on the ever changing dynamics inherent to any limit. According to Deleuze, the limits of a forest provided a clear example of this problem:

The limit of something is the limit of its action and not the outline of its figure. Even simpler example: you are walking in a dense forest, you're afraid. At last you succeed and little by little the forest thins out, you are pleased. You reach a spot and you say, "whew, here's the edge." The edge of the forest is a limit. Does this mean that the forest is defined by its outline? It's a limit of what? [...] The thing that shows that this is not an outline is the fact that we can't even specify the precise moment at which there is no more forest. There was a tendency, and this time the limit is not separable, a kind of tension towards the limit. It's a dynamic limit that is opposed to an outline limit. The thing has no other limit than the limit of its power [puissance] or its action. The thing is thus power and not form. The forest is not defined by a form, it is defined by a power: power to make the trees continue up to the moment at which it can no longer do so. The only question that I have to ask of the forest is: what is your power? That is to say, how far will you go? (Deleuze n. p.)

According to this view, a forest does not have a given outline: it is a dynamic body, and there are no geometrical limits to its edges. There is rather only tension and power. Such power might have a metaphysical expression, yet it can be also measured with the tools of science: forest power is an ecological force that spills over its sensible limits, and this overflowing force can be empirically tracked. This applies not only to the horizontal limits of the forest surface but also to the vertical tension existing between the forest and the sky, the biosphere and the atmosphere. There is no way of demarcating where one ends and where the other begins, because forest and sky constitute one another and engage in a continuous, dynamic space. Western scientists call this dynamic space 'ecology': a natural interaction. Amazonian animists call this space 'relation': a social engagement between two *human-like* entities we call 'forest' and 'sky'. What interests us here then is the Stoic observation that things are bodies, bodies with power, and that power can be either natural or social. As I shall show below, no matter which vantage point one takes: forest and sky always display an extraordinary power, and their respective powers and bodies are extraordinarily enmeshed. We all live within a turbulent space of forest-sky tensions.

Forest-Sky Relation in an Irreversible Time

If the idea of a geometric, tension-less space is a misleading measure of forest-sky relations, the time in which they exist sets much sharper limits to their mutual becoming. Newton's mechanist view of world dynamics – wherein everything is subject to a single law or force – saw no other time in things than the constant time of their acceleration towards a gravitational center. Things moved in space and time, their masses being attracted to one another. But time was external to things in Newton's *Principia,* and this is why the bodies of things had constant properties, unchangeable natures. As for Plato and Euclides, for Newton a forest would be a body of a given mass and a given outline moving in a given universal timeframe. A forest would not be for Newton any particular becoming; it would not have its own time.

Two hundred years later, Einstein's theory of *General Relativity* placed Newton's geometrical descriptions in relation to a spacetime curved continuum. The relations between things were then not only described as spatial relations between masses, but as the product of those masses traveling in a temporospatial curve. The main departure from Euclidean and Newtonian cosmology was the idea that time and space were not constant, but relative to the position of an observer traveling in spacetime. Some sounded theories suggested that time, for an observer traveling at a significant fraction of speed-light (the speed in which time travels in space), would pass slower than for a 'stationary' observer, and some models even demonstrated the reversibility of time under special conditions imposed upon the spacetime curve. The most paradoxical feature of Einstein's theories was perhaps that despite being aimed at describing relative phenomena, these descriptions were subjected to a limited set of universal laws, much as Newton's *Principia*.

General relativity has ever since opened many minds, but it has perhaps also disclosed the dangers of certain relativisms that are applied to actual phenomena. General relativity is not only a theory; it has also opened up a new way to think about reality. With all the virtues of relativist thinking, it should also be said that it has fostered misleading ideas that have permeated Western imaginaries. It is tempting to establish a connection between general relativism and the contemporary language of "alternative facts." But this would be an absurd comparison if one attended to the different degree of complexity of the two arguments. What holds true, however, is that the equations of time reversal and its symmetry, for instance, have been proven at theoretical and microscopic levels, but there is no empirical evidence that time can be reversed at a macroscopic level, as for instance the one on which climatic events take place: from Heisenberg's *Uncertainty Principle* to Prigogine's *Dissipative Structures*, science has after Einstein shown that no observer position can amend what is already happening on Earth. The beautiful formulae of general relativity cannot be applied to a cosmos marked by dramatic discontinuities. A forest ecology could never for instance be described with a set of formulae based on gradual and predictable change, nor would its time and space depend on any observer's position. A forest ecology constitutes one of the instances wherein slight changes lead to chaotic formations that can affect the whole atmospheric equilibrium, and these changes do not predictably or reversibly evolve in a temporospatial continuum. The time of a forest and our atmosphere cannot be reversed because "time" poses not a relative, but a drastic ecological limit to our life on Earth (Howe). This is not only a physical but also an ecopolitical question that could be addressed by both general relativists and climate change deniers. No spacetime wormhole will get us back to the moment when forests made our air breathable.

Cultivating (in) the Chaos

In the two preceding sections I have sketched a way to think about a forest-sky relation that is defined by the absence of fixed or pre-given spatial limits and the presence of rather narrow time limits. These two sections have then presented some theoretical conceptions of the forest-sky ecology which in the beginning I associated with the view of Newton's mother: the view of a cultivator. This perspective sees the agricultural space as something to be produced, and the agricultural time as something that will dramatically limit the possibilities of production of that agricultural space. The cultivator indeed manipulates the tensions existing between earth and sky and takes very seriously the time limits that her or his actions must take into account in order to produce a desired dynamics.

In agriculture, the atmosphere-biosphere interaction generally follows more or less predictable dynamics. This is why the cultivator knows that certain seeds planted in certain soils will produce certain plants under specific climatic circumstances within a specific timeframe. But we also mentioned that science, and in particular climate science and related fields, is unpacking the dramatic irregularities that the Earth's system's ecological dynamics has been showing in the past years. The cultivator of the twenty-first century is not only familiar with the rules of the earth-sky relation, but also aware of the chemo-industrial complex which apparently turns the atmospheric behavior into something rather unpredictable and rebellious. There is no more peacefulness in the countryside: the cultivator of today needs to be an expert in chaos.

However, the expertise in chaotic earth-sky interactions does not mean that no rules are to be inferred. It means rather that analytical foci and agricultural creativity have to be pushed somewhere else. There is a plausible order in current climatologic chaos that we may want to potentialize (Prigogine and Stengers). Molecular biologists have demonstrated that there are in fact certain sorts of communication between forms of life that are only enabled by chaotic dynamics, a process that could be called the creativity of far from equilibrium structures (13).

Now, let us imagine for a moment that this not only applies to molecules but also to persons. If one were to think about forms of human communication that emerge from the ongoing process of environmental collapse, then communication in chaos would become a question of anthropological interest. In the next section I will present the case of two very different kinds of cultivators, an Amazonian shaman and a climatologist, who have in the last years engaged in innovative forms of dialogue around the future of the rainforest. As it will be shown, then, it is possible to approach the ongoing processes of environmental degradation as contexts that foster new forms of cross-cultural connectivity.

Climatology and Animism

Since 2005, a group of microphysicists and climatologists have been developing the 'Biotic Pump Theory' (BPT), which has since its inception sparked intense controversy among atmospheric scientists (Gorshkov & Makarieva; Makarieva et al.). Unlike the widely accepted theory that holds that the Earth's rotation rate, the heating of the oceans, and atmospheric depth are the main drivers of air masses, the BPT suggests that a more powerful driver of winds might be found in the biosphere, in particular in tropical forests. According to the BPT, the condensation of water vapor released by trees creates a rapid depression – a low-pressure zone – that powerfully attracts moist, high-pressure masses of air, which can be 'pumped' along thousands of kilometers, from oceans and seas towards the forest.

One of the supporters of the BPT is the climatologist Antonio Nobre who, in recent years, has not only defended it to his colleagues but has also intensively tried to communicate the climatological importance of the Amazonian rainforest to a wider audience, with the hope of affecting the debate around environmental policies on an international level (Nobre, *REDD and PINC*, *Floresta e Clima*). In 2010, Antonio Donato Nobre gave a TedX talk titled *The Magic of the Amazon*, in which the scientist elaborated on the climatological relevance of the Amazonian rainforest. In the middle of this talk – with near a million views on the internet as of the time of writing, the scientist claimed that Amazonian indigenous views on the relation between rainfall patterns and the rainforest supported the BPT. In particular, he went on to compare how a Yanomami shaman and he himself saw the relation between forest trees and rain:

> I'd like to tell you a short story. Once, about four years ago, I attended a declamation, of a text by Davi Kopenawa, a wise representative of the Yanomami people, and it went more or less like this: "Doesn't the white man know that, if he destroys the forest, there will be no more rain? And that, if there's no more rain, there'll be nothing to drink, or to eat?" […]. This bugged me and I was befuddled. How could he know that? Some months later, I met him at another event and said, "Davi, how did you know that if the forest was destroyed, there'd be no more rain?" He replied: 'The spirit of the forest told us.' For me, this was a game changer, a radical change. I said, 'Gosh! Why am I doing all this science to get to a conclusion that he already knows?' Then, something absolutely critical hit me, which is, seeing is believing. Out of sight, out of mind (…) I mean, we, Western society, which is becoming global, civilized – we need to see. If we don't see, we don't register the information. We live in ignorance (…) Davi Kopenawa doesn't need this. He has something already that I think I missed. I was educated by television. I think that I missed this, an ancestral record, a valuation of what I don't know, what I haven't seen. (min: 14:51–16:51).

For his part, the shaman Davi Kopenawa has struggled for the last two decades to bring Yanomami cosmology to the "white people" (Kopenwa and Albert 133). Besides his activity as president of the *Comissão-ProYanomami* (Commission for the Yanomami People) and his numerous speeches given all over the world, an important part of this effort has been the release of the cosmological and ecopolitical manifesto *The Falling Sky: Words of a Yanomami Shaman* (Kopenawa and Albert). In this book, written with the help of his old friend, the anthropologist Bruce Albert, Kopenawa evokes in an autobiographical and detailed first person narrative his shamanic views on Yanomami cosmology, as well as his concerns regarding the social, economical and ecological danger in which the depredatory action of 'whites' has placed the Amazonian forest and its people.

Despite the climatologist references, it is rather difficult to establish direct equivalences between the shaman's and the scientist's environmental concepts and images. It holds true, as Antonio Nobre suggests in his talk, that there are some conceptual parallels between what some climate scientists supporting the BPT and Amazonian shamans say about the relation between trees and rain. However, one may wonder whether these evident parallels are enough to claim that scientists and shamans have come "to the same conclusion" (Nobre, *The Magic of the Amazon*). Here it is worth considering what Davi Kopenawa has actually said about the relation between Amazonian trees and rain:

> As soon as you cut down tall trees such as the *wari mahi* kapok trees and the *hawari hi* Brazil nut trees, the forest's soil becomes hard and hot. It is these big trees that make the rainwater come and keep it in the ground. The trees that white people plant, the mango trees, the coconut trees, the orange trees, and the cashew trees, they do not know how to call the rain. (Kopenawa and Albert 385).

Both the scientist and the shaman recognize that there is a relation between trees and rain, and that such a relation should pose certain limits to the human action on the Amazonian environment. But for all the apparent convergences, such a relation is strikingly different if we approach it from the shaman's or the scientist's perspective. By laying bare the physical causes and effects of micro-physical systems on climate, the work of Nobre is very different from the work of Kopenawa, who is negotiating with the sky through powerful *xapiri*-spirit beings (Kopenawa and Albert 131–32). Furthermore, it could be argued that it is not only the relation between trees and the rain they elicit that is different, but the very understanding of what actually defines a ['ecological'] relation (Viveiros de Castro 481).

It is worth recalling at this point that the BPT suggests that the climatological relation occurring at the limits of the atmosphere-biosphere is thought of as being driven by the mechanism of a 'pump'. The metaphor selected here seems crucial, since it reflects plainly the 'naturalist' aspiration to a full "mechanization of the world" (Descola 97). The relation between trees and rain is likewise one of the issues at stake for the shaman, but the 'calling' of rain performed by *some* trees (Kopenawa and Albert 385) puts such a relation not in mechanistic terms but in an animistic-relational logic where non-human beings are endowed with human agency and intentionality. Therefore, it is the concepts addressing the very nature of ecological relations that are different: trees and rain are indeed related for both the scientist and the shaman, but there is no conceptual agreement about what such a relation consists of.

Environmental Diplomacy

> The white people who once ignored all these things are now starting to hear them a little. This is why some have invented new words to defend the forest. Now they call themselves 'people of ecology' because they are worried to see their land getting increasingly hot. (…) this is why we understood the new white people words as soon as they reached us. I explained them to my people and they thought. 'Haixopë! This is good!' (Kopenawa and Albert 393)

Despite the beauty of the climatology-animism parabola, anthropological comparisons of scientific and shamanic forms of environmental thinking need to stress primarily the drastic differences existing between them. There is, however, an important common ground to both: namely, the fact that the scientist and the shaman both support a 'cultivator' perspective, that is, a position according to which forest-sky limits are seen as fluctuating tensions and our time to cope with these tensions very limited. This is why despite their differences they share a common ecopolitical struggle: the urgent protection of the rainforest as a measure for maintaining the stability of the whole Earth's atmosphere.

The globally concerned, cultivator's perspective is clearly on the side of the scientist, where the Biotic Pump Theory is devised to explain not local but global atmospheric dynamics. The theory states that forests powerfully attract moist air from the oceans and therefore play a much more important role in global patterns of rainfall than was previously imagined. In the case of South America, the role of the Amazonian forest in driving winds and rain would hypothetically affect the stability of the weather conditions of the whole continent, and it could even have global climatological consequences. Such a theory would also of course have implications that reach beyond the debate of specialists. If the theory gained significant acceptance, the role of human action in generating climate change through abusive management of forest resources would acquire a new, enhanced dimension in global economic and ecological debates (Nobre *REDD and PINC, The Magic of the Amazon, The Future Climate of Amazonia*).

From the shaman's perspective, the possibility of a falling sky, as evoked in the very title of his book, is likewise not conceived of as a local phenomenon.

It is the 'whole' sky – including that of the white people – that will collapse if humans continue to deplete the forests. In fact, several passages in the book recall that the land where the Amazon now stands is in fact the center of the ancient sky *hutukara,* which already fell apart in the Yanomami's mythological past. The present sky is more solid and secure than the old *hutukara,* but still remains fragile and unstable. According to Kopenawa's explanations, nowadays it is the work of shamans, who drink the *yokohana* powder and call the spirits of the forest, cosmological instances and climatological phenomena – e.g. *Mothokari* sun being, *Maari* rain being, *Omoari* dry season being, etc.– that "holds the sky up", thus preventing it from falling down again (Kopenawa and Albert 130).

The different views espoused above conceptualize from Yanomami and scientific perspectives the direct relation between terrestrial and atmospheric phenomena as well as the human responsibility determining the course of this interaction. Both views on the earth – sky relation resound with recent debates on the ecological intermingling of "cultural" and "natural" beings (Latour, *An Inquiry into the Modes of Existence*) and the anthropocene (Crutzen). The human interface connecting the ground and the sky has also been an issue for social sciences and philosophy in the recent years, and has led to a redefining from an anthropogenic point of view the dynamics of what scientists call "weather" (Ingold). Taking the anthropogenic reading of the sky a bit further, the view of the cultivator can even transcend the theoretical discussion to enter an ecopolitical reflection: if the causality of atmospheric events has to be seen from (human) life to the Earth's system, and not vice versa, then we may look at the air as a place both of life and of technological disruption, thus refocusing our current relation with the sky as a moment of responsibility (Szerszynski).

I argue that both the shaman and the scientist take this responsibility very seriously and accordingly try to cooperate in order to combat rainforest depletion. Their gestures (e.g. a TedX talk, a book) are therefore ecopolitical because they show awareness of the planetary scale of their ecological concerns and because they target their respective audiences. This is why the scientist, ten years before the above-mentioned Ted talk, already gave a presentation to an indigenous audience, in Manaus, where he exposed his findings on the forest climatology in an understandable language to non-scientists, and also stated his desire to "see" the forest and the sky "with the eyes of the spirits" (Nobre, *Floresta e Clima*). On the other hand, the shaman Davi Kopenawa has also very explicitly stated that his book, *The Falling Sky,* is an artifact devised exclusively to send his "words far away" and "penetrate the minds" of the white people. I have argued elsewhere that these efforts to reach out to others could be framed as part of an emerging "environmental diplomacy" (Arregui, *This Mess is a "World"!*), and that such forms of ecopolitical connection still need to be adequately explored and theorized from the perspective of the social sciences and humanities concerned with what is broadly understood as "climate change".

Decolonial Connections

I have elsewhere proposed to theorize the particular connections between the scientist and the shaman by approaching them as "mimicries" (Arregui, *Embodying Equivocations*). The reason for this approach is that the connective gestures I have followed are characterized by an attempt to communicate with the counterpart without presuming one has sufficient knowledge about the Other.

When for instance Antonio Nobre claims that he would like to 'see' the forest and the climate 'with the eyes of the spirits' (*Floresta e Clima* 39), he is arguably not only expressing a willingness, but also signaling a disposition to adopt another perspective. He made this very clear when he invoked Davi Kopenawa's take on the relation between forest trees and rain *(The Magic of the Amazon)*. One may argue that he was just addressing the shaman's perspective in a metaphorical sense, as a rhetorical gesture. And indeed, there is a deliberate *staging* in the way and the context in which the scientist makes such an affirmation. Yet the gesture remains anthropologically relevant, in my view, insofar as it discloses a strategy of science communication whereby two discourses, that of science and that of shamanism, may "resonate" with each other and thus gain "mutual amplification" (Prigogine and Stengers 46).

Furthermore, the scientist's gestures are built upon the recognition of the *lack of knowledge* about the Other – clearly expressed in Nobre's wondering: "how could he know that?" (*The Magic of the Amazon*, min: 14:51). This is why I suggest that the scientist's gesture should be addressed as being 'mimical', and not as a mere 'reference to', in as much as it displays a *disposition* to navigate the anthropological distance with respect to the counterpart, without necessarily undoing such distance by means of an absolutely certain knowledge about how things work in the context of the Other, i. e. shamanism.

The shaman also seems to be aware of the great anthropological distance existing between him and the world of the scientist. It was this awareness that led him, in 2000, to hold up, in the context of a shamanic ritual, the satellite image of the Earth's extension, the image of a planisphere (Albert 237). This gesture destabilized the usual form of "bringing down images" in conventional shamanic practices. That fixation of the image of the world in a rectangle of paper can be seen as an "innovative form of political shamanism" (238), which aims at engaging or at least experimenting with the conceptual imagination and the communicative formats of whites.

These kinds of gestures are not mere spectacle, but potentially ground-breaking, mimetic incursions into the relational logics of the Other. Mimicry can consist of bodily and practical gestures, as in the act of holding up the satellite image, or verbal, as for instance when Kopenawa called Antonio Nobre "the Einstein of the Amazon" (Milanez). The shaman made this comparison to a journalist from Sao Paulo who was interviewing him with regard to the Yanomami territorial conflicts. This comparison did not take place within a certain cultural context with a given pool of common referents; rather, it attempted to connect intuitively two different conceptual imaginaries. My interpretation is that Davi Kopenawa aimed at mimetically expressing his recognition towards someone from the context of the journalist – i.e. a 'white' scientist from the city of Sao Paulo– knowing that Einstein was a respected person in this context, but not necessarily knowing the stakes of Einstein's physical and cosmological theories.

The release of *The Falling Sky* is perhaps the best and most detailed example of what I would term an 'ecopolitical mimicry'. The very process of recording, transcription and the later publication of *The Falling Sky* is illustrative of an experiment in ecopolitical connectivity conducted by the shaman, with the complicity and support of the anthropologist Bruce Albert. The book in itself can be seen as a gesture, which is anthropologically interesting due to the rupturing character that the writing down of thoughts involves for a shaman. As has been said in an excellent review of the book (Cesarino), *The Falling Sky* asks what for anthropological analysis means the "ontological debasement of the written discourse when compared with the original form of [shamanic] knowledge production and transmission (dreams, visions, accounts, and spirit-songs)" (290).

To return to the main topic of this volume, the interesting aspect of the notion of 'mimicry' is perhaps the question of whether it helps to articulate the context of shamanism and the context of climatology with a decolonial perspective. The idea of mimesis has already been employed in order to describe how in colonial times indigenous peoples imitated the behavior of invaders in order to deal with and even trick them (Taussig). Yet there is another nuance I would like to address here. This nuance emerges from the distance I perceive in the difference that Bourdieu saw between the often-related concepts of 'mimesis' and 'imitation'. In his discussion about the idea of "habitus," Bourdieu identified imitation as a reflexive process and mimesis as a mirroring that was not subject to consciousness (Bourdieu 123). Yet as I have just shown, the kind of gestures addressed here are hardly amenable to either a closed dimension of conscious, intentional imitation, or a non-reflexive mimesis. Rather, a particular mixture of political intentionality and anthropological uncertainty seems to drive these connections. This is why I do not see the shaman's and the scientist's gestures as collapsing their differences or effectively closing an anthropological gap. On the contrary, the awareness of a distance seems to be what constitutes the disposition to 'export' their message to an anthropological domain as yet unknown. The 'decolonial' connection originates then in this double gesture of aiming to communicate with the Other and, at the same time, acknowledging the lack of knowledge about the Other's context. Mimicry is thus a connective gesture that *enacts* communicative intentionality in combination with a respectful attitude towards anthropological differences.

World Heritage at the End of the World

The scientist's and the shaman's decolonial, mimical connections show the great ecopolitical potential of the cultivator's perspective. This is a way to connect that displays a common interest in protecting the Amazonian rainforest, without imposing the criteria of one's own cultural context on the counterpart. It is worth noting that the type of protection stressed by these 'cultivators of the sky' is very different from the practices of preservation entailed in World Heritage politics. In this last section I will argue that the contrast between 'cultivator' and 'heritage'-driven perspectives can shed some light on the strategies that humans are currently devising in order to preserve those elements that are crucial for the survival and the well-being of the human and non-human forms of life.

First, there is in World Heritage processes an apparently unproblematic separation between 'natural' and 'cultural' heritage, even though experts in the field have expressed strong reservations about such a distinction (see Lowenthal; Del Mármol and Estrada in this volume). It is rather evident that for the cultivators examined here – the scientist and the shaman – the sky-forest relation would be alarmingly simplified if it were to be reduced to either a natural phenomenon or a purely cultural question. Both the shaman and the scientist seem to be aware that 'nature' and 'culture' are central notions of their counterparts' conceptual imagination, and accordingly express their ecological concerns in a manner that diplomatically articulates these two dimensions. In contrast to the heritagization of natural and cultural elements of the environment, cultivators see their technological action on the environment not as separating human culture from wild nature, but rather as recomposing the "natural-cultural hybrid" (Latour, *Nous n'avons jamais été modernes*) in which we are all immersed.

On the other hand, the cultivator's perspective stresses that a care or concern about something, i.e. the biosphere, must be manifested through cultivation. This departs from World Heritage Sites, which seem to have always been there, pregiven by human history. The logic of preservation in heritage processes is, as it were, Euclidean: sites are spatially limited, they have clear frontiers, within which UNESCO's legal framework operates. Moreover, these spatial limits are considered to respond to determined natural or cultural features, which correspond with UNESCO's criteria for preservation. There is no spatial tension in a heritage site's limits, for they are protected against any 'external' alteration that may endanger their cultural or natural *intrinsic* value. Heritage sites are also not subject to 'time'; they are in fact subtracted from time, their process of becoming is suddenly and legally stopped, and 'history' is turned into the objectified image of a past that must never be departed from.

It is not my aim to minimize the complexity of heritage processes, nor would I like to downplay the necessity of setting clear legal and spatial limits to protect certain landscapes, artifacts and symbols (the latter perhaps in terms of intangible cultural heritage). On the contrary, the overall suggestion of this chapter is that all these institutional measures should come in combination with what has been termed the 'cultivator' perspective. The reason as to why I suggest this can be put in very simple terms: the cultivators' perspective does not advocate looking after elements of the biosphere singularly and in isolation; rather, it advocates a cultivation of the *relation* between the different elements. In other words: it is not 'the forest' or 'the atmosphere' that humans should care about, but rather their friendly, productive interaction, which should be cultivated. Institutional measures to save sites or symbols will meet with little success if the forms of relation that originated these sites and symbols are not likewise protected.

In terms of environmental thinking, the difference between the 'preservation' of natural and cultural elements and the 'cultivation' of the relations between them may help to situate the role that humans play, or might want to play, in the ecological becoming of the planet. It is often assumed that climate change is leading the world to an environmental collapse. Yet little attention is being devoted to what 'collapse' actually means. It is certainly clear that at the end of our world starts another world where non-human species will live. In relational terms, there are then two ways of envisaging the prospect of an environmental collapse: either a future world without humans, or future humans dwelling in another world (see Danowski and Viveiros de Castro). So it does not matter how much effort we invest in protecting humanity (i.e. culture) or the world (i.e. nature), for it is not the permanence of these two elements separately that is at stake, but rather their current relation, which is running the risk of suffering a dramatic rupture. That our sky is behaving rebelliously is only one sign that such an ecological or relational rupture is underway. And it in all likelihood originated when humans neglected the careful gardening of the biosphere. Yet, as I have shown, there do remain contemporary cultivators, such as the shaman and the climatologist, who are voicing from very different cultural settings the necessity of caring more about the rainforest and its sky. For them, the Garden of Eden seems far from being the bucolic picture we have learnt to appreciate. From a cultivator's perspective, a 'natural paradise' cannot be represented by a static image; it should be rather signaled by something rebellious and dynamic. To my mind comes the wild, echoing and then fading scream of monkeys over the Amazonian canopy at sunset. It is these kind of gestures, coming from the forest, that reach the sky with the conciliatory noise of a life-generating relation we have inherited and which is now at risk of being silenced.

Works Cited

Albert, Bruce. *Yanomami: Back to the Image(s)*. Paris: Fondation Cartier, 2014.
Arregui, Aníbal G. "Embodying Equivocations: Ecopolitical Mimicries of Climate Science and Shamanism." *Anthropological Theory* (forthcoming).
—. "This Mess is a 'World'! Environmental Diplomats in the Mud of Anthropology." *Climate Change as the End of the World*. Ed. Rosalyn Bold. London: Palgrave Macmillan (forthcoming).
Bourdieu, Pierre. *Le sens pratique*. Paris: Éditions Minuit, 1980.
Cesarino, Pedro de N. "Ontological conflicts and shamanistic speculations in Davi Kopenawa's 'The falling sky'." *Hau: Journal of Ethnographic Theory* 4,2 (2014): 289–95.
Crutzen Paul J. "The Anthropocene." *Earth System Science in the Anthropocene*. Eds. Eckart Ehlers and Thomas Krafft. Berlin, Heidelberg: Springer, 2006. 13–18.
Danowski, Debora, and Eduardo Viveiros de Castro. "Is there any world to come?" *Supercommunity. e-flux*. 2015. 12 January 2016 <http://supercommunity.e-flux.com/authors/deborah-danowski/>.
Deleuze, Gilles. "On Spinoza. Lectures by Gilles Deleuze." 1981. 12 July 2017 <http://deleuzelectures.blogspot.co.at/2007/02/on-spinoza.html>.
Descola, Philippe. "Constructing natures. Symbolic ecology and social practice." *Nature and Society. Anthropological Perspectives*. Eds. Philippe Descola, and Gísli Pálsson. London: Routledge, 1996. 82–102.
Einstein, Albert. *Relativity. The Special and the General Theory*. Oxford and Princeton: Princeton University Press, 2015.
Gorshkov, Viktor and Makarieva Anastassia. "Biotic pump of atmospheric moisture as driver of the hydrological cycle on land." *Hydrology and Earth System Sciences* 11 (2007): 1013–33.
Heisenberg, Werner. *The Physical Principles of Quantum Theory*. Dover: Dover Publications, Inc., 1949.
Hornborg, Alf. "Animism, fetishism, and objectivism as strategies for knowing (or not knowing) the world." *Ethnos* 71,1 (2006): 21–32.
Howe, Cymene. "Timely." *Theorizing the Contemporary. Cultural Anthropology*. 2016. 12 July 2017 <https://culanth.org/fieldsights/800-timely>.
Ingold, Tim. *Being Alive. Essays on Movement, Knowledge and Description*. New York: Routledge, 2011.
Kopenawa, Davi and Bruce Albert. *The Falling Sky. Words of a Yanomami Shaman*. Cambridge, MA: The Belknap Press of Harvard University Press, 2013.
Latour, Bruno. *Nous n'avons jamais été modernes: Essai d'anthropologie symétrique*. París: La Découverte, 1991.
—. *An Inquiry into the Modes of Existence. An Anthropology of the Modern*. Harvard: Harvard University Press, 2013.
Layfield, David. "Turning carbon into gold: the financialisation of international climate policy." *Environmental Politics* 22,6 (2013): 901–17.
Makarieva, Anastassia et al. "Where do winds come from? A new theory on how water vapor condensation influences atmospheric pressure and dynamics." *Atmospheric Chemistry and Physics* 13 (2013): 1039–56.
Milanez, Felipe. "Garimpo na terra yanomami: violência e ganância." *Terra Magazine*. 27 October 2011. 2 June 2017 <http://terramagazine.terra.com.br/interna/0,,OI5437416-EI16863,00.html>.

Newton, Sir Isaac. *Newton's Principa. The Mathematical Principles of Natural Philosophy*. New York: Daniel Adee, 1848.
Nobre, Antonio D. "REDD and PINC: A new policy framework to fund tropical forests as global eco-utilities." *Beyond Kyoto: Addressing the Challenges of Climate Change – Science Meets Industry, Policy and Public* 8 (2009). 28 November 2017 <https://doi.org/10.1088/1755-1315/8/1/012005>.
—. "Floresta e Clima. Saber Indígena e Ciência." *Manejo do mundo: conhecimentos e práticas dos povos indígenas do Rio Negro, Noroeste amazônico*. Org. A. Cabalzar. Brasil: Instituto Socioambiental & Federação das Organizações Indígenas do Rio Negro, 2010. 38–45.
—. "The Magic of the Amazon: A River that flows invisibility all around us." TED Talk, 2010. 8 April 2015 <https://www.ted.com/talks/antonio_donato_nobre_the_magic_of_the_amazon_a_river_that_flows_invisibly_all_around_us/transcript>.
—. *The Future Climate of Amazonia*. Sao Paulo: Edition ARA, CCST-INPE e INPA, 2014.
Prigogine, Ilya. "Time, Structure and Fluctuation." Nobel Lecture, 1977. 12 July 2017 <http://www.nobelprize.org/nobel_prizes/chemistry/laureates/1977/prigogine-lecture.pdf>.
—., and Isabelle Stengers. *Order out of Chaos. Man's New Dialogue with Nature*. U.S. and Canada: Bantam Books, 1984.
Shear, Michael D. "Trump Will Withdraw U.S. From Paris Climate Agreement." *New York Times* 1 June 2017. 26 July 2017 <https://www.nytimes.com/2017/06/01/climate/trump-paris-climate-agreement.html>.
Szerszynski, Bronislav. "Life in the Open Air." *Issues in Science and Religion: What is Life?* Publications of the European Society for the Study of Science and Theology. Eds. Dirk Evers, Michael Fuller, Antje Jackelén and Knut-Willy Sæther. Springer, 2015. 27–41.
Taussig, Michael. *Mimesis and Alterity. A Particular History of the Senses*. London: Routledge, 1993.
Viveiros de Castro, Eduardo. "The relative native." *Hau: Journal of Ethnographic Theory* 3,3 (2013): 473–502.

Contributors

Aníbal Arregui holds a PhD in Social and Cultural Anthropology from the University of Barcelona (2013). From 2013 to 2015 he was postdoc researcher at the Graduate School *Kulturkontakt und Wissenschaftsdiskurs* at Rostock University, and presently he is Lecturer at the Department of Social and Cultural Anthropology, University of Vienna. He has conducted fieldwork in the lower Amazon region since 2006 in *quilombola* (maroon) and *ribeirinho* (mestizo) communities, focusing on local notions of 'body', 'technology' and 'environment'. Two representative publications are "Amazonian Quilombolas and the Technopolitics of Aluminum" (*Journal of Material Culture*, 2015) and "Embodying Equivocations: Ecopolitical Mimicries of Climate Science and Shamanism" (*Anthropological Theory*, forthcoming).

Romeo Carabelli is a research engineer at Citeres (Unité Mixte de Recherche, CNRS, and the University of Tours, France). He has an *Habilitiation à Diriger des Recherches* in architecture and geography from the *École Normale Superiéure* of Lyon. He focuses his activities on (re)territorialization processes of colonial legacies, mainly over contemporary configurations of scattered and multinational heritage in Northern Africa and former Portuguese colonies. Carabelli designs and manages research and cooperation projects regarding cultural heritage (architecture and landscape), mainly in the Mediterranean and the Global South.

Ronnie Ellenblum is Professor at the Department of Geography at The Hebrew University of Jerusalem and a Fellow of the Israeli Academy for Sciences and Humanities. He specializes in Medieval Geographies, Climate History, and the history of the Crusades. He is the author of *Frankish Rural Settlement in the Latin Kingdom of Jerusalem* (1998), *Crusader Castles and Modern Histories* (2005), and *The Collapse of the Eastern Mediterranean: Climate Change and the Decline of the East, 950–1072* (2012). Ellenblum heads the *Vadum Iacob* and the *Historic Cities* research projects.

Ferran Estrada is full professor at the Department of Social and Cultural Anthropology, University of Barcelona. His work focuses on the socioeconomic and cultural changes related to industrial development and the transformation of agriculture and livestock production in rural areas of Catalonia. He has studied the changes in the socioeconomic organization of production, as well as in household, family, kinship and alliance. More recently he has pursued research on heritage processes in rural areas, focusing on intangible cultural heritage. He is author of *Entre l'amor i l'interès: el procés matrimonial a la Val d'Aran* (1993, with Xavier Roigé and Oriol Beltran); *Les cases pageses al Pla d'Urgell. Família, residència, terra i treball durant els segles XIX i XX* (1998); *El mas al Montseny. La memòria oral* (2008, with Xavier Roigé), and *Transhumàncies del segle XXI. La ramaderia ovina i la transhumància a l'Alta Ribagorça* (2010, with Elisabet Nadal and Juan Ramón Iglesias).

Kerstin Knopf is Professor for Postcolonial Literary and Cultural Studies at the University of Bremen, Germany. She holds a PhD (2003) and a Habilitation (2012) from the University of Greifswald, Germany and she has taught North American literature, film, and media in Greifswald, Rostock and Mainz. Her main research interests are Indigenous film and literature worldwide; Postcolonial Studies focusing on North America, Australia, and Papua New Guinea; American and Canadian romantic literature; and American prison literature. She published *Decolonizing the Lens of Power: Indigenous Films in North America* (2008) and edited the volumes *North America in the 21st Century: Tribal, Local, and Global* (2011) and *Aboriginal Canada Revisited* (2008).

John J. Kucich is a professor of English at Bridgewater State University, Massachusetts. He serves as the editor of *The Concord Saunterer*, the journal of the Thoreau Society. He is the author of *Ghostly Communion: Cross-Cultural Spiritualism in Nineteenth-Century American Literature* (2004) and several recent essays on the intersections between Native and European American cultures in the eighteenth and nineteenth centuries. He is currently editing an essay collection on Thoreau's *The Maine Woods*.

Laure Lévêque is Ancienne élève de l'École Normale Supérieure, Professeur de Littérature française at the University of Toulon, France. She works, in a strictly transdisciplinary fashion, on the historical literature of the long nineteenth century, with a particular interest in the imaginary and ideological transmission and construction of cultural themes, the symbolic recomposition of social imaginaries and knowledges, and in the selection of the components forming the foundations of communal culture. She is the author of, among others, *Le roman de l'histoire* (2001), *Penser la nation, mémoire et imaginaire en révolutions* (2011), and *Rome et l'histoire. Quand le mythe fait écran* (avec Monique Clavel-Lévêque, forthcoming in 2017).

David Lowenthal is professor emeritus of geography and honorary research fellow at University College London. He has worked with heritage and conservation agencies and museums, and taught at a score of universities worldwide. In 2010, he was awarded the Forbes Lecture Prize by the International Institute of Conservation. Among his books are *West Indian Societies* (1972), *Geographies of* *the Mind* (1975), *Our Past Before Us: Why Do We Save It?* (1981), *The Past Is a Foreign Country* (1985), *The Politics of the Past* (1989), *The Heritage Crusade and the Spoils of History* (1996), *George Perkins Marsh, Prophet of Conservation* (2000), *The Nature of Cultural Heritage and the Culture of Natural Heritage* (2005), *Passage du temps sur le paysage* (2008), and (with others), *To Pass on a Good Earth: The Life and Work of Carl O. Sauer* (2014). His *The Past Is a Foreign Country – Revisited* (2015) won the 2016 British Academy Medal.

Hans-Jürgen Lüsebrink is Chair in Romance Culture and Intercultural Communication at the University of Saarbrücken, Germany. He has been guest professor in different Europan countries (France, Denmark, Poland, Austria) as well as in Canada, the U.S. and Africa (Senegal, Burkina Faso, Cameroon). His main research interests are the theory of intercultural communication, German-French cultural relations, European-non European cultural transfer, cultures and media in the Age of Enlightenment (mainly Almanacs, Encyclopedias, Popular media), as well as French Literature and media outside of Europe (mainly in Africa and in Quebec). His books include *Interkulturelle Kommunikation. Interaktion – Kulturtransfer – Fremdwahrnehmung* (2012) and *"Le livre aimé du peuple." Les almanachs québécois de 1777 à nos jours* (2014).

Gesa Mackenthun is Professor of American Studies at Rostock University. Her publications include *Fictions of the Black Atlantic in American Foundational Literature* (2004), *Metaphors of Dispossession. American Beginnings and the Translation of Empire, 1492–1637* (1997), and (co-edited with Bernhard Klein) *Sea Changes. Historicizing the Ocean* (2004). She was the initiator and first spokesperson of the graduate school "Cultural Encounters and the Discourses of Scholarship" funded by the German Research Foundation (2006–15). The resulting conference series she has edited (9 volumes so far) includes *Entangled Knowledge. Scientific Discourses and Cultural Difference* (2012, with Klaus Hock), *Agents of Transculturation* (2013, with Sebastian Jobs), and *Fugitive Knowledge* (2015, with Andreas Beer). Her upcoming book deals with nineteenth-century imperial archaeology, scientific constructions of American antiquity, and the indigenous response to this.

Camila del Mármol holds a PhD in Anthropology and works as tenure-track lecturer at the University of Barcelona, Spain. She has pursued ethnographic research in the Catalan Pyrenees, focusing on the development of heritage processes. Her areas of interest and publications include the transformation of political and economic structures in rural areas and its impact on social perceptions and cultural meanings. She has also conducted research on intangible heritage and food heritage in Catalonia. She is the author of *Pasados locales, políticas globales. Procesos de patrimonialización en un valle del Pirineo catalán* (2012), and co-editor of *The Making of Heritage. Seduction and Disenchantment* (2015).

Peter Probst is a professor of art history and anthropology at Tufts University in Boston, USA. He is a recipient of numerous grants, awards and fellowships, including the German Research Foundation, the Mellon Foundation, the Getty Foundation and Institute of Advanced Cultural Research in Vienna, Austria. Among his many publications is the prize winning *Osogbo and the Art of Heritage. Monuments, Deities and Money* (2011). His new book is a historiographical project, provisionally entitled "What is African Art? The Making and Unmaking of a Field."

Karl Steel is Associate Professor of English at Brooklyn College and the Graduate Center at the City University of New York. He has published on critical animal theory, posthumanism (most recently, the 'Medieval' chapter in the *Cambridge Companion to Posthumanism*), biopolitics and hunting, and ecocriticism. Since 2006, he has regularly contributed to *In the Middle*, a theory-oriented medieval studies blog. He is author of *How to Make a Human: Animals and Violence in the Middle Ages* (2011), and his second book, *Medieval Nonhumanisms: Sympathy, Edibility, and Helplessness*, is forthcoming with the University of Minnesota Press.

Jürgen Vogt is a freelance journalist and correspondent with his headquarters in Argentina. He studied Political Science at the University of Hamburg and the Otto-Suhr-Institute of the Free University of Berlin. His studies focused mainly on international relations, and the impact of the debt crisis in Latin America. He is a regular correspondent for the *tageszeitung* and since 1992 he has been a full-time editor and managing director for the monthly journal *Lateinamerika Nachrichten* in Berlin.

Stephanie Wodianka is Professor of Romance Literature at Rostock University, Germany since 2010. Her research interests include representations, practices and theories of the collective memory (literature, films, *chanson française*), the European meditative literature of the 17th century, the relations between aesthetics and the construction of (trans)cultural identities, and concepts and poetics of modern myth (e. g. *Zwischen Mythos und Geschichte*, 2009; *Metzler Lexikon Moderner Mythen*, 2014, *Inflation der Mythen?*, 2016). Since 2013 she has been chairing the interdisciplinary doctoral program on Cultural Encounters and the Discourses of Scholarship. Since 2014 she is member of the graduate school "Deutungsmacht und Deutungsmachtkonflikte in Religion und Belief systems" (both Rostock University). Currently, she is working on a project on cultural semiotics of the cardinal directions (e. g. "Histoire culturelle des points cardinaux," *Babel: Littératures plurielles,* 2015. Eds. Stephanie Wodianka and Sebastian Neumeister).